Advances in Information Security

Volume 56

Series Editor
Sushil Jajodia
Center for Secure Information Systems, George Mason University, Fairfax,
VA 22030-4444, USA

More information about this series at http://www.springer.com/series/5576

Sushil Jajodia • Paulo Shakarian
V.S. Subrahmanian • Vipin Swarup • Cliff Wang
Editors

Cyber Warfare

Building the Scientific Foundation

 Springer

Editors
Sushil Jajodia
George Mason University
Fairfax, Virginia, USA

Vipin Swarup
The MITRE Corporation
McLean, Virginia, USA

Paulo Shakarian
Arizona State University
Tempe, Arizona, USA

Cliff Wang
Information Sciences Directorate
Triangle Park, North Carolina, USA

V.S. Subrahmanian
Computer Science Department
University of Maryland
College Park, Maryland, USA

ISSN 1568-2633
Advances in Information Security
ISBN 978-3-319-36007-2   ISBN 978-3-319-14039-1 (eBook)
DOI 10.1007/978-3-319-14039-1

Printed on acid-free paper

Springer is part of Springer Science+Business Media (www.springer.com)

Preface

*It is imperative, going forward, that we broaden our
understanding of the science that underpins cybersecurity.*
—General (Ret.) Keith Alexander, Former Commander of
U.S. Cyber Command[1]

Modern society's increased reliance on computer systems, smartphones, and the Internet has provided a new target in a time of conflict. Indeed, cyber-warfare has already emerged as an extension of state policies—one needs to look no further than the headlines produced by Stuxnet, Aurora, or the cyber-attacks during the Russian-Georgian war than to gain an understanding of the emerging impact this domain has during a conflict.

While we have seen a plethora of advanced engineering concepts that directly affect cyber-warfare such as the inventions of the firewall, Metasploit, and even advanced malware platforms such as Flame, many of these concepts are built around best practices, rules-of-thumb, and tried-and-true techniques. While these inventions have been of high impact and significance, history has repeatedly taught us (in other disciplines) that the establishment of scientific principles leads to more rapid and remarkable progress.

Hence, this volume is designed to take a step toward establishing scientific foundations for cyber-warfare. Here we present a collection of the latest basic research results toward establishing such a foundation from several top researchers around the world. This volume includes papers that rigorously analyze many important aspects of cyber-conflict including the employment of botnets, positioning of honeypots, denial and deception, human factors, and the attribution problem. Further, we have made an effort to not only sample different aspects of cyber-warfare, but also highlight a wide variety of scientific techniques that can be used to study these problems. The chapters in this book highlight game theory, cognitive modeling, optimization, logic programming, big data analytics, and argumentation to name a few.

It is our sincere hope that this volume inspires researchers to build upon the knowledge we present to further establish scientific foundations for cyber-warfare and ultimately bring about a more secure and reliable Internet.

---

[1] http://www.nsa.gov/research/tnw/tnw194/article2.shtml.

About the Book

The first three chapters introduce some perspectives and principles of cyber warfare. In Chap. 1, Goel and Hong examine the use of cyber attacks as key strategic weapons in international conflicts, and present game-theoretic models for some cyber warfare problems. In Chap. 2, Elder et al. present a capability based on multi-formalism modeling to model, analyze, and evaluate the effects of cyber exploits on the coordination in decision making organizations. In Chap. 3, Sweeney and Cybenko describe how an attacker who controls the cyber high ground has a distinct advantage in achieving his mission objectives.

The next chapters explore cyber deception and game theoretic approaches. In Chap. 4, Al-Shaer and Rahman develop a game-theoretic framework for planning successful deception plans. In Chap. 5, Kiekintveld et al examine the use of game theory for network security, and present several game-theoretic models that focus on the use of honeypots for network security. In Chap. 6, Heckman and Stech describe cyber-counterdeception, and how to incorporate it into cyber defenses to detect and counter cyber attackers. In Chap. 7, Hamilton addresses the challenges of automatically generating cyber adversary profiles from network observations, even when the adversaries are using deception operations to disguise their activities and intentions. In Chap. 8, Shakarian et al. introduce a formal reasoning system that aids an analyst in the attribution of a cyber operation even when the available information is conflicting or uncertain.

Chapters 9–12 explore social and behavioral aspects of cyber security and cyber warfare. In Chap. 9, Marble et al. review the role of the human factor in cyber security, for both attackers and defenders. In Chap. 10, Ben-Asher and Gonzalez propose using a well-known, multi-agent, cognitive model of decisions from experience to study behavior in cyber-war. In Chap. 11, Puzis and Elovici examine the problem of finding visible nodes in a social network that are most effective at diffusing agents that reveal hidden invisible nodes. In Chap. 12, Paxton et al. review algorithms that discover community structure within networks, and compare them based on the analysis context.

Chapters 13 and 14 are based on large-scale field data from millions of real hosts. In Chap. 13, Dumitras presents results of empirical studies of real-world security using field data collected on over 10 million real hosts. In Chap. 14, Prakash discusses the use of graph mining techniques on large field datasets to solve a range of challenging cybersecurity problems. Finally, in Chap. 15, Ruef and Rohlf discuss how advancements in programming language technology can address fundamental computer security problems, and argue that current research techniques are insufficient to guarantee security.

Acknowledgements

We are extremely grateful to the numerous contributors to this book. In particular, it is a pleasure to acknowledge the authors for their contributions. Special thanks go to Susan Lagerstrom-Fife, senior publishing editor at Springer for her support of this project. We also wish to thank the Army Research Office for their financial support under the grant numbers W911NF-14-1-0116 and W911NF-13-1-0421.

Contents

Contributors

Myriam Abramson Information Technology Division, Naval Research Laboratory, Washington, DC, USA

Ehab Al-Shaer University of North Carolina at Charlotte, Charlotte, USA

Noam Ben-Asher Department of Social and Decision Sciences, Dynamic Decision Making Laboratory, Carnegie Mellon University, Pittsburgh, PA, USA

Joseph Coyne Information Technology Division, Naval Research Laboratory, Washington, DC, USA

George Cybenko Thayer School of Engneering at Dartmouth College, Hanover, NH, USA

Tudor Dumitraş Electrical and Computer Engineering Department, University of Maryland, College Park, MD, USA

Robert J. Elder System Architectures Laboratory, George Mason University, Fairfax, VA, USA

Yuval Elovici Telekom Innovation Laboratories and Department of Information Systems Engineering, Ben-Gurion University of the Negev, Beer-Sheva, Israel

Sanjay Goel University at Albany, State University of New York, New York, USA

Cleotilde Gonzalez Department of Social and Decision Sciences, Dynamic Decision Making Laboratory, Carnegie Mellon University, Pittsburgh, PA, USA

Samuel N. Hamilton Siege Technologies, Manchester, USA

Kristin E. Heckman The MITRE Corporation, McLean, VA, USA

Yuan Hong University at Albany, State University of New York, New York, USA

Paul Hyden Information Technology Division, Naval Research Laboratory, Washington, DC, USA

Christopher Kiekintveld Computer Science Department, University of Texas at El Paso, El Paso, USA

W. F. Lawless Paine College, GA, Augusta, USA

Alexander H. Levis System Architectures Laboratory, George Mason University, Fairfax, VA, USA

Viliam Lisý Agent Technology Center, Department of Computer Science and Engineering, Faculty of Electrical Engineering, Czech Technical University in Prague, Prague, Czech Republic

Julie L. Marble Advanced Physics Laboratory Senior Human Factors Scientist Asymetric Operations Sector, Johns Hopkins University, Laurel, MD, USA

Ranjeev Mittu Information Technology Division, Naval Research Laboratory, Washington, DC, USA

Geoffrey Moores Department of Electrical Engineering and Computer Science, U.S. Military Academy, West Point, NY, USA

Ira S. Moskowitz Information Technology Division, Naval Research Laboratory, Washington, DC, USA

Radek Píbil Agent Technology Center, Department of Computer Science and Engineering, Faculty of Electrical Engineering, Czech Technical University in Prague, Prague, Czech Republic

Simon Parsons Department of Computer Science, University of Liverpool, Liverpool, UK

Napoleon C. Paxton Information Technology Division, Naval Research Laboratory, Washington, DC, USA

B. Aditya Prakash Department of Computer Science, Virginia Tech., Blacksburg, VA, USA

Rami Puzis Telekom Innovation Laboratories and Department of Information Systems Engineering, Ben-Gurion University of the Negev, Beer-Sheva, Israel

Mohammad Ashiqur Rahman University of North Carolina at Charlotte, Charlotte, USA

Chris Rohlf Yahoo Inc., New York, USA

Andrew Ruef Trail of Bits, New York, USA

Stephen Russell Information Technology Division, Naval Research Laboratory, Washington, DC, USA

Paulo Shakarian Arizona Sate University, Tempe, AZ, USA

Ciara Sibley Information Technology Division, Naval Research Laboratory, Washington, DC, USA

Gerardo I. Simari Department of Computer Science and Engineering, Universidad Nacional del Sur, Bahìa Blanca, Argentina

Frank J. Stech The MITRE Corporation, McLean, VA, USA

Patrick Sweeney Thayer School of Engneering at Dartmouth College, Hanover, NH, USA

Bahram Yousefi System Architectures Laboratory, George Mason University, Fairfax, VA, USA

Chapter 1
Cyber War Games: Strategic Jostling Among Traditional Adversaries

Sanjay Goel and Yuan Hong

Abstract Cyber warfare has been simmering for a long time and has gradually morphed into a key strategic weapon in international conflicts. Doctrines of several countries consider cyber warfare capability as essential to gain strategic superiority or as a counterbalance to military inferiority. Countries are attempting to reach consensus on confidence building measures in cyber space while racing with each other to acquire cyber weaponry. These attempts are strongly influenced by the problem of clear attribution of cyber incidents as well as political imperatives. Game theory has been used in the past for such problems in international relations where players compete with each other and the actions of the players are interdependent. Problems in cyber warfare can benefit from similar game theoretic concepts. We discuss in this book chapter the state of cyber warfare, the key imperatives for the countries, and articulate how countries are jostling with each other in the cyber domain especially in the context of poor attribution and verification in the cyber domain. We present game theoretic models for a few representative problems in the cyber warfare domain.

1.1 Introduction

Cyber warfare started as a low intensity activity among nations and was initially used for nuisance attacks such as website defacement and denial of service attacks but it has developed into a fierce cyber arms race among countries. Cyber warfare now figures prominently in doctrines of major military superpowers and terrorist organizations. There have been cyber warfare incidents in the past where attacks were launched on Estonia and Georgia in context of political conflicts with Russia. There have also been attacks on South Korea and Japan related to regional political conflicts involving similar modes of attacks. Aside from these overt attacks, there have been several covert attacks involving espionage across different countries where both the

S. Goel (✉) · Y. Hong
University at Albany, State University of New York, New York, USA
e-mail: goel@albany.edu

Y. Hong
e-mail: hong@albany.edu

© Springer International Publishing Switzerland 2015
S. Jajodia et al. (eds.), *Cyber Warfare,* Advances in Information Security 56,
DOI 10.1007/978-3-319-14039-1_1

military and civilian infrastructure is targeted. There are suspicions that countries are attempting to intrude into the critical infrastructure of other countries to gain a strategic lever during conflict. There is also an apprehension that the Internet could be used to change national ideological and cultural values; along these same lines, a strong concern is that social media could be used to cause upheaval and overthrow governments. Countries are blaming each other for attacks and espionage while at the same time planning their own cyber warfare strategy. Mutual distrust among nations is driving them to invest in cyber warfare capabilities in order to gain strategic leverage over other countries while at the same time lobbying for slowing down the other countries. A big fear is cyber attack launched from a country by groups outside of government control could trigger a kinetic response.

There have been attempts at creating international treaties and laws related to cyber crime and cyber warfare but these are moving at a very slow pace while traditional military rivals jockey with each other to gain their own strategic advantage. A key impediment to building consensus on cyber warfare treaties is the inherent anonymity of the Internet that can camouflage the identity of the perpetrators and make it attribution of attacks to any specific individual, group, or nation uncertain. Attacks launched by actors who are not in direct control of the state can trigger a misdirected counter attack at a nation state. There is an additional problem of misdirection where attackers can deliberately leave a trail to implicate other parties for their activities. Countries are thus reluctant to sign any legal document that will hold them responsible for activities that can get misattributed to them through subterfuge and deceit of other countries.

Realizing the futility of attempting to forge a broad consensus on enforceable international treaties on cyber warfare and the urgency to cool down the torrid cyber arms race. There have been attempts at confidence building measures as a prelude to eventual signing of treaties. Efforts to create confidence-building measures to reduce the threat of cyber warfare are active in several international bodies including the United Nations (UN) and the Organization for Security and Cooperation in Europe (OSCE). States are attempting (or pretending) to cooperate with each other while at the same time competing with one another in the cyber arms race.

Game theory is well suited for analyzing relationships among multiple actors, who in this case include, nation states, non-state actors (terrorists, hacktivists, etc.), and supranational organizations (e.g., UN, OSCE, etc.). Since the seminal work of Von Neumann and Morgenstern (1944, 1994) "The Theory of Games and Economic Behavior", game theory has been used extensively for studying international relations. There are several areas where game theoretic models are suitable including security, economics, education, environment, human rights, and international law. In this chapter we focus on the security issues related to cyber warfare and formulate problems in the cyber warfare domain using game theoretical models. The chapter does not contain a deep mathematical development in this field but rather focuses on demonstrating the modeling of game theoretic concepts for cyber warfare.

The rest of the chapter is organized as follows: Sect. 1.2 provides a background of the problem including the adversaries (players), their strategic positions (options), and the key objectives (optimization function) to achieve. Sect. 1.3 discusses fundamental game theoretic concepts and some recent work on cyber warfare that includes game theoretic models. Sect. 1.4 discusses the models in details followed by a succinct conclusion.

1.2   Cyber Warfare

Definition of cyber attacks is contextual: depending on the actors, motivation, targets, and actions, they can be called cyber terrorism, cyber crime, cyber activism, etc. There are several distinct modes of conflicts related to cyber warfare. Understanding the relationships between actors, their behavior, and their motivations is essential in order to understand cyber warfare better and to reduce chances of a serious cyber conflict. We use game theoretic models to look at positions of the key players on each of these conflicts to understand the dynamics among the players in these conflicts. We select four modes of cyber conflict that are dominating international cyber politics for further analysis including: (1) social media wars that influences a country's internal politics often with a goal of fomenting social uprisings that can result in political change; (2) strategic war aimed at causing damage for the adversary as well as pillaging resources (e.g., industrial espionage); for this, countries are acquiring resources to conduct both espionage and develop tools that can be used to disable the adversarial activities occurring in critical infrastructure including power, communication, media, Internet, etc.; (3) ideological battle where fundamentalist organizations use the Internet to spew their ideology and to recruit members in other countries for their cause; (4) citizen-initiated war where a country's civilians directly attack another country's citizens and institutions as a part of larger conflict (ideological or kinetic).

Foreign intervention through social media has become a significant fear for countries leading to aggressive monitoring if not outright controlling of social media content. Some countries have already invested in censorship and control of the Internet mainly driven by intention to decrease political unrest or ideological and religion polluting. Social media-facilitated revolutions have driven some countries to the point of paranoia regarding control of online activity. If this type of distrust keeps growing, there is only one logical conclusion: separation of the Internet across country borders. A separated Internet could have severe consequences with negative impacts from the individual to national level from social relationships, educational pursuits, commerce, and tourism. In a lot of the authoritarian and corrupt regimes the conditions on the ground are ripe for popular revolutions. In the past, they have been kept in check through censorship and coercion. Social media has provided a forum for organizing large scale protests—which countries are prone to such attacks and which countries have incentives to sponsor such attacks.

The strategic war of targeting the resources has each country building up their cyber arsenals quietly while publicly denouncing similar activities by others. Each country considers cyberspace a natural place for gaining strategic military advantage. This is causing serious misgivings between different countries. For instance, the

United States is very concerned about Chinese reconnaissance into the power grid and at the same time attempting to gather intelligence from foreign networks. Similarly, businesses are constantly claiming intrusion by the Chinese for corporate espionage or stealing data. These illicit activities have been widely publicized by the media resulting in civilian unease and condemnation from the U.S. government. However, at the same time, it has been revealed that the U.S. ran one of the largest spying operations around the world sparing neither friend nor foe.

Terrorism fits naturally with game theory since when it is reduced to its simplest level, many terrorist events can be summed up to simple or complex strategic interactions. It can be examined both at a micro-level dealing with individual attack decisions and at a macro-level that involves overall strategy of the attacker (terrorist group) and defender (nation states). Each country seems to have their own terrorist problem; inciting such anti-national activities in other countries can backfire. Each country has their own terrorist foes that they are concerned with, e.g., Russia about Chechnya-based jihadi elements, the U.S. about Al Qaeda, India about Pakistan-based terrorist organizations, E.U. about jihadi elements from the Middle East, and China about Tibetan activities. While countries are being victims of terrorism, they are supporting terrorism in other countries. The link between sponsors and the victims can be established in order to formulate a strategy to counter cyber terrorism. Consider for instance a country has a chance to sponsor terrorism against a rival country. The choices are two fold i.e. sponsor or not to sponsor. The country against which it is targeted can either negotiate or retaliate. This creates a game theoretic problem.

There have been many incidents of citizen-initiated attacks against other countries either through tacit government support or through support of non-state actors. Examples of these types of incidents include hacker group activities in India and Pakistan. Similarly, there have been attacks by Russian citizens on Estonia and Georgia during conflicts. Citizen-initiated war typically starts with a strong rhetoric in the media and then takes a life of its own often outside of governmental control. Citizen-initiated attacks provide leverage to governments since they can absolve themselves at least partly in participating in an act of war but they may get out of control and lead to unanticipated disproportionate retaliation.

A key concerns for strategists is to prevent unexpected and unwarranted escalation of the war. The escalation can come from political reasons when the attacked nation is forced to have a forceful response to cater to public perception. Countries can deliberately force a response from other countries looking for an excuse for conflict. Non-state actors who launch attacks masquerading as a nation state can cause dangerous escalation in tension by launching cyber attacks purportedly from one nation state to another. This becomes especially potent since attribution is hard and distinguishing between an attack by a proxy representing the state and a non-state actor can be difficult. Given the shared security doctrines that exist among countries this conflict to escalate into a multi-county conflict. At some point a cyber attack will lead to a kinetic attack if tensions escalate sufficiently or phony cyber attacks will be used as a ruse to launch a kinetic attack. Attacks on the critical infrastructure have already escalated cyber warfare to the next level there have been mutual incriminations about surveillance and penetration into critical infrastructure networks among countries. Stuxnet worm that was used to launch attack on the centrifuges in the Iranian nuclear program has demonstrated the potency of critical infrastructure attacks leading each country to build their defensive capability and at the same time invest in offensive capabilities for deterrence.

Escalation of the social media war and information censorship may also escalate compelling countries to isolate them on the Internet leading to the fragmentation of the Internet that is also undesirable. Countries that consider the freedom of Internet a threat to the political structure and social fabric of society will start separating from the Internet. China has already insulated their citizens from the "objectionable content" of global Internet through stringent laws on admissible content on the Internet and aggressive censorship where they filter Internet traffic, block specific IP-addresses, and aggressively monitor the content on the Internet. Several other countries such as Russia, Iran, and Germany are making attempts to insulate their networks or data from other countries albeit for different reasons.

We formulate game theoretic problems related to some of these dynamic scenarios to better understand the dynamics and to determine optimum strategy. The overall goal of the endeavor is to support the creation of international treaties based on optimum strategies for each of the key player.

1.3 Game Theory

Game theory involves the formulation of a decision-making problem as a game in which two or more players make decisions such that the decisions of one player has an impact on the decision of the other player. The game is defined as a set of *strategies* and *payoffs* for each player. The players are assumed to be rational and their goal is to maximize their payoffs (utility) from participating in the game. All players also expect other players to be rational. Generally, rationality assumes perfect and complete information among players about the strategies and payoffs of each other. Complete information refers to the recognition of the identity of other players involved and the payoff for their particular strategies, whereas perfect information refers to the ability to observe the actions of other players. In the context of incomplete information, where players do not know their opponent's strategies, a Bayesian game based on a probability distribution of actions in the strategy set may be modelled (Harsanyi 1967).

There are three types of payoff functions: zero-sum; constant-sum; and non-zero sum. In zero-sum games the gains of one player are directly opposite to the losses of another. What one player wins, the other must lose. This assumes that opponent's evaluation functions are opposite. In constant-sum games, only one player will have a non-zero payoff at any one time, and in non-zero sum games no restrictions are applied to the payoff structure (Aumann and Maschler 1995). Hamilton et al. (2002) suggests that zero-sum assumptions are not reasonable in cyber warfare as state actors have different goals and priorities. Burke (1999) suggests a non-zero sum model is most realistic in the context of this type of information warfare.

The goal of the game is to find an equilibrium solution, i.e. the best outcome or payoff for the players considering the decisions of all other players. In classical optimization terms this is a local optima solution to the problem for a player. One of the most basic solution for a game is the minimax solution that minimizes a players' maximum expected loss. Nash Equilibrium, is achieved when a unique, optimal strategy for each player corresponding to every move of the opponent is available (Gibbons 1992). A strategy is said to be *pure* if the probability that the strategy will be chosen is 1 for a given scenario. In many cases, however, opponents do not have complete information or are uncertain about the structure of the game and a pure strategy is not evident. In this case, a stochastic model called the *mixed strategy* is used in which a probability associated with specific strategies are defined.

Games can be cooperative and non-cooperative. Cooperative games are usually modeled when mechanisms are available to enforce particular sets of behavior (source). Although we may assume cooperative strategies in cyber warfare (for example, cooperation among NSA and GCHQ), in this chapter we model non-cooperative games. We make policy recommendations to reduce problems of cyber warfare based on the conclusions derived from our non-cooperative models. Perfect information also involves the concept of *perfect recall*, or knowledge of the history of strategies chosen by each player. We expect the cyber warfare confidence building and treaty process to have perfect recall while cyber war strategy games to deploy offensive and defensive capabilities to have incomplete information. In the cases we model, however we make a simplification assumption of perfect information.

In general, games are either *static* or *dynamic*. In static games, decisions by all players are made simultaneously without knowledge of the decisions that other players have actually carried out. Dynamic games involve a series of games where the strategies can be re-evaluated based on previously made choices by the players involved. In the context of cyber warfare *dynamic* games may be present when intrusion tactics involve multiple steps and trials. At the same time, defense mechanisms may allow the recognition of previous attacks and influence future behavior in order to protect the systems. Sequence in time is thus an important component of cyber warfare (e.g. see Libicki 1997). It is also reasonable to assume static games, however, as many cyber attacks happen unbeknownst to those being attack. We create static models for several games.

1.3.1 Game Theory in International Relations

One of the key assumptions in game theory is that actors are non-altruistic and are purely driven by their own goals. The field of international relations is a quintessential representation of this assumption where nation-states are motivated only by their interests and are not guided by ethical or humanitarian concerns but are only concerned about maximizing their utility function (Evans and Newnham 1998; Hollis and Smith 1990). There are two areas of International Relations that can greatly improve the understanding of cyber warfare deterrence and arms race as well as international diplomacy. International relations scholars (Gleditsch 1990; Intriligator and Brito 1990; Bolks and Stoll 2000; Reuveny and Maxwell 1998) have extensively studied deterrence and arms races using game theoretic models. In its simplest form deterrence between two nation states can be studied where each threatens to retaliate to a potential attack by the other to prevent the other from launching the attack in the first place. The objective of the nation-states is to prevent destruction or domination by the other and each would feel more secure if it acquires weapons for protection. The acquisition of the weapons, albeit for defensive purposes, trigger the adversary into acquiring more weapons especially if the weapons are dual use leading to an arms race. This phenomenon where actions by a state to heighten its security can lead other states to respond with similar measures thereby escalating dangers of conflict rather than reducing them even though no one desires it is called the security dilemma and can be studied using game theoretic concepts. This phenomenon is studied extensively using the Prisoner's Dilemma game (Brams 1975; Clemens 1998; Dixit and Skeath 1999; Hamburger 1979; Powell 1999; Taylor 1995), which often results in a less than desirable outcome for each player. There has been very little research on the use of Game Theory for cyber warfare and cyber terrorism.

Matusitz (2009) suggests that game theory is particularly important and useful to apply to cyberterrorism. Jormakka and Mölsä (2005) present 4 distinct scenarios in which game theory may be applied in the context of information warfare. The first example includes a terrorist group (T) with certain requirements, holding hostages and threatening to cause destructive damage; and a government (G) wanting the terrorists to surrender. This game is modelled as a two-player static game of complete information, where each player has two strategies (e.g., accepting or rejecting the other's). Initially, this game ends with two Nash equilibriums with no unique solution as is typical in asymmetric warfare. If the game is repeated, and each player adopts a "bold" or single strategy, a dominated outcome can be obtained (i.e. outcome other than equilibrium). They also show that using a mixed strategy can prove effective against a dominative attack strategy. Finally they demonstrate an n-person game where an attacker is perpetrating a DoS attack on a network and each player has two strategies i.e. using the network or being idle. There is one attacker who wants to overload the network, and a number of other users who want to maintain the network functioning. This situation results in a payoff that is 0 for all players. After initial shutdown of the network, users will find another network in which to operate. Making this assumption the attacker ("vandal") cannot win. However, if the game is modeled as a dynamic game, and the vandal only overloads the network 50 % of the time, he can have some gain. Ma et al. (2011) develop a game theoretic model for interaction between government agencies and firms that are faced with cyber threats. They use the Crawford and Sobel (1982) "cheap talk" model. A similar model can be used to understand the interactions between the hacker groups and the Chinese government.

1.4   Problem Formulation

The basic game theory problem is that each country wants to deescalate cyber tension however they cannot trust the other adversaries and thus need to invest in cyber arsenals to catch up with the adversaries leading to the arms race where each party incurs a heavy loss. This can be explained by using the classical Prisoner's Dilemma problem—a two-person game. In this game both players have two strategies either to cooperate or to defect. If both players cooperate with each other they receive a low cost i.e. go to prison for 1 year. If one of them cooperates and the other defects, the prisoner who defects gets no cost i.e. goes free and the prisoner who cooperates gets a high cost i.e. 5 year prison term. If both of them defect then they both get a moderate cost of 3 years of prison term. Given the assumption that each player is only interested in self-gain and there is no trust with the other player the minimax strategy is to defect for both player (Table 1.1).

Table 1.1 Basic formulation for Prisoner's Dilemma

	Prisoner B stays silent (cooperates)	Prisoner B betrays (defects)
Prisoner A stays silent (cooperates)	Each serves 1 year	Prisoner A: 5 years Prisoner B: goes free
Prisoner A betrays (defects)	Prisoner A: goes free Prisoner B: 5 years	Each serves 3 years

In cyber arm race, if two nation states cooperate they have no cost (building a cyber arsenal). If both states defect i.e. they both have to build cyber arsenals, they have a moderate cost (building an arsenal). However if one cooperates (does not build an arsenal) and the other defects (builds an arsenal) the defecting state will have a low cost but the cooperating state will have a high cost (loss during conflict). Consequently, both states will choose to build an arsenal.

For instance, the U.S. and China may have been hacking and spying on each other for a long time (from traditional manners to computer based tactics), and try to gain the strategic military advantage in cyberspace. To build the cyber arsenal for the above purpose, increasing military expenditure becomes indispensable, however such military expense increase clearly affects their economics by appropriating the spending allocated for other areas such as construction, education and healthcare. Each of these two countries have two strategies: (1) reducing the military expenditure (cooperate), and (2) increasing expenditure to build up cyber arsenal (defect). Essentially, the rational strategy for them is to reduce cyber warfare expenditure for both countries by establishing a treaty (cooperate), then both of them are able to at least maintain the allocated expenditure in other areas—a win-win situation. However, countries may betray the treaty and privately increases the expenditure to build up cyber arsenal, and thus attempt to win the strategic military advantage in the cyber warfare. If the U.S. cooperates and China defects, the U.S. could easily win the advantage, and vice-versa. In reality, due to mutual lack of trust (each country is fear of the covert cyber activities from the other country), the cyber deterrence would indeed lead to an irrational result for the participated countries—both countries are strongly inclined to covertly increase its expenditure on building up the cyber arsenal (defect). Therefore, both countries have to invest considerable amount of expenditure on cyber warfare. Compared to the case of cooperation, both countries lose their payoff to some extent. (Table 1.2)

Table 1.2 Payoff matrix of "Prisoner's Dilemma" in cyber warfare

		United States	
		Reduces military expenditure (Cooperates)	Increases expenditure to build up cyber arsenal (Defects)
China	Reduces military expenditure (Cooperates)	Both countries can cut the expense on cyber arsenal, and thus save military expenditure	United State wins the strategic military advantage in cyberspace
	Increases expenditure to build up cyber arsenal (Defects)	China wins the strategic military advantage in cyberspace	Both countries spend considerable amount of money on cyber arsenal, and thus reduce expenditure on education, healthcare, construction, etc

Based on the "Prisoner's Dilemma", Nadiya Kostyuk (2013) studied another cyber conflict case between two powerful countries, e.g., the U.S. and China in cyber espionage that can hurt trade between the two. They are not likely to cooperate with each other, even though cooperation could bring mutual benefits to both countries. (Table 1.3) Please refer to the payoff matrix as below:

In the same article, Kostyuk (2013) showed that prisoner's dilemma can be also applied to the cyber warfare case between one powerful country and one less powerful country i.e Russia and Estonia. These two countries are also highly likely to choose "Do not cooperate", which is evidently a worsen case than both cooperate. (Table 1.4) Please refer to the payoff matrix given as below:

Besides the "Prisoner's Dilemma", we present another class model applicable to cyber warfare—zero-sum game. In zero-sum games, a player's gain (or losses) of utility is exactly balanced by the other player's utility losses (or gain). Hence, the total sum of gain and losses is equal to zero. For any two-player zero-sum game, if mixed strategy is allowed, the Nash Equilibrium can be found using linear programming (LP). As a key form of cyber warfare, anti-national cyber terrorism activities in a country are usually supported by another country, then the utility loss caused in the activities may lead to the activity supporter's payoff gain. Assuming that the payoff loss of one country equals the payoff gain of the other country, per the minimax theorem, the Nash Equilibrium—optimal (mixed) strategies for both countries on the international cyber terrorism activities can be derived by solving an LP problem.

For instance, each of two conflicting countries in cyber warfare have four different strategies regarding the support of cyber terrorism activities in the other country (attack) and counter cyber terrorism activities/mechanisms for itself (anti). The payoff for each combination of the players' strategies is balanced (an example is given in Table 1.5).

Each country aims at developing a cost-effective strategy to decide whether to spend money on overseas cyber terrorism activities and/or to establish its own counter

Table 1.3 Payoff matrix of "Digital Prisoner's Dilemma" (Two powerful nations). (Kostyuk (2013))

		United States	
		Cooperates	Does not cooperate
China	Cooperates	Likely Scenario:	Highly Unlikely Scenario:
		(1) individual hackers are punished	(1) U.S. denies responsibility
		(2) trade between the two nations continues	(2) U.S.—China relations worsen
			(3) Trade declines causing severe economic losses in the States
			(4) The number of cyber attacks coming from both countries increases
	Does not cooperate	Unlikely Scenario:	*Highly Likely Scenario:*
		(1) the U.S. continues experiencing losses in its intellectual property	(1) The attacks escalate
		(2) the U.S. could try applying sanctions against China	(2) U.S. relies on its adept domestic and international law enforcement arms
		(3) Mutual Legal Assistance Treaty is worthless	(3) China appears incapable of policing its cyberspace, making it vulnerable to internal attacks and eventually is forced to cooperate with the States

Table 1.4 Payoff matrix of "Digital Prisoner's Dilemma" (One powerful nation and one less powerful nation). (Kostyuk (2013))

		Estonia	
		Cooperates	Does not cooperate
Russia	Cooperates	Unlikely Scenario:	Highly Unlikely Scenario:
		(1) individual hackers are punished	(1) Russia denies responsibility
		(2) future hacks are deterred	(2) Russo—Estonian relations worsen
	Does not cooperate	Likely Scenario:	*Highly Likely Scenario:*
		(1) Estonia seeks help from Russia	(1) The attacks escalate
		(2) Mutual Legal Assistance Treaty is worthless	(2) Countries are incapable of policing its cyberspace—stepping stone nations for future attacks by third parties
			(3) Estonia seeks help from NATO or EU

cyber terrorism activities/mechanisms. Thus, we can formulate a zero-sum game for the cyber terrorism activities between two countries, where an optimal mixed strategy

Table 1.5 An example of zero-sum game in cyber warfare

	Attack and anti	Attack and no anti	No attack and anti	No attack and no anti
Attack and anti	(0, 0)	(50, − 50)	(− 10, 10)	(40, − 40)
Attack and no anti	(− 50, 50)	(0, 0)	(− 10, 10)	(40, − 40)
No attack and anti	(10, − 10)	(10, − 10)	(0, 0)	(0, 0)
No attack and no anti	(− 40, 40)	(− 40, 40)	(0, 0)	(0, 0)

in the Nash Equilibrium can be derived from the LP problem to facilitate the above decision-making. Furthermore, let us consider the dynamics between countries that have ability to sponsor cyber terrorism through non-state actors versus countries that are victims of such terrorism. The sponsoring country has three choices i.e. actively sponsor, control terror groups, do nothing. The defending country has three options prevent the attack, retaliate, and negotiate. The best scenario for the sponsoring nation is to bring the attacked country to a negotiating table without having to do anything. The best thing for the defending country is for cyber terrorism to not occur. There are different payoff's associated with each of the strategies of the defender and attacker. (Table 1.6) The matrix is shown below:

Table 1.6 State sponsorship of terrorism

		Defending nation		
		Prevent	Retaliate	Negotiate
Sponsoring nation	Sponsor non-state actors	(− 5, − 5)	(− 20, − 10)	(5, − 20)
	Control non-state actors	(− 5, 0)	(− 5, 0)	(4, − 20)
	Do nothing	(− 10, − 5)	(− 10, − 10)	(10, − 20)

1.5 Conclusion

Cyber warfare is becoming increasingly prevalent with multiple actors with several decision-making issues where they are interdependent on each other including, cyber arms race, agreeing to treaties, and dealing with cyber espionage and terrorism. In this chapter we draw from the field of international relations and terrorism to show examples of game theoretic models for cyber warfare. Game theory is well suited for this domain. We create models based on the prisoner's dilemma game. There are other game theoretic techniques that will work as well including stochastic games and multi-step games.

References

Aumann, Robert and Maschler (1995), Michael, "Repeated Games with Incomplete Information", MIT Press.

Brams, Steven J. (1975) "Game Theory and Politics", The Free Press: New York, NY.

Bolks, Sean and Stoll, Richard (2000), "The Arms Acquisition Process The Effect of Internal and External Constraints on Arms Race Dynamics", Journal of Conflict Resolution, Vol 44(5), pp. 580–603, Sage Publications.

Burke, Jonathan (1999), "Robustness of Optimal Equilibrium Among Overlapping Generations", Economic Theory, Vol. 14, pp. 311–330, 1999.

Clemens, Walter C. (1998) "Dynamics of International Relations: Conflict and Mutual Gain in an Age of Global Interdependence", Rowman & Littlefield Publishers: Lanham, MD.

Crawford, Vincent and Sobel, Joel, (1982), "Strategic Information Transmission", Econometrica, Vol 50(6), pp. 1431–1451.

Dixit, Avinash, and Skeath, Susan (1999) "Games of Strategy", W. W. Norton & Co.: New York, NY.

Evans, Graham, and Newnham, Jeffrey (1998) "Dictionary of International Relations", Penguin Putnam Inc.: New York, NY.

Gleditsch, Nils P. (1990) "Research on Arms Races", in Gleditsch, Nils P. and Njolstad, Olav (eds.), Arms Races: Technological and Political Dynamics, Sage Publications: Newbury Park, CA.

Gibbons, Robert (1992), "Game Theory for Applied Economists", Princeton University Press.

Hamburger, Henry (1979) "Games as Models of Social Phenomena", W. H. Freeman and Co.: New York, NY.

Hamilton, S. N., Miller, W. L., Ott, A., & Saydjari, O. S. (2002). The role of game theory in information warfare. *4th Information survivability workshop (ISW-2001/2002)*. Vancouver, Canada.

Harsanyi, John (1967), "Games with Incomplete Information Played by "Bayesian" Players, I-III, Part I, the Basic Model", Management Science, Vol 14(3), pp. 159–182.

Hollis, Martin, and Smith, Steve (1990). "Explaining and Understanding International Relations", Oxford University Press: New York, NY.

Intriligator, Michael D. and Brito, Dogobert L. (1990). "Arms Race Modeling: A Reconsideration", in Gleditsch, Nils P. and Njolstad, Olav (eds.), Arms Races: Technological and Political Dynamics, Sage Publications: Newbury Park, CA.

Jormakka, J., and Mölsä, J. V. (2005). Modelling information warfare as a game. *Journal of Information Warfare, 4*(2), 12–25.

Kostyuk, Nadiya (2013). "The Digital Prisoner's Dilemma: Challenges and Opportunities for Cooperation", published online at http://cybersummit.info/sites/cybersummit.info/files/The%20Digital%20Prisoner's%20Dilemma-Challenges%20and%20Opportunities%20for%20Cooperation_Nadiya%20Kostyuk%20.pdf.

Libicki, Martin (1997), "Defending Cyberspace, and Other Metaphors", National Defense University.

Ma Z. (Sam), Chen H. (Daisy), Zhang J., Krings A., & Sheldon F. (2011). Has the Cyber Warfare Threat Been Overstated?: A Cheap Talk Game-theoretic Analysis on the Google-hacking Claim? In *Proceedings of the Seventh Annual Workshop on Cyber Security and Information Intelligence Research* (pp. 42:1–42:1). New York, NY, USA.

Matusitz, J. (2009). A Postmodern Theory of Cyberterrorism: Game Theory. *Information Security Journal: A Global Perspective, 18*(6), 273–281. doi:10.1080/19393550903200474.

Powell, Robert (1999), "In the Shadow of Power", Princeton University Press.

Reuveny, Rafael and Maxwell, John (1998). "Free Trade and Arms Races", The Journal of Conflict Resolution, 42: 771–803.

Taylor, Alan D. (1995). "Mathematics and Politics: Strategy, Voting, Power and Proof", Springer-Verlag: New York, NY.

Von Neumann, John and Morgenstern, Oskar (1944). Theory of Games and Economic Behavior, Princeton University Press: Princestone.
Von Neumann, John and Morgenstern, Oskar (1994). "Theory of Games and Economic Behavior", John Wiley & Sons, Inc.:New York, NY.

Chapter 2
Alternatives to Cyber Warfare: Deterrence and Assurance

Robert J. Elder, Alexander H. Levis and Bahram Yousefi

Abstract Deterrence as practiced during the Cold War was largely defined in terms of capabilities to impose punishment in response to an attack; however, with growing concern over the proliferation of cyber technologies, deterrence has evolved to be understood more generally in terms of cost/benefit calculi, viewed from not only a national perspective, but also recognizing the importance of both friendly and adversary perspectives. With this approach, the primary instruments used for deterrence are those which encourage restraint on the part of all affected parties. The use of a multiple lever approach to deterrence offers a path to an integrated strategy that not only addresses the cost/benefit calculus of the primary attacker, but also provides opportunities to influence the calculus of mercenary cyber armies for hire, patriotic hackers, or other groups. For this multiple lever approach to be effective a capability to assess the effects of cyber attacks on operations is needed. Such a capability based on multi-formalism modeling to model, analyze, and evaluate the effect of cyber exploits on the coordination in decision making organizations is presented. The focus is on the effect that cyber exploits, such as availability and integrity attacks, have on information sharing and task synchronization. Colored Petri Nets are used to model the decision makers in the organization and computer network models to represent their interactions. Two new measures of performance are then introduced: information consistency and synchronization. The approach and the computation of the measures of performance are illustrated though a simple example based on a variation of the Pacifica scenario.

R. J. Elder (✉) · A. H. Levis · B. Yousefi
System Architectures Laboratory, George Mason University, Fairfax, VA, USA
e-mail: relder@gmu.edu

A. H. Levis
e-mail: alevis@gmu.edu

B. Yousefi
e-mail: byousefi@masonlive.gmu.edu

© Springer International Publishing Switzerland 2015
S. Jajodia et al. (eds.), *Cyber Warfare,* Advances in Information Security 56,
DOI 10.1007/978-3-319-14039-1_2

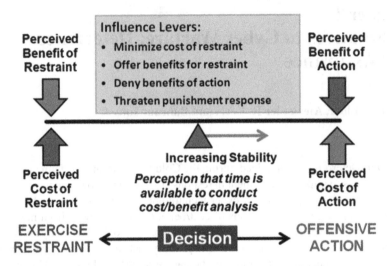

Fig. 2.1 Deter/Assure decision influences. (figure based on DO-JOC (2006))

2.1 Introduction

The evolving primary deterrence objective is to encourage restraint on the part of all affected parties, and the primary means is to establish mutual understanding among actors designed to prevent one actor from conducting actions or exhibiting behaviors that are so unacceptable to another that the responses become escalatory. In this context, the instruments of deterrence are not only the capabilities to impose punishment (threaten punishment response) or deny the effects of adversary actions (deny benefits of action), but also the means to identify friendly and competitor vital interests, to communicate with friends and adversaries, to validate mutual understanding of red lines, and to control escalation (minimize cost of restraint and offer benefits of restraint.). These Deter/Assure influences along with the influence levers are shown in Fig. 2.1.

Deterrence often fails because mutual understanding between actors is lost, or one actor's cost/benefit calculus drives an unacceptable behavior despite the threat of punishment. Therefore, a holistic approach to deterrence requires the US to identify both US and competitor vital interests, to establish a robust, open dialogue with competitors and friends, and to develop and maintain a range of actions to preserve the stability of the relationship. This naturally leads to the development of strategies designed to (1) assure friends and allies, (2) dissuade adversaries from developing capabilities that threaten national well being, (3) deter potential adversaries by encouraging restraint, denying benefits, and threatening to impose unacceptable cost, and (4) maintain capabilities to terminate conflict at the lowest level of destruction consistent with strategic objectives. Regardless of the decision maker, deterrence involves four primary considerations: (1) The perceived cost of restraint (calculus: costs of not taking an action); (2) The perceived benefits of restraint (calculus: benefits of not taking an action); (3) The perceived benefits of taking action (calculus: will action achieve the desired effect?); and (4) The perceived costs of taking action (calculus: how will the competitor respond?). Understanding how these factors are interrelated is critically important to determining how best to influence adversary decision-making.

The Deterrence Operation Joint Operating Concept (DO-JOC 2006) outlines a basic approach to deterrence and was a first attempt to apply Cold War lessons to post-Cold War challenges. The US Strategic Command has evolved this concept dramatically over the last three years and is in the process of updating the 2006 document. The DO-JOC postulates a series of critical assumptions for effective deterrence of adversarial actions and behaviors that can be applied to cyber deterrence: First, the United States is aware that an adversary (state or non-state) possesses a cyber attack capability that threatens its vital interests. Second, the adversary actions to be deterred result from deliberate and intentional calculations regarding alternative courses of action and their perceptions of the values and probabilities of alternative outcomes associated with those different courses of action. Finally, cyber deterrence must assume that at least some adversary values and perceptions relevant to their decision-making can be identified, assessed, and influenced by others. The DO-JOC goes on to note that some actors (both state and non-state) will be extremely difficult to deter; however, truly irrational actors are extremely rare. Their calculus may be very different from that of the United States but what constitutes rational behavior must be understood in their terms. The following examination of cyber deterrence accepts these fundamental assumptions and focuses on deterring rational actors from attacking US vital interests in or through cyberspace.

When most people think of deterrence, the first thought that comes to mind is the ability to impose significant punishment in retaliation for an attack. However, the Deterrence Operations JOC suggests that adversaries can also be deterred if they feel their actions will not achieve the desired benefits (denial; for example, through resilience) or that restraint from the action will achieve a better outcome than taking the action the US seeks to deter.

It is instructive to assess how the DO-JOC applies to cyber deterrence. General Larry Welch (2008) has stated that cyber deterrence is difficult unless an actor first understands its own critical vulnerabilities and takes action to protect them. Another important concept can be found in a report by the Air Force Scientific Advisory Board (AFSAB 2008) which argued that it is important to protect the United States from the *effects* of attacks rather than just protect the *targets* of the attacks, or attempt to blunt the attacks themselves. One might think of this protection against effects as "mission assurance" or "cyber resiliency" as contrasted with traditional "information assurance" which focuses on the protection of networks and systems, or cybersecurity which focuses on actions taken to deny the success of known attack vectors. From a deterrence perspective, the idea is to introduce uncertainty in the adversary's mind that the attacks will achieve the desired effects; if they don't, and there is a possibility that the source of the attack might be determined through forensic analysis or intelligence means, this potential denial of benefit of the attack, or loss of benefits that would result from exercising restraint should affect the adversary's decision calculus. The potential for attribution can be improved by "reducing the noise level" through improved security and defense of critical information, systems, networks, and infrastructure, making it easier to detect behaviors that might pose a threat to the United States. This could include establishment of protocols and standards that govern both the public and private sectors in areas that could affect United States vital interests. Daniel Geer (2010) addressed the need for policy choices that support risk management versus risk avoidance, clearly recognizing that our current risk avoidance approach to cyberspace is attractive, but impractical. He postulated that Americans want freedom, security, and convenience, but they can only have two of the three. The Nation must make choices to implement a cyber deterrence strategy; anything that sacrifices vitally important aspects of national and economic security in cyberspace for purposes of convenience simplifies the attack problem for a cyber adversary.

2.2 Applying Multi-Modeling to Cyber Deterrence

An approach based on multiformalism modeling (or multi-modeling) is proposed as an aid to applying the deterrence operations concept to cyberspace. In general, the models can provide insights into the calculus of potential adversaries and provide a means to evaluate courses of action which reduce the adversary's perceived cost of restraint (not taking an action which affects US vital interests), increase the adversary's perceived benefits from restraint, reduce the perceived benefits of taking actions unacceptable to the US, and/or increasing the perceived costs of taking actions which will lead to a US response.

It is clear that imposing punishment based on the effects of cyberspace actions is difficult because of our limited ability for attribution and the length of time it takes to conduct the forensic analysis. However, from a deterrence perspective, what the adversary perceives as the capability of the United States to attribute these actions is more important than the capability itself. Therefore, US strategy in this regard should raise doubts in the adversaries' calculus that such perpetrators can conduct their actions anonymously. From a denying benefits perspective, one approach is to increase the Nation's defensive or protection capabilities already embodied in US cyber security and information assurance programs. However, another way to deny benefits is to ensure that the United States can continue operations effectively in the areas that came under attack. This approach calls for resiliency across all sectors (Pflanz and Levis 2014); the military typically refers to this capability as *mission assurance*.

Turning to the concept of escalation control it is useful to recognize that cyber escalation control will likely involve activities that are not conducted directly in cyberspace. For example, cost of restraint to potential adversaries is affected by their perception of risk to their vital interests from the United States in any domain. Conversely, the United States might be able to influence an adversary's perceived benefit from restraint by taking full advantage of its superpower status to provide incentives which potential adversaries clearly recognize would be lost should they engage in major conflict with the United States. With proper messaging, the United States can place particular emphasis on the loss of benefits an adversary might expect should it attack US vital interests through cyberspace. This messaging issue is highlighted in a recent mass media article with the tile "The Decline of Deterrence: America is no longer as alarming to its foes or reassuring to its friends" (The Economist 2014).

As in other forms of deterrence, the means for cyber deterrence are capability posturing, visible activities, and messaging. There are many possible ways to posture US cyber capabilities for potential adversaries to see. For example, simulations can demonstrate the ability to continue governmental operations while under cyber attack. There are also a variety of visible activities that can be used to support the basic deterrence elements. For example, by conducting cyber warfare exercises the US demonstrates its readiness to act in cyberspace; and by demonstrating its forensics capabilities, even if not performed in real time, the United States can demonstrate its ability to attribute the sources of attack. The Department of Homeland Security, with its exercises conducted to prepare for both natural disasters and attacks, demonstrates US commitment to resiliency and incentivizes the entire Nation to establish measures which contribute to mission assurance across all sectors. And, finally, public messaging and private diplomacy allow the United States to explain to its friends and potential foes what the Nation considers to be unacceptable actions or behaviors in cyberspace, and the reasons for its own posturing and activities. All of these means can be modeled individually; the challenge is to understand and model their interactions.

Multi-modeling offers a structured approach to develop, analyze, and assess the multiple elements of a deterrence and assurance strategy as it applies to cyberspace. A key component of such an approach is to be able to assess the effects of cyber exploits on operations and compute measures that will enable the comparison of alternative strategies that are focused on mitigating the effects (i.e., denying benefits to the adversary). The use of multiple federated models brings together the expertise of subject matter experts across multiple domains; it can enable analysts to identify their own knowledge gaps; and allow improved information and knowledge sharing across different areas of expertise.

In the following sections a more detailed examination of the modeling approach and the definitions of several relevant measures of performance are described. The approach is illustrated using a vignette in which the effect of cyber exploits on a decision making organization (e.g., an Operations Center) is evaluated. The approach is showing great promise as a means to understand the complex interactions among the many actors that are affected by cyber exploits and thus support analysts and planners as they develop cyber deterrence strategies.

2.3 Multi-Formalism Modeling

Assessing the effect of cyber exploits on an organization's performance is a challenging problem. A cyber exploit is an action that affects the performance of an information system by taking advantage of its cyber vulnerabilities. The evaluation of the effectiveness of a decision making organization consisting of human decision makers supported by systems and interacting through networks is a complex issue: many interrelated factors affect the effectiveness of the overall system, e.g., the limited information processing capacities of the decision makers and the hardware and software characteristics of the systems. Consequently, models are needed of organizations performing well defined tasks and of their information systems, as well as performance evaluation measures and procedures for computing them. An integrated methodology that exploits multi-formalism modeling and is based on some earlier work has been developed and is described in this paper.

One of the key effects of cyber exploits is the degradation of the cohesiveness of organizations carrying out well-defined tasks in a coordinated manner. A mathematical description of coordination was developed for decision-making processes by Grevet and Levis (1988). When confronted with a particular task, organization members need to access information from the supporting systems and to interact with each other following well defined processes. Such is the case in operations centers such as Air Operations Centers, Air Traffic Control Centers, etc. When decision makers interact, they must have some protocol to recognize that they are working on the same task and sharing information that pertains to that task, i.e., that they are coordinated. Two measures for evaluating coordination were introduced: information consistency and synchronization. The latter measure relates to the value of information when the decision makers actually process it.

The approach taken is that of modular, horizontal multi-formalism (Gribaudo and Iacono 2014). A generic Petri Net model of an interacting decision maker is used (Levis 1992). That model has been extended to include systems that support the decision makers and communication networks that enable their interaction. The decision making organization is modeled as a Colored Petri Net (Jensen and Kristensen 2009) and is implemented in CPNTools (CPNTools 2014). The computer networks are modeled as queuing nets and implemented in OMNeT++ (OMNeT++ 2014). These two models, though expressed in a different modeling language (formalism), interoperate through an infrastructure, the Command and Control Wind Tunnel. This is shown in Fig. 2.2 (Hemingway et al. 2011). The validity of the interoperation of these two formalisms was established in Abu Jbara and Levis (2013) based on the approach described in Levis et al. (2012).

2.4 The Decision Making Organization Model

The decision making organizations under consideration consist of groups of interacting decision makers processing information received through systems that enable information sharing (e.g., a cloud) and who interact to produce a unique organizational

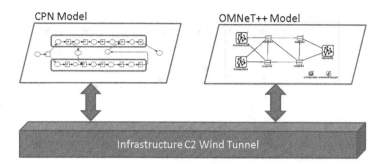

Fig. 2.2 Multi-formalism modeling and simulation architecture

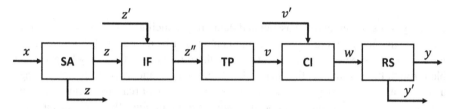

Fig. 2.3 The five stage decision maker model

response for each task that is processed. Each interacting organization member is modeled as consisting of a five-stage process as shown in Fig. 2.3.

The decision maker receives a signal x from the external environment or from another decision maker. The Situation Assessment stage (SA) represents the processing of the incoming signal x to obtain the assessed situation, z, which may be shared with other decision makers. The decision maker can also receive situation assessment signals z' from other decision makers within the organization; z' and z are then fused together in the Information Fusion (IF) stage to produce z''. The fused information is then processed at the Task Processing (TP) stage to produce v, a signal that contains the task information necessary to select a response. Command information from other decision makers is received as v'. The Command Interpretation (CI) stage then combines v and v' to produce the variable w, which is input to the Response Selection (RS) stage. The RS stage then produces the output y to the environment, or the output y' to other decision makers.

A Petri Net model is used to depict interactions between decision makers; the admissible interactions are limited to the four types shown in Fig. 2.4 in which only the interactions from the ith (DM_i) to the jth decision maker (DM_j) are shown. Similar interactions exist from the jth to the ith one. Furthermore, not all these interactions can coexist, if deadlocks are to be avoided (Remy et al. 1988).

A decision maker may have access to or select different systems and different algorithms that process the input depending on the type of signals received. The DM chooses an algorithm according to his area of expertise and the prevailing circumstances (timeliness, access to systems, etc.). Each algorithm is characterized by the

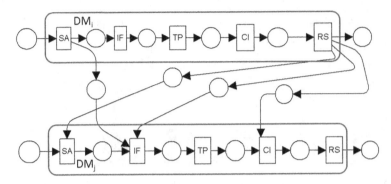

Fig. 2.4 Interacting decision making entities

accuracy of its output and the associated delay in producing it. The algorithms may
all reside in one system (e.g., at the command unit) or be located in different system
nodes; they may be accessible directly through an intranet or they may be accessible through the communication networks. There may be inconsistent or conflicting
assessments at the IF stages of the two units for a variety of reasons: using different
data sets (e.g., new vs. old data) or different assessment algorithms. A mechanism
would be needed to resolve such inconsistencies or conflicts. A similar argument is
made about the Response Selection stage where DMs have different algorithms for
generating a response.

2.5   On Measures

In order to assess the effect of cyber exploits, measures are needed. A set of new
measures is defined here that is computable from the Colored Petri net model of the
decision making organization. These measures were originally defined in Grevet and
Levis (1988).

To characterize the coordination for an interaction such as at the IF or CI stage
in the model of Fig. 2.5 order relations are defined on the set of tokens fired by the
corresponding transition:

Ψ_1 is a binary relation defined by:

$$((x, y, z)\Psi_1(x', y', z')) \leftrightarrow ((x = x') \text{ and } (z = z'))$$

Ψ_2 is a binary relation defined by:

$$((x, y, z)\Psi_2(x', y', z')) \leftrightarrow ((x = x') \text{ and } (z = z'))$$

Each token in the Colored Petri Net model is characterized by the triplet (T_n, T_d, C) where T_n is the time at which this input token was generated by the source, T_d
is the time at which a token entered the current processing stage, and the attribute C
characterizes the mission or task.

The firing of IF (or CI) is synchronized if and only if:

$$\forall i \in \{1, 2, \ldots, r\}(T_n^i, \; T_d^i, \; C^i)\Psi_1 \; (T_n^k \; T_d^k, \; C^k)$$

where i and k are two decision makers. This definition allows to discriminate between firings that are synchronized and firings in which one or several tokens arrive in their respective corresponding places with some delay.

The firing of IF (or CI) is *consistent* if and only if:

$$\forall (i, j) \in 1,2,\ldots,r \times 1,2,\ldots,r, (T_n^i, T_d^i, C^i)\Psi_2(T_n^j, T_d^j, C^j)$$

i.e., the data fused by a decision maker are consistent if they correspond to the same task or mission C. On this basis, the following definition for the coordination of an interaction is obtained: *The firing of a transition (such as IF) is coordinated if, and only if, it is synchronized and consistent.*

The definition of coordination applies to a single interaction. The definitions of the coordination of a single task, i.e., for a sequence of interactions concerning the same input, as well as for all tasks executed in a mission are as follows: The execution of a task is coordinated if, and only if, it is coordinated for all interactions that occur during the task. The execution of a mission is coordinated if, and only if, it is coordinated for all its tasks.

Consider a transition such as IF (or CI) with multiple input places. The $V(x_i, IF)$ denotes the vector that describes the colors of the tokens in the preset that have been generated as a result of the signal x_i (task or mission) produced by the external source. Then the *Degree of Information Consistency* (DIC) for stage IF and input task x_i is defined as:

$$d(x_i, IF) = \sum_{V(x_i,IF)} prob(V(x_i, IF))\frac{n(V(x_i, IF))}{z(V(x_i, IF))}$$

where $prob(V(x_i, IF))$ is the probability of having tokens with attributes generated by x_i in the input places of IF. Then let z be the number of subsets of two elements of $V(x_i, IF)$:

$$z(V(x_i, IF)) = \binom{r}{2} = \frac{r!}{2!(r-2)!}$$

and let n be the number of subsets of $V(x_i, IF)$ such that the two elements are equal.

By adding the degrees of information consistency for IF and CI and each task x_i and weighing by the probability of having that input task, the organizational degree of information consistency, DIC, for the tasks at hand can be evaluated:

$$DIC = \sum_{x_i} prob(x_i) \sum_{B=IF, CI} d(x_i, B)$$

This measure varies between 0 and 1, with 1 being the ideal information consistency of all interactions across all tasks.

The total processing time for a task by a decision maker consists of two parts: (a) the total time during which the decision maker actually carries out the task; and (b) the total time spent by the information prior to being processed. The latter time is due to two factors: (i) Information can remain unprocessed until the decision maker decides to process it with a relevant algorithm. Since an algorithm cannot process two inputs at the same time, some inputs will have to remain in queue for a certain amount of time until the relevant algorithm is available. (ii) Information can also remain unprocessed because the decision maker has to wait to receive data from another organization member. Consequently, an organization is not well synchronized when decision makers have to wait before receiving the information that they need in order to continue their task processing. Conversely, the organization is well synchronized when these lags are small.

The *Degree of Synchronization* for the organization, DOS, is given by:

$$DOS = \sum_{x_i} prob(x_i) \sum_{B=IF,CI} S(x_i; B)$$

where $S(x_i, B)$ is the total delay in transition B because of differences in the arrival time of the enabling tokens in its preset.

Two more measures were defined for evaluating the effect of cyber exploits on organizational performance.

Accuracy of the Organization $J(\delta)$ is the degree to which the organization produces desirable results (with lowest penalty) when using strategy δ. This is a global measure which ideally would be one but in realistic situations it is always less than one.

$$J(\delta) = \sum_{i} prob(x_i) \sum_{h} cost(y_h, y_{di}) prob(y_h|x_i)$$

where $\{x_i\}$ is the set of tasks and $\{y_h\}$ is the set of admissible responses from which the response y_h is selected for task x_i and y_{di} is the ideal response for input x_i. Cost(y_h, y_{di}) represents the cost associated with the organization's response.

Timeliness of the Organization $T(\delta)$ is the total response time of the organization from the time a task arrives to the time a response is produced, i.e., the task has been executed using strategy δ.

$$T(\delta) = E(elapsed\ time)$$

Up to this point, the model of an organization executing a set of tasks that arrive according to some probability distribution has been described. Also, measures of performance of the organization have been defined.

When fusion of data is performed by a decision maker it is possible that the available markings may allow multiple enablement of the IF (or CI) transition. Consequently, enablement rules need to be introduced at this point. Two alternative rules have been considered:

Rule 1 Transition IF (or CI) is enabled, if all its input places contain a token with the same value of the time attribute T_n. Rule 1 means that the transition IF (or CI)

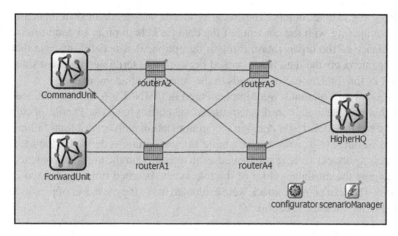

Fig. 2.5 OMNET++ Representation of the Communication Network

is enabled if and only if all its preset places contain at least a representation of the same input x_i.

Rule 2 The transition IF (or CI) is enabled if Rule 1 applies or if delays in receiving inputs from other organization members exceed a pre-specified limit.

2.6 The Network Model

A network model was implemented using OMNeT++ (2014) which is an extensible, modular, component-based C++ simulation library and framework, primarily for building network simulators. This is a discrete event simulation environment consisting of simple/compound modules with each module having a defined functionality (according to the relevant C++ class). Each module could be triggered with an appropriate event defined in its class. For the model of Fig. 2.5 the INET 2014 (2014) framework was used which supports different networking protocols including the four layers of the TCP/IP protocol. The framework provides simple/compound modules for all the four layers of the TCP/IP. The nodes in Fig. 2.5 contain in them the internal network structure for the corresponding entity (command unit, forward unit, and Higher HQ).

2.7 Modeling Cyber Exploits

Two types of cyber exploits were implemented for the computational experiments with the example described in Sect. 2.8: (1) Denial of Service attacks and (2) Integrity attacks. The Denial of Service is an attempt to make a network resource unavailable or render it too slow to be useful. This attack affects a localized region of the network topology, e.g., some routers. The Integrity attack, as was defined in this case, involves tampering with the contents of the data packets in order to compromise the performance of the organization through deception. It is usually the case that the attacker intercepts the data being passed between two terminals for a considerable amount of time; this sometimes leads to the detection of an anomaly.

The two types of attack were implemented in OMNeT++ for a predefined scenario that can generate coordinated attacks of both types. The Denial of Service exploits were modeled as a delay in a communication path or as a total failure of a network resource (e.g., a router) for a finite amount of time as defined in the scenario. The integrity attacks were implemented as an alteration in the message contents, i.e., by changing the attribute values of the tokens, at specified times as defined in the scenario. The results of the attack were evaluated using the measures of performance defined in the measures section.

2.8   A Pacifica Vignette

The island of Pacifica contains three sovereign countries: The Confederation of Washorgon States; The Republic of Nevidah; and The Peoples Republic of Califon. Califon is a Regional Hegemon in long-standing conflict with Nevidah over minerals and other economic issues. Nevidah is in mutual defense arrangement with Pacific nations including the USA. Washorgon traditionally maintains neutrality with Califon and Nevidah due to trade relationships and access to port facilities in Califon and Nevidah. The year is 2022; the Pacifica mineral fields are a major source of rare minerals. Califon has been conducting a campaign against Nevidah to obtain exclusive control of the mineral fields. Califon, seeks to limit US influence on Nevidah and the ability of US to provide assurance to Nevidah by exploiting the dependence of US forces on spectrum & cyber. The objective is to assess the effect of cyber attacks by Califon on a US Operations Center.

2.8.1   The Organization Model

The relevant components of internal organization structure of the Operations Center have been assumed to consist of the Situation Understanding Community of Interest (SU-COI), the Design and Plan COI (DP-COI) and the Command COI. (CC). It is assumed that all decision makers in each COIs share the same set of Situation Assessment (SA) and Response Selection (RS) algorithms (Fig. 2.6) and that they form a team. All the team members share the same goal. However, each team member may have a different area of expertise. For example, in the SU-COI different intelligence organization may be represented. The different areas of expertise have been modeled by assigning different probabilities for selecting the SA and the RS algorithms that a particular DM will use when an event occurs. Tables 2.1 and 2.2 reflect the assignment of probabilities for each DM in a COI.

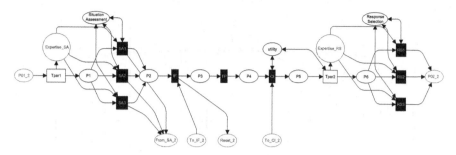

Fig. 2.6 Colored Petri net model of five-stage decision maker with three SA and three RS algorithms. (or processes)

Table 2.1 Probability of each individual DM selecting each SA algorithm for each incoming cyber event. (Expertise SA)

	SA algorithm 1	SA algorithm 2	SA algorithm 3
Event 1	p_{11}	p_{12}	p_{13}
Event 2	p_{21}	p_{22}	p_{23}
Event 3	p_{31}	p_{32}	p_{33}

Table 2.2 Probability of each individual DM selecting each RS algorithm for each identified cyber situation. (Expertise RS)

	RS algorithm 1	RS algorithm 2	RS algorithm 3
Situation 1	p_{11}	p_{12}	p_{13}
Situation 2	p_{21}	p_{22}	p_{23}
Situation 3	p_{31}	p_{32}	p_{33}

The COI teams may have different structures based on interactions between members. Two main structures were modeled: Collaborative (Fig. 2.7) and De-Conflicted (Fig. 2.8) as defined in Alberts and Hayes (2005).

The team designs in Figs. 2.7 and 2.8 were expressed in the form of Colored Petri Nets. In Fig. 2.9 the Petri net of the Design & Plan COI is shown. The hierarchical capabilities of Petri nets were used: each DM in Fig. 2.9 is represented by a substitution transition which contains the five-stage model of Fig. 2.6.

Since the team members receive some common inputs but each one can receive unique inputs, inconsistencies can occur that result in different situation assessments. Three mechanisms for resolving inconsistencies within a team have been postulated and modeled: (a) Repeat assessment for inconsistencies at the Information Fusion (IF) stage; (b) Utility maximizing decision at the Command Interpretation (CI) stage; and (c) Plurality voting at the Response Selection (RS) stage. If a decision maker encounters an inconsistency at the IF stage, the entire team will repeat the situation assessment. This may continue until a predefined time interval is exceeded tat which time the DM will continue with his own assessment even if it is not consistent with the assessment of other team members. If the DM faces conflicting data at the CI stage then he will select the option with the lowest associated cost. An example of the utility table that each decision maker uses is shown in Table 2.3.

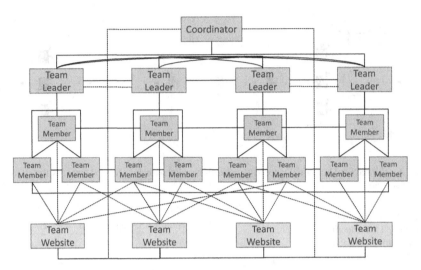

Fig. 2.7 Collaborative team structure. (Alberts and Hayes 2005)

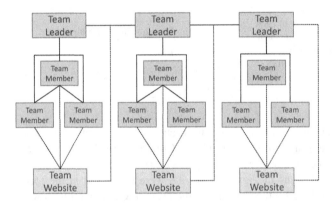

Fig. 2.8 De-conflicted team structure. (Alberts and Hayes 2005)

The team's final response in the case of any inconsistencies would be decided based on a plurality vote, i.e., the response that received the highest number of votes from the team members.

2.8.2 The Network Model and Cyber Exploits

The communication network that enables interactions among the organization members and also between the organization and the external environment has been modeled using the OMNeT++ simulation framework (OMNeT++ 2014). Each DM is assigned a dedicated terminal to work with. The implicit assumption is that

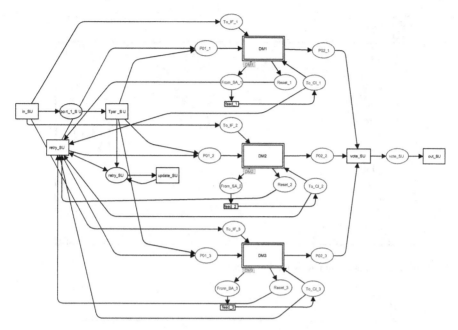

Fig. 2.9 Model of a three DM SU-COI team using the de-conflicted team design

Table 2.3 Cost of selecting a response for each situation

	Response 1	Response 2	Response 3
Situation 1	1	100	100
Situation 2	100	1	100
Situation 3	100	100	1

all the communications pass through network. The structure of the network model is shown in Figs. 2.10, 2.11 and 2.12.

The effects of two kinds of cyber exploits have been modeled: the effects on the organization's interactions of availability attacks such as denial of service and of integrity attacks in which data are modified by the attacker. The availability attacks were implemented by changing the communication channel's data rate during the execution of the scenario. The starting time of the attack (in the scenario timeline) and the reduction of channel throughput rate expressed as a percentage are two parameters characterizing the availability attack. The locality of the attack is another attribute.

The integrity exploits were implemented by the attacker modifying the data received by a DM. This could happen at the IF stage or the CI stage. Attributes of the integrity attack are the he probability of exploit being present during the scenario execution and the place in the organization model at which it occurs.

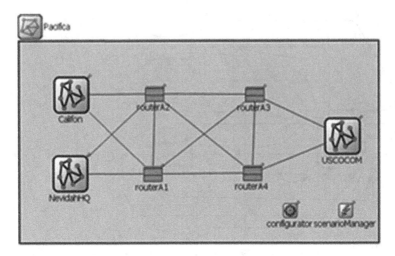

Fig. 2.10 The communication network. (top page)

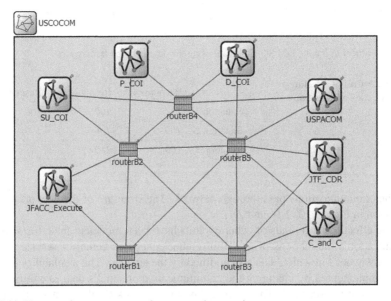

Fig. 2.11 The operations center network structure. (top page)

2.9   Computational Experiment and Results

For the Pacifica scenario in addition to the Situation Understanding COI and the Design and Plan COIs, additional entities were needed: the US Pacific Command (USPACOM), the Joint Task Force Commander (JTF_CDR), the Nevidah Comman-der (NCDR), the Capabilities and Constraints COI, and the Task Forces (Execute

Fig. 2.12 Network topology for the situation understanding community of interest

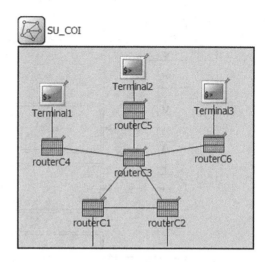

COI). These were represented by single nodes; only the SU and DP COIs were modeled by organizational structures. The SU COI was modeled with the de-conflicted team design while the Design COI and the Plan COI have collaborative organizational structures. The underlying architecture is an experimental architecture to effect Integrated Global Command and Control. The Petri net model of the complete organization (the top level) is shown in Fig. 2.13. All communications between the entities and within the entities occur through the network.

An activity model was developed to indicate the flow of data and of control and the resulting communications. A segment of the activity model is shown in Fig. 2.14.

The expertise probability tables for the decision makers, defined in Tables 2.1 and 2.2, were assigned the values shown in Tables 2.4 and 2.5.

Given this model, the Colored Petri net model of the organization and the OMNeT++ model of the network were executed on the C2 Wind Tunnel and data were collected so that the four Measures of Performance could be computed. The four measures were:

1. Accuracy of Organizational Response (*Accuracy*)
2. Timeliness of Organizational Response (*Timeliness*)
3. Degree of Information Consistency (*DIC*)
4. Degree of Synchronization (*DoS*)

These four measures provide us with a holistic view of organizational performance. The MOPs under normal condition (no exploit) are presented in Table 2.6 as a reference.

The availability attack is localized in the USPACOM network area and starts at scenario time t_{start} equal to 20. The throughput will be decrease from $10Mbps$ to $4Mbps$ for all the links directly connected to the main routers during the attack. The MOPs under availability exploit are summarized in Table 2.7.

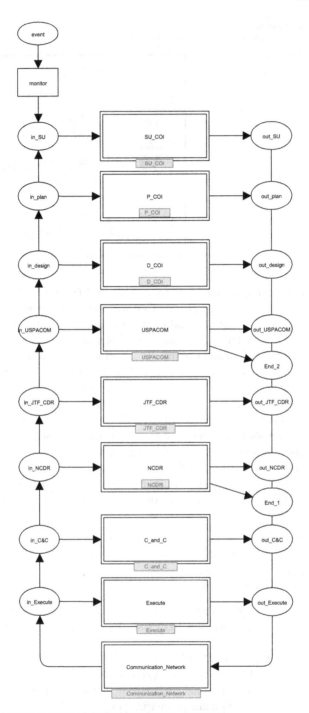

Fig. 2.13 The Petri net model of the Pacifica vignette. (top page)

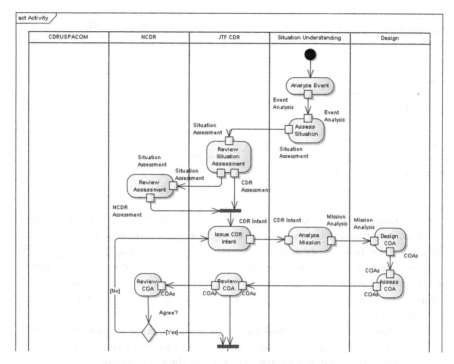

Fig. 2.14 Segment of the activity diagram describing the Pacifica scenario vignette

Table 2.4 Expertise of each DM at the SA stage

	SA algorithm 1	SA algorithm 2	SA algorithm 3
Event 1	0.9	0.05	0.05
Event 2	0.1	0.8	0.1
Event 3	0.2	0.1	0.7

Table 2.5 Expertise of each DM at the RS stage

	RS algorithm 1	RS algorithm 2	RS algorithm 3
Situation 1	0.9	0.05	0.05
Situation 2	0.1	0.8	0.1
Situation 3	0.2	0.1	0.7

The integrity attack is targeted on the Information Fusion (IF) stage of the fifth decision maker (DM-5) in the Planning COI team. The probability of the exploit being present is high ($p = 99\%$). The outcomes of the experiment are provided in Table 2.8.

Comparison of the results under normal conditions (Table 2.6) with no cyber exploits and the availability exploit (Table 2.7) displays an increase in operation time and degradation of organizational accuracy. A similar comparison between

Table 2.6 Performance
measures in the absence of
cyber exploits

Accuracy	Timeliness	DIC	DoS
0.71	294	0.94	7.35

Table 2.7 Performance
measures in the case of
availability attacks

Accuracy	Timeliness	DIC	DoS
0.53	301	1.00	7.35

Table 2.8 Performance
measures in the case of
integrity attack

Accuracy	Timeliness	DIC	DoS
0.65	308	0.93	7.88

Tables 2.6 and 2.8 shows that all the measures of performance were degraded when a focused integrity attack was made on a single decision maker in this large multi-person decision making organization. These results suggest that an integrity attack will cause performance degradation across the various measures while availability attacks prolong the mission and decrease the accuracy of the response but they will not affect the information consistency and synchronization of an organization, i.e., its coordination.

These results can now form the basis for assessing the effect of various vulnerabilities and provide needed information in developing a strategy for denying benefits of action and for determining the red lines for punishment responses.

2.10 Conclusions

A new approach based on multi-formalism modeling to model, analyze, and evaluate the effect of cyber exploits on the coordination in organizations has been presented. The focus is on the effect that cyber exploits have on the performance of a decision making organization when its ability to share uncorrupted information in a timely manner is degraded due to cyber exploits on the networks that support the interactions between organization members. Two new measures of performance, information consistency and synchronization, were used to demonstrate the effect of cyber exploits, as well as the traditional ones of accuracy and timeliness. The approach provides useful data for developing effective cyber deterrence and assurance strategies and for prioritizing elements of the four influence levers.

References

Abu Jbara A, Levis AH (2013) Semantically correct representation of multi-model interoperations. Proc. 26th International FLAIRS Conference, St Pete Beach, FL, May

AFSAB (2008) Defending and operating in a contested cyber domain, Air Force Scientific Advisory Board, Sztipanovits J Levis AH (eds) SAB-TR-08–01

Alberts DS, Hayes RE (2005) Campaigns of experimentation: Pathways to innovation and transformation. CCRP Publication Series, Washington, DC

CPN Tools (2014) http://www.cpntools.org

DO-JOC (2006) Deterrence Operation Joint Operating Concept, Version 2.0, Department of Defense, 2006 (Available at http://www.dtic.mil/futurejointwarfare)

Geer Jr., Daniel E., (2010) Cybersecurity and national policy, Harvard National Security Journal, vol. 1

Grevet JL, Levis AH (1988) Coordination in organizations with decision support systems. Proc. 1988 Symposium on C2 Research, Monterey, CA, June 1988, pp. 387–399

Gribaudo M, Iacono M (2014) An introduction to multiformalism modeling. In: Theory and Application of Multi-Formalism Modeling, Gribaudo M Iacono M (eds), IGI Global, Hershey, PA, pp. 1–16

Hemingway G, Neema H, Sztipanovits J, Karsai G (2011) Rapid synthesis of high-level architecture-based heterogeneous simulation: A model-based integration approach. Simulation, March

INET (2014) http://inet.omnetpp.org

Jensen K, Kristensen LM (2009) Coloured Petri Nets. Springer, Berlin

Levis AH (1992) A Colored Petri Net model of intelligent nodes. In: Robotics and Flexible Manufacturing Systems, Gentina JC Tzafestas SG (eds) Elsevier Science Publishers B. V., The Netherlands

Levis AH, Zaidi AK, Rafi MR (2012) Multi-modeling and meta-modeling of human organizations. *Proc. 4th Int'l Conf. on Applied Human Factors and Ergonomics—AHFE2012* San Francisco, CA, July

OMNeT++ (2014) http://www.omnetpp.org

Pflanz M, Levis AH (2014) On measuring resilience in Command and Control architectures. In: Suri N and Cabri G (eds) Engineering Adaptive and Resilient Computing Systems. Taylor & Francis, London

Remy PA, Levis AH, Jin VY (1988) On the design of distributed organizational structures. *Automatica*, 24(1) 81–86

The Economist (2014) 411(8885):23–26

Welch, Gen. Larry (2008) presentation to Cyber Warfare 2008, London, U.K., 31 March 2008

Chapter 3
Identifying and Exploiting the Cyber High Ground for Botnets

Patrick Sweeney and George Cybenko

Abstract For over 2000 years, military strategists have recognized the importance of capturing and holding the physical "high ground." As cyber warfare strategy and tactics mature, it is important to explore the counterpart of "high ground" in the cyber domain. To this end, we develop the concept for botnet operations. Botnets have gained a great deal of attention in recent years due to their use in criminal activities. The criminal goal is typically focused on stealing information, hijacking resources, or denying service from legitimate users. In such situations, the scale of the botnet is of key importance. Bigger is better. However, several recent botnets have been designed for industrial or national espionage. These attacks highlight the importance of where the bots are located, not only how many there are. Just as in kinetic warfare, there is a distinct advantage to identifying, controlling, and exploiting an appropriately defined high ground. For targeted denial of confidentiality, integrity, and availability attacks the *cyber* high ground can be defined and realized in a physical network topology. An attacker who controls this cyber high ground gains a superior capability to achieve his mission objectives. Our results show that such an attacker may reduce their botnet's footprint and increase its dwell time by up to 87 % and 155× respectively over a random or ill-informed attacker.

3.1 Introduction

A botnet is a collection of Internet connected computers that have been compromised to perform coordinated actions assigned by the controlling botmaster. Each compromised system in a botnet is known as a bot or zombie. Due to their massive scale and disruptive capability, botnets are frequently considered to be one of the largest threats to security on the Internet (Lee et al. 2010; Cooke et al. 2005). In fact, nearly all modern malware is essentially in the same class as a botnet, most notably having

P. Sweeney (✉) · G. Cybenko
Thayer School of Engineering at Dartmouth College, 8000 Cummings Hall,
Hanover, NH, 03755, USA
e-mail: sweenepj@gmail.com

G. Cybenko
e-mail: george.cybenko@dartmouth.edu

© Springer International Publishing Switzerland 2015

37

S. Jajodia et al. (eds.), *Cyber Warfare,* Advances in Information Security 56,
DOI 10.1007/978-3-319-14039-1_3

a command and control (C2) link back to a controlling entity. This makes a botnet a particularly appropriate platform for performing missions in cyberspace.

Recently, botnets have evolved to include not only end-user PC's, but also mobile devices, "smart" devices such as refrigerators, point-of-sale devices, and all manner of devices in the so-called "Internet of Things" (Bell 2014; Ashford 2013; Proofpoint 2014; Goodin 2013). As IP-based, Internet-connected devices become the norm, a clear consequence is that these new devices will become possible targets for attack. In essence, any Internet-connected system or device is a potential member of a botnet.

In addition to the expanding pool of vulnerable systems, the missions and modes of operation for botnets have likewise transformed. Whereas botnets were once primarily used for distributed denial of service (DDoS) attacks, they are now used to harvest information, mine bitcoins, send spam, and commit click-fraud – in many cases netting the botmaster significant profits. For example, the Gameover Zeus botnet with a payload of CryptoLocker generated approximately $ 27 million for the operator over a period of only 2 months (U.S. Department of Justice 2014).

Botnets can also be effectively harnessed for offensive cyber warfare applications against specific adversaries. The Internet has already witnessed some attacks of this type: Red October, Flame, APT1, and Snake to name a few (Global Research & Analysis Team (GReAT), Kaspersky Lab 2013; Kaspersky Labs 2012; Mcwhorter 2013; BAE Systems 2014). Unlike typical criminal botnets focused on profit, these botnets were designed to covertly commit systematic espionage. In terms of national interests, this is where the future of botnets lies.

Accordingly, it is vital to understand the ways in which botnets can be employed to perform missions that are motivated by national security and military interests such as monitoring and controlling the flow of an adversary's information. This paper describes a methodology for identifying and exploiting the *cyber high ground*— the set of physical systems from which cyber-based mission objectives can most effectively be achieved.

3.1.1   Our Contribution

Despite the fact that the military concept of "high ground" is over 2000 years old (Tzu 2013), it has not previously been rigorously defined for cyber operations. There are relatively few references to a "cyber high ground" or "information high ground" in the published literature (Krekel et al. 2012; Brewster 2014). These ambiguous references are focused more on strategic capability—that is, for example, whether the U.S. or China holds the "high ground" is a question of superior capability. We propose a cyber high ground concept that is literal and analogous to the height of a hill on a physical battlefield. This tactical cyber high ground provides a cyber attacker with actionable intermediate objectives as part of achieving a mission. To the best of our knowledge, this is the first attempt to identify and quantify a cyber high ground concept at this level of detail.

The remainder of the paper is organized as follows. Section 3.2 provides a brief example of our notion of the cyber high ground. Section 3.3 lays out mission categories that fall in the scope of this research. Finally, Sections 3.4 and 3.5 present our method of identifying the cyber high ground, and a use case with simulation results. Additional details and results can be found in the first author's Ph.D. thesis (Sweeney 2014).

3.2 Cyber High Ground Concept: An Example

Before an example is presented, we introduce our concept of a cyber high ground. We define a "mission set" to be a subset of systems in a network from which a cyber mission is executed. When evaluated for suitability as a mission high ground, the mission set is referred to as a candidate high ground. The optimal high ground, subsequently referred to simply as "the high ground," is the mission set that best achieves all mission objectives with minimal size. Given that context, systems that are a part of the high ground must possess one of two characteristics:

1. Effectiveness: they are situated appropriately within the targeted network to achieve desired collective goals or;
2. Stealth: they enable stealthy command and control with additional high ground systems.

Fig. 3.1 The design tradepsace explored in this research is primarily effectiveness vs. stealth. At the extremes, a highly effective botnet may not be stealthy at all, whereas a completely stealthy botnet won't be able to effectively complete a mission that requires some command and control. Somewhere in this tradespace is the cyber high ground

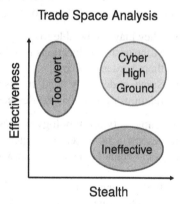

These two characteristics are more than likely opposed to each other so that designing a botnet to simultaneously achieve both effectiveness and stealth presents a trade space. Botnet design explores that trade space, seeking a high ground that comes closest to achieving all objectives within a tolerance that is acceptable to the botmaster, as in Fig. 3.1.

A scenario is developed in three parts as an example to illustrate our high ground concepts. The scenario involves an attacker who wishes to perpetrate an eavesdropping or man-in-the-middle (MITM) attack. Consider a set of target nodes, operated by a defender, that an attacker would like to eavesdrop on. That is, the attacker seeks to have a presence on the communication paths between every pair of target nodes. Whether the attacker wishes to observe the defender's netflows only, or perform

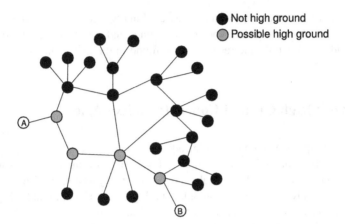

Fig. 3.2 In the first part of the scenario, an adversary simply wishes to eavesdrop on traffic between target nodes *A* and *B*. There are several locations from which this is possible, and given no further constraints any is equally well suited

more detailed inspection of the packets, they must be positioned in a location that allows access to the traffic. On a small scale, this offers some insight into the high ground—at least the attacker can eliminate nodes that are *not* high ground. Other considerations may play into the attacker's decision as well, such as:

- They may not be able to compromise an ideal network location;
- Some desirable locations may be behind a network defense perimeter that makes them harder to access;
- Some nodes may lend themselves to a higher level of stealth due to their relationship to defensive devices.

A simple network topology is presented as an undirected graph, where each node represents a host, server, router, or other network device. The graph represents physical connections on the network, and traffic is assumed to follow the shortest path.

In this scenario there are only two nodes of interest, and the attacker's mission is to eavesdrop on traffic between them. Figure 3.2 shows part 1 of the scenario, where the nodes of interest are A and B. In this part, the attacker has no constraints other than positioning his bots in a location that makes the eavesdropping mission possible. Being aware of the network topology, the attacker can quickly identify intermediate nodes that are on the shortest path from A to B, and mark those as feasible points to attack. There are several locations that meet the mission requirements, giving the attacker a relatively high probability of success in compromising and controlling a suitable node.

The second part of the scenario is shown in Fig. 3.3, where two additional constraints are levied upon the attacker. The first is due to the eavesdropping node being part of a botnet: it must report back to a C2 server at node C. The second constraint is that the defender has added a system at node D that with high probability detects

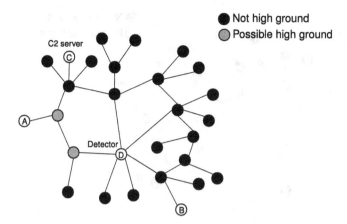

Fig. 3.3 The second part of the scenario adds two constraints including a C2 server that the eaves-dropping node must communicate with, and a detector node that detects C2 traffic. The attacker's eavesdropping locations are limited to those that will not route traffic through D

botnet C2 traffic. In order to maintain stealth of communications and avoid node D, eavesdropping nodes must be selected such that traffic is not routed through detector node D, thus reducing possible high ground options to the nodes shown. Note that the node between B and D is not a candidate high ground node because the shortest path route between that node and the C2 server passes through D which increases the probability of detection to an unacceptable level.

The final part of the scenario, shown in Fig. 3.4, presents the case where the attacker cannot easily contact the C2 server without routing traffic through a detector node. Note that the location of the C2 server has been changed from the previous configuration. Due to competing requirements of mission (eavesdropping and reporting to node C) and stealth (not alerting node D by having C2 paths pass through D), the high ground is limited such that no single node can simultaneously satisfy all the attacker's requirements. To deal with this situation the attacker uses an additional node as a relay for C2 traffic between the eavesdropping node and the C2 server. This provides added stealth while, perhaps counter intuitively, making the botnet larger. It is also important to note that a C2 structure is enforced on the botnet to ensure C2 traffic is routed for the most effective stealth.

From this scenario, we can identify some data points and metrics that are of interest to both the attacker and the defender:

- Where is the cyber high ground located for a particular mission/stealth profile?
- What level of mission effectiveness is achieved by the attacker?
- What level of stealth is achieved by the attacker?

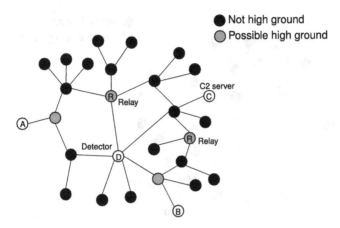

Fig. 3.4 In the final configuration, the adversary cannot accomplish the mission and avoid detection with just a single node. To do so requires one additional node to be used as a relay for C2 traffic. Note that two of several possible options (including options with more than one relay) are shown in the figure

Ultimately, both attacker and defender want to know the probability that the attacker can accomplish his mission if he achieves the high ground.

Like many questions about cyber security quantification, these are difficult to answer. The approach developed and presented in the remainder of the paper is one way to consistently measure these attributes, thus identifying a more informed design process.

3.3   Mission Types

Current botnets are associated with missions in which scale is of primary importance, such as DDoS attacks, spamming, mining virtual currency, click-fraud and harvesting private information. In these types of attacks, it is not as important where the bots are located on a network as that they exist in great numbers. If the locations of bots on a physical network are available as definable characteristics, that creates opportunities to use botnets for more subtle attacks and to be more strategic in developing stealthy C2 structures.

In addition to attacks that leverage scale, botnets with targeted deployment can participate in missions categorized into familiar types: denial of confidentiality, denial of integrity, and denial of availability (anti-CIA). This is expressed in Fig. 3.5

Denial of Confidentiality Botnets have already been observed harvesting information from systems they have co-opted. Their prolific nature leads to a very broad area of data collection that may be well suited for a wide-scale Internet sensing mission. On the other hand, if an attacker wishes to collect information on a specific set of targets, then a tailored botnet can provide a subtle and effective

		Effect Type		
		Anti-confidentiality	Anti-integrity	Anti-availability
Mission Type	Cyber espionage / snooping	X		
	Stealthy denial of service		X	X
	Control chokepoints	X	X	X

Fig. 3.5 Botnets designed with physical network configuration in mind can execute missions with specific anti-CIA effects

means to do so via a MITM or netflow monitoring attack. Mapping missions also fit into this category.

Denial of Integrity Botnets in practice execute forms of deception simply by hiding their existence on a system. This breakdown of trust in one's system is a denial of integrity at the most basic level. Once a botnet has co-opted a system, it is easy to recognize opportunities for deceiving the user with tampered information. Similar to denial of confidentiality attacks, however, a tailored botnet could perform denial of integrity remotely via a MITM attack against specific nodes. This requires both thoughtful insertion of the bots into locations that make the attack feasible, and possibly specialized capabilities such as the understanding a target system's communication protocols.

Denial of Availability Huge botnets are routinely engaged in DDoS attacks, and certainly a co-opted end node can be commanded to shut down, disrupt and/or delay services at the attacker's whim. A carefully inserted MITM attack bot could perform similar denial of service attacks with less overhead and fewer involved network nodes than a DDoS attack.

Our review of literature shows that these basic mission types are not considered when measuring botnet effectiveness. As mentioned previously, the primary metric of success in botnet design has thus far been solely size, or some derivative of size such as total available throughput or processing power (Wang et al. 2010; Dagon et al. 2007). In the next section, we present our method for designing and assessing botnets for the anti-CIA missions outlined here.

3.4 Identifying the Cyber High Ground

We propose evaluating both stealth and mission effectiveness in scenarios with a given network topology, and specific mission and stealth objectives. We intend to provide a means by which a cyber mission planner can input a set of desired effectiveness and stealth objectives for a given topology, and derive an optimal or approximately optimal cyber high ground.

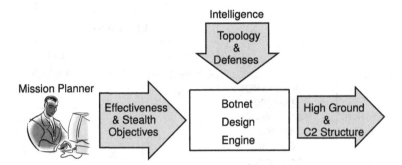

Fig. 3.6 Our botnet design engine takes effectiveness and stealth objectives provided by the mission planner and applies them to a known network topology (with known or estimated defenses). The output of the system is a listing of high ground nodes, C2 structure, and a quantified representation of the mission effectiveness and stealth provided for the mission

3.4.1 Concept Overview

The approach considered in this research begins with a mission that a person or organization, subsequently referred to as the *mission planner* or *attacker*, would like to perform on the *target network*. The mission planner identifies a prioritized set of effectiveness and stealth objectives that best fit the mission, and then submits them to the design engine. The design engine, using network topology data that includes physical systems, interconnections, targets, and possibly defensive information, produces an optimal or approximately optimal set of nodes that are the *cyber high ground* as well as an associated C2 structure. The framework is shown in Fig. 3.6. If this mission planner then controls the nodes in the cyber high ground and adheres to the optimized C2 structure, they have an optimized balance between accomplishing their mission and achieving the minimal probability of detection.

3.4.2 Characterizing Effectiveness

Given a specific mission, a botnet's effectiveness must be evaluated quantitatively. This step is necessary in order to identify the high ground among possible mission node sets.

A set of effectiveness primitives is used, with the intention that they can be generalized and combined into more complex missions. The mission planner defines a set of effectiveness objectives and attributes that best accomplish the mission, and these objectives affect the high ground.

Each objective is evaluated with respect to a candidate high ground H. Recall that a candidate high ground is a "mission set," or set of nodes that are members of a proposed botnet.

A basic effectiveness objective is a multi-target intercession objective. This concerns an eavesdropping or MITM attack with multiple targets, in which traffic routes between two or more specific target nodes is affected.

Attributes:

- Target list $(T = \{t_1, ..., t_n\})$: a set of 2 or more targets that are the subject of the attack.
- Effectiveness robustness $(R_{effectiveness})$: the desired number of nodes covering each route.

The effectiveness of a botnet toward meeting a multi-target intercession objectives is measured through a ratio of actual route coverage to desired route coverage. It is linearly tempered by the desired effectiveness robustness. If an objective is to monitor a set of T target nodes as they communicate with one another, then the total number of undirected shortest path routes in the network is $|T|(|T|-1)/2$. Any subset of routes that intersects the candidate high ground yields a mission effectiveness component of:

$$
Effectiveness \ (H) = \frac{2}{|T|(|T|-1)} \sum_{i=1}^{|T|} \sum_{j=i+1}^{|T|} \min\left(1, \frac{|r(t_i, t_j) \cap H|}{R_{effectiveness}}\right) \quad (3.1)
$$

where $r(t_i, t_j)$ is the set of nodes on the route that traffic takes between targets t_i and t_j. A term in the summation is less than 1 if H does not meet the effectiveness robustness goal for a target pair and equals 1 if the goal is achieved or surpassed so that no credit is given for over acheiving the desired coverage.

3.4.3   Characterizing Stealth

Stealth objectives are related to communication, not to specific mission activity. Each stealth objective, like the effectiveness objectives, is evaluated with respect to a candidate high ground H.

Depending on the botnet's mission, a mission planner can set stealth objectives using simple primitives. The most basic notion of stealth is to minimize the use of network resources, especially those instrumented to detect botnet C2 traffic.

An additional required ingredient for the model is:

- Quantitative expression for the probability of detection $(Pr_{detection})$: this models the likelihood of botnet detection based on how many C2 messages a detector observes. In this work, a linear model is used (more observed C2 messages leads to a linearly higher probability of detection with a maximum of 1).

In order to calculate a stealth objective score, the candidate high ground H is required as well as the suggested botnet communication structure, O, which is a set of edges in the botnet overlay network that represent communication routes. U is the set of nodes that are suspected to be detectors. The resource use, u_i, is determined for each node in U by simulating transmission of a single message to every member of

H using the communication structure O. Each time a resource is traversed or bot sends/receives a message, its total use is increased by one unit.

The overall stealth objective score is computed as the average probability of detection across all resources:

$$Stealth\,(H, O) = \left(1 - \frac{1}{|U|} \sum_{\forall u_i} Pr_{detection}(u_i)\right) \tag{3.2}$$

3.4.4 Finding the Optimal High Ground and C2 Structure

Once a botnet's effectiveness and stealth objectives are identified, they are used to design a botnet that provides the optimal effectiveness and stealth. Therefore the remaining task is to translate objectives into high ground and associated C2 structure, O (i.e. which nodes communicate with which nodes).

Recall that the probability of detecting C2 traffic on a defended node is dependent on how many messages it observes. Therefore it is critical in designing an optimal C2 structure to minimize the use of nodes that are suspected or known to host detectors. Without O, the stealth objectives could not be quantified and therefore the high ground could not be identified.

In a centralized C2 botnet, O would consist of a set of edges from one node (the C2 server) to each other node. However, a centralized C2 structure is suboptimal for managing stealth based on resource use. Instead, a technique is used to algorithmically determine the C2 structure with the lowest risk of detection The technique computes a minimal spanning tree with respect to risk, and is subsequently called a risk-minimal spanning tree (RMST). RMST is simply a special case of a P2P structure in which bots are given very specific peer lists for communication.

To determine the RMST C2 structure in an automated fashion, the following procedure is used:

1. Initialize edges in the topology's adjacency matrix with low but non-zero cost of traversal,
2. Assign high cost to traversing edges into and out of nodes that host detectors or are suspected to host detectors,
3. Generate a matrix containing the cost to traverse the shortest routes between each pair of nodes in the botnet overlay,
4. Determine the minimal spanning tree among the overlay nodes, yielding the RMST C2 structure.

Once the RMST is determined, the attacker should route C2 traffic along its edges, which are edges in the overlay network. By definition, this C2 structure imparts minimal hits on the detectors/high cost nodes.

Finally, for a given set of mission effectiveness objectives $\{E_1, ..., E_n\}$ and stealth objectives $\{S_{n+1}, ..., S_m\}$, the goal is to find the candidate high ground, H, that maximizes:

$$H_{optimal} = \arg\max_{H} \left[\sum_{i=1}^{n} E_i P_i + \sum_{j=n+1}^{m} S_j P_j \right] \quad (3.3)$$

where P_i and P_j are normalized weights that represent the mission planner's assigned priorities for the desired mission and stealth objectives, and

$$\sum_{k=1}^{m+n} P_k = 1$$

Exhaustively trying all combinations of nodes in a topology to find the optimal high ground is infeasible as the number of nodes increases. In fact, optimizing a single intercession objective with minimal size and $R_{effectiveness} = 1$ is nontrivial. Identified by Karp as the NP-complete "hitting set" problem, it says for a family $\{U_i\}$ of subsets of $\{s_j, j = 1, 2, ..., r\}$, there is a set W such that, for each i, $|W \cap U_i| = 1$ (Karp 1972). In this case, U_i represents the routes of interest, and W constitutes the mission cyber high ground. Therefore methods for approximating the solution are desired. In this research, a simulated annealing optimization algorithm has been used.

3.5   Simulation and Results

To demonstrate the benefits of identifying and controlling the high ground, a use case is developed and presented. The use case takes place on a measured network topology derived from RocketFuel data (Spring et al. 2004; Rocketfuel 2013). The topology is the Level 3 (US) internet service provider (ISP) topology which has 5328 nodes and 11,346 edges.

3.5.1   Use Case Description

In this use case, a legitimate entity (the defender) is performing a mission on a network topology. The defender's mission leads to target nodes being randomly scattered on the topology along with detector nodes for defense.

Target nodes are set to perimeter nodes, considering that they are most representative of a legitimate user sourcing or sinking data on a network. Detectors are set to interior nodes (i.e. routers) as they are in a position to observe traffic flows and look for botnet C2 activity. Both target nodes and detectors are controlled by the defender.

The attacker is designing a botnet to intercede traffic between target nodes while remaining stealthy. The locations of detectors is known. In this context, the attacker develops three objectives for the mission:

Objectives

- E_1 = multi-target intercession with T = *target list*.
- S_2 = minimize size of high ground/botnet.
- S_3 = avoid using resources proportionally according to known risk.

Factors

Two parameters are varied in this use case:

1. *Percentage of target nodes T, $|T|$:* 5 %, 10 % of total nodes in topology.
2. *Percentage of detectors, $|D|$:* 5 %, 10 % of total nodes in topology.

Design Approaches

Several design approaches are used for comparison, including:

Random/Peer-to-peer: This is a naïve approach to design, where the attacker assumes nothing about the topology. Nodes are randomly added to the proposed high ground until an acceptable effectiveness is reached. Stealth is largely ignored, as nodes in the high ground communicate randomly to others as is typical of a peer-to-peer botnet.

   Several out-degrees for each bot are explored, including 2, 3, 4, 5, and $N - 1$, where N is the size of the botnet, essentially creating a centralized botnet structure.

Basic Heuristic: This is a partially informed approach, where the attacker adds nodes to the high ground based on their degree. Beginning with the highest degree nodes on the target network, nodes are added to the high ground until a target effectiveness score is reached. Stealth is achieved by adopting an RMST C2 structure.

Advanced Heuristic: This approach is similar to the basic heuristic technique except nodes are added to the high ground in order of decreasing mission-betweenness. Mission-betweenness is a measure of how central a node is to the defender's target nodes. Stealth is again achieved by adopting an RMST C2 structure.

Optimized: This approach, which has been discussed in depth, is another informed technique to which the other approaches are compared.

The target effectiveness score is set by the optimized approach, and serves as the baseline that the other design approaches must achieve.

Repetitions

Each configuration is executed ten times with random seeds. Randomness for additional repetitions comes from designation of the target set, T, and detectors on the topology.

Summary of Experiments

Table 3.1 summarizes the combinations of factors for this use case. A simulation is executed using each design approach for each set of factors.

Table 3.1 Summary of experiment factors. $|T|$ and $|D|$ are defined as a percentage of total nodes in the topology, and $P_1 - P_3$ are the objective priority weights for E_1, S_2 and S_3 respectively

Configuration	$|T|$ (%)	$|D|$ (%)	P_1	P_2	P_3
2.1	5	5	0.65	0.05	0.30
2.2	5	10	0.65	0.05	0.30
2.3	10	5	0.65	0.05	0.30
2.4	10	10	0.65	0.05	0.30

3.5.2 Results

There are three natural ways to compare results, holding one of each constant out of the effectiveness, size, and stealth. Because of the non-linearity of the stealth objective (recall that sometimes a larger botnet exhibits more stealth, sometimes less) it is more challenging to include. Comparing on the basis of effectiveness and size, however, is more intuitive and effectiveness is selected as the basis for comparison in the following paragraphs.

Tables 3.2 through 3.5 list the results of the simulations for where the effectiveness objective E_1 is held constant between design approaches. The E_1 level is set by the optimized approach first, and then the alternative approaches are used to achieve the same level.

In each configuration, the optimized approach provides a noticeable reduction in high ground size, as can be seen in Tables 3.2 and 3.3. It must be noted that the although the advanced heuristic design approach produced a larger high ground on average, in some individual cases it was quite competitive. The basic heuristic approach does not fare well. Although nodes with a high degree centrality have an increased chance of being on a path of interest when there is more cross communication between nodes, this approach is still crude and doesn't take into account important information about the locations of targets.

Finally, the randomly designed botnet performs terribly, requiring up to 10+ times the number of nodes that an optimized design requires. To put the high ground

Table 3.2 This table shows the high ground magnitude, in number of nodes, for each combination of factors in the use case, and for each design approach. The effectiveness score, E_1 is shown as it forms the basis of comparison for the different design approaches. The numbers are averaged over ten repetitions. Additionally, each of the ten repetitions for the random case is an average of ten executions given a single target and detector layout

Factors				$|H|$ (mean)			
Conf	$|T|$ (%)	$|D|$ (%)	E_1	Optimized	Advanced heuristic	Basic heuristic	Random
2.1	2	2	0.9956	128.6	219.5	1081.0	1580.0
2.2	2	4	0.9927	157.1	230.0	1035.9	1467.1
2.3	4	2	0.9948	213.3	250.4	762.8	1520.3
2.4	4	4	0.9917	248.3	267.3	749.6	1427.9

sizes into perspective, consider that the network on which the mission is taking place has 5328 nodes. As the attacker is forced to increase the size of the botnet,

Table 3.3 This table shows a percentage reduction in high ground size that an optimized design brings for each combination of factors in the use case. It is interpreted as, the optimized design reduces the required size of the botnet by the listed percentage, while maintaining the same effectiveness. For example, in configuration 2.1, the optimized design approach reduced the botnet size by 91.86 % compared to the random design approach

Factors			Optimized $|H|$ reduction percentage		
Conf	$|T|$ (%)	$|D|$ (%)	Advanced heuristic (%)	Basic heuristic (%)	Random (%)
2.1	2	2	41.41	88.10	91.86
2.2	2	4	31.70	84.83	89.29
2.3	4	2	14.82	72.04	85.97
2.4	4	4	7.11	66.88	82.61

Table 3.4 This table shows the composite stealth scores for each combination of factors in the use case. The effectiveness score, E_1 is shown as it forms the basis of comparison for the different design approaches. The values are averaged over ten repetitions. Scores for random design with out degree (OD) equal to 2, 4, and 5 are omitted because the scores were very similar to the scores with $OD = 3$

Factors				Composite stealth score				
Conf	$|T|$ (%)	$|D|$ (%)	E_1	Optimized	Advanced heuristic	Basic heuristic	Random (OD = 3)	Random centralized
2.3	2	2	0.9956	0.9970	0.9946	0.9587	0.7185	0.8231
2.6	2	4	0.9927	0.9960	0.9921	0.9541	0.7177	0.8244
2.9	4	2	0.9948	1.0000	0.9871	0.9800	0.7240	0.8274
2.12	4	4	0.9917	0.9988	0.9850	0.9766	0.7199	0.8264

Table 3.5 This table shows the improvement in dwell time that an optimized design has over the other design alternatives in the use case. It is interpreted as, the optimized botnet can exist on the network for the the given number of times as long as the alternative design while exhibiting the same level of stealth. For example, in configuration 2.1, the botnet designed using the optimized approach can exist on the network $65\times$ as long as the botnet designed with a random/centralized approach. Note that "Inf" means that that the optimized design achieved a perfect score, so it can't be compared accurately to the other designs

Factors			Optimized improvement in dwell time			
Conf	$|T|$ (%)	$|D|$ (%)	Advanced heuristic	Basic heuristic	Random (OD = 3)	Random centralized
2.1	2	2	1.8	14.1	110.4	65.0
2.2	2	4	2.0	11.7	82.4	47.9
2.3	4	2	Inf	Inf	Inf	Inf
2.4	4	4	12.4	19.4	270.3	156.8

the saturation level on the network goes up as a percentage of nodes required to compromise. A randomly designed botnet of size 1580 means nearly 30 % of the network nodes have to be controlled by the attacker to accomplish the mission. An optimized botnet meeting the same mission objectives could occupy only 128 nodes, yielding a saturation level of only 2.4 %.

The least improvement is attained over the advanced heuristic approach (only 7.11 % in configuration 2.4). This shows there is some merit to the advanced heuristic approach, and supports a logical conclusion that nodes exhibiting high mission-centricity are of high value to an attacker.

Increases in dwell time, as shown in Tables 3.4 and 3.5, are achieved across all combinations of factors. A botnet's dwell time considers that for each message sent by the attacker's botnet, there is a probability of stealth, i.e. the probability that the botnet is not detected, which is $1 - Pr_{detection}$. To determine the probability of non-detection for multiple messages, the probability of non-detection for a single message is raised to the power of the number of messages in the series. Comparing the result to the probability of non-detection for other designs, the power becomes the improvement factor for dwell time. More succinctly:

$$Improvement = \frac{log(Score_{alternative})}{log(Score_{optimized})} \qquad (3.4)$$

For example, if the optimized design improves the dwell time of the botnet by 10 vs. an alternate design approach, that means that the optimized botnet could send 10x more C2 messages to all bots with the same probability of detection.

Dwell time is impacted primarily by two factors: the size of the botnet and the detector-avoidance capability. As the botnet gets larger, more message traffic is naturally generated in order to send a message to each bot. If those messages additionally do not follow intelligent routing, they will intersect the detectors indiscriminately.

In some cases, an optimized botnet can achieve perfect stealth—i.e. it can route C2 messages around all detectors when the locations of detectors are known. In nearly every case, as can be seen in Table 3.5, the optimized botnet shows a significant improvement in dwell time over other design approaches.

One case where the optimized approach reveals an advantage occurs when there is a smaller number of detectors. In many cases, the ability to not only route around detectors but also place bots in locations that make such routing easier is a distinct advantage unique to the optimized design. See, for example, cases 2.1 vs. 2.2 and 2.3 vs. 2.4. In each comparison, as the saturation of detectors increases from 2 to 4 %, the advantage that the optimized design provides decreases (with one exception) as it becomes more challenging to avoid the prolific detectors.

A second observation of interest comes from comparing case 2.2 vs. 2.4. While the number of detectors remains consistent at 4 %, there is nearly a 3–6× increase in dwell time against the advanced heuristic and random design approaches as the number of targets increases from 2 to 4 %. This is due partially to a differential in size increases for the design approaches, but also due to the ability to place bots in locations that facilitate both effectiveness and stealth at the same time.

3.5.3 Summary Points

- In this use case, it may be sufficient for a mission planner to use the advanced heuristic design approach. However, the optimized design approach does improve performance somewhat over every alternative.
- The basic heuristic approach is likely insufficient. While it's true that nodes with higher degree are more likely to be used by the distributed communications architecture of the targets, poor effectiveness scores were still achieved with this relatively naïve approach.
- For an equally effective botnet, the optimized design approach reduces the attacker's botnet size by 24, 77, and 87 % as compared to advanced heuristic, basic heuristic, and random design, respectively, when averaged across all sets of factors.
- For an equally effective botnet, the optimized design approach increases dwell time by 5×, 15×, and up to 155× over the advanced heuristic, basic heuristic, and random designs, respectively, when averaged across all factors. Cases where the optimized approach achieved perfect stealth are not included in the avearge.
- Figure 3.7 charts the scores for a quick-look comparison.

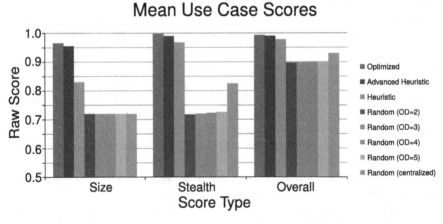

Fig. 3.7 This chart shows a quick-look comparison of scores for the different design approaches in the use case. The first column shows the high ground size scores, which are essentially (1-the saturation required for the attacking botnet). For example, a botnet requiring 1300 nodes on a 5328 node network would have a saturation of approximately 25 %, for a score of approximately 0.75. The second column shows the stealth score, and the rightmost column shows the total score which is the priority-weighted sum of all the mission planner's objective scores

3.6 Defensive High Ground

To this point, the high ground has been considered from the perspective of the attacker. It is arguable that in physical warfare, there is a single high ground that affords the same benefit to both the attacker and the defender. On a cyber battlefield, that is not necessarily the case.

Recall from Fig. 3.4, we proposed two possible sets of high ground nodes for the attacker. In each set, there is one node to perform the intercession mission and one to act as a relay to the C2 server.

Next, consider what objectives the defender has upon the shared topology. The primary objective, of course, is the mission performed by nodes A and B. Secondary, but of equal importance, is ensuring the mission is unimpeded by the attacker. In order to do so, the defender must detect the attacker's botnet activity (and then presumably act upon it). This leads to a simplified, derived requirement for the defender's high ground: detect the attacker's C2 messages.

The detector D is in fact the defender's proposed high ground at the outset. The defender has designated mission nodes A and B, along with detector D. In reality, D is placed with some degree of forethought as it does prevent the attacker from achieving a single-node high ground. However, it is impossible for the defender to know that a priori, and as we have seen it is still trivial for the attacker to achieve his objectives.

Figure 3.8 illustrates some potential high ground nodes for the defender that will allow detection of the attacker's C2 messages given the current state of the topology. A keen observer will note that a detector placed directly adjacent to the C2 server is ideal in this simplified topology; however we must recall that detectors are to be placed prior to an attacker's intrusion onto the network, which renders that trivial placement impossible. The broader observation is that the original detector location D is instrumental in deriving the attacker's high ground, which in turn generates a revised defensive high ground orthogonal to the original. In other words, the defender's high ground depends on the attacker's high ground—and the attacker's high ground depends on the defender's!

An unfortunate outcome of this analysis is that the defender is at a distinct disadvantage simply because they "play first" by placing detectors in anticipation of an attack. If the attacker can discern the location of the detectors, he will be able to meet his effectiveness and stealth objectives with high probability. The two basic recourses the defender has are to:

1. Assume that detector placement will be discovered by the attacker and fully instrument *all* non-mission nodes as detectors, or
2. Assume that the detector placement will not be discovered by the attacker, and instrument *some* non-mission nodes.

Neither of these options is particularly attractive. The first option, instrumenting all nodes, is not only unrealistic but impossible without allowing for cohabitation of attacker and defender on the same node. The merits of this particular arrangement

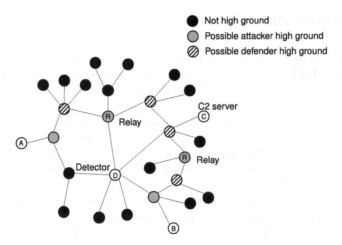

Fig. 3.8 In the example presented earlier, the defender's initial proposed high ground was only node D. This figure shows how the possible high ground for the defender has changed in light of the attacker's optimal botnet design. There are several locations identified that may be part of the defender's high ground, however it is dependent on the attacker's high ground and cannot be determined a priori

are the subject of other work, and not addressed here. Regardless, it is a significant investment for the defender both in initial setup and management of the large number of detectors.

The second option is more manageable, but the efficacy depends on good operational security. Recent events show that our adversaries are very good at learning information about our cyber systems that we would prefer not to divulge, so it is hard to take on faith that detectors can remain anonymous.

Nevertheless, this is the only viable option (for a static defense—dynamic relocation of detectors may also be effective but costly in terms of effort). Consequently, as we advance our own techniques for obtaining intelligence about the cyber battlefields on which we intend to operate, we must become equally adept and denying that information to our adversaries. Without doing so we will concede the high ground to the attacker and, at best, have diminished capability to detect their activity and, at worst, miss it entirely.

3.7   Conclusions

This research explores several optimization criteria for botnet cyber attack based on a well-defined, quantitative notion of "cyber high ground" which is introduced with basic examples and then demonstrated through use case simulation. To our knowledge, this is the first attempt to define this concept at the level of physical systems and yet it is critical to cyber operations that involve covert and subtle espionage on adversary networks.

Moreover, the definition and quantification of advanced anti-CIA cyber missions is explored. While traditional botnet missions have focused on scale and throughput, subtle denial of confidentiality, integrity, and availability rely more on acquiring and holding key network locations. This work has suggested stealth and effectiveness objectives that are quantifiable and measurable, as well as providing a process for optimizing a botnet across those objectives.

Through use case simulation, it has been shown that using an optimized approach to botnet design can generate botnets that are significantly more stealthy than those designed randomly or via heuristic approaches.

Finally, this research has pushed the limits of the science of botnet design to an extent that it has not previously been explored. Hopefully, with additional effort in future work, this science will develop to inform us as both attackers and defenders, and give a superior edge in designing and deploying cyber weapons such as botnets. Additional results, details and use cases can be found in (Sweeney 2014).

3.8 Release Statement

The views expressed in this article are those of the authors and do not reflect the official policy of the United States Air Force, Department of Defense, or the U.S. Government. Approved for Public Release; Distribution Unlimited: 88ABW-201404819.

References

Ashford, W., Jan. 2013. Computerweekly - huge botnet infecting smartphones in china. URL http://www.computerweekly.com/news/2240176104/Huge-botnet-infecting-smartphones-in-China

BAE Systems, 2014. Snake Campaign & Cyber Espionage Toolkit. Tech. rep.

Bell, L., Jan. 2014. The Inquirer - 24,000 Android devices are hit by XXXX.apk mobile botnet. URL http://www.theinquirer.net/inquirer/news/2322028/24-000-android-devices-are-hit-by-xxxxapk-mobile-botnet

Brewster, M., May 2014. The Canadian Press - NATO Scrambles to take the Cyber High Ground. URL http://www.londoncommunitynews.com/news-story/4503489-nato-scrambles-to-take-the-cyber-high-ground/

Cooke, E., Jahanian, F., McPherson, D., 2005. The zombie roundup: Understanding, detecting, and disrupting botnets. Proceedings of the USENIX SRUTI Workshop.

Dagon, D., Gu, G., Lee, C. P., Lee, W., Dec. 2007. A Taxonomy of Botnet Structures. Twenty-Third Annual Computer Security Applications Conference (ACSAC 2007), 325–339.

Global Research & Analysis Team (GReAT), Kaspersky Lab, Jan. 2013. Securelist - the "red october" campaign - an advanced cyber espionage network targeting diplomatic and government agencies. URL http://www.securelist.com/en/blog/785/The_Red_October_Campaign_An_Advanced_Cyber_Espionage_Network_Targeting_Diplomatic_and_Government_Agencies

Goodin, D., Dec. 2013. Arstechnica - credit card fraud comes of age with advances in point-of-sale botnets. URL http://arstechnica.com/security/2013/12/credit-card-fraud-comes-of-age-with-first-known-point-of-sale-botnet/

R.M. Karp. 1972. Reducibility among combinatorial problems. R.E. Miller, J.W. Thatcher (Eds.), Complexity of Computer Computations, Plenum Press, New York, pp. 85–104.

Kaspersky Labs, May 2012. Kaspersky - kaspersky lab and itu research reveals new advanced cyber threat. URL http://usa.kaspersky.com/about-us/press-center/press-releases/kaspersky-lab-and-itu-research-reveals-new-advanced-cyber-threa

Krekel, B., Adams, P., Bakos, G., 2012. Occupying the information high ground: Chinese capabilities for computer network operations and cyber espionage.

Lee, W., Wang, C., Dagon, D., 2010. Botnet Detection: Countering the Largest Security Threat.

Mcwhorter, D., 2013. APT1: Exposing One of China's Cyber Espionage Units. Mandiant. com. URL http://scholar.google.com/scholar?hl=en&btnG=Search&q=intitle:APT1:+Exposing+one+of+China's+cyber+espionage+units#0

Proofpoint, Jan. 2014. Proofpoint - more than 750,000 phishing and spam emails launched from "thingbots" including televisions, fridge. URL http://www.proofpoint.com/about-us/press-releases/01162014.php

Rocketfuel, 2013. Rocketfuel: An ISP Topology Mapping Engine. URL http://www.cs.washington.edu/research/networking/rocketfuel/

Spring, N., Mahajan, R., Wetherall, D., Anderson, T., Feb. 2004. Measuring ISP Topologies With Rocketfuel. IEEE/ACM Transactions on Networking 12 (1), 2–16.

Sweeney, P. J., 2014. Designing effective and stealthy botnets for cyber espionage and interdiction: Finding the cyber high ground. Ph.D. Thesis, Thayer School of Engineering, Dartmouth College, Hanover NH.

Tzu, S., 2013. The art of war. Orange Publishing.

U.S. Department of Justice, June 2014. U.S. Leads Multi-National Action Against "Gameover Zeus" Botnet and "Cryptolocker" Ransomware, Charges Botnet Administrator. URL http://www.justice.gov/opa/pr/2014/June/14-crm-584.html

Wang, P., Aslam, B., Zou, C., 2010. Peer-to-Peer Botnets: The Next Generation of Botnet Attacks. Electrical Engineering, 1–25.

Chapter 4
Attribution, Temptation, and Expectation: A Formal Framework for Defense-by-Deception in Cyberwarfare

Ehab Al-Shaer and Mohammad Ashiqur Rahman

Abstract Defense-by-deception is an effective technique to address the asymmetry challenges in cyberwarfare. It allows for not only misleading attackers to non-harmful goals but also systematic depletion of attacker resources. In this paper, we developed a game theocratic framework that considers *attribution, temptation* and *expectation*, as the major components for planning a successful deception plan. We developed as a case study a game strategy to proactively deceive remote fingerprinting attackers without causing significant performance degradation to benign clients. We model and analyze the interaction between a fingerprinter and a target as a signaling game. We derive the Nash equilibrium strategy profiles based on the information gain analysis. Based on our game results, we design *DeceiveGame*, a mechanism to prevent or to significantly slow down fingerprinting attacks. Our performance analysis shows that *DeceiveGame* can reduce the probability of success of the fingerprinter significantly, without deteriorating the overall performance of other clients. Beyond the DeceiveGame application, our formal framework can be generally used to synthesize correct-by-construction cyber deception plans against other attacks.

4.1 Introduction

4.1.1 Challenges of Cyberwarfare

Despite the persistent improvement in cybersecurity in the past decade or so, the gap between sophisticated attacks and existing cyber defense capabilities is ever increasing. As it is sufficient for attackers to find one path to achieve the goal, however, the defender must secure all paths to guarantee security. In addition, unlike kinetic warfare, adversaries have the freedom to plan and execute their attack but victims can only defend because it is often infeasible for defenders to identify or trace back the attacker in cyber space. This asymmetry in cyber warfare plays a key role in fueling

E. Al-Shaer (✉) · M. A. Rahman
University of North Carolina at Charlotte, Charlotte, USA
e-mail: ealshaer@uncc.edu

M. A. Rahman
e-mail: mrahman4@uncc.edu

© Springer International Publishing Switzerland 2015

S. Jajodia et al. (eds.), *Cyber Warfare,* Advances in Information Security 56,
DOI 10.1007/978-3-319-14039-1_4

this arm race to the adversaries advantage. To address this asymmetry challenge in cyberwarfare, it is important to design defense mechanisms that does not only detect or prevent attackers but they also can cause damage to the adversary as a counter attack by, for example, increasing the attack cost significantly, and/or depleting attackers resources. Defense-by-deception offers strong foundations to develop sophisticated cyber defense that can cause a significant damage on the adversary mission provides invaluable means to monitor and learn about the attackers strategies and techniques.

4.1.2 Cyber Deception Foundations

In this research, we define cyber deception as sequence of planned actions/events that divert the adversaries from reaching their goal attack to either any random but "unharmful state(s), or a desired state by the defender. In the first case, deception is used to basically avoid the attack (temporally or permanently). In the second case, deception is used to learn about the attackers tactics and techniques. In either case, defense-by-deception can effectively reduce the attack surface and security risk because it will decrease the possibility of attack success and the impact. A successful defense-by-deception must satisfy the following conditions: (1) *correct* to satisfy the goals above, (2) *affordable* to limit/control the cost and overhead, (3) stealthy to stay undetectable by adversaries. The last condition represent the main distinction between cyber deception and moving target defense.

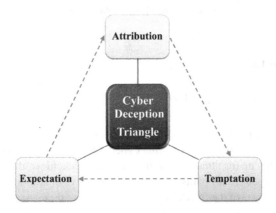

Fig. 4.1 Cyber deception triangle

In this paper, we explore a formal framework to generate a correct-by-construction cyber deception planning. We characterize three components/phases for systematically synthesizing cyber deception plans, which comprises: (1) *attribution* to predict attacker information such as IP sources and motivation/goals, (2) *temptation* to provide means to keep adversary highly attracted to pursue her goals, and (3) *expectation* to guarantee that the deception systems exhibits the normal behavior as perceived by adversaries. Figure 4.1 shows the triangle of deception that represents the interaction of these three components. As a case study, we developed a game theoretic framework (called DeceiveGame) to deceive fingerprinting attackers. The goal of the framework is to ensure (1) target misidentification by remote fingerprinters, and (2) attackets resource depletion by maximizing number of probes required to identify a target. We developed a probabilistic risk ranking metric based on information theory to identify attackers attribution. In specific, if the fingerprinting "information gain computed from the traffic sent by a specific source increases above a certain threshold, we classify this source as a fingerprinter or scanner. Other means to achieve attribution includes, for example, monitoring traffic that hits the honeynet (unused IP address) or based on IDS alarms. As fingerprinting attackers usually require multiple scanning probes to identify a target with a reasonable confidence, the DeceiveGame in this case initiates misleading responses in order to eventually exhaust the scanners with number of testing probes and make the target misidentified. To satisfy attackers "expectation or "temptation in this framework by constructing deceiving responses such as they are logically valid, and they contribute positively to adversary information gain, respectively.

4.1.3   Deceiving Fingerprinting Attacker: a Case Study

Fingerprinting is the process of determining the OS of a remote machine. To exploit a vulnerability of a remote machine, an attacker must know the machine's platform and the running services in advance such as OS type, version, installed patches, etc.

Active fingerprinters send an arbitrary number of crafted probes and analyzes the responses (e.g., Nmap, XProbe2, etc. (Fyodor 2007; Arkin and Yarochkin 2003)) and a number of tests are carried out on the outgoing packets from the target. The test results are compared with the known signatures in order to identify the OS platform of the target.

A number of counter-fingerprinting tools have been proposed in the literature, such as Scrubber, IP Personality, Morph, HoneyD, OSfuscate, IPMorph, etc. (Smart et al. 2000; Prigent et al. 2009; Roualland and Saffroy 2001; Zhang and Zheng 2009; Adrian 2008). However, the goal of these tool is avoiding fingerprinting rather than misdirecting the attacker to specific state or depleting her resources. In addition, the existing counter-fingerprinting tools alter outgoing packets of each connection irrespective of the sender's behavior. This *exhaustive defense mechanism* results in a significant *performance degradation* mainly with respect to throughput and connection quality.

These techniques make modifications on different TCP/IP fields in the packet header, among them some are critical for performance. For example, the modifications on *Initial Window Size*, *Time-To-Live* (TTL), and *Don't Fragment Bit* (DF) can make a significant throughput degradation. If the receive-window size is too small, then the sender will be blocked constantly as it fills out the receive window with packets before the receiver is able to acknowledge (Poduri and Nichols 1998).

If the initial window size is too large, the sender will spend a long time to retransmit the entire window every time a packet loss is detected by the receiver (Tcp optimizer, speed guide 2011).

Similarly, if the TTL value is too small, packets may not reach the distant destination. Throughput degradation can also happen if the DF bit is reset, because this
breaks the maximum transmission unit (MTU) discovery.

Moreover, the existing counter-fingerprinting techniques make significant computational overhead for defenders. IP-layer defense mechanisms (*e.g.*, scrubbing)
require fragment reassembly and re-fragmentation. Any modification in IP header
requires adjustment of the header checksum.

All of these works increase the end-to-end communication latency significantly.

Our presented counter-fingerprinting deception technique uses a game-theoretic
approach to performs dynamic sanitization on selective packets in order to increase
the distortion of the fingerprinter's knowledge while managing her expectation and
temptation and with limited acceptable overhead on benign users. We define a game
model for the fingerprinting process and corresponding countermeasure between a
fingerprinter and a target machine. Using a *signaling game* framework (Gibbons
1992), we analyze the interactions between the fingerprinter and the target, while
obtaining both pooling and separating equilibria.

This analysis gives us the opportunity to find potential solutions for evading or
delaying fingerprinting, and to get the best strategy for the target. Using our equilibrium analysis, we design a defense mechanism called *DeceiveGame*, to deceive
fingerprinting. As our game model takes the performance of benign clients into
consideration, *DeceiveGame* balances between security and overhead.

We performed experiments to evaluate the performance of *DeceiveGame*, by
comparing it to the non-strategic exhaustive counter-fingerprinting mechanism. We
found that in some scenarios, our tool reduces the overhead by 60 % compared to
the exhaustive defense, while it keeps the probability of successful fingerprinting
satisfactorily low.

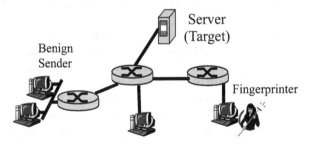

Fig. 4.2 Fingerprinting system model. A *server* (*target*) provides services to several hosts. A
fingerprinter tries to figure out the OS of the target

4.2 Fingerprinting: System Model

As shown in Fig. 4.2, we study a network where the *target* is a server that provides
services (e.g., web services) to its client. Hence, many hosts communicate with the
target to access the service. We call these hosts *senders*. We assume that an attacker

tries to identify the OS of the target in order to use the information for launching attacks against the target. We call the attacker *fingerprinter*. A fingerprinter is also a sender. The target wants to defend against fingerprinting. Thus, the target (as a *defender*) needs to deal with benign senders and fingerprinters simultaneously, while it does not know explicitly about the sender type. In our model, a *probe* denotes a particular type of packet that is sent to the target by benign senders or fingerprinters.

The attacker is able to attack different targets and it may have different levels of interest (or benefit) in them. However, the attacker has a certain interest in a particular target. Hence, in this paper, we focus on a single target. The attacker has a certain interest in a particular target, while the target can consider all senders as a single entity (i.e., the target can only care about received probes, not the number of senders). Hence, in this paper, we focus on modeling the interaction between one fingerprinter and one target.

Table 4.1 A list of symbols

Symbol	Definition
n, m	Number of tests and probes, respectively
x	Amount of effort (or time) put for fingerprinting
$\mathbb{N}, \mathbb{M}$	Sets of tests and probes, respectively
$\mathbb{N}_x, \mathbb{M}_x$	Sets of tests and probes used within time x, respectively
g_i	Potential information gain from ith test
G	Average information gain required for successful fingerprint
d_i	It denotes whether or not test i is defended by the target
$\pi(x)$	Probability of success in fingerprinting in x effort
$\sigma(x)$	Cost of fingerprinting in x effort
$\phi(x)$	Information gain possible from the probes sent in x effort, if no defense is taken against them
$\theta(x)$	Belief of the target about the sender type (being a fingerprinter)
$\psi(x)$	Potential defense cost due to taking defense against $\mathbb{N}_x$
Q	Acceptable performance degradation (due to defense)

4.2.1 Fingerprinting Game Period

We assume that the fingerprinter should launch and complete the fingerprinting in a period of time smaller than T_M. We define T_M as the maximum time bound for fingerprinting. The reason behind this assumption is that we consider other defense mechanisms like *moving target defense* working on the target, in addition to the counter-fingerprinting mechanism.

In the case of a moving target defense mechanism, the target's logical identification is intelligently or randomly changed (e.g., the change of IP address (Michalski 2006;

Al-Shaer et al. 2012)). We assume that the target moves at each T_M interval. If there is no secondary defense mechanism for the target, then T_M can be very large.

In a particular time instance, several senders can connect to the target. The sessions of some senders do overlap. A sender can start communication (*i.e.*, fingerprinting) at any time during a particular T_M. Hence, T_F is the period during which the fingerprinting process continues. T_F cannot be more than T_M.

Though there is variable communication latency, we assume that the sending time is the same as the receiving time. Table 4.1 summarizes the notation used throughout this paper.

Table 4.2 A list of tests used to fingerprint remote operating system

ID (i)	Name	g_i	v_i	b_i	q_i	Related Probes
1	DF: IP don't fragment bit	1.1	1	1	1	Any of {1–6}
2	T: IP initial time-to-live (TTL)	2.5	0.9	1	1	Any of {1–12, 15}
3	W: TCP initial window size	4.7	1	1	1	Any of {1–6, 8}
4	S: TCP sequence number	1	1	1	0	Any of {1, 7, 8, 12}
5	A: TCP acknowledgment number	1.2	1	1	0	Any of {7–9, 11, 12}
6	F: TCP flags	1	1	0	–	Any of {7–9, 11, 12}
7	O: TCP options' order	5	1	1	0	Any of {1–6, 8}
8	RD: TCP RST data checksum	0.7	1	1	0.5	Any of {1–9, 12}
9	CC: Explicit congestion notification	0.3	0.9	0	–	{15}
10	CD: ICMP response code	0.9	0.5	1	0.5	{13, 14}
11	SP: TCP initial sequence number (ISN)	3	0.5	1	0	Any 4 of {1–6}

4.2.2 Fingerprinting Tests

We assume that a fingerprinter utilizes n types of *tests* for fingerprinting. Let, $\mathbb{N} = \{1, 2, 3, \cdots, n\}$ is the set of tests. For each test type $i \in \mathbb{N}$, we define the following traffic analysis properties that are useful for cyber deception triangle:

1. *Information gain* (g_i): This property denotes the potential information gain Greenwald and Thomas (2007) from the result of the test i, which in turn expresses the strength of the test in fingerprinting. We briefly describe the calculation of information gain in the appendix. A test is a simple or composite step for checking one or multiple TCP/IP header field value(s), sometimes response behaviors, with known results. Usually a particular test is possible from different probes. These probes often give different information gains for the test. However, we do not count some of these probes as they give significantly lower gains compared to the remaining probes. The probes that we count for a test usually give very similar gains. Hence, we consider the average of these gains as the gain expected from the test. Note that g_i basically represents the information gain considering how much uncertainty the test i can remove if the test is done alone. A test may

not give the same information gain given prior successful tests. This can happen, especially, when two or more tests depend on the same TCP/IP fields or response behaviors. We address this issue later in the paper. Using this property, we craft the deception responses to achieve both attribution and temptation. For attribution, an increasing trend of reuest/response information gain indicates that someone is constantly attempting to learn about the target. To manage temptation and expectation, we avoid too deep obfuscation of the deception responses in order to maintain the information gain increasing trend but at slower rate before the target is misidentified.

2. *Credibility* (v_i): The credibility value ($0 \leq v_i \leq 1$) shows whether the test i is plausible as a valid TCP/IP packet. The credibility depends on the credibility of the probe(s) used for this test.

   Moreover, if a test requires a group of probes, the test's credibility is considered as low. Because, the specific order or the fixed collection of the probes can give an easy sign of a fingerprinting act. This property is very useful for attack attribution as the lower the credibility score the more likely it is a fingerprinter.

3. *Visibility of Defensibility* (b_i): It is a boolean value denoting whether the test i can be defended, so that the sender does not get potential information gain from the test. There can be some tests, which are not possible to defend without revealing an active defense/deception. *I.e.*, information hiding will be expressive to attackers. This property is used to ensure attackers' expectation of the target responses. Although hiding some of these field will confuse or mislead the attacker, our deception mechanism is prompted not to use it because it will jeopardize the stealthiness and expectation conditions of cyber deception.

4. *Impact on performance* (q_i): Defending different tests makes different impact on the performance of the sender and target. For example, defending against *TCP initial sequence number* does not degrade the sender's performance, whereas defending against *initial TTL* might have very bad impacts on the performance. We refer this as the *defense cost*, which is crucial in the case of benign senders. This is used to ensure that the overhead is affordable in real-life operational environment. We assume three qualitative values for q_i, *i.e.*, {1, 0.5, 0}, that define high, medium and no impact, respectively.

Table 4.2 presents a number of tests. We cite these tests from Fyodor (2007), since the tests done by Nmap are comprehensive and well known. The table also shows the properties of the tests. For example, the test 7 has information gain 5 and high credibility ($v_i = 1$). This test is defensible ($b_i = 1$) and it will not cause any performance degradation ($q_i = 0$).

4.2.3 Fingerprinting Probes

We assume that there are m types of probes. Let, $\mathbb{M}$ is the set of probes, *i.e.*, $\mathbb{M} = \{1, 2, 3, \cdots, m\}$. We denote the credibility of a probe j using f_j. This property shows whether the probe j is credible enough, so that the target would like to respond to it (*e.g.*, whether the probe is a valid TCP/IP packet). For example, if a probe j is sent towards a closed port, its credibility can be assumed to be zero. Any probe without three-way handshaking are also not valid ($f_j = 0$), while TCP SYN based probes are valid TCP/IP packets (*i.e.*, $f_j = 1$). The test's credibility depends on the probe(s) used for the test.

Usually the response of a probe can give more than one test result. Hence, the potential gain possible from the probe j is $\sum_{i \in \mathbb{N}_j} g_i$. Here, $\mathbb{N}_j$ is the set of tests ($\mathbb{N}_j \subseteq \mathbb{N}$), which are carried out from the probe j.

Table 4.3 A list of probes used by a fingerprinter.

j	Name	f_j	Comment
1–6	Pkt1-6	1	SYN, different TCP Options (*e.g.*, MSS, SACK, NOP, WScale, Timestamp) are selected in a order
7	T2	1	DF, Options (MSS, SACK, timestamp)
8	T3	1	SYN, FIN, URG, PSH, same Options as T2
9	T4	1	DF, ACK, same Options as T2
10	T5	0	SYN, same Options as T2, to closed ports
11	T6	0	Similar to T4 but to closed ports
12	T7	0	FIN, URG, PSH, same Options as T2, to closed ports
13–14	IE1-2	0	ICMP (different values for TOS and Code), DF
15	ECN	1	SYN, ECE, CWR, ECN, Options (MSS, SACK, etc.)

Table 4.3 shows some of the probes used in Fyodor (2007) with their properties. The set $\mathbb{M}$ includes all kinds of packets in addition to the probes used by a fingerprinter. The information gain may be possible from the responses to the packets sent by a benign sender. Since the benign sender does not do fingerprinting, the accumulated gain from its packets is typically less than that from the probes used by the fingerprinter.

4.2.4 Information Gain Computation

Greenwald and Thomas presented the process of calculating the information gain for a fingerprinting test presented in (Greenwald and Thomas 2007). The process is very briefly described here for the readers.

Let X be a random variable that describes the classification of the OS of a target system. The entropy in X is the amount of uncertainty existing in classifying an unknown system. Let X can take n possible values, where n is the number of all possible operating systems. Each value has the probability $p(x_j)$, $1 \le j \le n$. So, the entropy is calculated as follows:

$$H(X) = -\sum_{j=1}^{n} p(x_j) \log_2 p(x_j)$$

Let $Test_i$ be a random variable that describes the result of applying the test i to the probe response from a target system. The conditional entropy of X (i.e., $H(X|Test_i)$) is calculated given that $Test_i$ is successful. The mutual information of X and $Test_i$ is the amount of information one gains about X if it knows the result, $Test_i$. This is termed as *Information Gain*. This can be simply defined as the difference between the entropy before taking the test and the entropy conditioned on the value of the test. The conditional entropy $H(X|Test_i)$ is computed as follows, where $Test_i$ is considered to take on n_i values, each $(test_{i_k})$ with probability $p(test_{i_k})$, $1 \leq k \leq n_i$:

$$H(X|Test_i) = -\sum_{k=1}^{n_i} p(test_{i_k}) \sum_{j=1}^{n} p(x_j|test_{i_k})\log_2 p(x_j|test_{i_k})$$

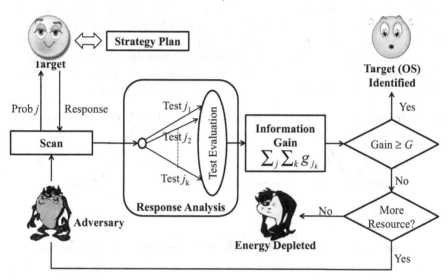

Fig. 4.3 The process of fingerprinting and the corresponding defense idea

Thus, the Information gain on X by $Test_i$ is

$$H(X;Test_i) = H(X) - H(X \mid Test_i)$$

In our model, g_i denotes $H(X;Test_i)$. To calculate information gain one needs three probabilities: $p(x_j)$, $p(test_{i_k})$ with $1 \leq k \leq n_i$, and $p(x_j \mid test_{i_k})$ with $1 \leq j \leq n$ and $1 \leq k \leq n_i$. The information gain shown in Table 4.2 is derived by assuming that each OS is equally likely $p(x_j) = 1/n$. We know that OS distributions are not uniform usually.

Though the given OS distribution might change the gain values (Greenwald and Thomas 2007), which in turn may change the course of playing the game, our game model and the solution process remain the same. Moreover, the administrator of the target network knows the OS distribution in the network, while the attacker may not know the correct one. Hence, the target has an advantage over the attacker in playing the game.

4.3 Deceiving Fingerprinting: Game Model

Game theory models strategic situations, in which the success of one player in making choices depends on the choices of other players (Gibbons 1992). The key point of our game-theoretic analysis is to consider the strategic behaviors of the target as well as the sender (especially from a fingerprinter's point of view). Moreover, game theory will help us to deal with the lack of knowledge about the type of the sender, *i.e.*, whether it is benign or malicious.

In Fig. 4.3, we present the interactions between a fingerprinting attacker and a target. An attacker usually keeps scanning until the OS of the target is identified or the attack resource is depleted. The target has a strategy to respond to all incoming packets without an explicit distinction between benign and malicious traffic. The DeceiveGame in the target uses the belief score of individual sources to determine if it can send a normal response or twist the response to deceive the attacker. Eventually, if the attacker can gain sufficient information about the system, the target (its OS) is identified from the attacker perspective or misidentified from the defender perspective. Otherwise the attacker's resource/energy can be consumed.

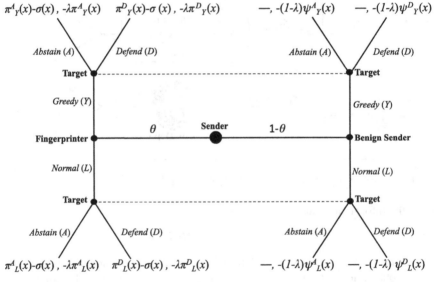

Fig. 4.4 Representation of a fingerprinting attack as a *signaling game*. The players are a *target* and a *sender*. The belief of the *target* about the *sender* type (i.e., whether a *benign sender* or a *fingerprinter*) is modeled by θ (see Sect. 4.3.2). *Dashed lines* show the uncertainty of the *target* about the type of the *sender*. The *target* observes the actions of the *sender*, i.e., *normal* (L) and *greedy* (Y). The actions of the *target* (i.e., *abstain* (A) and *defend* (D)) are represented on each *leaf* of the *tree* (see Sect. 4.3.1). The *leaves of the tree* represent the payoffs of the players (see Sect. 4.3.3). The first value is the fingerprinter's payoff. Note that we do not show payoff for the *sender* if the *target* believes that it is a *benign sender*

Here, DeceiveGame may not misguide the attacker to untrue identity, but instead it may send responses that reveals different contradictory identities (e.g., the OS platform) to bring the overall information gain low and keep the attacker trying. Although this strategy might help to avoid the attack by confusing the adversary, it can be easily detected by the attacker because it is unexpected behavior. Although our framework supports this strategy, it can also be used to control the degree of distortion in the information gain due to deceiving responses in order to balance between temptation and expectation.

We model fingerprinting using a *signaling game* with a target and a sender (*i.e.*, a benign sender or a fingerprinter) as players. Our choice of the signaling game is based on the *dynamic* and *incomplete information* nature of the fingerprinting attack where the action of one player is conditioned over its belief about the type of the opponent as well as its observation on the actions of other player. As it is shown in Fig. 4.4, we can represent the signaling game, similar to two connected trees where branches and roots represent the available actions for a given player and the belief about the type of the opponent respectively. We define a fingerprinting game for each connection (or a set of connections that are suspected for coming from a single botnet). We assume that if several connections exist, there are as many fingerprinting games running in parallel. We analyze a single fingerprinting game in the following. We describe different strategies for the fingerprinter and the target. Next, we address how the belief of the target about the type of the sender is updated. Finally, we introduce their payoffs.

4.3.1 Strategy Model

Fingerprinter's Strategy: In the fingerprinting game, the fingerprinter determines the amount of information gain it receives by the probes.

Let x be the amount of time spent by a sender for communicating with the target. From the fingerprinter's perspective, this is the time already given for fingerprinting the target. We name x as *effort*. Hence, we use *effort* and *time* interchangeably throughout the paper. We assume that the fingerprinter's cost of sending probes is trivial with respect to the time spent for fingerprinting. The value of x is bounded within 0 and T_F.

We use $\hat{x}_i$ to denote the earliest time instance when the target receives a probe whose response potentially gives result for the test i.

We know that a single probe can do multiple tests and multiple probes can do the same tests. Hence, $\mathbb{N}_x$ ($\mathbb{N}_x \subseteq \mathbb{N}$) is the set of tests possible from the probes in $\mathbb{M}_x$. The sizes of $\mathbb{M}_x$ and $\mathbb{N}_x$ are nondecreasing with the time (*i.e.*, x). The relationship between the probe set $\mathbb{M}_x$ and the test set $\mathbb{N}_x$ is expressed as below:

$$\mathbb{N}_x = \bigcup_{j \in \mathbb{M}_x} \{i_{j,1}, ..., i_{j,k}\}, \text{where } 0 \leq k \leq m \tag{4.1}$$

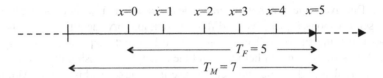

Fig. 4.5 An example showing the relation between T_M, T_F and x, when the maximum time for fingerprinting the target is $T_M = 7\,Sec$ and the time of the game between the fingerprinter and the target is $T_F = 5$ s

Here, $\{i_{j,1}, ..., i_{j,k}\}$ is the set of tests that are possible from the probe j. We know that there are few tests that require the responses of multiple probes. A test of this kind is usually associated with a specific set of probes. Hence, for such a test i, $\mathbb{N}_x$ includes i, if and only if each of the probes required for computing i exists in $\mathbb{M}_x$. This is also fair to assume that, in order to defend the test i, it is enough to sanitize the response of one of the probes (*e.g.*, the last received one) associated to the test.

To illustrate the above model we consider the case where $m = 7$ and $n = 10$, *i.e.*, $\mathbb{N} = \{1, 2, \cdots, 10\}$ and $\mathbb{M} = \{1, 2, \cdots, 7\}$, as shown in Fig. 4.5. In this example, we assume T_M is 7 seconds, T_F is 5 seconds, and a probe is sent per second. At $x = 1$, the sender sends (*i.e.*, the target receives) the probe 2, which can give result for the tests 1 and 4. Thus, $\hat{x}_1 = 1$ and $\hat{x}_4 = 1$, while $\mathbb{M}_1 = \{2\}$ and $\mathbb{N}_1 = \{1, 4\}$. At $x = 2$, the sender sends the probe 6, which can give results for the tests 3 and 4. So, $\hat{x}_3 = 2$, while already we saw $\hat{x}_4$. Then, $\mathbb{M}_2 = \{2, 6\}$ and $\mathbb{N}_2 = \{1, 3, 4\}$.

We define the set of actions for the sender (i.e., a fingerprinter) as $s_F = \{Greedy, Normal\}$. When the fingerprinter plays *Greedy*, it is avaricious for information and it sends probes to get more information from the target. On the other hand, with the *Normal* strategy the fingerprinter sends the probes that can give little or no information gain. Note that the expected behavior from a benign sender is *Normal*, because it communicates to the target only to receive a service. We define a simple threshold-based mechanism to distinguish these two strategies. In this respect, we define G as a portion of the total potential information gain (*i.e.*, $\sum_{i \in \mathbb{N}} g_i$) as the average gain that is required to identify the OS of the target. We use G^B and G^F to denote the total expected gain within the game period with respect to a *benign* sender and a *fingerprinter*, respectively. Obviously, according to the expected behavior, $G^B < G \le G^F$.

Let us assume that a fingerprinter selects a probe from the probe set at each step (at a particular x during T_F) of the game. Considering G^B, we define $\phi(x)$ as the observed behavior from the sender at x. We also define $\phi^B(x)$ as the expected behavior from a benign sender. The accumulated potential information gain asked by the sender till x is represented by $\phi(x)$, where $\phi(x) = \sum_{i \in \mathbb{N}_x} g_i$.

The expected behavior $\phi^B(x)$ is computed as follows:

$$\phi^B(x) = \sum_{i=0}^{x} \phi_0^B r^i \tag{4.2}$$

Here ϕ_0^B is the initial value, while $\phi_0^B r^i$ is the expected increment of gain at time i. The value of r ($0 < r < 1$) is approximately computed considering the equality:
$$\sum_{i=0}^{T_M} \phi_0^B r^i = G^B.$$

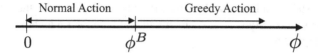

Fig. 4.6 Strategy of the sender. The sender is playing *Greedy* if it asks information more than ϕ^B. Otherwise it plays *Normal*

The reason behind taking this equality is that with the time, the increase in asking gain (*i.e.*, the rate of asked gain) is expected to be reduced due to the using of same types of packets multiple times.

The target expects the total asked gain within a particular time (effort) to be limited. As shown in Fig. 4.6, we assume that if $\phi(x) > \phi^B(x)$, the sender plays *Greedy*, otherwise it plays *Normal*.

Target's Strategy We define the set of actions for the target as $s_T = \{Defend, Abstain\}$. The action *Defend* means that the target defends the test, *e.g.*, by sanitizing the response of the associated probe (or by sending confusing or misleading response), so that the sender does not receive information from the test. In the case of *Abstain*, the original response remains unmodified and the sender receives information associated to the test. The term $d_i(x)$ denotes the target's strategy against the test i at x. We consider $d_i = 1$ when target decides to *Defend*, while $d_i = 0$ in the case of *Abstain*. The target's strategy is to select one of these actions, so that (i) the success in fingerprinting by the sender is low (as far as possible) when it is a fingerprinter, and (ii) the defense cost (*i.e.*, the performance degradation experienced by the sender) is reasonably low, if it is a benign sender.

The target may require to take action against a particular test i more than once, since multiple probes often have the same test in common or multiple times the same probe might be sent.

We consider that the subsequent defense strategy for the same test will remain the same (*i.e.*, $d_i(x_i) = d_i(\hat{x}_i)$, where $x_i > \hat{x}_i$) during T_F. Moreover, since a probe usually give results for more than one test, the target often require to take decisions for multiple tests at a time.

The fingerprinting game is played at each time instance x when a probe is received at the target. Then, the optimal strategy of the target will be defined (i.e., whether play *Defend* or *Abstain*) by finding the equilibrium of the signalling game. We present the equilibrium in Sect. 4.4.2.

4.3.2 Belief Model

In our fingerprinting game, the target does not know whether the sender is a finger-printer or a benign sender. The strategy of the target depends on its belief about its opponent, as shown in Fig. 4.4. We define $\theta(x)$ $(0 \leq \theta(x) \leq 1)$ as the belief of the target about the sender type at x. A larger value of θ denotes a higher possibility of being a fingerprinter.

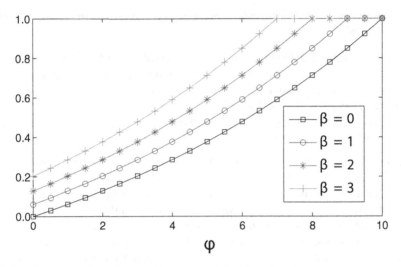

Fig. 4.7 The impact of ϕ and β on θ. Here, we consider $G^F = 10$

The value of θ is updated with x, particularly after receiving a probe (*i.e.*, watching the sender's action). In order to update $\theta(x)$, we use $\phi(x)$.

$$\theta(x) = \min\left(1, \frac{e^{(\beta+\phi(x))/G^F} - 1}{e - 1}\right) \tag{4.3}$$

Note that we take into account the initial value of the belief (*i.e.*, $\theta(0)$) using the nonnegative value β. The larger is β, the higher is the initial belief about the sender towards being a fingerprinter. Typically, β is very small, even zero, compared to G^F. We consider the exponential function of the potential information gain to compute belief, so that a small increase in gain has more effect on belief if accumulated gain is already high. Because, though the probes used by benign senders also have information gain, the accumulated gain is expected to be low. Other convex function can be used given the target's objectives. The more the target is keen about its security, the higher the initial value of θ. Figure 4.7 shows the impact of ϕ and β on θ. A list of known (or expected) benign and malicious hosts can be used to set the prior belief about a sender. The belief value is used for defining the attack attribution (i.e., scanner vs. benign, specific scanned service, motive etc).

4.3.3 Payoff Model

Benefit Let P be the benefit that the fingerprinter will receive if it succeeds in fingerprinting, and $\pi(x)$ be the *probability of success* after giving x effort. Then, the *expected benefit* for a fingerprinter is $\pi(x)P$. The value of P captures the importance of the target. We assume that both players perceive the same importance of the target. In our model, we assume that P is equal to 1. Hence, the expected benefit of the fingerprinter is $\pi(x)$. We now describe the calculation of $\pi(x)$.

If a probe for a test i is sent at $\hat{x}_i$ effort, we use the term $\pi_i(\hat{x}_i)$ for representing the probability of success received from the test. We already mentioned that the potential information gain from a test may depend on the prior tests. We use the notation $g_i(\hat{x}_i)$ representing the information gain received from the test i, given the tests done prior to $\hat{x}_i$. Hence, $\pi_i(\hat{x}_i)$ is computed as follows:

$$\pi_i(\hat{x}_i) = \frac{g_i(\hat{x}_i) - g_i(\hat{x}_i)d_i(\hat{x}_i)b_i}{G} \tag{4.4}$$

Here, $g_i(\hat{x}_i)$ is the potential information gain from the test i, if it is successful, taking into account the already successful (not defended) tests till $\hat{x}_i$ ($\{k \mid (k \in \mathbb{N}_{\hat{x}_i})$ and $(d_k(.) = 0)\}$). If we assume that the dependency is negligible, *i.e.*, the information gain is independent of the prior successful tests, then $\forall_x \ g_i(x) = g_i$. This will simplify Eq. (4.4) as follows:

$$\pi_i(\hat{x}_i) = \frac{g_i - g_i d_i(\hat{x}_i)b_i}{G} \tag{4.5}$$

The target selects the optimal $d_i(\hat{x}_i)$ at the equilibrium, which depends on b_i, v_i, q_i, $\hat{x}_i$, and the *belief* (θ) about the sender type. The belief follows the prior behavior of the sender based on the probes received by the target. We compute the cumulative probability of success after x effort as follows:

$$\pi(x) = \sum_{i \in \mathbb{N}_x} \pi_i(\hat{x}_i), \text{ where } \hat{x}_i \leq x \tag{4.6}$$

The benefit is used to provide temptation and keeping the attacker engaged. Attackers must perceive some benefit (even if it is fake) in order to for the game to continue. We consider a *zero-sum benefit model*. The more benefit, *i.e.*, the probability of success, the fingerprinter receives ($\pi(x)$), the less benefit the target obtains ($-\pi(x)$).

Cost Let $\sigma(x)$ be the cost incurred by the fingerprinter after a given x effort. The cost of processing or transmitting a packet is very trivial to be considered in the fingerprinting cost. Since all the probes and tests are already known, the fingerprinter only cares about the time it gives for fingerprinting. We define $\sigma(x)$ as a simple linear concave function of x as follows:

$$\sigma(x) = \alpha_0 + \alpha_1 x \tag{4.7}$$

Here, α_0 is the initial cost of attacking a target and α_1 is the cost per time unit. These coefficients take the same unit as of the budget. If we take the initial cost as 0 ($\alpha_0 = 0$) and the cost per time unit as 1 ($\alpha_1 = 1$), then the cost is just the time. The cost equation can be quadratic or even exponential. However, these types of cost equations will make a fingerprinter to fingerprint within a short time, $i.e.$, a higher probing rate, which is subject to catch by an IDS.

We know that defending a test i may incur cost ($i.e.$, the impact on performance), which is denoted by q_i. Hence, the defense cost at $\hat{x}_i$ for the test i is:

$$\psi_i(\hat{x}_i) = \frac{q_i d_i(\hat{x}_i) v_i}{Q} \tag{4.8}$$

Here, Q represents the defense cost that is intolerable in terms of the minimum level of performance. The use of v_i in computing $\psi_i(x)$ expresses the fact that less credible probes are not expected to be sent by a benign sender. Hence, there is no need to consider the defense cost due to defending the tests associated to these probes. The cumulative defense cost after x effort is computed as follows:

$$\psi(x) = \sum_{i \in \mathbb{N}_x} \psi_i(\hat{x}_i), \text{ where } \hat{x}_i \leq x \tag{4.9}$$

The cost and benefit can be both used in our framework to deplete the attacker resources.

Payoff We model the fingerprinter's payoff by u_F as follows:

$$u_F(x) = \pi(x) - \sigma(x) \tag{4.10}$$

Note that both $\pi(x)$ and $\sigma(x)$ are normalized values between 0 and 1. We also model the target's payoff by u_T as shown in the below:

$$u_T(x) = -\lambda \pi(x) - (1 - \lambda)\psi(x) \tag{4.11}$$

We use λ ($0 \leq \lambda \leq 1$) to denote the preference of defense over the defense cost. If the target does not have a specific choice, then λ is 0.5.

In Fig. 4.4, we show the payoffs of the fingerprinter and the target at a particular x for different combinations of strategies. In the case of $Greedy$ (Y) strategy of the sender at x, let us assume that the target chooses $Abstain$ for the test corresponds to Y. Then the received benefit by the fingerprinter is $\pi_Y^A(x) = g_Y/G$, since $d_Y = 0$ in Eq. (4.4). In this case, the target has no defense cost, $i.e.$, $\psi_Y^A(x) = 0$ (see Eq. (4.8)). If the target chooses $Defend$ ($i.e.$, $d_Y = 1$), then the fingerprinter receives the benefit, $\pi_Y^D(x) = (g_Y - g_Y b_Y)/G$ and the target pays the defense cost, $\psi_Y^D(x) = q_Y v_Y$.

4.4 Analysis of the Fingerprinting Game

In this section, we first introduce the methodology for solving a signaling game. Then we present the equilibria of our game and their interpretations.

4.4.1 Analysis Methodology: Perfect Bayesian Equilibrium

To predict the outcome of the fingerprinting game, one could use the well-known concept of *Nash Equilibrium* (NE): A strategy profile constitutes a Nash equilibrium if none of the players can increase its payoff by unilaterally changing its strategy. In the case of *incomplete information games* (*e.g.*, signaling games), the players are unaware of the payoffs of their opponents. Hence, we adopt the concept of *Perfect Bayesian Equilibrium* (Gibbons 1992).

Definition 1 A *perfect Bayesian equilibrium* consists of strategies and beliefs satisfying the following requirements:

1. At each information set, the player with the move must have a belief about which node in the information set has been reached by the play of the game.
2. Given their beliefs, the players' strategies must be sequentially rational.
3. At information sets on the equilibrium path, beliefs are determined by Bayes' rule and the players' equilibrium strategies.
4. At information sets off the equilibrium path, beliefs are determined by Bayes' rule and the players' equilibrium strategies where possible.

Moreover, an equilibrium is called a *separating equilibrium* in signaling game, if each sender type sends a different signal. An equilibrium is called a *pooling equilibrium* if the same signal is sent by all types.

4.4.2 Fingerprinting Game: Results

Considering the above definition of the perfect Bayesian equilibrium, we solve the fingerprinting game to find possible *separating* and *pooling* equilibria. Theorem 1 and Theorem 2 identify the best strategies for the players in the fingerprinting game. Due to the limited space, we refer the reader to our technical report available in (Rahman et al. 2013) for the proof of theorems.

Theorem 1 [(*Greedy*, *Normal*), (*Defend*, *Abstain*)][1] *is the only separating equilibrium of the fingerprinting game.*

Theorem 1 shows that at the separating equilibrium the target defends (*i.e.*, plays *Defend*) if the sender (expected to be a fingerprinter) plays *Greedy*. It plays *Abstain* if the sender (expected to be benign) plays *Normal*. Theorem 2 presents the pooling equilibrium along with necessary conditions. Here, the target believes that the sender plays *Greedy* for each given type and the expected behavior of the target is *Defend* at this equilibrium. In this case, the posterior probability of a sender

---

[1] The sender strategy profile (a, b) means that it plays a for the type θ and b for the type $1 - \theta$. In case of the target, (a, b) means that it plays a following the *Greedy* action and b following the *Normal* action of the sender.

being a fingerprinter is θ. If the senders of both types would play *Normal* and the posterior probability of a sender being a fingerprinter would be assumed as μ, the expected behavior of the target would be *Abstain*.

Theorem 2 *[(Greedy,Greedy), (Defend,Defend), θ]*
and [(Normal,Normal), (Abstain,Abstain), μ] are the pooling equilibrium of the fingerprinting game, if the following conditions hold:

1. $\theta/(1 - \theta) \geq (1 - \lambda) \, q_Y \, v_Y/(\lambda \, g_Y \, b_Y/G)$
2. $\mu/(1 - \mu) \leq (1 - \lambda) \, q_L \, v_L/(\lambda \, g_L/G)$
3. $g_L = 0 \ or \ b_Y = 0$

4.5 *DeceiveGame* Mechanism

The existing counter-fingerprinting mechanisms do not follow any dynamic strategy in defense mechanism. They always take same strategy, *i.e.*, defend a particular probe irrespective of its potential impact, the possible sender type, and the target's belief. We design a mechanism, named *DeceiveGame*, that follows optimal strategy selection based on the equilibrium analysis of the fingerprinting game to deceive attackers. *DeceiveGame* can be implemented on the target or between the sender and the target similar to firewall. This mechanism operates at the network layer, because it requires to work on the TCP/IP headers of the packets. *DeceiveGame* intercepts packets, applies necessary modifications to the outgoing packets, and forwards the packets to the sender.

4.5.1 *Strategy Selection Mechanism*

DeceiveGame determines the appropriate response strategy against each received probe. Though a benign sender's behavior is mostly *Normal*, it can sometimes behave *Greedy*. On the other side, a fingerprinter can sometimes act *Normal* to fool the target. Hence, it is important to consider the belief to determine the attacker attributions and obtain the optimal strategy. Since in the pooling equilibrium the belief is considered explicitly, we apply Theorem 2 in *DeceiveGame*. We divide $\mathbb{S}$, the set of tests that are possible from the received probe, into two sets: $\mathbb{S}_1$ and $\mathbb{S}_2$. The first set consists of the tests, which are already seen in the earlier received probes, while the second set represents the new tests. Since the actions corresponding to the tests in $\mathbb{S}_1$ have been already selected and applied on the tests, the same strategy will be followed for them. Hence, we need to find the actions for the tests in $\mathbb{S}_2$. We sort the tests in $\mathbb{S}_2$ considering their properties.

We defend the packets, which are not valid ($v = 0$) or have no defense cost ($q = 0$). For the rest of the tests, we apply Theorem 2 to select the optimal strategies. Trivially, the value of μ is the same as θ.

Note that the values for different game parameters, such as G, ϕ_0^B, λ can be defined based on the guidelines and prior knowledge. For example, the small value of λ shows that the target is very sensitive to performance degradation. More discussions about the parameter selections can be found in. In order to defend a probe, *DeceiveGame* modifies the appropriate fields (or behaviors) in the response to the received probe based on the strategy set $\mathbb{D}$.

4.5.2 Implementation Issues

The tests can be defended in different ways. In some cases, *DeceiveGame* can do normalization in the responses similar to the methodology of protocol scrubber (Smart et al. 2000). In some cases, it can choose random values. For the probes having low credibility, *e.g.*, the probes sent without three way hand-shaking or towards closed ports, can be defended easily by sending no reply. Since these defense methods are not the aim of the paper, their description is not given here.

4.6   Evaluation

We evaluated *DeceiveGame* in two stages. First, we analyzed the performance of the tool against conventional fingerprinting mechanisms. We also analyzed some important characteristics of the defense mechanism. Then, we verified whether our tool can evade Nmap (Fyodor 2007).

4.6.1   Performance and Characteristic Analysis

We analyzed *DeceiveGame* using emulation and simulation experimentations. Various fingerprinting scenarios were created where fingerprinters and benign senders send packets to the target. Experiments were done under three different options: (1) without defense ($d = 0$), (2) using exhaustive defense ($d = 1$), which represents the existing defense strategies, and (3) using our proposed *DeceiveGame*. We evaluated the results using the following metrics: (1) *effectiveness* that measures the probability of fingerprinting success, (2) *overhead* that measures the potential defense cost realized by the target as a result of sanitizing responses, and (3) *intrusiveness* that measures the number of defended probes.

Methodology In our experiments, we created a random traffic that contained all the fingerprinting probes as shown in Table 4.3. The probe type can be selected based on four fingerprinting models (*i.e.*, attack models) as follows: (1) *naive fingerprinter* that selects probes in an increasing order of information gain, (2) *greedy fingerprinter* that first selects the probes with higher information gain, (3) *random fingerprinter*

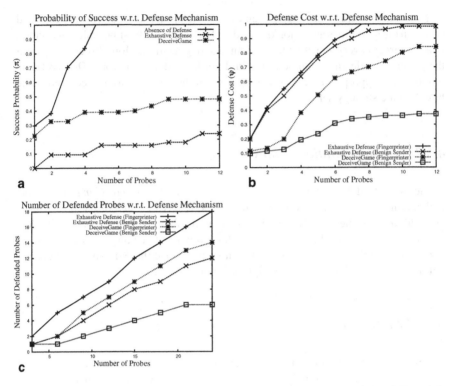

Fig. 4.8 a Comparison of general defense mechanisms w.r.t. success of fingerprinting, **b** Potential defense cost in different defense mechanisms, **c** Number of probes/tests defended in different defense mechanisms

Table 4.4 Parameter values used in simulations

n	m	G	G^B	G^F	ϕ_0	β	Q	λ	T_M
16	20	7	$0.5 \times G$	$1.5 \times G$	$0.5 \times G^B$	0	3	0.5	25s

that selects probes randomly from the unused tests using uniform distribution, and (4) *hybrid fingerprinter* that is a combination of the previous models. In hybrid model, a fingerprinter can start attacking with random model and next it can choose greedy model after spending 50 % of its possible efforts. We used the random model in the experiments unless the fingerprinting model is explicitly specified. The properties of the tests and associated probes are the same as those shown in Tables 4.2 and 4.3, respectively.

We assume that all other packets do not provide any information gain (*i.e.*, entail no fingerprinting test). We generate benign traffic using archives of web traffic (The internet traffic archive 2008).

Table 4.4 shows the values that we considered for different game parameters. We already conducted simulations with other values and the results showed the similar behaviors as in the following.

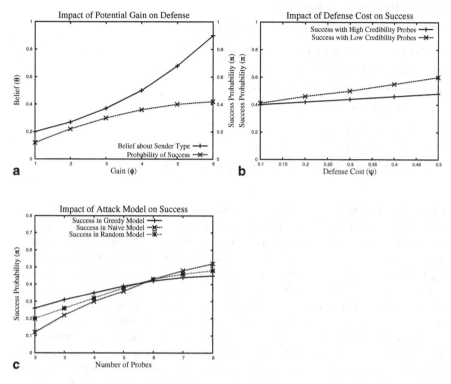

Fig. 4.9 Impact of **a** the potential information gain on the probability of success, **b** the potential defense cost on the probability of success, **c** different attack models (*i.e.*, the order of the probes based on potential gain) on the probability of success

Performance Analysis Figure 4.8a shows that the potential success of fingerprinting (*i.e.*, $\pi(x)$) in the case of *DeceiveGame* is close to that of the exhaustive defense mechanism and it is within the 20–25 % difference. This success probability does not allow for a successful determination of the target. Note that repeating a probe multiple times does not increase the fingerprinting success as it does not contribute to the information gain. While *DeceiveGame* performs reasonably well in defeating fingerprinting, it remains highly efficient in reducing the defense cost (*i.e.*, $\psi(x)$) incurred by the exhaustive defense mechanism. Figure 4.8b and c show the associated results. Figure 4.8b shows that *DeceiveGame* reduces the overhead up to 60 % as compared to the exhaustive mechanism. Figure 4.8c shows that DeceiveGame defends fewer number of probes (as well as tests) than the exhaustive mechanism, especially in the case of benign senders. These results prove that our mechanism is able to discriminate between benign senders and fingerprinters, and it adjusts the defense mechanism accordingly in order to outperform conventional fingerprinting countermeasure mechanisms.

Table 4.5 The output (partial) of Nmap

OS Fingerprinting Command: nmap -O -v 152.15.106.207
Nmap Output without DeceiveGame:
MAC Address: D4:BE:D9:9A:74:3A (Dell)
Running: Microsoft Windows 7 | Vista | 2008
OS details: Microsoft Windows 7 Professional, ⋯
Nmap Output while DeceiveGame is running:
MAC Address: D4:BE:D9:9A:74:3A (Dell)
Too many fingerprints match this host to give specific OS details

Characteristic Analysis We analyzed the impact of potential information gain of the fingerprinter on the target's belief about the sender type and thus on the fingerprinter's success. We observed (as shown in Fig. 4.9a that with the increase of the potential gain, the rate of increasing the belief (θ) that the sender is a fingerprinter becomes high. The impact of the potential defense cost on the success probability is shown in Fig. 9b in two different credibility levels. The more is the cost (*i.e.*, performance degradation) for defending a test, the higher is the success probability from the test. However, in the case of a low-credible probe, this impact is insignificant (as discussed in Sect. 4.3.3). The impact of attack model (*i.e.*, greedy, naive, and random) on the fingerprinting success is presented in Fig. 4.9c. We observed that sending probes with higher information gain (e.g., in greedy model) obtain lower success probability in the long run. Because even a small increase in the potential gain might create a significant impact on the belief, given that the accumulated gain is high.

Accuracy We implemented the prototype of *DeceiveGame* using *C* programming language. We used *Win Divert* Basil (2012), a user-mode packet capture-and-divert package for windows, in this implementation. The implemented prototype was installed in a host, *A*, where Windows 7 OS was running. We installed Nmap (Fyodor 2007) in another host, *B*. We tried to fingerprint *A* from *B* in two ways: with and without executing *DeceiveGame* on *A*. The outputs of both cases are presented in Table 4.5. We found that *DeceiveGame* successfully disrupted Nmap from understanding the OS of *A*. In this experiment, we observed that the belief about the sender (i.e., θ) reached high (close to 1) within 3 probes sent by Nmap. As a result, most of the probes are defended.

4.7 Related Work

A number of tools have been proposed to evade from fingerprinting. The TCP/IP stack normalization approach was introduced with Scrubber (Smart et al. 2000), which is the first well-known counter-fingerprinting tool. It removes ambiguities from TCP/IP traffic that gives clues to a host's operating system. IP Personality

Roualland and Saffroy (2001) and other tools such as (Zhang and Zheng 2009; Wang 2004, Prigent et al. 2009) introduced the idea of emulating different personalities to evade fingerprinting tools. IpMorph Prigent et al. (2009) is built combining the concept of Scrubber and IP Personality. OSfuscate Adrian (2008) is a small counter-fingerprinting tool that allows to change some registry values in order to reconfigure the TCP/IP stacks. However, none of these above mentioned tools offer a strategic framework for cyber deception and they all treat a benign sender similarly to a fingerprinter.

4.8   Conclusion

Defense-by-deception offers a game changing paradigm that reverses the asymmetry in cyberwarfare because it allows for (1) avoiding attacks proactively, (2) learning the attackers' strategies, and (3) attacking the attackers by depleting their resources during the attack. A successful cyber deception planning requires estimating attack attributions, engaging attacker by temptations, and matching attackers' expectation. We presented a formal game-theocratic framework that integrates these three components in order to deceive remote fingerprinting attackers. Defense against remote OS fingerprinting is the precaution against potential remote attacks. Since a sender can be a benign one rather than a fingerprinter, always defending can cause considerable performance degradation in the case of benign senders. Our proposed game-theoretic defense mechanism, *DeceiveGame* takes the sender type into consideration and performs selective defense actions based on the belief about the type. Therefore, the proposed mechanism is suitable for defense against an unknown opponent. Most importantly, *DeceiveGame* works differently against a fingerprinter and a benign sender. It keeps the fingerprinting success low in the case of a fingerprinter, while it creates less performance degradation in the case of a benign sender. We evaluated our tool prototype by simulating different known probes. We found that the tool outperforms conventional defense mechanisms by reducing the overhead up to 60 %, while the probability of fingerprinting success remains reasonably low.:

References

Adrian. Osfuscate 0.3. 2008. Available in http://www.irongeek.com.
O. Arkin and F. Yarochkin. A fuzzy approach to remote active operating system fingerprinting. 2003. Available in http://www.sys-security.com/archive/papers/Xprobe2.pdf.
E. Al-Shaer, Q. Duan, and J. H. Jafarian. Random host mutation for moving target defense. In *SECURECOMM*, 2012.
Basil. Windivert 1.0: Windows packet divert. 2012. Available in http://reqrypt.org/windivert. html.
Fyodor. Remote os detection via tcp/ip fingerprinting (2nd generation). 2007. Available in http://insecure.org/nmap/osdetect/.
L. Greenwald and T. Thomas. Evaluating tests used in operating system fingerprinting. In *LGS Bell Labs Innovations*, 2007.

R. Gibbons. Game theory for applied economics. In *Princeton University Press*, 1992.

J. Michalski. Network security mechanisms utilizing network address translation. In *Journal of Critical Infrastructures*, volume 2, 2006.

K. Poduri and K. Nichols. Simulation studies of increased initial tcp window size. In *Internet Draft by IETF*, 1998.

G. Prigent, F. Vichot, and F. Harroue. Ipmorph: Fingerprinting spoofing unification. In *Journal in Computer Virology*, volume 6, Oct 2009.

M. Rahman, M. Manshaei, and E. Al-Shaer. A game-theoretic solution for counter-fingerprinting. Technical Report, 2013. Available at http://www.manshaei.org/files/TR-Deceive- Game.pdf.

Roualland and Jean-Marc Saffroy. Ip personality. 2001. Available in http://ippersonality. sourceforge.net.

M. Smart, G. R. Malan, and F. Jahanian. Defeating tcp/ip stack fingerprinting. In *USENIX Security*, Aug 2000.

Tcp optimizer, speed guide. 2011. Available in http://www.speedguide.net/tcpoptimizer.php.

The internet traffic archive. 2008. Available in http://ita.ee.lbl.gov/html/traces.html.

K. Wang. Frustrating os fingerprinting with morph. 2004. Available in http://www.synacklabs. net/projects/morph/.

X. Zhang and L. Zheng. Delude remote operating system (os) scan by honeyd. In *Workshop on Computer Science and Engineering*, Oct 2009.

Chapter 5
Game-Theoretic Foundations for the Strategic Use of Honeypots in Network Security

Christopher Kiekintveld, Viliam Lisý and Radek Píbil

Abstract An important element in the mathematical and scientific foundations for security is modeling the strategic use of deception and information manipulation. We argue that game theory provides an important theoretical framework for reasoning about information manipulation in adversarial settings, including deception and randomization strategies. In addition, game theory has practical uses in determining optimal strategies for randomized patrolling and resource allocation. We discuss three game-theoretic models that capture aspects of how honeypots can be used in network security. Honeypots are fake hosts introduced into a network to gather information about attackers and to distract them from real targets. They are a limited resource, so there are important strategic questions about how to deploy them to the greatest effect, which is fundamentally about deceiving attackers into choosing fake targets instead of real ones to attack. We describe several game models that address strategies for deploying honeypots, including a basic honeypot selection game, an extension of this game that allows additional probing actions by the attacker, and finally a version in which attacker strategies are represented using attack graphs. We conclude with a discussion of the strengths and limitations of game theory in the context of network security.

5.1 Introduction

We are increasingly reliant on an infrastructure of networked computer systems to support a wide range of critical functions in both civilian and military domains. A major challenge we currently face is securing these networks against malicious

C. Kiekintveld (✉)
Computer Science Department, University of Texas at El Paso, El Paso, USA
e-mail: cdkiekintveld@utep.edu

V. Lisý · R. Píbil
Agent Technology Center, Department of Computer Science and Engineering, Faculty of Electrical Engineering, Czech Technical University in Prague, Prague, Czech Republic
e-mail: viliam.lisy@agents.fel.cvut.cz

R. Píbil
e-mail: radek.pibil@agents.fel.cvut.cz

© Springer International Publishing Switzerland 2015
S. Jajodia et al. (eds.), *Cyber Warfare,* Advances in Information Security 56,
DOI 10.1007/978-3-319-14039-1_5

attackers ranging from individuals to criminal organizations and nation states. The diverse and constantly evolving nature of the threat and the tactics used by attackers demand that we develop a similarly diverse and adaptive array of countermeasures for securing networks. In addition, we need to develop the mathematical foundations and scientific understanding of security necessary to accurately model the threat and to effectively deploy these countermeasures. The science of security focuses not on identifying specific vulnerabilities or attack/defense techniques, but rather on studying more fundamental principles of security.

A important feature of many security problems is that they involve aspects of deception, information hiding, or information manipulation. For example, the first stage in executing an attack on a network is typically reconnaissance–scanning a network and using fingerprinting techniques to gain information about the connectivity and configuration of the network infrastructure and individual hosts. Intrusion detection also involves manipulating information on both sides; attackers try to disguise their activities to make it difficult to distinguish between attacks and legitimate activity, while network operators try to detect attacks and learn as much as possible about the behavior of attackers. Some code injection vulnerabilities can be mitigated by randomizing code and instruction sets (Kc et al. 2003), which can be viewed as another use of information hiding. We will focus here on examples that involve deploying honeypots (i.e., fake computer systems) to attract the attention of attackers to gain information about the attackers and waste their resources.

We argue that game theory provides a valuable theoretical foundation as well as specific models and algorithms that can be applied to many problems in network security and cyber warfare. Game theory studies decision-making problems with multiple interacting decision makers (also called agents or players), including adversarial situations where two or more agents have opposing goals. Security problems almost always involve interactions between multiple agents with differing goals (e.g., an attacker and a network administrator), so game theory is a natural framework to apply to these situations. Game theory is also particularly well-suited to reasoning systematically about uncertainty, strategic randomization, and information manipulation in the context of adversarial agents. The notion of mixed strategies that allow players to randomize their actions is central to game theory, and many solution concepts can provide guidance on exactly *when and how* to randomize in cases where a uniform random strategy is suboptimal. Game theory also emphasizes the beliefs that players hold, both about the state of the world and their mental models of how other players will act. Reasoning about such beliefs is an important aspect of understanding deception at the deepest level.

Here we present several game-theoretic models that focus on the strategic use of honeypots in network security. These models involve deception in the sense that honeypots are fundamentally about deceiving attackers into attacking fake targets, and they also involve deception in the sense that randomization is necessary in the optimal strategies. Honeypots serve several purposes in protecting networks, including early detection of attacks, collecting detailed information about attacker behaviors and capabilities, distracting attackers and wasting resources, and making it more difficult for attackers to gain an accurate understanding of the configuration of a network.

However, they are limited resources, and there are strategic decisions about how to deploy them to maximize the benefit in terms of improve security. Our models address these resource allocation questions for honeypots at varying levels of abstraction.

We begin by briefly introducing background material on game theory, and then on two classes of games that are closely related to network security problems: security games (Kiekintveld 2009; Tambe 2011) and deception games (Spencer 1973). We then describe our basic model, the honeypot selection game, followed by our extension of this model that includes additional probing actions that attackers can use to detect whether a particular machine is a honeypot or not. The next model considers a richer representation of attacker behavior in the form of attack graphs; we consider the problem of optimizing honeypot deployments to interdict possible attack plans in this representation. We conclude by discussing issues related to using game theory for network security, including strengths and weaknesses of the approach and opportunities for future work.

5.2 Background

We begin by introducing some basic background material on game theory; for a more thorough introduction, see (Shoham and Leyton-Brown 2009). We then discuss two classes of games from the literature that are particularly relevant to cyber warfare.

5.2.1 Game Theory

Game theory is used in many disciplines as a framework for modeling situations with more than one decision maker (player) (Osborne 2004; Shoham and Leyton-Brown 2009). One of the important features of games is that there is no straightforward way to define the optimal action for a given player, because the best action depends on the behavior of the other players. Advances in game theory have led to many different ways of modeling games with different features, and solution concepts and algorithms for reasoning about strategy choices and outcomes.

The elements of a game model include:

1. The **players** who participate in the game
2. The **strategies** available to each player
3. The **payoffs** to each player for each combination of strategy choices (outcome)
4. (optional) Information about the sequences of moves made by the players
5. (optional) A definition of what information players have when making moves

One way of representing games is the *normal form*, often depicted using a matrix such as the one shown in Fig. 5.1. This example is a simple security game with two players, an attacker and a defender. The defender's strategies are represented by the rows: defend target 1 (top), or defend target 2 (bottom). The attacker's strategies are the columns: attack target 1 (left), or attack target 2 (right). Each cell in the matrix

Fig. 5.1 A an example of a
game in normal form

Security Game

2 players
2 targets
1 defender resource

	Target 1	Target 2
Target 1	1, -1	-2, 2
Target 2	-1, 1	2, -1

gives the payoffs for one of the four possible outcomes. For example, the upper left
cell is the case where both the attacker and defender choose target 1, resulting in a
payoff of 1 for the defender and −1 for the attacker.

Another important concept in game theory is *mixed strategies*, which allow players
to randomize their play by selecting according to a probability distribution over their
pure strategies. For example, a defender using a mixed strategy in the example game
could choose target 1 60 % of the time and target 2 40 % of the time. It is clear
that randomization is important in many games as a way to keep an opponent from
predicting what strategy will be played. In the well-known game of "Rock, Paper, and
Scissors," any predictable strategy can be easily defeated, and players must be able
to select different actions to be unpredictable; mixed strategies capture this type of
behavior in games. Mixed strategies can also be interpreted as a form of deception or
information hiding, where the information that is hidden is what the player's strategy
choice will be.

Games can be analyzed in many ways, but typically the goal is to predict what
behaviors are likely to be observed when the game is played, or to identify a strategy
for a player to play that will result in a high payoff (of course, selecting a good
strategy may also involve making predictions about what the other players will do).
Methods for analyzing games are known as solution concepts, including the well-
known concept of Nash equilibrium. A *Nash equilibrium* is a profile of strategy
choices for all players such that every player is playing optimally, given strategies
of the other players. This concept requires that every player correctly predicts the
strategies of the other players, and plays an optimal strategy in response (known as
a best response). In a Nash equilibrium, every player could announce their strategy
choice, and no player would have an incentive to change to a different strategy. Nash's
seminal result showed that such equilibria always exist in finite games as long as
players are allowed to play mixed strategies that allow randomization (Nash 1951).

In addition to the basic normal form representation, game theory includes a large number of richer representations that can be used to describe sequential interactions between players, the structure of the (imperfect) information that players have available when making decisions, and other complexities of a particular situation. There are also many different solution concepts beyond Nash equilibrium. Some are extensions of Nash equilibrium to more complex game representations, and others are refinements that place additional restrictions on the behaviors of the players. Still others use different types of reasoning to find solutions, or are motivated by descriptive goals such as predicting the play of human players in games. A thorough review is beyond the scope of this article, but we will discuss a few specific models and concepts that are most closely related to security.

5.2.2   Security Games

Security problems often involve making complex decisions in adversarial settings where the interests of attackers and defenders are directly opposed. A recent line of research has adopted game theory as a framework for randomizing security deployments and schedules in homeland security and infrastructure protection domains. Security games (Kiekintveld 2009; Tambe 2011) provide a general model for resource allocation decisions in adversarial settings where attackers can observe and exploit patterns in the deployments of resources. This model has been successfully used to randomize the deployment of security resources in airports (Pita et al. 2008; Pita 2011), to create randomized schedules for the Federal Air Marshals (Tsai et al. 2009), and to randomized patrolling strategies for the United States Coast Guard (Shieh et al. 2012).

The example in Fig. 5.1 is a very simple example of a security game. More generally, a security game specifies a set of possible targets (e.g., flights, train stations, inbound roads to an airports). The attacker picks one of these targets, while the defender uses resources to protect the targets. However, the defender has limited resources and cannot protect all of the targets, and therefore must select only a subset to protect. The payoffs in the game specify four values for each target, two for the defender and two for the attacker. The pairs of values correspond to whether or not there is a defender assigned to the target or not. The defender receives a higher value for the case where the target is protected than when it is unprotected, while the attacker receives a higher value if the target is unprotected. A special class of games, *zero-sum games*, is often used to model purely adversarial settings in which the payoffs of the players are exactly opposite (i.e., one player wins exactly the amount that the other player loses). Security games have a similar structure in that payoffs move in the opposite direction, but they allow for more variation in the payoffs than zero-sum games.

It is common in security games to model the attacker as having the capability to observe and learn about the defender strategy before deciding on an attack. This is a realistic assumption for many domains, since attackers typically use surveillance and other information gathering actions during the course of planning an attack, so they are likely to have significant knowledge of the defenses protecting a target before deciding to attack. The Stackelberg security game model incorporates this assumption by assuming that the defender moves first and commits to playing any mixed (randomized) strategy. The attacker observes exactly what this mixed strategy is, and then calculates and optimal target to attack using this knowledge. This is the worst case in a sense, since it assumes that the attacker gains perfect information about the defense strategy. Other models have also been explored in the literature, including simultaneous moves and cases with various types of imperfect observations for the attacker.

The key question in security games is to decide how the defender should allocate limited protective resources to maximize protection against an intelligent attacker who reacts to the security policy. The optimal deterministic strategy is simply to protect as many of the most valuable targets as possible. However, a randomized strategy can use deterrence to improve the overall level of protection by spreading the resources out over a larger set of targets. Since the attacker does not know exactly which targets will be protected (only the probabilities), the attacker has some risk of being unsuccessful when attacking a larger set of targets. Essentially, the defender is able to gain an advantage by concealing information about the defense strategy using randomization. However, a strategy that optimally conceals information is the uniform random policy that uses the same probability to protect every target. This is also not optimal for the defender; the defender should weight the probabilities so that the more important targets are protected with higher probability. The crux of the game-theoretic solution for a security game is to find a weighted randomized strategy for allocating the security resources that optimally balances between allocating more resources to higher-valued targets and hiding information about the policy using randomization to increase risk for the attacker.

Strategic decision-making in cyber warfare poses many of the same fundamental challenges as protecting physical infrastructure: limited resources, the need to manipulate the information an attacker can gain through surveillance, and the need to learn about an attacker's strategy. We believe that game theory can be used to address many of these challenges in cyber domains, building on the success of security games. One promising area is developing better strategies for using honeypots and other deception strategies in network security. We describe some out our initial research on game-theoretic models for deploying honeypots to illustrate this approach below.

5.2.3   Deception Games

Deception has been studied in many forms in the game theory literature. It often takes the form of using randomized strategies to hide information from an opponent, as in the security games described above. Another example is found in game theory models of poker, which naturally generate bluffing behaviors as part of randomized Nash equilibrium strategies. In these strategies, it is optimal for players to sometimes make bets with poor cards so that it is more difficult for an opponent to infer information about the cards a player is holding based on their bidding strategy.

Another model that has received some attention in the game theory literature models deception more directly using actions intended to confuse an opponent. A formal model of *deception games* was first introduced in (Spencer 1973). One player is given a vector of three random numbers drawn from the uniform distribution on unit interval. This player is allowed to modify one of the three numbers to any other number from the same unit interval. The modified vector of numbers is shown to the second player. The second player chooses one of the three numbers, and receives the original value of the number at that position as a reward (i.e., the value before the modification made by player 1). So, the second player prefers to choose higher values, but the first player can try to deceive the second player by making one of the small values in the vector appear large. The open question stated in the original paper is whether there is a better strategy for the second player than randomly choosing one of the numbers. This question was answered in (Lee 1993) proving that if the changer plays optimally, the second player cannot play better then random. Several similar questions about various modifications of the model were published in the next years, but the results generally apply only to the specific game formulations and they do not present the complete strategies to play the game. Our model for selecting honeypots builds on this deception game model, though it is not identical in the details.

5.3   Honeypots

A honeypot is a computer system deployed in a computer network specifically to attract the attention of possible attackers. They do not store valuable information, and are designed to log as much information about system behavior as possible for analysis after an event. Honeypots can help to increase system security in several ways (Spitzner 2003): (1) The presence of honeypots can waste the attacker's time and resources. The effort an attacker spends to compromise the honeypot and learn that it does not contain any useful information directly takes away time and resources that could be used to compromise valuable machines. (2) Honeypots serve an intrusion detection role, and can provide an "early warning" system for administrators, providing more time to react to attacks in progress. A particularly important case of this is detecting "zero day" attacks and previously unknown vulnerabilities. (3) Once an attacker compromises a honeypot, the network administrator can analyze all of the attacker's actions in great detail, and use the information obtained to better protect the network. For example, security gaps used in an attack can be patched, and new attack signatures added to antivirus or intrusion detection systems.

We consider the use of honeypots from an adversarial perspective, where network administrators and attackers both reason strategically. In general, a network administrator will try to maximize the probability that an attacker chooses to attack a honeypot rather than a real service. However, attackers are increasingly aware of the possibility of honeypots, and actively take steps to identify and avoid them. For example, once they gain access to a system, they can use multitude of methods to probe the system and rule out the possibility that they are in a honeypot before they continue with their attack (e.g., (Dornseif and Holz 2004)). To be effective against more sophisticated attackers, honeypots must be sufficiently disguised that they are not obvious (i.e., they cannot simply present the most vulnerable possible target).

Honeypots can be classified into low interaction and high interaction variants. A *low interaction* honeypot is relatively simple, and therefore it can be added to the network at low cost (Cohen 2000), but even simple probing by the attacker will reveal it is not a real system. A *high interaction* honeypot is much more expensive to create and maintain. For example, to increase believability realistic user activity and network traffic may need to be simulated. High interaction honeypots in particular are a limited resource and it is important to optimize how they are deployed.

5.4   The Honeypot Selection Game

In Pibil et al. (2012) we introduced the *Honeypot Selection Game* to model situations where an attacker decides which machines or services in a network to attack, and a defender decides what types of honeypots to add to the network. One of the important features of real-world networks is that they have many different types of machines with different configurations (available services, hardware, etc.). Some categories of machines are more important than others, both to the owner of the network and as targets for the attacker. For example, a database server containing valuable military information may have a much higher value than a standard laptop. To model this we classify machines into categories of *importance* that are assigned values to represent the gain/loss associated with a successful attack. One of the decisions that the defender makes when deploying honeypots on a diverse network is how to disguise the honeypots—in other words, which category of machine should each honeypot be designed to look like?

We represent a *configuration* of the network using a vector of values representing the apparent importance of each machine. The defender knows the values of each of the real machines in the network, and extends the vector by adding honeypots. For each honeypot, the defender selects the value of the machine that will be observed by the attacker (e.g., by configuring the honeypot to emulate machines of that category). We assume that both players have knowledge of the typical configurations of the network, so the players can calculate the probability that the configuration is the actual configuration of the network. We assume that the defender adds a fixed number of honeypots to the network, and that the attacker knows the number of honeypots. This is a worst case assumption about the attacker, and the model could be generalized to allow for imperfect information about the number of honeypots, though it makes the problem more difficult to solve.

Consider the example shown in the Fig. 5.2 with two machines that have importance values 4 and 3. The administrator has one honeypot and needs to decide how to assign it a value. He could assign it a value of 5 to make it appear very attractive (e.g., by making it appear to contain valuable data and exposing obvious vulnerabilities). The attacker observes the unordered vector of values by doing a scan of the

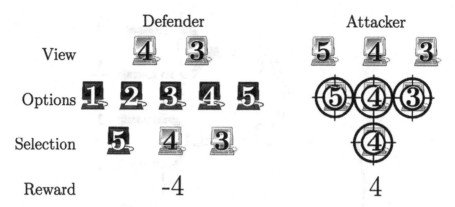

Fig. 5.2 Example run of the Honeypot Selection Game. The defender selects one honeypot to add to a network with two targets. The attacker attacks a single target and cannot distinguish honeypots from real hosts

network, including the value of the honeypot: (5,4,3). A naïve attacker might attack the machine with the highest value (5), therefore attacking the honeypot. However, a sophisticated attacker might reason that this is "too good to be true" and choose instead to attack the next best machine, with a value of 4. If the attacker chooses a real machine to attack, he obtains a reward and the network administrator is penalized. If the attacker chooses to attack a honeypot, he does not obtain any reward and possibly is penalized for disclosing his attack strategy.

From this example, we can see that assigning all honeypots a maximal value may not be the optimal strategy. We search for a solution in the form of a Nash equilibrium, which is a pair of mixed strategies such the neither player can benefit be changing to a different strategy. To find a Nash equilibrium we can formulate this as an optimization problem (due to the specific structure of the game), and use linear programming to find a solution; for details of the formulation and optimizations that speed up the search see (Pibil 2012). For very simple games we can also visualize and solve the game models using Gambit, a well known toolkit for game theory. An example of a game tree using gambit is shown in Fig. 5.3.

The typical form of a solution can be seen in Fig. 5.4a (left), which shows the probability that the defender will use a honeypot with each different value from 1 to 4 for a scenario with uniform random values for the machines in the network (full details of the experiments are presented in (Pibil 2012)). In general, higher values are used more frequently but the optimal probability values depend on the details of a specific problem. If we assume that all network configurations are equally probable than the optimal strategy for the defender in the situation from Fig. 5.2 is to add the honeypot with value 4. The strategy for the attacker is than to select a target randomly with uniform probability.

In Fig. 5.4b we present the results for the defender's expected value against three different types of attackers as the number of honeypots increases. The box line is an attacker who always chooses the maximum value (i.e., an optimistic attacker who

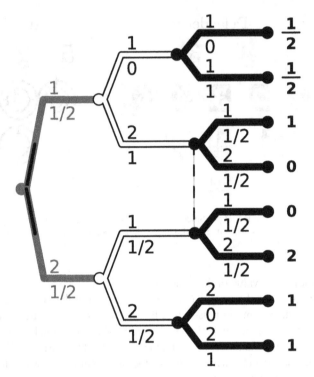

Fig. 5.3 The game tree of a Honeypot Selection Game rendered by Gambit with one real service, one honeypot and a domain 1, 2. Light gray edges are random choices, white edges are defender's actions and black edges the attacker's actions. Services corresponding to actions are above the branches, while probabilities are under them

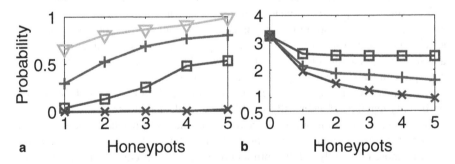

Fig. 5.4 **a** An example of the structure of a typical solution, where each line represents a honeypot value from 1–4, with higher lines corresponding to higher values. The number of honeypots allowed varies along the x axis. **b** The defender's expected utility against three different types of attackers as the number of honeypots allowed increases. (Cross: Nash equilibrium attacker, Plus: random attacker, Box: Maximum attacker)

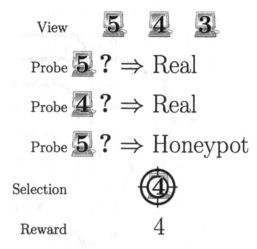

Fig. 5.5 Demonstration of the attacker's actions in Honeypot Selection Game with Probes

ignores the possibility of honeypots). The plus line is an attacker who chooses a target at random, without respect to the value of the target. The cross line is an attacker who accounts for honeypots and plays according to the Nash equilibrium of the game (Fig. 5.5).

5.5   Honeypot Selection with Attacker Probes

There are many opportunities for interesting extensions to this basic model. One that we have explored in detail allows attackers to execute *probe* actions to further analyze the machines on a network to determine whether or not they are honeypots. This is intended to model the real behaviors of attacker in networks who use various strategies such as traffic analysis to identify likely honeypots (Dornseif and Holz 2004).

To capture this situation in the formal game theoretic model, we introduce additional probe actions for the attacker. Prior to executing the attack on the selected target, the attacker executes a limited number of probing actions on the hosts of his choice. The result of the probe is an observation of whether the probed host is real, or a honeypot. This observation is closely, but not perfectly, correlated with the real nature of the host. The probing methods are typically not perfect and the defender can even disguise real servers as honeypots in order to deter the attackers (Rowe et al. 2007). The probes are executed sequentially and the attacker can use the results of the earlier probes to decide which host to probe next. After the probing phase, the attacker has to combine the information acquired by the probing and his believe about the strategy deployed by the defender to pick one target to attack.

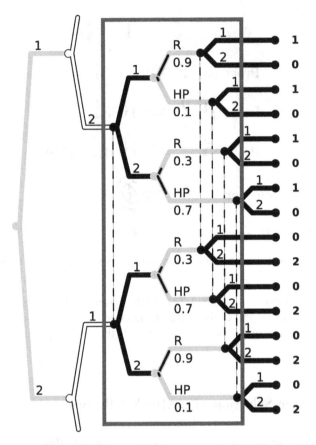

Fig. 5.6 An example of part the Gambit game tree for an example of the Honeypot Selection Game extended with probing actions. The area in the box represents a probing action for the attacker and the observation revealed by nature

An example showing part of the game tree with probing actions for the attacker is shown in Fig 5.6. Comparing this figure with the game tree for the basic honeypot selection game we can see that the game is much larger, due to the additional levels of actions for the attacker when selecting probes. In addition, the information sets are significantly more complex, since the attacker can gain different types of information during the game. While we can still formulate and solve these games using linear programming, the size of the game poses additional computational challenges that increase with the number of probing actions allowed.

For the game with probes with also compute the optimal solution in the form of a Nash equilibrium. Similar results to those in the previous section are presented in Fig. 5.7. The strategy for the defender is shown in the plot on the left. When the defender takes into account the probing of the attacker, the optimal strategy uses the most important honeypots more often than in the case without probes. This

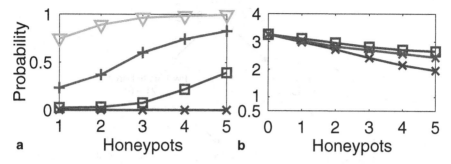

Fig. 5.7 a An example of the structure of a typical solution for the version of the game with probes, where each line represents a honeypot value from 1–4, with higher lines corresponding to higher values. The number of honeypots allowed varies along the x axis. **b** The defender's expected utility against three different types of attackers as the number of honeypots allowed increases. (Cross: Nash equilibrium attacker, Plus: random attacker, Box: Maximum attacker)

is mainly because the rational attacker directs the probes to the most promising targets and probing a honeypot typically has higher error probability than probing a real machine. The expected payoff for the defender against the same three types of attackers (maximum, random, and Nash equilibrium) is shown on the right.

5.6   Honeypot Strategies for Games on Attack Graphs

The models discussed above use a relatively simple representation of the attacker strategies, with the attackers choosing only which machines to attack. However, richer models of attacker behavior are highly desirable, particularly when viewing honeypots as a mechanism for learning about the plans or behaviors of attackers. One useful modeling paradigm that captures a broader range of attacker behavior is attack graphs (sometimes restricted to attack trees). Attack graphs represent all the known attack vectors that can be used to compromise the security of a system. Several different types of attack graphs have been proposed in the literature, but they share the basic idea of representing sequential attack plans in which attackers use various actions to gain privileges on certain machines in a network, which in turn may allow new attack actions.

One advantage of adopting the attack graph formalism is that there are several existing tools that can automatically analyze a computer network to generate attack graphs based on known vulnerabilities. For example, the network scanning tools Nessus[1] and OpenVAS[2] scan the network (or individual hosts) for open ports, installed software versions and similar characteristics, and based on large databases of

---

[1] http://www.nessus.org.
[2] http://www.openvas.org.

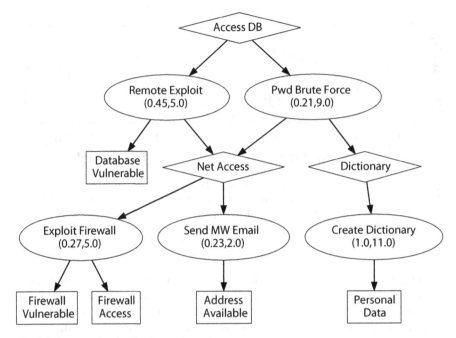

Fig. 5.8 An example of a simple attack graph

known vulnerabilities identify the ones that are present in the network. Vulnerability databases can also provide additional structured data that is useful for creating models, such as assessing the probability of success or the expected cost of exploiting specific vulnerabilities. The vulnerabilities found by network scanners can then be merged to create attack graphs using rule-based tools, such as MulVAL (Ou et al. 2006) or NetSPA (Pibil et al. 2006). A very simple example of an attack graph is shown in Fig. 5.8.

Existing work mainly uses attack graphs to identify the optimal subsets of vulnerabilities to fix on the network, in order to perfectly secure the network against the known attacks or to optimize some aggregate measure of the overall security of the network. In game-theoretic models, attack graphs can be used to model complex behavior of the attackers. Based on analysis of the attacker behaviors we can consider the optimal strategies for the defender, which can include various policies or configuration changes to the network, such as adding honeypots to the network or modifying firewall rules.

If both the administrator and the attacker have perfect knowledge about the network and the security measures deployed on the network, the defender can optimize the security measures with respect to the expected reaction of the attacker. For example, the defender can try to identify the best possible set of rules for the firewalls in the network. For each such set, the defender can (1) evaluate the restrictions to the usability of the network, (2) generate the attack graph representing all possible attacks after the new rules are applied and based on that, (3) compute the optimal attack with respect to the time or skill level required by the attacker. Among all the evaluated options, the defender can choose the one that achieved the desired tradeoff between security and usability.

In the honeypot selection game, we can use the more detailed modeling of the attacker's behavior allowed by the attack graphs to better determine the importance of a host in the network. Instead of an abstract number representing the importance of a host, we can use the attack graph to evaluate the role of the host in the potential attacks. For example, we can estimate how costly the attacks using a specific host are in comparison to the attacks that do not use this host. We can estimate how many options for attack continuation compromising each of the hosts will open. If analysis of the attack graph identifies a key node where an attacker might try to exploit a particular vulnerability, adding several honeypots to the network that appear to replicate this key node can result in a high probability that the attacker chooses to attack one of the honeypots before attacking the real machine.

We assume that the defender can choose a subset of honeypots from a fixed set of alternatives. There are endless number of possible configurations of the honeypots and their placement into the network; hence, in our initial investigation we restrict the defender to use only honeypots that completely copy the configuration and connectivity of an existing host on the network. This restriction has several advantages. First, copying an existing machine and obfuscating the useful data on the machine can be done almost automatically with a substantially lower costs than configuring a brand new host. Second, it can create much more believable honeypots that will make it hard for the attacker to distinguish them from the production systems. Third, if the attacker uses some unknown exploit on the honeypot, we know that the same exploit is available on one of the production machines. We can check these machines to determine if they were compromised in the same way, and try to remove the vulnerability and/or update the attack graph to include it in further analysis. Fourth, we do not introduce any fundamentally new attack vectors to penetrate the network. A honeypot can take the place of a production machine in the attack plan, which is a the desired effect, but we do not open any new opportunities for the attacker. Hence, it is virtually impossible that we are reducing the security of the network. Moreover, the attack graph created for the original network perfectly represents the possible attack on the modified network, if we abstract the exact machine on which the individual attack actions are performed. As a result, the effect of adding each subset of honeypots to the network is only modifying the probabilities that certain attack actions use a honeypot and not the attack graph itself.

Copying each of the hosts has different initial and maintenance costs for the defender. The attacker has costs, for example, for the time he spends attacking and the possibility of disclosing a zero-day exploit to the defender. The players generally do not care about these costs of their opponents. Furthermore, the defender often values his sensitive data more than the attacker trying to steel them. Therefore, we model the game as a non-zero-sum game and we use the Stackelberg equilibrium as the solution concept for the game.

In a Stackelberg game, we assume that the attacker knows the action selected by the defender. In this case, he knows what hosts on the network have been copied as honeypots, but we assume that he does not know which particular instance of certain type of host is the real one and which is the honeypot. Based on that, he can derive the probability that each of his actions will interact with a honeypot and use this information in computing the optimal attack to perform on the network. The optimal set of honeypots for the defender to add to the network is the one that motivates the attacker to select the attack that is least harmful to the defender. The attacker will either pick less valuable targets or have a high probability of being discovered.

The main challenge that this model poses is the computational complexity of computing optimal solutions. We have proposed a method for computing the optimal attack by transforming the problem into standard problems previously solved in artificial intelligence (Lisy and Pibil 2013) as well as a more efficient problem specific method (Durkota and Lisy 2014). Both of these methods can be extended to take into account the probability of interacting with a honeypot in computing optimal attack strategies. While the optimal solvers are still only able to solve small networks, the game theoretic models build on top of these solvers can use the fact that the same problem with mild modifications is solved repetitively to provide many improvement, such as reusing partial results and deriving strong heuristics.

Either way, solving the optimal attack problem is NP-hard if both the cost and probability of success of attack actions are considered. Therefore, it may be very interesting to integrate approximate solvers with error guarantees, such as (Buldas and Stepanenko 2012), to the game theoretic models. However, this requires investigating new solution concepts which would be able to deal with this uncertainty.

5.7 Discussion

We now discuss some of our observations related to deploying game-theoretic models and solution methods for network security and cyber warfare. We first highlight some of the more important strengths of the approach:

- Game theory provides a strong theoretical/mathematical foundation for modeling adversarial decision, including security
- The models assume intelligent adversaries that adapt to defensive strategies
- Game theory offers models of deception and strategic randomization that can be used to systematically identify good strategies for manipulating information
- There are many existing models and algorithms that can be leveraged for analysis
- Modeling player's beliefs play a central role, including recursive modeling of the beliefs and strategies of the other players

There are also a number of challenges in using game theory for security, including:

- Network security problems are often very complex with combinatorial action/belief spaces, resulting in scalability problems for analyzing the games
- Large models contain many parameters, and these may be difficult to estimate efficiently using available data

- Game theory models are best suited to maximizing expected results, rather than providing guaranteed performance
- Some types of game models and solution concepts make implausible assumptions including perfect rationality and perfect knowledge

We begin by highlighting some of the features of game theory that make it a promising direction for establishing a stronger scientific approach for security. The main feature of game theory is that it explicitly models all of the agents in a scenario, including their available actions and the values that they assign to the various outcomes. This is a rich modeling framework, and it is able capture how players will *adapt and respond* to the actions of other players. In contrast, many other security decision making frameworks really on a *fixed* notion of the threat or risk, such as a probability that an attacker will attempt a particular type of attack. Such models are more limited than game-theoretic models because they do not offer predictions of how the threat will change as the defensive strategy changes. A model with a fixed threat is roughly equivalent to a myopic best response calculation in game theory (i.e., given my current prediction about the threat, what is the optimal defensive strategy?). Game theoretic models offer the possibility of thinking further ahead to anticipate responses by an opponent, and even calculating the equilibria that are fixed points of the best-response dynamics and other evolutionary processes.

There are challenges in constructing a useful game-theoretic model that captures the important features of a problem at the right level of abstraction, and it should be emphasized that game theory may not be useful for all security problems. In some cases the solution to a problem may be trivial or immediately obvious due to the symmetry or other structure in the problem. For example, if one wants to make it difficult to discover the IP address of a machine and all IP addresses are functionally identical, assigning the addresses using a uniform random policy is trivially the best solution.

Game theory is also not very useful in situations where a guaranteed solution is desirable (e.g., formally proving that systems will never enter undesirable states, or that a cryptographic protocol is secure). However, we argue that often there is no such thing as 100 % security, or it is cost prohibitive relative to the value of the resource being protected. For these situations we must accept results based on expected outcomes, accepting an appropriate level of risk. Game theory is best suited to models problems where there are complex interactions between different strategies, and it is necessary to make choices that maximize the *expected* value of a specific course of action. For these cases the solutions to the game will balance risk and cost by selecting strategies with high expected values.

Constructing a useful game theoretic model can also be difficult due to the complexity that arises in many security domains. Computer networks are very complex in that they comprise large numbers of different types of interconnected devices, running different software and services, and with different owners. These machines are constantly communicating in varying patterns using complex protocols. Modeling these systems can easily lead to combinatorial spaces, such as selecting subsets of the hosts in a network, or generating all possible routes/paths through a network, or modeling different combinations of software and services that could be present on a host. When decisions are being made for these systems, it is easy to generate models that are intractable due to the size of the game. A model may be intractable to solve due to limited scalability of the solution algorithms, and the models may also be problematic to specify due to the number of parameters.

There is reason for optimism in developing game theory models for very complex domains. Much of the progress in security games has been driven by advances in algorithms for scaling to very large problem instances, including some where the strategy spaces involve large networks (Jain 2011; Tsai et al. 2013). In addition, there has been dramatic progress on algorithms for solving poker and related games, with new algorithms able to solve games that are several orders of magnitude larger than the best algorithms from just a few years ago (Sandholm 2010). These scalable solution algorithms are based on key ideas such as iterative solution methods that avoid enumerating the full strategy space (Bosansky 2013), and automated abstraction methods that can simplify large games to more tractable versions (Sandholm and Singh 2012). We believe that applying such techniques to network security games could lead to similar advances and allow for many new applications of game theory for network security.

A related challenge for modeling cyber security domains is that these domains are very dynamic, and the details of the decision problems are constantly changing. Computer networks are not static entities; hosts may join or leave the network, network infrastructure and routing may change, the configurations of individual hosts are updated as software and services are added, removed, or updated. The nature of the threat also changes as new vulnerabilities are discovered or new attackers with different goals and capabilities attempt to compromise a network in different ways. These changes mean that the relevant models for decision making must also be updated on a continual basis so that they are still relevant.

The dynamism of cyber security domains presents opportunities for using learning in combination with game theory. Many previous security games models have focused on terrorism, and there is very limited data available to construct and validate the models since there are very few examples of terrorist attacks. In cyber security, interactions between defenders and attackers are much more frequent, with results in a much larger amount of data that can be used to specify models and to improve them over time. The field of empirical game theory (Kiekintveld 2008) has introduced methods for constructing game-theoretic models using data. There is also a large body of work on multi-agent learning (Fudenberg and Levine 1998) that is relevant for situations where multiple agents interact frequently and can learn about the behavior of other agents. Both of these are promising directions for future research on making dynamic games applicable to cyber security.

Another issue that game theory raises that is of particular interest for cyber security is accurately modeling the behavior of agents that are not perfectly rational. Research on behavioral game theory focuses on developing descriptive models that accurately predict human behavior in games (Camerer 2003). The solution concepts studied in behavioral game theory differ from Nash equilibrium and other traditional concepts in that they do not model perfectly rational players, but rather seek to accurately describe the behavior of real players. These solutions concepts are of great interest for analyzing security games because they may offer more accurate predictions about the behavior of attackers.

In addition, behavioral models open new directions for reasoning about deception in security games. A solution concept that assumes perfect rationality can suggest deceptions that involve randomizing to hide information, but it cannot suggest deceptions involving false beliefs because such beliefs are inherently irrational because the definition of rationality usually includes correct Bayesian reasoning. However, behavioral models can include imperfect reasoning, including the possibility of false beliefs. Therefore, an agent with an accurate behavioral model of an opponent could develop deception strategies that exploit the imperfect reasoning of the opponent, leading to a wider range of possible deception strategies including creating false beliefs for the opponent.

5.8   Conclusion

We see great potential for game theory to play a role in both the theoretical foundations and practical applications of security. One area where it seems particularly relevant is modeling and analyzing strategic manipulation of information, including randomization and deception tactics. Indeed, the growing area of security games has already produced several notable successes in applying game theory to randomize security policies to improve security for physical infrastructure. There is also a small but growing number of game theoretic models that have been developed for cyber security.

We discuss a series of game models that consider optimizing the way honeypots can be used in network security. These range from the basic honeypot selection game to an extended version that allows for probing behaviors, to models that include attack graphs as a more detailed representation of attacker behavior. The models capture many of the salient features of deploying honeypots, though it is certainly possible to enrich them further. The primarily limitation of these models is the scalability of the current solution algorithms, but applying techniques from other state of the art methods in computational game theory could improve the algorithms significantly. We also argue that new research on learning in dynamic game models and behavioral solution concepts that model humans will be important for improving our understanding of deception at a fundamental level, and will allow new applications of game theory for cyber security.

Acknowledgements   This research was supported by the Office of Naval Research Global (grant no. N62909-13-1-N256), and the Czech Science Foundation (grant no. P202/12/2054). Viliam Lisý is a member of the Czech Chapter of The Honeynet Project.

References

B. Bosansky, C. Kiekintveld, V. Lisy, J. Cermak, and M. Pechoucek. Double-oracle algorithm for computing an exact nash equilibrium in zero-sum extensive-form games. In *Proceedings of the 12th International Conference on Autonomous Agents and Multiagent Systems (AAMAS 2013)*, 2013

A. Buldas and R. Stepanenko. Upper bounds for adversaries' utility in attack trees. In J. Grossklags and J. Walrand, editors, *Decision and Game Theory for Security, volume 7638 of Lecture Notes in Computer Science*, pages 98–117. Springer Berlin Heidelberg, 2012.

C. F. Camerer. *Behavioral Game Theory: Experiments in Strategic Interaction*. Princeton University Press, 2003.

F. Cohen. A mathematical structure of simple defensive network deception. *Computers & Security*, 19(6):520–528, 2000.

M. Dornseif and T. Holz. Nosebreak-attacking honeynets. In *2004 IEEE Workshop on Information Assurance and Security*, 2004.

K. Durkota and V. Lisy. Computing optimal policies for attack graphs with action failures and costs. In *STAIRS 2014: Proceedings of the Seventh Starting Ai Researchers' Symposium*, page (to appear). IOS Press, 2014.

D. Fudenberg and D. K. Levine. *The Theory of Learning in Games*. MIT Press, 1998.

K. Ingols, R. Lippmann, and K. Piwowarski. Practical attack graph generation for network defense. In *Computer Security Applications Conference, 2006. ACSAC'06. 22nd Annual*, pages 121–130. IEEE, 2006.

M. Jain, D. Korzhyk, O. Vanek, V. Conitzer, M. Pechoucek, and M. Tambe. A double oracle algorithm for zero-sum security games on graphs. In *International Conference on Autonomous Agents and Multiagent Systems*, 2011.

G. S. Kc, A. D. Keromytis, and V. Prevelakis. Countering code-injection attacks with instruction-set randomization. In *Proceedings of the 10th ACM Conference on Computer and Communications Security*, CCS '03, pages 272–280, New York, NY, USA, 2003. ACM.

C. Kiekintveld. *Empirical Game-Theoretic Methods for Strategy Design and Analysis in Complex Games*. PhD thesis, Universit y of Michigan, 2008.

C. Kiekintveld, M. Jain, J. Tsai, J. Pita, F. Ordonez, and M. Tambe. Computing optimal randomized resource allocations for massive security games. In *AAMAS-09*, 2009.

K. Lee. On a deception game with three boxes. *International Journal of Game Theory*, 22(2):89–95, 1993.

V. Lisy and R. Pibil. Computing optimal attack strategies using unconstrained influence diagrams. In G. Wang, X. Zheng, M. Chau, and H. Chen, editors, *Intelligence and Security Informatics, volume 8039 of Lecture Notes in Computer Science*. Springer Berlin Heidelberg, 2013.

J. Nash. Non-cooperative games. *The Annals of Mathematics*, 54(2):286–295, 1951.

M. J. Osborne. *An Introduction to Game Theory*. Oxford University Press, 2004.

X. Ou, W. Boyer, and M. McQueen. A scalable approach to attack graph generation. In *Proceedings of the 13th ACM conference on Computer and communications security*, pages 336–345. ACM, 2006.

R. Pibil, V. Lisy, C. Kiekintveld, B. Bosansky, and M. Pechoucek. Game theoretic model of strategic honeypot selection in computer networks. In J. Grossklags and J. Walrand, editors, *Decision and Game Theory for Security*, volume 7638 of *Lecture Notes in Computer Science*. Springer Berlin Heidelberg, 2012.

J. Pita, M. Jain, C. Western, C. Portway, M. Tambe, F. Ordonez, S. Kraus, and P. Parachuri. Depoloyed ARMOR protection: The application of a game-theoretic model for security at the Los Angeles International Airport. In *AAMAS-08 (Industry Track)*, 2008.

J. Pita, M. Tambe, C. Kiekintveld, S. Cullen, and E. Steigerwald. GUARDS—game theoretic security allocation on a national scale. In *AAMAS-11 (Industry Track)*, 2011.

N. C. Rowe, E. J. Custy, and B. T. Duong. Defending Cyberspace with Fake Honeypots. *Journal of Computers*, 2(2):25–36, Apr. 2007.

T. Sandholm. The state of solving large incomplete-information games, and application to poker. *AI Magazine*, Special Issue on Algorithmic Game Theory, 2010.

T. Sandholm and S. Singh. Lossy stochastic game abstraction with bounds. In *ACM Conference on Electronic Commerce (EC)*, 2012.

E. Shieh, B. An, R. Yang, M. Tambe, C. Baldwin, J. Direnzo, G. Meyer, C. W. Baldwin, B. J. Maule, and G. R. Meyer. PROTECT : A Deployed Game Theoretic System to Protect the Ports of the United States. *AAMAS*, 2012.

Y. Shoham and K. Leyton-Brown. *Multiagent Systems: Algorithmic, Game-Theoretic, and Logical Foundations*. Cambridge University Press, 2009.

J. Spencer. A deception game. *American Mathematical Monthly*, page 416–417, 1973.

L. Spitzner. *Honeypots: tracking hackers*. Addison-Wesley Professional, 2003.

M. Tambe. *Security and Game Theory: Algorithms, Deployed Systems, Lessons Learned*. Cambridge University Press, 2011.

J. Tsai, Y. Qian, Y. Vorobeychik, C. Kiekintveld, and M. Tambe. Bayesian security games for controlling contagion. In *In Proceedings of the ASE/IEEE International Conference on Social Computing(SocialCom)*, 2013.

J. Tsai, S. Rathi, C. Kiekintveld, F. Ordó nez, and M. Tambe. IRIS—A tools for strategic security allocation in transportation networks. In *AAMAS-09 (Industry Track)*, 2009.

Chapter 6
Cyber Counterdeception: How to Detect Denial & Deception (D&D)

Kristin E. Heckman and Frank J. Stech

Abstract In this chapter we explore cyber-counterdeception (cyber-CD), what it is, and how it works, and how to incorporate counterdeception into cyber defenses. We review existing theories and techniques of counterdeception and relate counterdeception to the concepts of cyber attack kill chains and intrusion campaigns. We adapt theories and techniques of counterdeception to the concepts of cyber defenders' deception chains and deception campaigns. We describe the utility of conducting cyber wargames and exercises to develop the techniques of cyber-denial & deception (cyber-D&D) and cyber-CD. Our goal is to suggest how cyber defenders can use cyber-CD, in conjunction with defensive cyber-D&D campaigns, to detect and counter cyber attackers.

6.1 What it Is Denial and Deception (D&D)?

Deception is fundamentally psychological. Deceptive actions by one actor influence the behaviors of another actor, so deception is a form of influence and persuasion, although the target of the deception may be completely unaware of being persuaded or influenced. (Boush et al. 2009; Laran et al. 2011)[1] We refer to the deceptive actor as the *ATTACKER* because this chapter focuses on the cyber attacker's use of

---

---

[1] Boush et al. (2009). Market research shows consumer resistance or susceptibility to persuasion can be driven by processes that operate entirely outside the conscious awareness of the consumer; e.g., Laran et al. (2011).

K. E. Heckman (✉) · F. J. Stech
The MITRE Corporation, 7515 Colshire Drive, McLean, VA 22102, USA
e-mail: kheckman@mitre.org

© Springer International Publishing Switzerland 2015
S. Jajodia et al. (eds.), *Cyber Warfare,* Advances in Information Security 56,
DOI 10.1007/978-3-319-14039-1_6

103

Table 6.1 D&D Methods matrix. Source: Adapted from Bennett and Waltz (1999)

Deception objects	D&D Methods	
	Deception: Mislead (M)-Type Methods Revealing	Denial: Ambiguity (A)-Type Methods Concealing
Facts	Reveal facts Reveal true information to the target Reveal true physical entities, events, or processes to the target	Conceal facts (Dissimulation) Conceal true information from the target Conceal true physical entities, events, or processes from the target
Fictions	Reveal fictions (Simulation) Reveal to the target information known to be untrue Reveal to the target physical entities, events, or processes known to be untrue	Conceal fictions Conceal from the target information known to be untrue Conceal from the target physical entities, events, or processes known to be untrue

denial and deception, and we refer to the target of the *ATTACKER*'s deception as the *DEFENDER* given our argument for the defensive use of cyber-CD.

Deceptions should have a tangible purpose: namely, *ATTACKER* deceives *DEFENDER* to cause *DEFENDER* to behave in a way that accrues advantages to *ATTACKER*. This is *ATTACKER*'s deception goal, and *DEFENDER*'s actions in response to the deception are what create the *ATTACKER*'s desired deception effect. While the constituents of deception concepts and plans are psychological, the consequences of executing those plans are physical actions and reactions by *ATTACKER* and *DEFENDER*. So deceptions are interactions between the deceptive *ATTACKER* and the deception target *DEFENDER*; and these interactions have both conceptual psychological, as well as behavioral physical action aspects.

This causal relationship between psychological/conceptual state and physical/behavioral action is created by the two essential deception methods:

- Denial: *ATTACKER* behavior that actively prevents *DEFENDER* from perceiving information and stimuli, this is, using hiding and concealing techniques that generate ambiguity in *DEFENDER*'s mind about what is and is not perceived as real;
- Deception: *ATTACKER* behavior that provides misleading information and reveals deceptive stimuli to actively reinforce *DEFENDER*'s perceptions, cognitions, and beliefs. This generates a mistaken certainty in *DEFENDER*'s mind about what is and is not real, making *DEFENDER* certain, confident, and ready to act—but wrong.

In this chapter, we use *denial*, *hiding*, and *concealing* as synonymous; and *deception*, *misleading*, and *revealing* as synonymous. As we discuss below, deception may entail concealing facts or fictions; and revealing facts or fictions (Table 6.1).

6.2   What Is Counterdeception?

McNair (1991) offered a "concept for counterdeception," that is, in assessing the actions and intentions of the enemy or adversary, "to effectively avoid falling prey to enemy deception efforts, a commander must accurately identify the enemy operation as deceptive, and avoid taking the action his opponent desires him to take."[2] Whaley (2006, 2007a) claims the term *counterdeception* is merely convenient shorthand for "the detection of deception" and was coined in 1968 by William R. Harris of the Center for International Studies at Harvard University.[3] All definitions of *counterdeception* link it to the function of intelligence, that is, of understanding the behavior and objectives of the adversary, as contrasted with *denial and deception*, which is the operational function of influencing the perceptions, beliefs, and behaviors of the adversary (e.g., Bennett and Waltz 2007; Gerwehr and Glenn 2002; Whaley 2006, 2007b).

Bennett and Waltz (2007) define counterdeception in terms of the defender's actions that counterdeception must support: "counterdeception is characterized [by]. . . *awareness* [of the adversary's deception capabilities and operations], *detection and exposure* [of specific deception techniques and tactics by the adversary], *and discovery and penetration* [of the adversary's deception intentions and objectives]." Bennett and Waltz define the purposes of counterdeception as determining the deceiver's real and simulated capabilities, and determining the deceiver's deception intentions:

> The purpose of counterdeception is to find the answers to two fundamental and highly interdependent questions. First, counterdeception must . . . penetrate through the deception to discern the adversary's real capabilities and intentions, in other words, to answer the question: What is real? Simultaneously, analysts and decision-makers must determine what the adversary is trying to make them believe in order to consider the second question: What does the adversary want you to do? The answers to these two questions are absolutely essential to the success of one's own strategies, policies, and operations.

Unfortunately, Barton Whaley's (2007b) analysis of many historical cases of military and political deception reached a striking conclusion— *the odds overwhelmingly favor the deceiver, no matter how shrewd the victim*: "the deceiver is almost always successful regardless of the sophistication of his victim . . . it is the irrefutable conclusion of the historical evidence." But Whaley offers some hope for counterdeception: "the avoidance of victimization" by deception "requires [a] decisional model, specifically one designed to analyze the signals of stratagem [i.e., deception] . . . To detect deception, one must, at the minimum, know to look for those specific types of clues

---

[2] McNair (2000).

[3] Whaley (2007d) further wrote: "Counterdeception is . . . now standard jargon among specialists in military deception. This useful term was coined in 1968 by Dr. William R. Harris during a brainstorming session with me in Cambridge, Massachusetts." Harris's papers, while widely influencing other scholars of deception and counterdeception, are hard to come by. Epstein (1991) cites Harris (1968). Other relevant Harris counterdeception papers Epstein cited include Harris (1972); and Harris (1985).

that point to deception ... they are an essential part of the counterdeception analyst's toolkit."[4] We will describe one such counterdeception model in this chapter.

Gerwehr and Glenn's (2002) research echoes Whaley's recommendations on counterdeception: the counterdeception analyst must understand the strengths and weaknesses of the deceiver's methods, and identify ways to exploit specific weaknesses to detect corresponding indications of deception. They write: "[a] key finding ... is that different counterdeception methods can and should be applied toward different deception techniques. ... experimentation should be done to define these relationships. ... A body of thoroughly vetted experimentation and analysis is needed that clearly prescribes what sorts of counterefforts to employ to stave off particular types of deception."[5] We return to the issue of experimentation and its role in developing counterdeception techniques at the end of this chapter.

6.3   What Is Counter-Deception?

It is important to distinguish *counterdeception* from *counter-deception*. That is, *counterdeception* is the analysis of the actions and intentions of an adversary's denial and deception operations, typically by the defender's intelligence organization; while *counter-deception* is a deception operation run by the defender's deception organization to expose or exploit an adversary's deception operations. *Counter-deception* is necessary to engineer successful *counter-deception* operations; while conversely *counter-deceptions* can be useful tools for extending and amplifying the *counterdeception* analysis of the deceptive adversary.

Rowe (2004) described *counter-deception*: "defending information systems, planning to foil an attacker's deceptions with deceptions of our own. ... Besides the intrinsic suitability of a deception, we must also consider how likely it fools an attacker."[6] Rowe (2006) uses the term "second-order deceptions" to mean what we term *counterdeception*: "recognition by an agent of one or more ... first-order deceptions. ... detection of deception affects perceptions about who participates, why they do it, and the preconditions they recognize."

---

[4] Boush et al. (2009), in *Deception in the Marketplace: The Psychology of Deceptive Persuasion and Consumer Self Protection,* advocate "deception protection" for consumers (Chap 1) to help them "detect, neutralize and resist the varied types of deception" in the marketplace.

[5] Bodmer et al. (2012) noted Chinese cyber deception in cyber wargaming (p. 82): "reports of the People's Liberation Army (PLA) advancing their cyber-deception capabilities through a coordinated computer network attack and electronic warfare integrated exercise." We found no references explicitly to cyber exercises of *cyber-counterdeception*.

[6] Rowe used the term *counterdeception*, we believe he meant what we term here *counter-deception*; Rowe (2004). Rowe (2003) proposed a counterplanning approach to planning and managing what we term *counter-deception* operations. A recent description of counter-deception, "a multi-layer deception system that provides an in depth defense against ... sophisticated targeted attacks," is Wang et al. (2013).

A recent research award (Wick 2012), titled "Deceiving the Deceivers: Active Counterdeception [sic.] for Software Protection," described a *counter-deception* system to deceive cyber attackers with decoys:

> To better protect [DoD operations and infrastructure] critical systems, we propose to design and build an "active counterdeception" software protection system... CYCHAIR consists of two complementary technologies. The first [provides] the ability to easily generate large numbers of reusable, extensible and highly reconfigurable decoys. These decoys serve multiple purposes: first of all, they serve to increase the adversary's workload while confusing them as to the manner and location of the real targets. Secondly, they serve as intelligence gatherers, recording all the adversarial interactions. These records are fed to the second piece of the system, an inference engine we call LAIR (Logic for Adversarial Inference and Response). These inferences can be used to automatically trigger dynamic reconfiguration of the decoys (to further frustrate and slow down the adversary), and used as recommendations to the human-in-the-loop for additional active responses to the attack.

In other words, the use of decoys in CYCHAIR is a cyber-*counter-deception* *(Cyber-C-D)* operation intended to counter stealthy and deceptive cyber attackers, while the LAIR component enhances the effectiveness of the defenders' deceptive decoys. The system provides secondary counterdeception elements ("intelligence gatherers, recording all the adversarial interactions") but the clear objective of this system is *counter-deception*.[7]

6.4 What Is Cyber-CD?

In some respects, cyber-CD is nothing new. Cyber attackers use denial techniques to hide worms, viruses, and other malware inside innocuous code. Anti-virus systems use signature-based detection (i.e., known patterns of data within executable code) to search for malicious viruses or other types of malware. These signatures are widely shared among cyber defenders to defeat cyber attacker denial tools and techniques. Exploiting the known signatures of malicious code to expose hidden attacks is a basic form of cyber-CD.

Cyber attacker cyber-D&D goes far beyond planting malicious code inside innocuous code. Attacker cyber-D&D tactics are extensive (Fig. 6.1), and complex (e.g., they may either reveal *or* conceal facts, or reveal *or* conceal fictions, or they may conceal facts *and* reveal fictions), so cyber defenders need considerable cyber-CD capabilities to detect these various tools and techniques using cyber-D&D in the attack.

Additionally, cyber-CD must help defenders understand the attackers' possible intentions and objectives. If the cyber defenders also use cyber-D&D in the defense, the cyber-CD effort assists in shaping the defensive cyber-D&D plans and operations, as well as supporting the cyber defender generally. For example, to convince the cyber

---

[7] For a general analysis of denial techniques in cyber-*counter-deception (cyber-C-D)*, see Yuill et al. (2006).

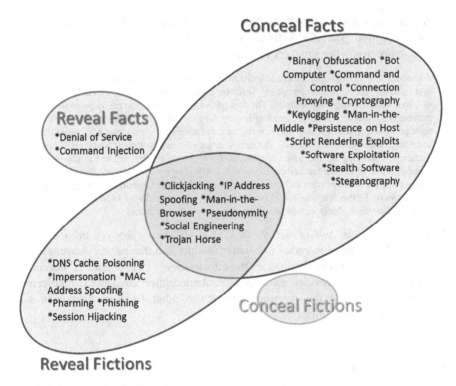

Fig. 6.1 Attacker cyber-D&D tactics

attacker that their offensive cyber-D&D tools, tactics, and techniques are succeeding in deceiving the defenders, counterdeception might support what Whaley (2006) terms the counterdeception "triple cross," that is, detecting the adversary's deception, and turning the detected deception against the adversary, using defensive cyber-D&D tools, techniques, tactics, and procedures (TTTPs).

Recently, *The Economist* described a cyber-CD and defensive cyber-D&D operation to protect a bank from cyber fraud (*The Economist* 2014). An American bank created "Honey Bankers:" non-existent bankers with cyber identities, with fake e-mail addresses and plausible biographies, with supporting biographical details on bogus bank web pages not linked to the rest of the bank's website. An attacker, using offensive cyber-D&D to conceal their own identity, sending a transfer request to one of these fictional "Honey Bankers" aliases, is thus exposed as a likely fraudster. The bank then blocks the sender's internet address, pending further investigation. The bank's defensive cyber-D&D tactic, the "Honey Bankers," also serves a defensive cyber-CD function, that is, by tempting fraudsters, the bank exposes them as something other than legitimate customers.

In short, cyber-CD provides the means and methods to identify the cyber-D&D TTTPs cyber attackers are using (Fig. 6.1), and, having identified possible cyber-D&D TTTPs, investigate hypotheses to understand what the attacker's possible intent may be in using cyber-D&D. Because many of the cyber attacker's D&D tools and tactics are designed to be "lost in the noise" of normal operations of the cyber systems defending the enterprise, a key component of cyber-CD is maintaining high resolution characterizations of what constitutes normal operations (i.e., "the noise"), and even more detailed descriptions of anomalies, including known and suspected cyber attacks (i.e., "the signals" that must be detected and described), including detailed descriptions of prior use of cyber-D&D TTTPs by attackers.

Cyber defenders may share information on cyber attackers and their methods that helps defenders detect hidden attacks and weapons. Mandiant's reports (Mandiant 2010, 2011, 2013) on advanced persistent threats (APTs) and their tactics and campaigns help defenders to recognize the indicators and behavioral signatures of these stealthy APT attackers. For example, Mandiant published profiles of malware families that the Chinese APT1 intelligence unit has developed and used in *"APT1: Exposing One of China's Cyber Espionage Units, Appendix C: The Malware Arsenal."* The profiles show how APT1 used each tool and how the malware behaves when deployed. Mandiant also published *"APT1: Exposing One of China's Cyber Espionage Units, Appendix F: APT1 SSL Certificates,"* which lists the self-signed X.509 certificates used by APT1 to encrypt malware communications. Mandiant explained that "detection of these SSL certificates may indicate an APT1 malware infection." Mandiant also published digital Indicators of Compromise (IOCs), "an open, extendable standard for defining and sharing threat information in a machine readable format. . . . IOCs combine over 500 types of forensic evidence with grouping and logical operators to provide advanced threat detection capability." Altogether, Mandiant published "more than 3,000 indicators to bolster defenses against APT1 operations." Cyber-CD greatly benefits from the publication and exploitation of detailed indicator data that cyber-CD can use to recognize and identify cyber-D&D TTTPs.

The STIX and TAXII systems, sponsored by the office of Cybersecurity and Communications at the U.S. Department of Homeland Security, offer mechanisms for defenders to identify and share, among other threat indicators, attacker cyber-D&D TTTPs:

> Structured Threat Information eXpression[8] (STIX) is a collaborative community-driven effort to develop a standardized language to represent structured cyber threat information. The STIX Language conveys the full range of potential cyber threat information.
> The Trusted Automated eXchange of Indicator Information[9] (TAXII) enables sharing of actionable cyber threat information across organization and product/service boundaries. TAXII . . . exchanges . . . cyber threat information for the detection, prevention, and mitigation of

---

[8] STIX and the STIX logo are trademarks of The MITRE Corporation. The STIX license states: The MITRE Corporation (MITRE) hereby grants you a non-exclusive, royalty-free license to use Structured Threat Information Expression (STIX™) for research, development, and commercial purposes. Any copy you make for such purposes is authorized provided you reproduce MITRE's copyright designation and this license in any such copy (see http://stix.mitre.org/).

[9] TAXII and the TAXII logo are trademarks of The MITRE Corporation. The TAXII license states: The MITRE Corporation (MITRE) hereby grants you a non-exclusive, royalty-free license to use Trusted Automated Exchange Indicator Information (TAXII™) for research, development, and

cyber threats. TAXII . . . empowers organizations to achieve improved situational awareness about emerging threats, enabling organizations to share the information they choose with the partners they choose.

More complex defender cyber-CD methods, beyond recognizing and identifying indicators of cyber-D&D, are necessary for more complex cyber-D&D methods. For example, methods are needed to infer possible intentions and objectives of cyber-D&D. In the next section we describe the basic components needed for counterdeception and how they relate to D&D. Several counterdeception theories have described methods and processes to implement these components. We describe one such counterdeception theory and suggest how it might be adapted to cyber-CD. We also describe the essential elements and necessary steps of counterdeception analysis.

6.5 What Are the Components of Counterdeception?

Counterdeception capabilities have been described by Bennett and Waltz (2007) and Whaley (2006, 2007d, 2012; Whaley and Busby 2002). Notably, neither Bennett and Waltz nor Whaley described the capabilities needed for cyber-CD.[10] Bennett and Waltz in their 2007 book, *Counterdeception: Principles and Applications for National Security,* described both counterdeception *functions* and the components and capabilities of an *organizational counterdeception system.* The functional capabilities they describe are:

- identifying an adversary's deception operations;
- negating, neutralizing, diminishing, or mitigating the effects of, or gain advantage from, the adversary's deception operation;
- exploiting knowledge of the adversary's deception;
- penetrating through the deception to discern the adversary's real capabilities and intentions;
- determining what the adversary is trying to make you believe–What does the adversary want you to do?

An organization must have a variety of counterdeception systems, Bennett and Waltz argue, to perform effective counterdeception functions. These counterdeception organizational system capabilities include:

- fundamental counterdeception technical methods;
- system architecture to support counterdeception operations;
- counterdeception planning and collection strategies;
- counterdeception information processing systems for:

---

commercial purposes. Any copy you make for such purposes is authorized provided you reproduce MITRE's copyright designation and this license in any such copy (see http://taxii.mitre.org/).

[10] Other than a few references to detecting deception in social engineering situations, we found no research on cyber-counterdeception, per se, in general searching of the scholarly literature.

- analysis methodology and workflow:
  - processing filters and knowledge bases;
  - computational analytic support tools;
  - analytic tool workflow.
- counterdeception analysis, decision support, and production systems:
  - deception analytic flow;
  - considering alternatives analysis;
  - deception warning.
- counterdeception system performance & effectiveness measures.

Whaley's (2007d) *Textbook of Political-Military Counterdeception: Basic Principles & Methods* defines "counterdeception ... as the detection of deception—and, by extension, the possible triple-cross of the deceiver. . . . Ideal counterdeception reveals the truth behind the lie, the face beneath the mask, the reality under the camouflage. Good counterdeception spares us from unwelcome surprises. This term may be extended to also mean 'triple-cross' of the detected deceiver. . . the active measures to turn an opponent's deception back upon himself." Whaley (2012) also refers to counterdeception analysis as "incongruity analysis," and credits this label to the aforementioned William Harris.[11]

Whaley notes the significant differences between the deceiver, weaving the web of deceit, and the counterdeception detective, unraveling the web, thread by thread:

> The analyst faced with deception [must] think more like a detective solving a mystery [and be able to] think . . . into the mind of a deceptive opponent . . . The mental process whereby . . . generally all deception planners. . . design deception operations is mainly or entirely linear and one-dimensional like a connect-the-dots game. Conversely . . . intelligence analysts [detecting deceptions] . . . solve the mystery largely using a process that is logically non-linear and three-dimensional, similar to solving a crossword puzzle.

Whaley differentiates the type of analytic thinking needed for counterdeception analysis from what he terms "conventional analysis:"

> Conventional analysts, by working from a mainly linear cause-to-effect deductive model, tend to quickly (and often prematurely) lock onto the most obvious cause. Conversely, abductive [counterdeception] analysts, engineering backward from an observed effect to discover its most likely cause, tend to explore alternative hypotheses before circling in on the one that most closely fits the evidence. Essential to this abductive process is that it is non-linear, cycling through successive feedback loops, which assure at least some open-minded analysis of the competing hypotheses (ACH). . . . Our two types of . . . analysts will differ in their reaction to deception. Whenever deception is present, the deductive type of analyst predictably tends to directly focus on the most obvious cause—just as the deceiver had planned. Conversely, the abductive analyst is better positioned to perceive those special telltale incongruities (anomalies or discrepancies) that always distinguish each real object and event from its simulation—its counterfeit. . .

---

[11] Some (e.g., Bennett and Waltz 2007) would credit "incongruity analysis" to R. V. Jones, and his theory of spoofing and counter-spoofing. See Jones (2009), pp. 285–291: "the perception of incongruity—which my ponderings have led me to believe is the basic requirement for a sense of humour—[concluding]. . . the object of a practical joke [is] the creation of an incongruity."

Whaley describes counterdeception capabilities in terms of general principles, specific methods, operations for verification and falsification, and operations beyond detection and verification.

Whaley conceives of counterdeception as requiring the capability to apply several general principles to analysis. First, counterdeception analysis is largely the mirror-image of deception planning and execution: "the characteristics of the things hidden and displayed and categories of analysis are the same. The only difference... is that the process by which the deceiver plots a deception follows a different (although related) logical path than the process by which the [counterdeception] analyst unravels it." One consequence of this symmetry is that Whaley advocates counterdeception analysts should have experience in planning deceptions. McPherson (2010) makes this point emphatically for military units: "An effective cell brought together to identify adversary deception should be drawn from individuals who already understand how to operationally plan deception."

Second, Whaley argues "the deception detective's job is, at least in theory, [easier than the deceiver's]." Whaley describes what he terms the 'counterdeception analyst's advantage' in terms of capabilities to detect the observable indications of simulation and dissimulation:

> Whoever creates a deception simultaneously creates all the clues needed for its solution. Moreover, every deception necessarily generates a minimum of two clues, at least one about the real thing being hidden and at least one other about the false thing being shown.
>
> 1) Whenever deceivers create a deception they simultaneously generate all the clues needed for its detection. These give the [counterdeception] detectives additional chances for discovering the [deception] operation.
> 2) Each of these deception-generated clues is an incongruity—an incongruous characteristic that distinguishes the false thing from the real one it seeks to replace.
> 3) Every deception has two fundamental parts. These are dissimulation (hiding) and simulation (showing). Dissimulation hides or conceals something real and simulation shows or displays something false in its place. In theory both hiding and showing take place simultaneously, even if one is only implicit.
> > Corollary 3a) Ideally, the deceiver should hide and show simultaneously.
> > Corollary 3b) If this isn't possible, at least always hide the real before showing its false substitute.
> > Corollary 3c) And if doing so, allow enough time for the thing being hidden to have plausibly reappeared somewhere else.
> 4) Each of these parts is incongruous with its previous reality. Thus every deception creates at least two incongruities. One represents a built-in inability to hide all the distinctive characteristics of the thing being hidden. The other represents an inherent inability to show all the characteristics of the thing being shown in its place. Each part, therefore, creates a decisive clue for the [counterdeception] detective.
> 5) Consequently, although the deceiver has only one opportunity to "sell" his deception operation, the [counterdeception] detective (analyst) has two chances to detect it, two clues that lead directly to a solution.

Whaley observes that there are actually many specific methods (he lists twenty) that take advantage of the 'counterdeception analyst's advantage' and enable the detection of deception:

There are dozens of specific theories, principles, and methods for detecting deception. Most tend to be overlooked by the great majority of political-military intelligence analysts—they have simply not yet been adopted by our analyst's teaching and training schools and courses. However, all have been adopted in one or more other disciplines, particularly by consistently successful analysts who deal more or less regularly with deception.

Simply detecting deception is insufficient for successful counterdeception, and Whaley stresses the need for capabilities to verify deception hypotheses, and to falsify alternative hypothesis (i.e., disprove the "reality" presented by the deceiver and prove it is not real). The capability to assess multiple alternative competing hypotheses is widely seen as a requirement for effective counterdeception analysis.[12] Whaley notes "the cost may be prohibitive—economically, psychologically, ethically, socially, or politically—but it can be done." He describes several specific methods that provide help to test alternative hypotheses; providing verification and falsification capabilities, passive versus active measures, tripwires, traps, lures, and provocations.

Whaley (2012) recently proposed a set of four skills for detectives (i.e., intelligence and deception analysts) that must be used in sequence to solve any mystery: the ability to perceive incongruities; the ability to form a hunch or hypothesis that explains those incongruities; the ability to test the hypothesis to determine how closely it fits the current conception of reality; and the ability to weigh the relative merits of any alternative or competing hypotheses. If this four-step process successfully explains and eliminates all of the incongruities, then the mystery is solved. More likely, this process will uncover new incongruities, and the process iterates. Each cycle of this four-step process will produce either an increasingly close match with reality or an entirely new model of reality or a new point of view. The counterdeception model described below follows Whaley's four-step process.

Finally, Whaley stresses the need for actions before, during, and after detection of deceptions. Before and during detection of deception, he argues that anticipation of deceptions and proactive counter-measures can reduce susceptibilities and vulnerabilities to deceptions, and help to negate or counter-act the effects of deceptions. After deception detection and verification, the friendly side should consider using the detection as the basis for the "triple-cross," that is, leading the deceiver to believe the deception has worked, while the deceiver's belief is actually being exploited by the friendly side.

---

[12] For example, Heuer (1981). Whether or not deception is detected, assessing hypotheses regarding the adversary's possible courses of action against the evidence provides useful insights into adversary intentions. Heuser (1996) wrote, : "The [counterdeception] cell would be tasked to … [look] at the data from the enemy's point of view. They would need to place themselves in the mind of the enemy, determine how they would develop a deception plan and see if evidence supports it. … The enemy may not be employing a deception plan, but the process will aid in exploring different enemy courses of action that may have been overlooked.," Bruce and Bennett (2008) wrote: "the failure to generate hypotheses increases vulnerability to deception… One key to Why Bad Things Happen to Good Analysts has been conflicting organizational signals regarding promotion of overconfidence ("making the call") versus promotion of more rigorous consideration of alternative hypotheses and the quality of information;" in George and Bruce (2008).

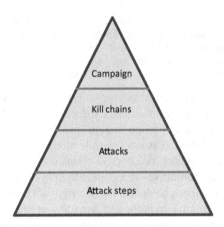

Fig. 6.2 High-Level model of cyber intrusions

Whaley observes that "these special actions require close and continuing liaison and coordination among the intelligence analysts, the planners, operations staff, and even the commander. . . close institutionalized cooperation between intelligence and operations at the top. . . [and] direct liaison links across organizational hierarchies at all levels of intelligence analysts and intelligence collectors." These organizational liaison and coordination links require additional capabilities to effectively perform counterdeception. Cyber-CD capabilities need to be both psychologically and organizationally complex because cyber attackers use complex attack kill chains and intrusion campaigns and adapt cyber-D&D TTTPs to conceal them.

6.6   Cyber Attacker Kill Chains & Intrusion Campaigns

Cyber intrusion tactics and strategies have advanced considerably over the last two decades. Analysts have drawn on empirical observations to formulate high-level models of cyber intrusions. The four-tiered pyramidal model of intrusions in Fig. 6.2 depicts various granularities of abstractions in such models.

Starting from the bottom, an attack step represents an atomic or primitive unit of execution in cyber intrusions. Examples include an action to corrupt a log file or escalate a process privilege.

The second level, a cyber attack, typically consists of a carefully orchestrated set of attack steps. It requires the attacker to sequence the steps and string them together in careful ways, with the outputs of each step used as inputs to subsequent steps. Thus, analysts typically model attacks by a formalism such as an attack tree.

Next in the pyramid is the cyber kill chain, Hutchins generally recognized as a useful, high-level meta-model of attacks (Hutchnis et al. 2011). The kill chain models the distinct phases of cyber intrusions, starting with reconnaissance and ending with execution and maintenance. A kill chain for a particular intrusion may consist of multiple attacks mapped to its various phases.

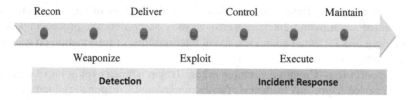

Fig. 6.3 Cyber kill chain for computer network intrusions

At the top of the pyramid is the cyber campaign: a strategic construct used by decision makers in articulating and achieving strategic objectives. The small size of the pyramid's apex conveys that strategic campaigns are few and far between. A government may organize a single strategic cyber campaign over a given (extended) time period. That campaign may encompass multiple kill chains, with each kill chain consisting of numerous attacks and each attack in turn consisting of many attack steps.

Cyber attackers use denial, or hiding, tactics throughout this hierarchy, and particularly to conceal the steps, attacks, and chains at the lower levels of the pyramid. Cyber attackers also may use deceptions to "cover" cyber campaigns. That is, the attacker may attempt to mislead victims and bystanders as to the true objectives, targets, or extent of cyber-attack campaigns. For example, the objectives, targets, and extent of the Stuxnet cyber campaign are still debated.[13] This use of denial and deception argue for the development and application of cyber-CD capabilities in cyber defenses.

Cyber attackers, such as state-actor advanced persistent threats (APTs) and advanced cyber criminals, employ a cyber-attack strategy, divided into phases, called the kill chain. Figure 6.3 illustrates the concept of a cyber kill chain for computer network intrusions, originally formulated by Lockheed Martin,[14] to inform computer network defense (CND) operations.

For a network intrusion to succeed, the attacker completes each step of the kill chain. Steps prior to a successful exploit offer opportunities for cyber defenders to detect intrusion attempts, while defenders deploy incident response and forensics after an exploit. These sets of steps are often referred to as "left of exploit" and "right of exploit," respectively. To the extent the attackers use cyber-D&D TTTPs the greater the utility of cyber defender counterdeception capabilities to support detection and response.

Hutchins et al. (2011), who applied the "kill chain" concept to cyber attacks, define the kill chain phases as:

---

[13] See, for example (Lachow 2011; Sanger 2012; Langner 2013; Lindsay 2013).

[14] Although originally referred to as the "Intrusion Kill Chain" by the authors of the related seminal paper, the concept is now more generally referred to as "Cyber Kill Chain." See http://www.lockheedmartin.com/us/what-we-do/information-technology/cyber-security/cyber-kill-chain.html.

1. *Reconnaissance*—Research, identification, and selection of targets, often represented as crawling Internet websites such as conference proceedings and mailing lists for email addresses, social relationships, or information on specific technologies.
2. *Weaponization*—Coupling a remote access Trojan with an exploit into a deliverable payload, typically by means of an automated tool (weaponizer). Increasingly, client application data files such as Adobe Portable Document Format (PDF) or Microsoft Office documents serve as the weaponized deliverable.
3. *Delivery*—Transmission of the weapon to the targeted environment. The three most prevalent delivery vectors for weaponized payloads by APT actors ... are email attachments, websites, and USB removable media.
4. *Exploitation*—After the weapon is delivered to the victim host, exploitation triggers intruders' code. Most often, exploitation targets an application or operating system vulnerability, but it could also more simply exploit the users themselves by convincing them to execute a file they downloaded from the Internet.
5. *Installation*—Installation of a remote access Trojan or backdoor on the victim system allows the adversary to maintain persistence inside the environment.
6. *Command and Control (C2)*— Typically, [since firewalls deny incoming traffic for initiating connections,] compromised hosts must beacon outbound to an Internet controller server to establish a C2 channel. Once the C2 channel is established, intruders have "hands on the keyboard" access inside the target environment. The next step is to enable their mission by uploading the appropriate set of tools.
7. *Actions on Objectives*—Only now can intruders take actions to achieve their original objectives. While data exfiltration is among the most common objective, there are other equally concerning actions including data corruption, denial of service, lateral movement, misattribution, corruption of physical systems, and deception.

Croom (2010) suggests that a defender can mitigate the impact of the attacker's cyber kill chain by disrupting any single phase (italics added):

> For the defender, the most important lessons of the kill chain are that it clearly shows that the adversary must progress successfully through every stage before it can achieve its desired objectives, and *any one mitigation* disrupts the chain and defeats the adversary. The more mitigations the defenders can implement across the chain, the more resilient the defense becomes.[15]

6.7 Cyber Defender Deception Chains and Deception Campaigns

Defensive cyber-D&D teams can plan strategically against attacker campaigns as well as defending tactically against independent incidents. Key to cyber-D&D strategy is

---

[15] Croom (2010). The author, Lieutenant General Charles Croom (Ret.) is Vice President of Lockheed Martin Information Systems and Global Solutions.

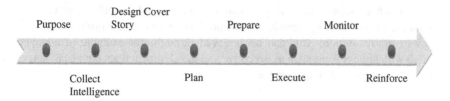

Fig. 6.4 Deception chain

allowing the attacker apparent success that is covertly under the control of defenders. In the short term, "success" will reduce the adversary's incentive to innovate (i.e., since the attacker's kill chain is apparently working), and provide defenders with a channel to manipulate adversary action in pursuit of a deception goal beyond the integrity of their own cyber operations. To enable this cyber-D&D strategy, we propose the use of a "deception chain" that encompasses the phases of planning, preparation, and execution of cyber-D&D operations (Fig. 6.4). Defenders can use this deception chain to develop adaptive and resilient deceptive courses of action (COAs) in addition to other defensive responses. The deception chain is based on the ten-step process for planning, preparing, and executing deception operations defined by Barton Whaley (2007c).

Cyber-CD plays a major role in the second step (*Collect Intelligence*) and secondarily in aiding the security of the other deception chain steps (e.g., by aiding the defender to *Plan, Monitor,* and *Reinforce* the defensive cyber-D&D by furnishing information on the attacker's offensive cyber-D&D). That is, cyber-CD detects and describes the capabilities of the attacker's use of cyber-D&D. While a great deal more intelligence is collected about the adversary for the deception chain (e.g., the attacker's general and specific beliefs about the defenders capabilities), cyber-CD is essential to defeating the attacker's use of cyber-D&D TTTPs.

Defenders can instantiate an instance of the deception chain at each phase of the attacker's kill chain. The deception chain, much like an attacker's kill chain, is naturally recursive and disjoint. Deception operations require continual reexamination of the objectives, target, stories, and means throughout the planning, preparation, and execution phases. The defender's deception team must be prepared to respond to the dynamics of the adversary as well as friendly situations.

Given this, an intrusion campaign could include several deception chains, each of which would address the defender's operational or tactical goals based on its assessment of the attacker's operational and tactical goals from its corresponding kill chain activities. Organizations can also use intrusion campaigns to assess the attacker's strategic goals, and use these findings to shape the strategic goal of a deception campaign, that is, what the organization expects to achieve at a strategic level by utilizing deception against a particular intrusion campaign. For example, if campaign analysis suggests that a particular intrusion campaign is seeking to obtain as much information as possible about a product in development, the organization's deception campaign might be to convince the adversary that the product's planned release has been significantly delayed due to technological difficulties, and that the corporation is considering abandoning the product because of the prohibitively high costs of the resolution. This can be achieved through, for example, a honeypot seeded with honeytokens such as executive and development team email exchanges, technical reports, and budget estimates.

6.8 Applying Cyber-CD in Deception Campaigns

Assuming cyber attackers will use both denial (or hiding) and deception (or misleading) TTTPs in their attack campaigns, cyber defenders must develop TTTPs to counter both of these. That is, defenders must develop capabilities for counterdenial, to reveal what is hidden, and for counterdeception, to determine what is actually real from what is false (i.e., the detection of deception). As Whaley (2007b) concluded from his analysis of many historical cases of military and political deception, the odds overwhelmingly favor the deceiver, no matter how shrewd the target of the deception. Figure 6.5 shows this disparity conceptually. Unless the defender uses effective counterdenial and counterdeception TTTPs at the appropriate opportunities, most of the advantages accrue to the attacker (i.e., see the six gray-shaded cells). But when the defender's counterdenial and counterdeception capabilities are appropriately matched against the attacker's use of D&D TTTPs, the advantages accrue to the defender (i.e., see the two blue-shaded cells).

6.9 A Cyber-CD Process Model

D&D TTTPs are difficult to detect because they exploit the defender's reasoning errors, cognitive limitations, and concomitant biases. The most important reasoning errors contributing to victims' susceptibility to deception are:

- reasoning causally from evidence to hypotheses,
- failure to entertain a deception hypothesis,
- biased estimates of probabilities, and
- failure to consider false positive rates of evidence.

The first two errors involve considering too few alternative hypotheses due to incomplete generation or premature pruning, which can involve misestimates of probabilities. The sources and effects of biases arising from mental estimates of probabilities are well-known.[16] Two biases are particularly debilitating for detecting deception: bias due to making conclusions that support preconceptions, assuming a piece of evidence is consistent with too few hypotheses; and mirror imaging—assuming an adversary is likely to choose a course of action that appeals to the observer.[17]

---

[16] Gilovich et al. (2002) and Dawes (2001).
[17] Heuer (1981) and Elsässer and Stech (2007).

Attacker: Denial & Deception Moves	Defender: Counterdenial & Counterdeception Moves		
	2. Naïve—No Counterdeception and No Counterdenial	4. Counterdenial Moves	6. Counterdeception Moves
1. Unwitting—No Denial or Deception	No advantage No advantage	Disadvantage: Suspects denial hiding that is not present Advantage: Perceives unwarranted intrusiveness	Disadvantage: Suspects deception that is not present Advantage: Perceives unwarranted paranoia
3. DENIAL: Covering—Hiding	Disadvantage: Misses denial hiding of critical information Advantage: Conceals critical information	Advantage: Perceives hidden critical information Disadvantage: Critical information exposed	Disadvantage: Suspects deception that is not present; misses denial hiding Advantage: Conceals critical information; perceives unwarranted deception detection
5. DECEPTION: Misleading—Deceiving	Disadvantage: Misled by deception Advantage: Misleads and hides critical information	Disadvantage: Misled by deception Advantage: Perceives what is hidden Disadvantage: Critical information exposed Advantage: Misleads	Advantage: Perceives what is hidden and is not misled Disadvantage: Denial and deception fail; critical information exposed

Fig. 6.5 Matrix of attacker's Denial & deception moves versus defender's counterdenial and counterdeception moves

Two major analysis shortcomings impairing counterdeception analysis are poor anomaly detection (i.e., missing anomalies or prematurely dismissing anomalies as irrelevant or inconsistent) and misattribution (i.e., attributing inconsistent or anomalous events to collection gaps or processing errors rather than to deception). The first shortcoming results when analysts have insufficiently modeled the normal environmental patterns so that unusual events and anomalies can be detected and measured, and when there is a lack of familiarity with the indicators of D&D TTTPs so that the linkages between unusual and anomalous events and possible use of D&D TTTPs are missed.

To recognize deception, the analyst must consider the deceiver's alternative courses of action (COAs) and overcome biases that lead to inappropriately weighing

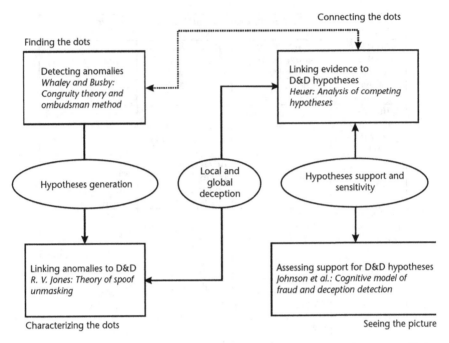

Fig. 6.6 Conceptual schematic for counterdeception analysis process. (Source: Bennett and Waltz (2007), based on Stech and Elsäesser (2007)

evidence that seems to support one of only a few alternative COAs. The analyst must estimate the likelihood of these COAs as new evidence is received, while simultaneously considering the likelihood that evidence is deceptive.[18] The most promising techniques to reduce bias in probabilistic assessments is to require a subject to perform and document a systematic analysis of the evidence, considering on the one hand that the evidence is veridical, and on the other hand, that the evidence may be deceptive.

Stech and Elsässer (2007) proposed a counterdeception process model (Fig. 6.6), integrating a variety of counterdeception theories,[19] to help analysts avoid the biases that make deception succeed. This process model estimates the likelihoods of deceptive and veridical information by following four analysis processes sequentially, with possible recursion:

Finding the dots: Detecting anomalies and inconsistencies between expectations about the evidence that will be observed and the actual observations.

Characterizing the dots: Linking anomalies to possible D&D TTTPs, and deceptive manipulations of the environment and evidence of possible adversary deception tactics.

---

[18] See Fischhoff (1982).
[19] See Stech and Elsässer (2007).

Connecting the dots: Testing hypotheses about adversary D&D COAs against evidence of (global and local) D&D TTTPs and COAs without D&D. Assess sensitivity and support for alternative hypotheses and recollect evidence as needed.

Seeing the picture: Recommending actions to test the D&D hypotheses and exploit adversary D&D.

The first step of the process, *Finding the dots*, addresses the detection of anomalies using techniques based on Whaley and Busby's congruity-incongruity and ombudsman theory—asking if the anomalies have possible D&D utility. Detection of anomalies (incongruities) is not necessarily evidence of deliberate deception, hence the importance of having a well-understood baseline of the "normal" (no D&D) operational environment, and the incidence of anomalies and incongruities from non-D&D causes, as well as from D&D TTTPs. Anomalies and incongruities in the absence of D&D may result from sensor malfunctions, unintentional distortion or corruption of data or information during transmission, atypical behavior of users in the cyber environment, or analytical errors. Deception often succeeds because the deception victim explains away anomalies and fails to attribute them to D&D TTTPs, so the first step is to find the anomalous dots and consider if they may be due to D&D.

The second step, *Characterizing the dots*, involves linking anomalies to D&D TTTPs. The counterdeception process uses R. V. Jones's (1995) concepts of unmasking spoofs by examining anomalies through multiple information channels. D&D becomes harder and more detectable as more channels must be spoofed. D&D that is extremely successful in some channels may be very weak or even absent in others.

Between the second and thirds steps the counterdeception process shows "local and global deception." This is a key distinction in counterdeception analysis. A local deception represents D&D due to local conditions such as concealment of network traffic due to "local deception," (i.e., failures of local systems), rather than to "global deception," such as traffic masking and obfuscation created by an attacking adversary. Evidence of "local deceptions" will be sporadic, apparently random, widely distributed, and at best, weakly linked to various hypothetical adversary COAs; while "global deceptions" will have the opposite characteristics.

The third and fourth steps, *Connecting the dots* and *Seeing the picture*, use Heuer's analysis of competing hypotheses (ACH) to assess the likelihood that the observed anomalies are associated with a probable deceptive course of action (COA), and to evaluate the level of support for each identified D&D and no-D&D hypothesis. As support for hypothetical D&D COAs is found, the counterdeception analyst may wish to re-collect new information (i.e., finding new dots, indicated by the dashed line connecting the first and the third steps) in light of the possible adversary COAs and the indicators they suggest (Johnson et al. 2001).

Stech and Elsässer adapted Heuer's ACH for counterdeception; the most significant adaptations to Heuer's original eight-step outline for the analysis of competing hypotheses (Heuer 1999) are:

- Adding the "other" or "unknown" hypothesis to Heuer's step 1, that is, "Identify the possible hypotheses to be considered." This modification supports Bayesian analysis of the alternative hypotheses.

- Making sure that Heuer's step 2, "Make a list of significant evidence and arguments for and against each hypothesis," considers not only the case where evidence supports a hypothesis, $p(E|H_i)$, but also the likelihood of observing that same evidence if the hypothesis is not true, $p(E|\neg H_i)$.
- Specifically considering deception-related COAs in Heuer's steps 4, "Refine the ACH matrix," and 5, "Draw tentative conclusions about the relative likelihood of each hypothesis."
- Adding the concept of conducting operational "experiments" to Heuer's step 8, "Identify milestones for future observation that may indicate events are taking a different course than expected," in order to provide additional intelligence that would reveal evidence of deliberate deception.

The first two adaptations support the use of Bayesian belief networks to model the alternative COAs and to perform sensitivity analysis in order to analyze the diagnosticity of the evidence, part of Step 3 in Heuer's ACH. The last two adaptations support the comparisons of possible COAs, which might include D&D, or not; and to identify possible ways to react to the adversary to create operational experiments, which help identify possible adversary intentions and objectives.

Some suggestions for training intelligence analysts to detect deception are consistent with this model. Hobbs (2010), for example, recommended methods like this for use by the International Atomic Energy Agency (IAEA) analysts assessing inspections of nuclear facilities and evidence of possible deception.

While there seem to be no cyber-CD case studies openly available with which to illustrate the counterdeception analysis process concept shown in Fig. 6.6, a detailed case study of the analysis of a stealthy cyber attacker provides some evidence of most of the steps shown in the counterdeception process concept, applied to a cyber case. In a series of papers, Mandiant (2013) has exposed an advanced persistent threat (APT) as a Chinese cyber intelligence unit. That is, Mandiant penetrates the APT's attempt to remain stealthy and to conceal their identity, to reveal who the APT probably is. Mandiant's analyses steps can be related to the steps in the counterdeception process concept to show how key elements of the counterdeception process can be applied to detecting an adversary using cyber-D&D to conceal actions and identity.

Background: Mandiant published information on the most prolific APT in 2010, but did not identify it as "APT1" until 2013, when it averred APT1 was a Chinese intelligence gathering unit,[20] Unit 61398, one of 20 APT groups in China probably associated with cyber espionage. Mandiant wrote "APT1 is a single organization of operators that has conducted a cyber-espionage campaign ... since at least 2006.... Against nearly 150 victims." Mandiant identified the intent and objectives of APT1 as cyber espionage theft of "hundreds of terabytes ... of valuable intellectual property,

---

[20] "2nd Bureau of the People's Liberation Army (PLA) General Staff Department's (GSD) 3rd Department, which is most commonly known by its Military Unit Cover Designator (MUCD) as Unit 61398." Unit 61398 functions as "the Third Department's premier entity targeting the United States and Canada, most likely focusing on political, economic, and military-related intelligence," Stokes et al. (2011).

stealing … technology blueprints, proprietary manufacturing processes, test results, business plans, pricing documents, partnership agreements, and emails and contact lists." The industries targeted by APT1 match industries China identified as strategic to growth, including four of seven strategic emerging industries that China identified in its 12th Five Year Plan.

Finding the dots & Detecting anomalies: Mandiant identified several indicators linking APT1 to China, Shanghai, and a particular neighborhood in Shanghai:

- Mandiant observed that in 97%, out of the 1,905, APT1 Remote Desktop sessions the operator's keyboard layout setting was "Chinese (Simplified)—US Keyboard … [and] display Simplified Chinese fonts.
- 98% of 832 IP addresses logging into APT1 controlled systems using Remote Desktop resolved back to China.
- 100% of the 614 distinct IP addresses used for an APT1 attacker tool (HTRAN) communications were registered in China, and 99.8% were registered to one of four Shanghai net blocks.
- APT1 targeted dozens of organizations simultaneously; once APT1 establishes access to a victim's network, they continue to access it periodically over several months or years to steal large volumes of valuable intellectual property.
- APT1 maintained access to victims' networks for an average of 356 days. The longest time period was at least 1,764 days, or four years and ten months.
- APT1 deletes compressed archives after they pilfer information, leaving solely trace evidence.
- APT1 does not target industries systematically but steals from an enormous range of industries on a continuous basis.

Altogether, Mandiant has published over 3,000 digital indicators for APT1 activities, including domain names, APT1 group nicknames, IP addresses, and malware hashes, over 40 families of malware, X.509 encryption certificates used. All these indicators help the cyber-CD analysts to find the dots of cyber-D&D TTTPs.

Characterizing the dots & Linking anomalies to D&D: Mandiant's report describe the APT1 attack kill chain in detail, including APT1's use of various stealth cyber-D&D TTTPs:

- Spear phishing emails, APT1's most commonly used technique, containing a malicious attachment or a hyperlink to a malicious file, often in.zip format, with plausible file titles (e.g., Oil-Field-Services-Analysis-And-Outlook.zip).
- Subject line and text in the spear phishing email body are usually relevant to the email recipient.
- APT1 creates webmail accounts using real peoples' names familiar to the recipient (e.g., colleagues, a company executive, an IT department employee, or company legal counsel) and uses these accounts to send spear phishing emails.
- Deceptive email interactions:

"In one case a person replied, "I'm not sure if this is legit, so I didn't open it." Within 20 min, someone in APT1 responded with a terse email back: "It's legit."

- Dropper files (e.g., files that appear to be, for example, a .pdf, but are actually an .exe with hidden file type extensions).
- Backdoor software, typically APT1 custom-made, installed that allows APT1 to communicate out and then send commands to the victim's system remotely. Note that the use of APT1 custom backdoor software rather than the publicly available backdoors, such as Poison Ivy and Gh0st RAT, allows analysts to test for "local deception" (e.g., publically available malware) versus "global deception" (e.g., one of APT1's custom malware backdoor tools, of which there are over forty known instances).
- Detection of MD5 hashes associated with APT1 malware.
- Installation of stealthy "beachhead backdoors," which give APT1, a toe-hold to perform simple tasks, retrieve files, gather basic system information, trigger execution of other more significant capabilities, such as a standard backdoor, followed by installation of "standard backdoor" tools, which give APT1 "intruders a laundry list of ways to control victim systems."
- APT1 backdoor covert communications mimic legitimate Internet traffic (e.g., MSN Messenger, Jabber/XMPP, Gmail Calendar) as well as the HTTP protocol to hide traffic with APT1 command and control from the victims.
- APT1 backdoors use SSL encryption so that communications are hidden in an encrypted SSL tunnel. APT1 public SSL certificates provide indications.
- APT1 predominantly uses publicly available tools to dump password hashes from victim systems to obtain legitimate user credentials.
- APT1 attackers use passwords that are either pattern-based, such as the keyboard pattern "1qaz2wsx," or highly memorable, such as using "rootkit" as a password on the information security research site rootkit.com.
- APT1 primarily hides in the normal environment and uses built-in operating system commands to explore a compromised system and its networked environment. Possible use of batch scripts in this reconnaissance may provide indicators.
- Lateral movement to other systems on the victim's network, connecting to shared resources, execute commands using the publicly available "psexec" tool, behaving like legitimate system administrators.
- Maintaining APT1 presence with more backdoor installations, stealing valid usernames, passwords, and VPN credentials and impersonating legitimate users.
- Using two email-stealing utilities that Mandiant labeled as unique to APT1: GETMAIL and MAPIGET.
- APT1's use of grammatically incorrect English phrases (File no exist; Shell is not exist or stopped!) sometimes provides cyber-D&D indicators.

These cyber-D&D TTTPs have been linked to specific APT1 campaigns and attacks against various specific strategic targets, for the objectives of exfiltrating very large volumes of stolen intellectual property.

Connecting the dots & Linking evidence to D&D hypotheses: Mandiant did express two alternative competing hypothesis (probably facetiously):

- "A secret, resourced organization full of mainland Chinese speakers with direct access to Shanghai-based telecommunications infrastructure is engaged in a multi-year, enterprise scale computer espionage campaign right outside of Unit 61398's gates, performing tasks similar to Unit 61398's known mission."
- "APT1 has intentionally been conducting a years-long deception campaign to impersonate Chinese speakers from Shanghai in places where victims are not reasonably expected to have any visibility—and without making a single mistake that might indicate their."

More seriously, Mandiant correlated evidence and indicators for APT1 activity and TTTPs with evidence from imagery, open sources, open Internet communications and files, and various AP T1 activity "pocket litter," with the specific signatures of the Chinese PLA cyber military intelligence Unit 61398.

- From January 2011 to January 2013 Mandiant observed 1,905 instances of APT1 actors logging into their hop infrastructure from 832 different IP addresses with Remote Desktop. Of the 832 IP addresses, 817 (98.2 %) were Chinese and belong predominantly to four large net blocks in Shanghai. Registration for two of these net blocks serve the Pudong New Area of Shanghai, where PLA Unit 61398 is headquartered. Unit 61398 is partially situated at Datong Road 208 in Pudong New Area of Shanghai.
- One APT1 personality uses the password "2j3c1k" which Mandiant suggests stands for 2nd Bureau [Unit 61398], 3rd Division, 1st Section.
- APT1's combination of a relatively high number of "Shanghai" registrations with obviously false registration examples in other registrations suggests a partially uncoordinated domain registration campaign in which some registrants tried to fabricate non-Shanghai locations but others did not; e.g., a registration that included a website production company address located in Shanghai across the river from PLA Unit 61398.

Mandiant's main hypothesis is that APT1 is actually identified as a specific Chinese PLA cyber espionage unit, PLA Unit 61398.

Seeing the picture & Assessing support for D&D hypotheses: Mandiant's report states two hypotheses:

- We believe the facts dictate only two possibilities:
  - Either
    A secret, resourced organization full of mainland Chinese speakers with direct access to Shanghai-based telecommunications infrastructure is engaged in a multi-year, enterprise scale computer espionage campaign right outside of Unit 61398's gates, performing tasks similar to Unit 61398's known mission.
  - Or
    APT1 is Unit 61398.

Mandiant's primary hypothesis is that the nature of APT1's targeted victims and the group's infrastructure and tactics align with the mission and infrastructure of PLA Unit 61398. Given the mission, resourcing, and location of PLA Unit 61398, Mandiant concludes that PLA Unit 61398 is APT1.

While not an ACH matrix, Mandiant provided the following table of "Matching characteristics between APT1 and Unit 61398:" (Table 6.2)

Table 6.2 Matching characteristics between APT1 and Unit 61398 (Source: Mandiant 2013)

Characteristic	APT1 (as directly observed)	Unit 61398 (as reported)
Mission area	Steals intellectual property from English-speaking organizations Targets strategic emerging industries identified in China's 12th Five Year Plan	Conducts computer network operations against English-speaking targets
Tools, tactics, and procedures (TTPs)	Organized, funded, disciplined operators with specific targeting objectives and a code of ethics (e.g., we have not witnessed APT1 destroy property or steal money which contrasts most "hackers" and even the most sophisticated organize crime syndicates)	Conducts military-grade computer network operations
Scale of operations	Continuously stealing hundreds of terabytes from 141 organizations since at least 2006; simultaneously targeting victims across at least 20 major industries Size of "hop" infrastructure and continuous malware updates suggest at least dozens (but probably hundreds) of operators with hundreds of support personnel	As part of the PLA, has the resources (people, money, influence) necessary to orchestrate operation at APT1's scale Has hundreds, perhaps thousands of people, as suggested by the size for their facilities and position within the PLA
Expertise of personnel	English language proficiency Malware authoring Computer hacking Ability to identify data worth stealing in 20 industries	English language requirements Operating system internals, digital signal processing, steganography Recruiting from Chinese technology universities
Location	APT1 actor used a Shanghai phone number to register email accounts Two of four "home" Shanghai net blocks are assigned to the Pudong New Area Systems used by APT1 intruders have Simplified Chinese language settings An APT1 persona's self-identified location is the Pudong New Area	Headquarters and other facilities spread throughout the Pudong New Area of Shanghai, China
Infrastructure	Ready access to four main net blocks in Shanghai, hosted by China Unicom (one of two Tier 1 ISPs in China) Some use of China Telecom IP addresses (the other Tier 1 ISP)	Co-building network infrastructure with China Telecom in the name of national defense

The counterdeception analysis process would recommend the counterdeception version of the ACH Matrix. That is, a single hypothesis "column" for APT1 = Unit 61389, another for APT1 $\neq$ Unit 61398, and a third for "Other Hypothesis." All evidence would be assessed with respect to its likelihood, or unlikelihood, of being observed if the given hypothesis were true, and also if the hypothesis were false, to assess diagnosticity of the evidence. For the "Other Hypothesis," all evidence would be treated as neither supporting or ruling out "Other Hypothesis," to provide a neutral baseline against which to compare the other hypotheses. Then the overall likelihood of the two primary hypotheses can be compared to the neutral baseline "Other Hypothesis," to see if either hypothesis is strongly supported by the evidence.

6.10 Wargaming Cyber-D&D and Cyber-CD

Cyber-D&D can be used by cyber attackers or defenders. How well would cyber-CD support defensive cyber-D&D against a cyber attacker? As suggested earlier, the many dimensions of cyber-D&D and cyber-CD suggest no simple processes will succeed in the highly interactive cyber conflict engagements. Cyber wargame exercises allow cyber defenders to practice their interactive cyber defensive capabilities (i.e., cyber-CD and cyber-D&D) against skilled adversaries in a controlled environment. Since the use of cyber-D&D in passive and active cyber defense is relatively new, and cyber-CD is at best conceptual, testing cyber-D&D and cyber-CD tactics, techniques, procedures, and tools (TTPTs) can demonstrate the strengths and weaknesses of these cyber defenses in controlled environments before they are used against cyber adversaries in the wild. Cyber wargame exercise of cyber-CD and cyber-D&D TTPTs also provide a useful environment to explore areas for further research and development of cyber defensive measures.[21]

Kott and Citrenbaum (2010)[22] described the traditional uses of wargames in business and military operational and decision analyses to: explore likely outcomes and unanticipated plan effects; identify possible reactions and counteractions; characterize evolution of market and environmental attitudes; identify alternative plan implementations; explore possible actions, reactions, and counteractions of opposing forces; estimate likely outcomes of operational plans. Traditionally, military wargames focused on forces, weapons, movements, and fires; while business wargames focused on marketing, investments, revenues, and profits.

---

[21] There is nothing new in proposing deception versus counterdeception in RED versus BLUE wargames or applying these wargames to the cyber domain; see, for example, Feer (1989) and Cohen et al. (2001).

[22] Some recent wargame examples are described in Alberts et al. (2010). Joint Chiefs of Staff (2006) recommends wargaming plans and courses of action for information operations. Wargaming by DOD may be less frequent than suggested by doctrine and history, e.g., regarding the 2008 Russian invasion of Georgia a U.S. Army War College analysis concluded "U.S. intelligence-gathering and analysis regarding the Russian threat to Georgia failed. . . . No scenarios of a Russian invasion were envisaged, wargamed, or seriously exercised;" p. 72, Cohen and Hamilton (2011).

A cyber wargame exercise in a sandbox environment is one method an organization can use to better understand how to utilize cyber-D&D TTTPs and to be prepared for an adversary with a D&D capability by applying cyber-CD.

6.10.1 Exercise Basics

Like kinetic wargames, cyber wargames are conducted to achieve one or more objectives. Wargaming objectives can vary from training, to testing the utility of a new network defense tool, testing the efficacy of recent modifications made to the network sensor infrastructure, testing the skills of the organization's cyber intelligence analysts (Wheaton 2011)[23] so that future training can be appropriately developed, learning strategy and testing strategies (Calbert 2007), to rehearsals of critical operations.[24]

Cyber wargames are organized around a scenario that is intended to simulate a relevant reality.[25] Scenarios can range from using collaborative cyber mission systems to conducting a multinational military operation (Heckman et al. 2013), to assuming an adversary already has credential access to the organization's network, but is attempting to establish persistence and exfiltrate sensitive information while engaging in defense evasion. The scenario should permit for a clear end to the wargame exercise while ensuring that there is sufficient gameplay to achieve the wargame's objective(s).

Cyber wargames include a number of players divided into three teams: RED, WHITE, and BLUE. The RED team represents adversarial elements, such as malicious cyber attackers with hands-on-keyboards, cyber intelligence analysts, or the head of a nation-sponsored organization that manages or hires such attackers and analysts. The BLUE team represents friendly elements, such as computer network defenders, cyber intelligence analysts, or the head of an organization that is currently undergoing a cyber attack. Specific team assignments are derived from the scenario. WHITE provides the game control and umpires questions and issues that arise as the game is played. WHITE usually serves as the conduit and filter between the RED and BLUE players and the "real world" to ensure that realistic game play is not mistaken by others outside the game as real-world events. Conversely, WHITE allows RED and BLUE access to real-world assets and resources that would be allowed within the rules of the game. WHITE's role during actual play is discussed further below.

---

[23] Wheaton (2011) recommends a game-based approach to teaching strategic intelligence analysis to increase learning, improve student performance, and increase student satisfaction.

[24] For example, Pérez (2004) wrote: "The risks vs. benefits of committing [military rescue] forces must be weighed and war-gamed carefully between all civilian/military leaders prior to committing the military arm [to a hostage rescue mission]. "

[25] Even when wargames are designed to explore future concepts and capabilities, they must provide a realistic basis for these innovations and a realistic environment for the exploration. See, for example, Rosen 1991; Murray and Millet 1996, 2000; Scales and Robert 2000; Knox and Murray 2001; and Fisher 2005

Along with their role as wargames opponents to BLUE teams, RED teams and RED teaming can be used to identify and reduce cyber risks and exposures by deliberately challenging the organization's plans and programs and to test the organization's assumptions. As a result, RED teams help guard against surprise and catastrophic consequences. RED teams rely on upon creativity, intuition, and subject matter expertise to test organizational assumptions and systems (Gowlett 2011). Research comparing RED and BLUE teams in a terrorism-counterterrorism wargame suggests RED teams, on the offensive against defending BLUE teams will usually test the BLUE team's mettle; RED teams tend to make far more use of internal team expertise, are more creative, focus on fewer courses of action, and use external expertise less than BLUE opponents (Woolley 2009, 2010, 2011).

When a cyber wargame involves denial and deception or counterdeception, the scenario requirements will determine whether there will be one or more BLUE cyber-D&D or cyber-CD teams playing defensively, or whether there will be one or more RED cyber-D&D or cyber-CD teams playing offensively.

The D&D and the CD team(s) should interact closely with their team counterparts (e.g., BLUE for the BLUE cyber-D&D or cyber-CD team(s)) to ensure continuity and informed team play. For example, a BLUE cyber-D&D team can benefit greatly from close interaction with a BLUE player representing a cyber-intelligence analyst. Intelligence is a key component in planning and executing defensive cyber-D&D operations. If a BLUE cyber-CD team is playing, it should be part of the defensive cyber intelligence element, but closely linked to the BLUE cyber-D&D team, as well as to the BLUE security operations team.

Wargames can be played synchronously or asynchronously. However, given that deception is fundamentally psychological, asynchronous play does not lend itself as well to D&D and CD as synchronous play.[26] The RED and BLUE teams are humans interacting with each other in a cyber environment, and if D&D and/or CD is being used, the scenario should be designed to afford such psychological interplay. The scenario should also allow the interaction to be direct. That is, both the RED and BLUE players are in direct communications. For example, a RED player masquerading as an member of an instant messaging (IM) system hypothetically might send a BLUE player a phishing link in an IM. The RED and BLUE interaction is more likely to be indirect, mediated by the technical elements of the cyber environment. That is, RED implants exploits that are triggered when BLUE players engage with the cyber environment. Similarly, BLUE indirectly interacts with RED when baiting the RED players with honeytokens BLUE knows will attract RED's interests.

The WHITE team provides overall game control which includes enforcing the rules of engagement and ensuring that RED and BLUE make continual forward progress. The WHITE team also manages requests for information (RFI) from the

---

[26] On the other hand, counterdeception analysis can be performed synchronously in live exercises or asynchronously on "cold cases." That is, an asynchronous counterdeception reconstruction of D&D operations from forensic materials, historical records, and other materials can be readily performed. Such asynchronous analyses are common in counter-fraud, cheating detection, art forgery analysis, malingering, etc. For example, see Stech and Elsässer (2007).

teams, and provides the teams with injects. WHITE stimulates both teams on a turn-by-turn basis or intermittently as required by the scenario with injects tailored to encourage RED and BLUE play likely to fulfill the objectives of the wargame. Injects can include the results of actions taken by the team receiving the inject or those taken by the other team which, in reality, would be visible to the team receiving the inject, as well as scenario activities which stimulate game play. It is also important that the WHITE players monitor the actions and interactions of the RED and BLUE players. WHITE solicits updates from the teams regarding their situational awareness and current plans, as well as an assessment of the other team, such as their capabilities, objectives, and plans. WHITE also enforces the "lanes in the road" i.e., the roles assigned in the wargame for RED and BLUE players.

WHITE also simulates those elements of the cyber environment that are impractical to replicate or simulate in the cyber wargame environment. For example, WHITE might provide both the RED and BLUE operators with simulated cyber intelligence on the other team. WHITE also adapts and modifies the cyber environment as needed to facilitate the continuation of the wargame play. For example, WHITE might play the role of a high authority and require BLUE to use cyber-D&D TTPTs against the RED opponent.

Because cyber-D&D and cyber-CD wargames are interactive, they offer less scientific control of variables than pure experiments, but they offer more control and more measurement opportunities than observations in the wild. That is, wargame exercises may create specific experimental conditions, e.g., experimentally control access by the RED or BLUE players to various resources in the cyber environment. Wargame exercises, relative to observations in the wild, also offer greater opportunities to collect and measure RED and BLUE behaviors and interactions. Just as experimental study of Internet threats has yielded valuable insights and tools for monitoring malicious activities and capturing malware binaries (Dacier et al. 2010 Jajodia et al. 2010), wargame exercises offer opportunities for control and manipulation to better understand offensive and defensive interactions, such as the use of cyber-D&D and cyber-CD.

6.11 The Future of Cyber-Counterdeception in Active Cyber Defense

Information warfare (IW), post-Stuxnet's cyber attack on physical infrastructure, is a possible future threat, especially as less powerful adversaries attempt to gain an asymmetric advantage in conflict. How governmental and private sector capabilities and operations for active cyber defenses will be integrated and coordinated against such threats has been an issue since at least 1997:

> While offensive IW remains within DOD's realm, defensive IW is truly a national issue and must involve the private sector. The interagency arena is absolutely critical to the success of defensive IW. While DOD can be a major player in this area, it cannot lead. Leadership in this area must come from the White House. IW is emerging as an inexpensive, yet effective

means to directly target the U.S. homeland. The U.S. must plan for this contingency in a coherent and coordinated manner and a sound organizational underpinning is a fundamental pillar to both a DOD and national IW architecture. (Fredericks 1997)

In 1999, on behalf of the Office of the Secretary of Defense (OSD), the National Security Agency, and the Defense Advanced Research Projects Agency, RAND's National Defense Research Institute published *Securing the U.S. defense information infrastructure: a proposed approach* (Anderson 1999). RAND's proposal strongly featured cyber deception as a defensive measure to counter IW attacks on the nation's defense networks. Fifteen years later, in 2014, it is unlikely that the extensive use of deceptive cyber defenses proposed by RAND have been implemented, for defense networks, or other critical information infrastructures.

In 2012, the Defense Science Board Task Force on Resilient Military Systems concluded the:

> cyber threat is serious and that the United States cannot be confident that our critical Information Technology (IT) systems will work under attack from a sophisticated and well-resourced opponent utilizing cyber capabilities ... the DoD needs to take the lead and build an effective response to ... decrease a would-be attacker's confidence in the effectiveness of their capabilities to compromise DoD systems. This conclusion was developed upon several factors, including the success adversaries have had penetrating our networks; the relative ease that our Red Teams have in disrupting, or completely beating, our forces in exercises using exploits available on the Internet; and the weak cyber hygiene position of DoD networks and systems. (Defence Science Board 2012)

While the fundamental principles of denial and deception and counterdeception seem relatively constant, in the future, the landscapes and dynamics of D&D and CD tools and techniques will be constantly evolving as the "arms races" between the deceivers and the deception detectives goes on. As new tactics to conceal evolve, procedures to reveal will be developed. These pressures will be particularly acute in the cyber realm, where the virtual can evolve many times faster than the physical. Changes in technologies, policies, social interactions, even global politics will force changes in the landscapes and dynamics of the cyber-D&D versus cyber-CD contests.

Whaley offers a comforting constant in the midst of these swirling dynamics of the deception-counterdeception arms race landscapes:

> ... it's fair to say that in the majority of cases, most of the overall costs of detecting deception are prepaid by already existing intelligence capabilities. ... consistently effective deception analysis doesn't require more analysts or a bigger budget but simply different recruitment criteria, teaching tools, training procedures, and operational protocols. (Whaley 2007f in Arquilla and Borer 2007)

In surveying these landscapes and dynamics, Bennett and Waltz (2007) noted the "deception and counterdeception disciplines are not static," and described five key factors influencing the future of these contests:

1. *Human nature and the threat of deception will persist:* The deceiver holds a significant advantage over both the naïve and the sophisticated victims, and the

advantages of deception, especially in asymmetric contests, are too great to be overlooked in future cyber contests.[27]

2. *The role and morality of deception will be debated:* The debate regarding the use of cyber-D&D will continue and has already influenced discussions of cyber defenses.[28] This factor (along with the first) offers an advantage for the future of counterdeception. But as distasteful as deception may be in Western democratic societies, few in those societies tend to naysay the virtues of enhancing capabilities to detect deceptions. As deception continues to be controversial, advocates of enhancing counterdeception are likely to benefit. Since other societies (e.g., Marxist-Leninist, Islamic, Eastern) may have varying moral histories and perspectives regarding deception,[29] the use of deception against Western cultures will likely continue, resulting in a continuing need for better counterdeception capabilities.

3. *Channels for deception will continue to grow:* This is especially likely in the cyber realm, simply because the rate of innovation and evolution are accelerated there, and because the cyber realm continues to intersect (if not actually harbor) more and more important components of real life. Notwithstanding, as cyber-D&D TTTPs are innovated and evolved, channels and TTTPs for cyber-CD will also grow. Cyber forensics, defenses, and capabilities for cyber-CD will benefit from the growth of such channels. Bennett and Waltz (2007) wrote: "Counterdeception analysts will also benefit from the expansion of open source channels, because they also provide greater breadth of context, and additional independent means to validate information, increasing the likelihood of detecting . . . incongruities that may tip off a deception."

---

[27] Bennett and Waltz (2007) cite the National Intelligence Council's (2000, p. 9) conclusion regarding the future use of deception: "most adversaries will recognize the information advantage and military superiority of the United States in 2015. Rather than acquiesce to any potential US military domination, they will try to circumvent or minimize US strengths and exploit perceived weaknesses [though] greater access . . . to sophisticated deception-and-denial techniques. . ."

[28] See, for example, Bodmer et al. (2012): "There is a very well-developed legal framework to deal with intruders, and as one of the "good guys" your responses are bound by that framework. You can expect to work closely with legal counsel to ensure that your operation is legal. . . But this does not mean that there are no ethical consequences to your actions. Even if your specific [cyber-D&D] operation does not push ethical boundaries, taken collectively, the actions of you and your colleagues just may."

[29] What Whaley (2007e) found (as might be expected) is subtle: Some cultures are clearly more deceptive than others but only during given slices of time. No single culture has excelled in deceptiveness throughout its history; while the Chinese since the 1940s have shown high levels of military-political deceptiveness, this is not true throughout Chinese history. In a given culture and time, levels of deceptiveness can be quite different across major disciplines of military, domestic politics, foreign diplomacy, and commercial business. Sometimes ends justify means, practical considerations of greed and survival sometimes override religious, moral, or ethical objections to deception. High, medium, and low levels of deceptive behavior were found in every culture at different times and regardless of its level of technology. We found no comparisons of counterdeception capabilities across cultures comparable to Whaley's analysis of cultural deceptiveness.

Table 6.3 Deception & Counterdeception Relevant Information and Quantum Science and Technologies. (Source: Bennett and Waltz 2007)

Enabling and emerging applied technologies	Potential deception or counterdeception applications
Agent-based learning, autonomy and intelligence; machine-to-machine collaboration	Automated real-time computer net-work deception, attack and adaptation (agent lying); agent counterdeception (agent deception detection) and response
Digital data embedding; steganography	Concealment of messages and data within public information sources
Digital imaging and image processing	Creation of virtual imagery (still and video with audio) of a deception that is indistinguishable from reality
Quantum computing	Exponentially enhanced cryptography and cryptanalysis; tamper-proof cryptography for anti-deception information protection
Quantum sensing	Remote discrimination of cover, concealment, & deception; detection of nanoscale sensor networks

4. *Methods for employing deception will grow:* As the science and technology available as channels for deception are innovated and evolved, deception art will be adapted to these new channels (Table 6.3). Since the deceiver may have to learn a great deal about such new channels of deception to conceal realities, present convincing ploys, and control leakage of anomalies and incongruities, it is possible that every new deceptive use of such innovative channels will offer a greater than normal number of incongruities, anomalies, and "tells," conferring Jones and Whaley's "counterdeception analyst's advantage" on cyber-CD efforts.[30]

5. *Deception will increase in both global reach and influence:* Given a shrinking, hyper-connected globe, with influences at the speed of social media and Internet news, and highly intertwined virtual and physical dimensions, it is perhaps safe to say almost any notable human behavior *will increase in both global reach and influence.* That said, as the stakes at risk to deception increase in cyber contests, we would expect the pressures will also increase to enhance effective cyber-CD.

---

[30] Not all observers agree with Jones's and Whaley's concept of a "counterdeception analyst's advantage" over deceivers, and some tend to see the deception-counterdeception contest in terms of (to use Handel's (2005) characterization), "the persistent difficulty involved in attempting to expose deception" i.e., more along the lines of Fig. 6.5, above (Matrix of Attacker's Denial & Deception Moves versus Defender's Counterdenial and Counterdeception Moves). For example, Scot Macdonald (2007) sees the deceivers as generally holding the advantages over deception detectives as new tools, technologies, channels, and environments become available.

The rapid growth of the global cyber security industry is fairly clear evidence of these pressures.[31]

While Bennett and Waltz (2007) point to the growing influence and reach of deception in the future, cyber-D&D and cyber-CD will also become far more personal than in the past. The increasing overlap of our physical and cyber identities will continue to shift our personal landscapes and dynamics regarding deceptions and their detection. The opportunities and the challenges for cyber deception and for counterdeception cyber forensics keep changing, as Bloom (2013) summarized:

> Knowledge will continue to explode about what people buy and have bought, where they are and where they have been, with whom we communicate, and so on. Such knowledge will facilitate data mining both for individuals, groups of people, and all people. Greater predictive validity may well occur ... especially if there's massive cross-referencing of an individual's data with that of presumed friends, families, and associates. But there also will be greater deception and counterdeception possibilities for the more ingenious of good and bad actors. (Bloom 2013)

Unlike traditional counterintelligence, "Almost every action in the cyber realm can be recorded, detected, identified, analyzed, replayed, tracked, and identified" (Bodmer et al. 2012). This provides an abundance of potential intelligence for counterdeception analysts, which can then be used against adversaries in counter-deception operations. Bodmer et al. (2012) described nine observables which can be used to assess an adversary's level of capability:

1. *Attack origin points:* Awareness that an adversary has penetrated the organization is key. It is then important to determine how the adversary gained access, and from where the attack originated.
2. *Numbers involved in the attack:* To get an understanding of the adversary's sophistication, motive, and intent, it is helpful to study the victim of the attack: their function, role, accesses, and how this relates to the history of the organization's attacks.
3. *Risk tolerance:* This relates to the amount of effort taken by the adversary to conceal their presence. Adversaries with a high risk tolerance may not alter logs or wipe systems. Whereas adversaries with a low risk tolerance are more likely to alter logs, corrupt applications, or wipe systems.
4. *Timeliness:* This observable is reflective of the adversary's level of understanding of the organization and/or the organization's infrastructure. It can be measured by determining, for example, how quickly the adversary moved through each system; the amount of search time to locate information which was then exfiltrated; access

---

[31] An ad hoc search on "growth of the global cyber security industry" yielded a 2014 estimate of about $77 billion, and a 2019 estimate of about $ 156 billion, i.e., more than doubling in 5 years, or roughly seven times faster growth than estimates of the growth of the global economy over the 2014–2019 time frame. See http://www.asdnews.com/news-53610/Global_Cyber_Security_Market_to_be_Worth_$76.68bn_in_2014.htm; http://www.marketsandmarkets.com/PressReleases/cyber-security.asp; and http://www.conference-board.org/pdf_free/GEO2014_Methodology.pdf.

time stamps which might suggest a pattern or geolocation of the adversary; or whether the attack was scripted.

5. *Skills and methods:* Determining the skill level and methods used to gain access, leave, and maintain persistence, requires access to activity logs from hosts as well as the organization's network. To evaluation skills and methods, it is important to know what the adversary used during the attack, for example, the vulnerability/exploit, tools, data transfer techniques, and logging alteration or deletion technique.

6. *Actions:* To assess the adversary's actions, it is necessary to identify the total number of systems that were accessed, and at what times, to identify a possibly pattern. This may help assess the adversary's possible motives, intent, and objectives.

7. *Objectives:* Identifying the adversary's objectives based on what the organization has lost, will facilitate attributing affiliations to the adversary.

8. *Resources*: One means of measuring the adversary's resources is via the observables collected, such as the availability (e.g., open source, freeware, commercial, illegally purchased) and cost of the tools used, the length of time spent accessing the organization's resources, and the types of information being taken/stolen.

9. *Knowledge sources*: Public security sites, underground forums, public forums, hacker group private sites, and social networking sites can be used by defenders to track, attribute, or learn more about a specific threat.

This ability to capture actions in the cyber realm will surely not diminish in the future. Cyber-D & D & CD practitioners can leverage these nine observables as a starting point in the dynamic process of assessing adversary capability maturity. As adversary TTTPs evolve, so must the defender's 'metrics.' Defenders likewise will need to develop a dynamic set of metrics for measuring *their* cyber-D&D and cyber-CD capabilities. Any organization practicing cyber-D&D, cyber-CD, and cyber-C-D should strive to grow their capability maturity over time. As more organizations, and adversaries, grow their cyber-D&D, cyber-CD, and cyber-C-D capability maturity, the deception and counterdeception disciplines will in turn mature.

In the "arms race" between deceivers and detectors, deceivers may eventually become cognizant of the detector's intelligence gathering means and methods, and simply work around them. That is, deceivers will show cyber-CD analysts, via their own intelligence collection capabilities, exactly what they expect to see and help them to deceive themselves. Given that all deception is inherently psychological, it is key that deception detectors are trained in self-deception and cognitive biases.[32] The detection organization's best defense against a capable adversary is a capable cadre of D&D, CD, and C-D professionals.

---

[32] See, for example Caverni and Gonzalez (1990) and Yetiv (2013).

Adversaries are likely to bring more, and more effective, cyber-D&D to future cyber warfare,[33] cyber crimes, and cyber terrorism. The dynamics of the cyber and technology innovation landscapes offer tremendous opportunities in the future to the cyber deceiver. But they also offer potential opportunities to the cyber deception detectives. Until nations adopt cyber-D&D defenses, however, and leverage those experiences into cyber-CD defensive capabilities, it may well be that these future opportunities and advantages will go solely to the cyber attackers.

References

Alberts, David S., Reiner K. Huber, & James Moffat (2010) NATO NEC C2 Maturity Model. Washington, DC: DoD Command and Control Research Program.

Anderson, Robert H. et al. (1999) Securing the U.S. Defense Information Infrastructure: a Proposed Approach. Santa Monica, CA: RAND.

Arquilla, John & Douglas A. Borer, eds. (2007) *Information Strategy and Warfare: A Guide to Theory and Practice*. New York: Routledge.

Bennett, M., & E. Waltz (2007) *Counterdeception Principles and Applications for National Security*. Norwood, MA: Artech House.

Bloom, Richard (2013) *Foundations of Psychological Profiling: Terrorism, Espionage, and Deception*. Boca Raton, FL: Taylor & Francis Group.

Bodmer, Sean, Max Kilger, Gregory Carpenter, & Jade Jones (2012) *Reverse Deception: Organized Cyber Threat Counter-Exploitation*. New York: McGraw-Hill.

Boush, David M., Marian Friestad, & Peter Wright (2009) *Deception in the Marketplace: The Psychology of Deceptive Persuasion and Consumer Self Protection*. New York: Routledge Taylor & Francis.

Bruce, James B. & Michael Bennett (2008) "Foreign Denial and Deception: Analytical Imperatives," in George, Roger Z. & James B. Bruce (2008) *Analyzing Intelligence: Origins, Obstacles, and Innovations*. Washington, DC: Georgetown University Press.

Calbert, Gregory (2007) "Learning to Strategize," in Kott, Alexander and William M. McEneaney (2007) *Adversarial Reasoning: Computational Approaches to Reading the Opponent's Mind*. Chapman & Hall/CRC: Boca Raton, FL.

Caverni, Fabre & Michel Gonzalez, eds. (1990) *Cognitive Biases*. New York: Elsevier

Cohen Ariel & Robert E. Hamilton (2011) The Russian Military and the Georgia War: Lessons and Implications. ERAP Monograph, June 2011, Carlisle Barracks PA: Strategic Studies Institute, U.S. Army War College.

Cohen, Fred, Irwin Marin, Jeanne Sappington, Corbin Stewart, & Eric Thomas (2001) *Red Teaming Experiments with Deception Technologies*. Fred Cohen & Associates, November 12, 2001. http://all.net/journal/deception/experiments/experiments.html.

Croom, Charles (2010) "The Defender's 'Kill Chain'," *Military Information Technology*, Vol. 14, No. 10, 2010. http://www.kmimediagroup.com/files/MIT_14-10_final.pdf

Dacier, Marc, Corrado Leita, Olivier Thonnard, Van-Hau Pham, & Engin Kirda (2010) "Assessing Cybercrime Through the Eyes of the WOMBAT," in Jajodia, Sushil, Peng Liu, Vipin Swarup,

---

[33] One 2009 report suggested the Chinese will employ integrated network electronic warfare which includes "using techniques such as electronic jamming, electronic deception and suppression to disrupt information acquisition and information transfer, launching a virus attack or hacking to sabotage information processing and information utilization, and using anti-radiation and other weapons based on new mechanisms to destroy enemy information platforms and information facilities." Krekel (2009).

& Cliff Wang, eds. (2010) *Cyber Situational Awareness: Issues and Research*. New York: Springer.

Dawes, R.M. (2001) *Everyday Irrationality: How Pseudo Scientists, Lunatics, and the Rest of Us Systematically Fail to Think Rationally*. Boulder, CO: Westview Press.

Defense Science Board (2012) Task Force Report: Resilient Military Systems and the Advanced Cyber Threat. Washington, DC: Department of Defense.

Elsässer, Christopher & Frank J. Stech (2007) "Detecting Deception," in Kott, Alexander & William M. McEneaney, eds. (2007) *Adversarial Reasoning: Computational Approaches to Reading the Opponent's Mind*. Boca Raton FL: Taylor & Francis Group.

Epstein, Edward Jay (1991) *Deception: The Invisible War Between the KGB and the CIA*. New York: Random House.

Feer, Fred S. (1989) *Thinking-Red-in-Wargaming Workshop: Opportunities for Deception and Counterdeception in the Red Planning Process*. Santa Monica, CA: RAND, May 1989.

Fischhoff, B., (1982) "Debiasing," in Kahneman, D., P. Slovic, & A. Tversky, eds. (1982) *Judgment under Uncertainty: Heuristics and Biases*. Cambridge UK: Cambridge University Press, 1982, pp. 422–444.

Fisher, David E. (2005) *A Summer Bright and Terrible: Winston Churchill, Lord Dowding, Radar, and the Impossible Triumph of the Battle of Britain*. Berkeley CA: Shoemaker & Hoard.

Fredericks, Brian (1997) "Information Warfare: The Organizational Dimension," in Robert E. Neiison, ed. (1997) *Sun Tzu and Information Warfare*. Washington, DC: National Defense University Press.

Gerwehr, Scott, & Russell W. Glenn (2002). *Unweaving the Web: Deception and Adaptation in Future Urban Operations*. Santa Monica, CA: RAND.

Gilovich, T., D. Griffin, & D. Kahneman (2002) *Heuristics and Biases*. Cambridge UK: Cambridge University Press.

Gowlett, Phillip (2011) *Moving Forward with Computational Red Teaming*. DSTO-GD-0630, March 2011, Joint Operations Division, Defence Science and Technology Organisation, Canberra Australia.

Harris W. R. (1968) "Intelligence and National Security: A Bibliography with Selected Annotations." Cambridge MA: Center for International Affairs, Harvard University.

Harris W. R. (1972)"Counter-deception Planning," Cambridge MA: Harvard University.

Harris W. R. (1985)"Soviet Maskirovka and Arms Control Verification," mimeo, Monterey CA: U.S. Navy Postgraduate School, September 1985.

Handel, Michael (2005) *Masters of War: Classical Strategic Thought*. London: Frank Cass–Taylor & Francis

Heckman, K. E., M. J. Walsh, F. J. Stech, T. A. O'Boyle, S. R. Dicato, & A. F. Herber (2013). Active Cyber Defense with Denial and Deception: A Cyber-wargame Experiment. *Computers and Security, 37*, 72–77. doi: 10.1016/j.cose.2013.03.015

Heuer, Jr., Richards J. (1981) "Strategic Deception and Counterdeception: A Cognitive Process Approach," *International Studies Quarterly*, v. 25, n. 2, June 1981, pp. 294–327.

Heuer, Jr., Richards J. (1999) "Chapter 8, Analysis of Competing Hypotheses," *Psychology of Intelligence*, Washington, DC: Central Intelligence Agency. https://www.cia.gov/library/center-for-the-study-of-intelligence/csi-publications/books-and-monographs/psychology-of-intelligence-analysis/

Heuser, Stephen J. (1996) *Operational Deception and Counter Deception*. Newport RI: Naval War College, 14 June 1996.

Hobbs, C. L. (2010) *Methods for Improving IAEA Information Analysis by Reducing Cognitive Biases*. IAEA Paper Number: IAEA-CN-184/276. http://www.iaea.org/safeguards/Symposium/2010/Documents/PapersRepository/276.pdf

Hutchins Eric M., Michael J. Cloppert, & Rohan M. Amin, "Intelligence-Driven Computer Network Defense Informed by Analysis of Adversary Campaigns and Cyber Kill Chains," 6th Annual International Conference on Information Warfare and Security, Washington, DC, 2011. http://www.lockheedmartin.com/content/dam/lockheed/data/corporate/documents/LM-White-Paper-Intel-Driven-Defense.pdf.

Jajodia, Sushil, Peng Liu, Vipin Swarup, & Cliff Wang, eds. (2010) *Cyber Situational Awareness: Issues and Research*. New York: Springer.

Johnson, Paul E., S. Grazioli, K. Jamal, and R. G. Berryman (2001) "Detecting Deception: Adversarial Problem Solving in a Low Base-rate World," *Cognitive Science*, v.25, n.3, May-June.

Joint Chiefs of Staff (2006) Joint Publication 3–13 *Information Operations*. Washington, DC: Department of Defense.

Jones, R.V. (1995) "Enduring Principles: Some Lessons in Intelligence," *CIA Studies in Intelligence*, v. 38, n. 5, pp. 37–42.

Jones, R. V. (2009) *Most Secret War*. London: Penguin. Croom (2010).

Knox, MacGregor & Williamson Murray (2001) *The dynamics of Military Revolution 1300–2050*. Cambridge UK: Cambridge University Press.

Kott, Alexander, & Gary Citrenbaum, eds. (2010). *Estimating Impact: A Handbook of Computational Methods and Models for Anticipating Economic, Social, Political and Security Effects in International Interventions*. New York: Springer.

Krekel, Bryan (2009) *Capability of the People's Republic of China to Conduct Cyber Warfare and Computer Network Exploitation*. McLean VA: Northrop Grumman Corporation.

Lachow, Irving (2011) "The Stuxnet Enigma: Implications for the Future of Cybersecurity," *Georgetown Journal of International Affairs*. 118 (2010–2011). http://heinonline.org/HOL/Page?handle?=?hein.journals/geojaf11&div?=?52&g_sent?=?1&collection?=?journals#442.

Langner Ralph (2013) *To Kill a Centrifuge A Technical Analysis of What Stuxnet's Creators Tried to Achieve*. Hamburg: The Langner Group, November 2013. http://www.langner.com/en/wp-content/uploads/2013/11/To-kill-a-centrifuge.pdf.

Laran, Juliano, Amy N. Dalton, & Eduardo B. Andrade (2011) "The Curious Case of Behavioral Backlash: Why Brands Produce Priming Effects and Slogans Produce Reverse Priming Effects," *Journal of Consumer Research*, v. 37, April 2011.

Lindsay Jon R. (2013) Stuxnet and the Limits of Cyber Warfare. University of California: Institute on Global Conflict and Cooperation, January 2013. http://www.scribd.com/doc/159991102/Stuxnet-and-the-Limits-of-Cyber-Warfare (a version published in *Security Studies*, V.22–3, 2013. https://78462f86-a-6168c89f-s-sites.googlegroups.com/a/jonrlindsay.com/www/research/papers/StuxnetJRLSS.pdf).

Macdonald, Scot (2007) *Propaganda and Information Warfare in the Twenty-first Century: Altered Images and Deception Operations*. New York: Routledge.

Mandiant (2010) M-Trends: the Advanced Persistent Threat. https://www.mandiant.com/resources/mandiant-reports/

Mandiant (2011) M-Trends 2011. http://www.mandiant.com/resources/m-trends/

Mandiant (2013) APT1: Exposing One of China's Cyber Espionage Units. http://intelreport.mandiant.com/Mandiant_APT1_Report.pdf and Appendices.

McNair, Philip A. (1991) *Counterdeception and the Operational Commander*. Newport, RI: Naval War College.

McPherson, Denver E. (2010) Deception Recognition: Rethinking the Operational Commander's Approach. Newport RI: Joint Military Operations Department, Naval War College.

Murray, Williamson & Allan R. Millett (1996) *Military Innovation in the Interwar Period*. Cambridge UK: Cambridge University Press.

Murray, Williamson & Allan R. Millett, (2000) *A War To Be Won, Fighting the Second World War*. Cambridge, MA: Harvard University Press.

National Intelligence Council (2000) *Global Trends 2015: A Dialogue About the Future with Nongovernment Experts*. Washington, DC: National Intelligence Council, NIC 2000–02, December 2000.

Pérez, Carlos M. (2004) *Anatomy of a Rescue: What Makes Hostage Rescue Operations Successful?* Thesis, Naval Postgraduate School: Monterey, CA, September 2004.

Rosen, Stephen Peter (1991) *Winning the Next War: Innovation and the Modern Military*. Ithaca, NY: Cornell University Press.

Rowe, N. C. (2003) "Counterplanning Deceptions To Foil Cyber-Attack Plans," *Proceedings of the 2003 IEEE Workshop on Information Assurance*, West Point NY: United States Military Academy, June 2003.

Rowe, N. C. (2004) "A model of deception during cyber-attacks on information systems," *2004 IEEE First Symposium on Multi-Agent Security and Survivability*, 30–31 Aug. 2004, pp. 21–30.

Rowe, N. C. (2006) "A Taxonomy of Deception in Cyberspace," *International Conference on Information Warfare and Security*, Princess Anne, MD.

David E. Sanger (2012) *Confront and Conceal: Obama's Secret Wars and Surprising Use of American Power*. Crown: New York.

Scales, Jr., Robert H. (2000) *Future Warfare: Anthology, Revised Edition*. Carlisle Barracks, PA: U.S. Army War College.

Stech, F., and C. Elsässer (2007) "Midway Revisited: Detecting Deception by Analysis of Competing Hypothesis," *Military Operations Research*. 11/2007; v. 12, n. 1, pp. 35–55.

Stokes, Mark A., Jenny Lin, & L.C. Russell Hsiao (2011) "The Chinese People's Liberation Army Signals Intelligence and Cyber Reconnaissance Infrastructure," Project 2049 Institute, 2011: 8, http://project2049.net/documents/pla_third_department_sigint_cyber_stokes_lin_hsiao.pdf

The Economist (2014) "Banks and Fraud: Hacking Back–Bankers go Undercover to Catch Bad Guys," *The Economist*, April 5th 2014. http://www.economist.com/news/finance-and-economics/21600148-bankers-go-undercover-catch-bad-guys-hacking-back

Wang, Wei, Jeffrey Bickford, Ilona Murynets, Ramesh Subbaraman, Andrea G. Forte & Gokul Singaraju (2013) "Detecting Targeted Attacks by Multilayer Deception," *Journal of Cyber Security and Mobility*, v. 2, pp. 175–199. http://riverpublishers.com/journal/journal_articles/RP_Journal_2245-1439_224.pdf

Whaley, Barton (2006) *Detecting Deception: A Bibliography of Counterdeception Across Time, Cultures, and Disciplines, 2nd Ed*. Washington, DC: Foreign Denial & Deception Committee, March 2006.

Whaley, B. (2007a). *The Encyclopedic Dictionary of Magic 1584–2007*. Lybrary.com.

Whaley, B. (2007b). *Stratagem: Deception and Surprise in War*. Norwood, MA: Artech House.

Whaley, B. (2007c). Toward a General Theory of Deception. In J. Gooch & A. Perlmutter, eds. *Military Deception and Strategic Surprise*. New York: Routlege.

Whaley, B. (2007d). *Textbook of Political-Military Counterdeception: Basic Principles & Methods*. Washington, DC: Foreign Denial & Deception Committee, August 2007.

Whaley, B. (2007e). *The Prevalence of Guile: Deception Through Time and Across Cultures*. Washington DC: Foreign Denial & Deception Committee, August 2007.

Whaley, B. (2007f) "The One Percent Solution: Costs and Benefits of Military Deception," in Arquilla, John & Douglas A. Borer, eds. (2007) *Information Strategy and Warfare: A Guide to Theory and Practice*. New York: Routledge.

Whaley, B. (2012). *The Beginner's Guide to Detecting Deception: Essay Series #1. Foreign Denial & Deception Committee*, Office of the Director of National Intelligence, Washington, DC. Unpublished manuscript.

Whaley, Barton, & Jeff Busby (2002) "Detecting Deception: Practice, Practitioners, and Theory," in Godson, R., and J. Wirtz, eds. (2002) *Strategic Denial and Deception: The Twenty-First Century Challenge*, New Brunswick, NJ: Transaction Publishers.

Wheaton, Kristan J. (2011) "Teaching Strategic Intelligence Through Games," *International Journal of Intelligence and CounterIntelligence*, 24:2, 367–382.

Wick, Adam (2012) "Deceiving the Deceivers: Active Counterdeception for Software Protection," DOD SBIR Award O113-IA2–1059, Contract: FA8650–12-M-1396. http://www.sbir.gov/sbirsearch/detail/393779

Woolley, A. W. (2009) *"Which Side Are You On? How Offensive and Defensive Strategic Orientation Impact Task Focus and Information Search in Teams,"* Working Paper 548, May 2009, Carnegie Mellon University, Tepper School of Business: Pittsburgh PA. http://repository.cmu.edu/tepper/548.

Woolley, A. W. (2010) *"Is it Really Easier to be the Bad Guys? The Effects of Strategic Orientation on Team Process in Competitive Environments."* Working Paper, June 2010, Carnegie Mellon University, Tepper School of Business: Pittsburgh PA. https://student-3k.tepper.cmu.edu/gsiadoc/wp/2009-E26.pdf.

Woolley, A. W. (2011) "Playing Offense vs. Defense: The Effects of Team Strategic Orientation on Team Process in Competitive Environments," *Organizational Science*, v.22,n.6, Nov-Dec 2011, pp. 1384–1398.

Yetiv, S. (2013) *National Security Through a Cockeyed Lens: How Cognitive Bias Impacts U.S. Foreign Policy*. Baltimore, MD: Johns Hopkins University Press.

Yuill, Jim, Dorothy Denning, & Fred Feer (2006) "Using Deception to Hide Things from Hackers: Processes, Principles, and Techniques," *Journal of Information Warfare*. 5,3: pp. 26–40.

Chapter 7
Automated Adversary Profiling

Samuel N. Hamilton

Abstract Cyber warfare is currently an information poor environment, where knowledge of adversary identity, goals, and resources is critical, yet difficult to come by. Reliably identifying adversaries through direct attribution of cyber activities is not currently a realistic option, but it may be possible to deduce the presence of an adversary within a collection of network observables, and build a profile consistent with those observations. In this paper, we explore the challenges of automatically generating cyber adversary profiles from network observations in the face of highly sophisticated adversaries whose goals, objectives, and perceptions may be very different from ours, and who may be utilizing deceptive activities to disguise their activities and intentions.

7.1 Introduction

Cyber warfare is at its essence, information warfare. While the overall goal of a cyber mission may be to achieve specific objectives, the sub-goals consist mainly of the gathering of information or the manipulation of adversary information in order to achieve an information advantage. As such, subterfuge and deception are the primary tools of most cyber warriors and take many forms, from luring adversaries into honey pots and manipulating their perceptions, to misleading attack attribution efforts by laying clues that point to an innocent party.

Currently, analyzing such manipulations and obfuscations remains largely adhoc, relying on the solo efforts of individual cyber analysts with very little in terms of infrastructure support. In this chapter, we explore the challenges of automatically analyzing streams of sensor data that may contain only trace amounts of data related to cyber adversary activities, and deduce likely adversary profiles. This is fundamentally different from traceback where the goal is to clearly identify adversary identity; instead, an adversary profile identifies characteristics such as goals, resources, and previous actions. The profile can also be leveraged to identify likely future activities based on what has been observed so date. Cyber adversary profiling, which on the

S. N. Hamilton (✉)
Siege Technologies, Manchester, USA
e-mail: samuel.hamilton@siegetechnologies.com

© Springer International Publishing Switzerland 2015
S. Jajodia et al. (eds.), *Cyber Warfare,* Advances in Information Security 56,
DOI 10.1007/978-3-319-14039-1_7

Fig. 7.1 Technology enablers
for automated cyber profiling

surface may sound like an impossible task, is being done on a daily basis by human
analysts that are only exposed to a fraction of the detailed data an automated tool
can process. It is our belief that an automated tool in this domain will not replace
the human analyst in the foreseeable future. Instead, it will act as a valuable tool
for presenting likely hypotheses, with accompanying data to show why specific
adversary profiles were identified, what an adversary has likely been trying to do,
and what that adversary may do in the future. In this sense, it will act to complement
a human analyst with its ability to process massive amounts of data in which subtle
traces of adversary behavior may be lingering, while still taking advantage of the
significant potency of human judgment and domain expertise.

Ideally, each adversary profile should be ranked by likelihood and threat level, and
presented to the user. Adversary models can also be compared with a list of known
adversary profiles for potential match identification. The net result is an automated,
systematic mechanism for detecting not only network attacks, but the most critical
information for combating cyber attacks long term: who is attacking, what do they
want, and how will the try to get it.

Figure 7.1 shows the primary technology enablers for automated cyber profiling.
Driving the process is an ontology of possible adversary characteristics. This ontology drives four basic technologies. The first generates hypothesis adversary profiles.
Each profile can be used to extrapolate possible adversary actions that would be
consistent with the goals and resources of the hypothesized adversary. Expected network observables, given those actions, can then be deduced. Once a set of expected
network observables has been generated for a given hypothesized adversary, you can
rate the likelihood that this adversary has actually been present in the network by
comparing deduced observables against actual observables.

Each of the four primary technologies, along with the adversary characteristics technology itself, represents a significant area of ongoing research. The remainder of this paper is dedicated to a discussion of the issues involved in each of the technical areas as they relate to automated adversary profiling.

7.2   Adversary Ontology

Early work on cyber profile characteristic modeling or ontology generation concentrated on broad adversary characteristics. For example in (Hamilton et al. 2001a) the authors break cyber adversaries into categories such as hacker types (broken down by sophistication level), insider threats, organized crime, funded and unfunded terrorist activities, and nation state threats. Threat levels have been further abstracted into a general threat Matrix that models adversary commitment in terms of Intensity, Stealth, and Timeframe, and adversary resources in terms of technical personnel, cyber and kinetic knowledge, and access (Dugan et al. 2007). These generalized characteristics can be very useful, and represent an excellent starting point for driving an automated adversary profile tool. On their own, however, the difference between the high level of abstraction represented in these taxonomies and the low abstraction level represented in actual network observables is too great. Additionally, these abstractions have generally concentrated on adversary capabilities, mostly ignoring characteristics such as goals and motivations. As adversary goals are critical for both utilizing a profile to predict future behavior, and for deducing what adversary profile is likely from past behavior, representing adversary goals and motivations is critical and necessary.

There is a body of work on adversary modeling to draw from related to course of action generation that more concretely define adversary profiles. Generally speaking these works have concentrated on defining adversary capabilities such that in individual circumstances possible actions can be generated (Boddy et al. 2005, Wang et al. 2006). General capability models that can be made specific enough to anticipate effects at the network level include:

- *Access*. This includes physical access and/or cyber access on a system-by-system basis. In some cases these accesses may imply an insider threat.
- *Knowledge*. Knowledge of the network, mission, deployed defensive resources, defender techniques, tactics and procedures, etc.
- In (Hamilton and Hamilton 2008) higher-level goals and motivations were also represented, and support for seamless blending of cyber and kinetic missions were supported. Example general goals include:
- *Data Exfiltration*. This category can be further broken down in terms of data size and type, as well as the time sensitivity of the data (which effects the appropriate mechanisms for exfiltration).
- *Launching Pad*. Adversaries may not care about compromising the targeted facility at all, and may only plan to use it to attack another facility.

- *Mission Interference.* Adversaries may choose to compromise resources with a specific mission degradation effect in mind.
- *Embarrass.* This includes defacing public resources, interfering with services, etc.
- *Mischief.* Adversaries may have a revenge motivation or a general dislike for the target and be aiming to cause general mischief.
- *Data Compromise.* Deletion, or Modification data without discovery in various locations, with various time sensitivities.
- *Gain Resource.* Adversaries may be attempting to gather a specific resource or capability, such as access or knowledge.

In (Hamilton and Hamilton 2008) there was some attempt to tie these more concrete representations to the more abstract ontology represented in works such as (Hamilton et al. 2001a) and (Dugan et al. 2007) through modeling abstract concepts such as risk tolerance, exposure sensitivity, and generalized resource models (financial and technological) but further work is necessary in this area.

Ideally, the set of specific goals and objectives should be automatically derivable from a more general ontology given specific network characteristics. Mission characteristics, if available, would also be highly useful. Note that there is a significant difference between the generation of more specific adversary characteristic definitions such as goals and objectives, and actual course of action generation. First, the goals and objectives are generally at a higher abstraction level than actions (such as install RootKit, or Launch DDOS attack); second, goals and objectives, unlike courses of action, do not carry with them proposed mechanisms for achieving the desired effects.

7.3 Adversary Hypothesis Generation

Once an ontology of adversary characteristics has been identified, a set of hypothesized adversary profiles needs to be generated that can then be tested against actual network observables to determine likelihood. Profiles can created from the ontology by defining which elements are relevant for a particular hypothesized adversary, and potentially the degree for which it is true. In some cases, more fidelity is required than a simple true or false value. For example, when setting the risk tolerance for a particular adversary, a simple Boolean value is insufficient; instead a value range is more appropriate.

We anticipate that the generation of a set of hypothesized adversaries is a step that would happen more than once during the adversary profiling process. Instead, we view the entire process as cyclical in nature. Adversary profiles are generated, judged, and then the results of that judging help generate the next set of potential adversaries to be considered.

Figure 7.2 Shows this basic process. The implication is that there are really two phases to adversary profile generation. The first phase is a bootstrapping process, which initializes the process by generating initial adversary profiles.

Fig. 7.2 Automated Cyber
Profiling Technologies

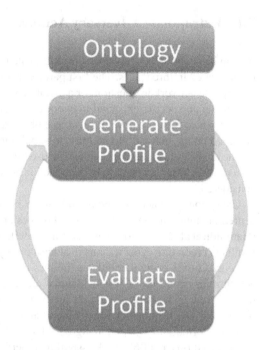

The second phase occurs cyclically after a series of one or more adversary profiles have been evaluated. This enables information generated by the evaluation process to help more intelligently guide the adversary hypothesis generation process.

If an adversary is represented as a set of features selected from the ontology, then the techniques relevant to adversary profile generation are well defined. Essentially, the problem becomes the same as a traditional optimization problem. A feature space can be extracted from the ontology, and the evaluation of adversary likelihood is the score to be optimized. Thus, genetic algorithms (Schmitt 2001), simulated annealing (Kirkpatrick et al. 1983), or other well studied optimization approaches can be leveraged. All of these algorithms are designed such that as part of their process they generate new hypothesis feature sets given previous feature set evaluations. Therefore, hypothesis profiles can be generated automatically within the context of these algorithms. All that is left is addressing the bootstrapping process, since this is a necessary component to traditional optimization approaches. In most cases, we expect that seeding the algorithms with cyber adversary profiles at least partially derived from actual adversaries will lead to the best results, though a random seeding may do better at identifying the characteristics of previously unknown groups. The specific seeding strategy that is appropriate depends on the optimization strategy being utilized.

Note that while optimization stratagems are well studied, the appropriate technique and implementation is highly dependent on the feature set and the speed of the feature set evaluation process. Thus, there is still significant work to be done on how to generate hypothesis profiles by leveraging optimization techniques once a specific ontology and evaluation mechanism is defined.

7.4   Extrapolate Adversary Actions

We envision the cyber adversary profile evaluation described in Fig. 7.2 will be implemented in three parts. The first part extrapolates a set of adversary actions for the specific network in question for a given cyber adversary profile. The second step is to generate specific expected network observables for these action sets, and the third step is to measure how closely these observables match what has actually been observed on the network. In addition to supplying an adversary likelihood measure for the analyst, this measurement can be used in the optimization algorithm referred to in the previous section to help generate the next set of adversary hypotheses to be considered.

Cyber course of action generation is an area that has been receiving an increasing degree of attention. One of the first techniques proposed was game theoretic search (Hamilton et al. 2001a, 2008), which was extended into a viable system with credible results in predicting cyber actions in at least one cyber exercise (Meyers et al. 2002). More traditional game theoretic techniques have also been applied, which leverage equilibrium equations to try to identify optimal actions and strategies. This is a rapidly growing body of work, well summarized in (Roy et al. 2010). A fair amount of the early work embraced unrealistic assumptions, such as that the adversary has perfect information (Lye and Wing 2002), or at least never has any misinformation (Alpcan and Baser 2006). Work assuming imperfect, inaccurate information is much more rare, and usually assumes a zero sum game where all parties have symmetric goal sets. Generally speaking, the action sets and state representations are extremely limited in equilibrium equation oriented course of action generation, as the space of possibilities explored must be fairly heavily constrained to converge on a solution in a reasonable amount of time. Due to this, we believe it would be extremely challenging to leverage this body of work for course of action generation specific enough to derive sets of expected network observables.

In addition to game theoretic approaches, traditional planning algorithms have also been utilized (Boddy et al. 2005). This has many of the same advantages as game theoretic search in that actions can be motivated by a set of goals and translated into a set of actions specific enough to generate hypothesized network observables without invoking the same degree of algorithmic complexity associated with equilibrium equation based solutions. In fact, in terms of depth of analysis, planning based solutions can be considered superior to game theoretic search because it can search deeper by only considering actions by a single party. Of course, this eliminates the possibility of modeling deception and other multi-party dynamics, which we consider a significant liability.

Currently, we believe game theoretic search remains the most promising technology to generate action sets from adversary profiles with sufficient fidelity to be able to translate into expected sets of network observables. Automated course of action generation is far from a solved problem in the cyber domain, however, and it is extremely plausible that new developments may change that perspective.

7.5   Deduce Expected Observables

Once a set of expected actions has been derived from a hypothesized cyber adversary profile, it is necessary to generate a set of expected network observables. The appropriate abstraction level must be low level enough to measure how likely it is the observables have occurred, but high level enough to cover a range of possible instantiation mechanisms. The need to cover a range of possible instantiations invalidates most traditional approaches to traffic generation such as LARIAT (Charles et al. 2010) or Skaion's TGS, or even more modern approaches such as was utilized in DARPA's Anomaly Detection at Multiple Scales (ADAMS) program (Glasser and Lindauer 2013). Note that network traffic is simply one example of a relevant cyber observable. Any cyber relevant observations would be considered in scope.

There are some attempts at standardization of cyber observable definition formats that might be applicable in that they represent observables concretely enough to measure, but without the degree of specifics inherent in actual traffic or sensor output generation that would cause pattern matching to fail. Mitre's CybOX language is one such example. These languages are by necessity very general, and a significant degree of work would be required to leverage any one of these languages to produce observable sets from action sets.

Course of Action generation technologies that have attempted to explicitly model observables instead of adapting simplifying assumptions such as perfect information have also addressed this issue, generally preferring to represent observables in their own format instead of leveraging any of the attempts at standardization. This decision is driven by the fact that course of action technologies of the type reviewed in the previous section can be extremely computationally expensive, so a representation crafted to be efficient and compact within the course of action generation framework is quite a sensible decision. An added benefit is that the same course of action algorithm used to identify what a hypothesized adversary likely has already done, can also be used to identify what that same adversary is likely to do in the future.

7.6   Rate Adversary Likelihood

Once a series of observables has been generated, it must be matched against actual observed traffic to determine the likelihood of the adversary profile associated with its expected observable set. Very little work exists in matching abstract observable definitions of the type used in course of action generation engines, or in matching high abstraction level observable definitions, to observed low level observable instances.

Our current expectation is that this requires more than simply a translation from a high level observable definition to a low level instantiation followed by pattern matching within observed traffic. The actual observation set represented by traffic and sensor output is too large, and the number of possible instantiations derivable from a single high level observable definition are too large. Instead, we expect success to come from an inverted approach. Instead of translating from the high level observable definition into a concrete traffic snippet (or other cyber observable) we believe more success will be found by translating the low level observable into a higher level of abstraction. This would enable standard pattern matching mechanisms to be employed with reasonable scaling effects (due to the reduction of data size post translation).

A simple initial segmentation would be to abstract and bin observables on a host-by-host basis, such that observable lists become independent chronologically ordered vectors of observables. This would allow parallel pattern matching techniques to be applied, and percentage of matches could be used to judge likelihood of a hypothesized adversary profile being active in your network. To be resilient to minor chronological ordering issues, DNA matching techniques that allow for order swapping or event insertion effects while still generating a similarity score could be utilized.

7.7 Conclusions

Overall, we believe that automated adversary profiling could and should be a critically important part of our national cyber strategy. Identifying who is attacking us, why they are attacking us, and what they are likely to do next are critical components to defending our nations interests, and the amount of information necessary for human analysts to process in order to develop intelligent conclusions in real time is simply too massive to reliably and effectively accomplish without automated help. While there is much work to do to bring about this objective, we believe that the technological advances necessary to bring about this vision are feasible, and would represent an important step toward providing our cyber warriors the tools necessary to combat the ever increasing threats to our nations critical cyber assets world-wide.

References

T. Alpcan and T. Baser, "An Intrusion Detection game with Limited Observations", Proceedings of the International Symposium on Dynamic Games and Applications, 2006.

M. Boddy, J. Gohde, T. Haigh, and S. Harp. "Course of Action Generation for Cyber Security Using Classical Planning", ICAPS, 2005.

W. Charles V., C. Connelly, et. al. "Generating client workloads and high-fidelity network traffic for controllable, repeatable experiments in computer security." In Recent Advances in Intrusion Detection, pp. 218–237, 2010.

D. P. Dugan, S. R. Thomas, et. al., Categorizing Threat: Building and Using a Generic Threat Matrix: Sandia National Laboratories, 2007.

J. Glasser, B. Lindauer, "Bridging the Gap: A Pragmatic Approach to Generating Insider Threat Data", IEEE Security and Privacy Workshop, 2013.

S. N. Hamilton, W. Hamilton. "Adversary Modeling and Simulation in Cyber Warfare", International Information Security Conference, p. 461–475, 2008.

S. N. Hamilton, W. L. Miller, A. Ott, and O. S. Saydjari, The Role of Game Theory in Information Warfare, The Information Survivability Workshop, 2001a.

S. N. Hamilton, W. L. Miller, A. Ott, and O. S. Saydjari, "Challenges in Applying Game Theory to the Domain of Information Warfare", The Information Survivability Workshop, 2001b.

S. Kirkpatrick; Gelatt Jr, C. D.; Vecchi, M. P. (1983). "Optimization by Simulated Annealing", Science 220 (4598): 671–680.

K. Lye and J. Wing, Game Strategies in Network Security, Proceedings of the Foundations of Computer Security, 2002.

K. Meyers, O. S. Saydjari, et. al., ARDA Cyber Strategy and Tactics Workshop Final Report, 2002.

S. Roy, C. Ellis, S. Shiva, D. Dasgupta, V. Shandilya, Q. Wu, "A Survey of Game Theory as Applied to Network Security". In Proceedings of the 2010 43rd Hawaii International Conference on System Sciences (HICSS '10).

Schmitt, Lothar M. "Theory of Genetic Algorithms", Theoretical Computer Science 259: 1–61, 2001.

L. Wang, S. Noel, S. Jajodia, "Minimum-cost network hardening using attack graphs", Computer Communications, Vol. 29, No. 18, pp. 3812–3824, 2006.

Chapter 8
Cyber Attribution: An Argumentation-Based Approach

Paulo Shakarian, Gerardo I. Simari, Geoffrey Moores and Simon Parsons

Abstract Attributing a cyber-operation through the use of multiple pieces of technical evidence (i.e., malware reverse-engineering and source tracking) and conventional intelligence sources (i.e., human or signals intelligence) is a difficult problem not only due to the effort required to obtain evidence, but the ease with which an adversary can plant false evidence. In this paper, we introduce a formal reasoning system called the InCA (Intelligent Cyber Attribution) framework that is designed to aid an analyst in the attribution of a cyber-operation even when the available information is conflicting and/or uncertain. Our approach combines argumentation-based reasoning, logic programming, and probabilistic models to not only attribute an operation but also explain to the analyst why the system reaches its conclusions.

8.1 Introduction

An important issue in cyber-warfare is the puzzle of determining who was responsible for a given cyber-operation—be it an incident of attack, reconnaissance, or information theft. This is known as the "attribution problem" (Shakarian et al. 2013). The difficulty of this problem stems not only from the amount of effort required to find forensic clues but also the ease with which an attacker can plant false clues to

P. Shakarian (✉)
Arizona Sate University, Tempe, AZ, USA
e-mail: shak@asu.edu

G. I. Simari
Department of Computer Science and Engineering, Universidad Nacional del Sur,
Bahía Blanca, Argentina
e-mail: gis@cs.uns.edu.ar

G. Moores
Department of Electrical Engineering and Computer Science, U.S. Military Academy,
West Point, NY, USA
e-mail: geoffrey.moores@usma.edu

S. Parsons
Department of Computer Science, University of Liverpool, Liverpool, UK
e-mail: s.d.parsons@liverpool.ac.uk

© Springer International Publishing Switzerland 2015

S. Jajodia et al. (eds.), *Cyber Warfare,* Advances in Information Security 56,
DOI 10.1007/978-3-319-14039-1_8

mislead security personnel. Further, while techniques such as forensics and reverse-engineering (Altheide 2011), source tracking (Thonnard et al. 2010), honeypots (Spitzner 2003), and sinkholing 2010 are commonly employed to find evidence that can lead to attribution, it is unclear how this evidence is to be combined and reasoned about. In a military setting, such evidence is augmented with normal intelligence collection, such as human intelligence (HUMINT), signals intelligence (SIGINT) and other means—this adds additional complications to the task of attributing a given operation. Essentially, cyber-attribution is a highly-technical intelligence analysis problem where an analyst must consider a variety of sources, each with its associated level of confidence, to provide a decision maker (e.g., a military commander) insight into who conducted a given operation.

As it is well known that people's ability to conduct intelligence analysis is limited (Heuer 1999), and due to the highly technical nature of many cyber evidence-gathering techniques, an automated reasoning system would be best suited for the task. Such a system must be able to accomplish several goals, among which we distinguish the following main capabilities:

1. Reason about evidence in a formal, principled manner, i.e., relying on strong mathematical foundations.
2. Consider evidence for cyber attribution associated with some level of probabilistic uncertainty.
3. Consider logical rules that allow for the system to draw conclusions based on certain pieces of evidence and iteratively apply such rules.
4. Consider pieces of information that may not be compatible with each other, decide which information is most relevant, and express why.
5. Attribute a given cyber-operation based on the above-described features and provide the analyst with the ability to understand how the system arrived at that conclusion.

In this paper we present the InCA (Intelligent Cyber Attribution) framework, which meets all of the above qualities. Our approach relies on several techniques from the artificial intelligence community, including argumentation, logic programming, and probabilistic reasoning. We first outline the underlying mathematical framework and provide a running example based on real-world cases of cyber-attribution (cf. Sect. 8.2); then, in Sects. 8.3 and 8.4, we formally present InCA and attribution queries, respectively. Finally, we discuss conclusions and future work in Sect. 8.6.

8.2 Two Kinds of Models

Our approach relies on *two separate models of the world*. The first, called the **environmental model** (EM) is used to describe the background knowledge and is probabilistic in nature. The second one, called the **analytical model** (AM) is used to analyze competing hypotheses that can account for a given phenomenon (in this case, a cyber-operation). The EM *must be consistent*—this simply means that there must

EM	AM
"Malware X was compiled on a system using the English language."	"Malware X was compiled on a system English-speaking country Y."
"Malware W and malware X were created in a similar coding sytle."	"Malware W and malware X are related."
"Country Y and country Z are currently at war."	"Country Y has a motive to launch a cybre-attack against country Z."
"Country Y has a significant investment in math-science-engineering (MSE) education."	"Country Y has the capability to conduct a cyber-attack."

Fig. 8.1 Example observations—EM vs. AM

exist a probability distribution over the possible states of the world that satisfies all of the constraints in the model, as well as the axioms of probability theory. On the contrary, the AM will allow for contradictory information as the system must have the capability to reason about competing explanations for a given cyber-operation. In general, the EM contains knowledge such as evidence, intelligence reporting, or knowledge about actors, software, and systems. The AM, on the other hand, contains ideas the analyst concludes based on the information in the EM. Figure 8.1 gives some examples of the types of information in the two models. Note that an analyst (or automated system) could assign a probability to statements in the EM column whereas statements in the AM column can be true or false depending on a certain combination (or several possible combinations) of statements from the EM. We now formally describe these two models as well as a technique for *annotating* knowledge in the AM with information from the EM—these annotations specify the conditions under which the various statements in the AM can potentially be true.

Before describing the two models in detail, we first introduce the language used to describe them. Variable and constant symbols represent items such as computer systems, types of cyber operations, actors (e.g., nation states, hacking groups), and other technical and/or intelligence information. The set of all variable symbols is denoted with $\mathbf{V}$, and the set of all constants is denoted with $\mathbf{C}$. For our framework, we shall require two subsets of $\mathbf{C}$, $\mathbf{C}_{act}$ and $\mathbf{C}_{ops}$, that specify the actors that could conduct cyber-operations and the operations themselves, respectively. In the examples in this paper, we will use capital letters to represent variables (e.g., X, Y, Z). The constants in $\mathbf{C}_{act}$ and $\mathbf{C}_{ops}$ that we use in the running example are specified in the following example.

Example 1 The following (fictitious) actors and cyber-operations will be used in our examples:

$$\mathbf{C}_{act} = \{baja, krasnovia, mojave\} \tag{8.1}$$

$$\mathbf{C}_{ops} = \{worm123\} \tag{8.2}$$

■

The next component in the model is a set of predicate symbols. These constructs can accept zero or more variables or constants as arguments, and map to either

$\mathbf{P}_{EM}$: $origIP(M,X)$ Malware M originated from an IP address belonging to actor X.

      $malwInOp(M,O)$ Malware M was used in cyber-operation O.

      $mwHint(M,X)$ Malware M contained a hint that it was created by actor X.

      $compilLang(M,C)$ Malware M was compiled in a system that used language C.

      $nativLang(X,C)$ Language C is the native language of actor X.

      $inLgConf(X,X')$ Actors X and X' are in a larger conflict with each other.

      $mseTT(X,N)$ There are at least N number of top-tier math-science-engineering universities in country X.

      $infGovSys(X,M)$ Systems belonging to actor X were infected with malware M.

      $cybCapAge(X,N)$ Actor X has had a cyber-warfare capability for N years or less.

      $govCybLab(X)$ Actor X has a government cyber-security lab.

$\mathbf{P}_{AM}$: $condOp(X,O)$ Actor X conducted cyber-operation O.

      $evidOf(X,O)$ There is evidence that actor X conducted cyber-operation O.

      $motiv(X,X')$ Actor X had a motive to launch a cyber-attack against actor X'.

      $isCap(X,O)$ Actor X is capable of conducting cyber-operation O.

      $tgt(X,O)$ Actor X was the target of cyber-operation O.

      $hasMseInvest(X)$ Actor X has a significant investment in math-science-engineering education.

      $expCw(X)$ Actor X has experience in conducting cyber-operations.

Fig. 8.2 Predicate definitions for the environment and analytical models in the running example

true or false. *Note that the EM and AM use separate sets of predicate symbols—* however, they can share variables and constants. The sets of predicates for the EM and AM are denoted with $\mathbf{P}_{EM}, \mathbf{P}_{AM}$, respectively. In InCA, we require $\mathbf{P}_{AM}$ to include the binary predicate $condOp(X, Y)$, where X is an actor and Y is a cyber-operation. Intuitively, this means that actor X conducted operation Y. For instance, $condOp(baja, worm123)$ is true if $baja$ was responsible for cyber-operation $worm123$. A sample set of predicate symbols for the analysis of a cyber attack between two states over contention of a particular industry is shown in Fig. 8.2; these will be used in examples throughout the paper.

A construct formed with a predicate and constants as arguments is known as a *ground atom* (we shall often deal with ground atoms). The sets of all ground atoms for EM and AM are denoted with $\mathbf{G}_{EM}$ and $\mathbf{G}_{AM}$, respectively.

Example 2 The following are examples of ground atoms over the predicates given in Fig. 8.2.

$$\mathbf{G}_{EM} : origIP(mw123sam1, krasnovia),$$

$$mwHint(mw123sam1, krasnovia),$$

$$inLgConf(krasnovia, baja),$$

$$mseTT(krasnovia, 2).$$

$$\mathbf{G}_{AM} : evidOf(mojave, worm123),$$

$$motiv(baja, krasnovia),$$

$$expCw(baja),$$

$$tgt(krasnovia, worm123). \qquad \blacksquare$$

For a given set of ground atoms, a *world* is a subset of the atoms that are considered to be true (ground atoms not in the world are false). Hence, there are $2^{|\mathbf{G}_{EM}|}$ possible worlds in the EM and $2^{|\mathbf{G}_{AM}|}$ worlds in the AM, denoted with $\mathcal{W}_{EM}$ and $\mathcal{W}_{AM}$, respectively.

Clearly, even a moderate number of ground atoms can yield an enormous number of worlds to explore. One way to reduce the number of worlds is to include *integrity constraints*, which allow us to eliminate certain worlds from consideration—they simply are not possible in the setting being modeled. Our principle integrity constraint will be of the form:

$$\text{oneOf}(\mathcal{A}')$$

where $\mathcal{A}'$ is a subset of ground atoms. Intuitively, this says that any world where more than one of the atoms from set $\mathcal{A}'$ appear is invalid. Let $\mathbf{IC}_{EM}$ and $\mathbf{IC}_{AM}$ be the sets of integrity constraints for the EM and AM, respectively, and the sets of worlds that conform to these constraints be $\mathcal{W}_{EM}(\mathbf{IC}_{EM})$, $\mathcal{W}_{AM}(\mathbf{IC}_{AM})$, respectively.

Atoms can also be combined into formulas using standard logical connectives: conjunction (*and*), disjunction (*or*), and negation (*not*). These are written using the symbols $\wedge, \vee, \neg$, respectively. We say a world (w) *satisfies* a formula (f), written $w \models f$, based on the following inductive definition:

- if f is a single atom, then $w \models f$ iff $f \in w$;
- if $f = \neg f'$ then $w \models f$ iff $w \not\models f'$;
- if $f = f' \wedge f''$ then $w \models f$ iff $w \models f'$ and $w \models f''$; and
- if $f = f' \vee f''$ then $w \models f$ iff $w \models f'$ or $w \models f''$.

We use the notation $formula_{EM}, formula_{AM}$ to denote the set of all possible (ground) formulas in the EM and AM, respectively. Also, note that we use the notation $\top, \bot$ to represent tautologies (formulas that are true in all worlds) and contradictions (formulas that are false in all worlds), respectively.

8.2.1 Environmental Model

In this section we describe the first of the two models, namely the EM or environmental model. This model is largely based on the probabilistic logic of (Nilsson 1986), which we now briefly review.

First, we define a *probabilistic formula* that consists of a formula f over atoms from $\mathbf{G}_{EM}$, a real number p in the interval $[0, 1]$, and an error tolerance $\varepsilon \in [0, \min(p, 1 - p)]$. A probabilistic formula is written as: $f : p \pm \varepsilon$. Intuitively, this statement is interpreted as "formula f is true with probability between $p - \varepsilon$ and $p + \varepsilon$"—note that we make no statement about the probability distribution over this interval. The uncertainty regarding the probability values stems from the fact that certain assumptions (such as probabilistic independence) may not be suitable in the environment being modeled.

Example 3 To continue our running example, consider the following set Π_{EM}:

$f_1 = govCybLab(baja) : 0.8 \pm 0.1$

$f_2 = cybCapAge(baja, 5) : 0.2 \pm 0.1$

$f_3 = mseTT(baja, 2) : 0.8 \pm 0.1$

$f_4 = mwHint(mw123sam1, mojave) \wedge compilLang(worm123, english) : 0.7 \pm 0.2$

$f_5 = malwInOp(mw123sam1, worm123)$

    $\wedge\ malwareRel(mw123sam1, mw123sam2)$

    $\wedge\ mwHint(mw123sam2, mojave) : 0.6 \pm 0.1$

$f_6 = inLgConf(baja, krasnovia) \vee \neg cooper(baja, krasnovia) : 0.9 \pm 0.1$

$f_7 = origIP(mw123sam1, baja) : 1 \pm 0$

Throughout other examples in the rest of the paper, we will make use of the subset $\Pi'_{EM} = \{f_1, f_2, f_3\}$. ∎

We now consider a probability distribution Pr over the set $\mathcal{W}_{EM}(\mathbf{IC}_{EM})$. We say that Pr *satisfies* probabilistic formula $f : p \pm \varepsilon$ iff the following holds: $p - \varepsilon \leq \sum_{w \in \mathcal{W}_{EM}(\mathbf{IC}_{EM})} Pr(w) \leq p + \varepsilon$. A set Π_{EM} of probabilistic formulas is called a *knowledge base*. We say that a probability distribution over $\mathcal{W}_{EM}(\mathbf{IC}_{EM})$ satisfies Π_{EM} if and only if it satisfies all probabilistic formulas in Π_{EM}.

It is possible to create probabilistic knowledge bases for which there is no satisfying probability distribution. The following is a simple example of this:

$condOp(krasnovia, worm123) \vee condOp(baja, worm123) : 0.4 \pm 0;$

$condOp(krasnovia, worm123) \wedge condOp(baja, worm123) : 0.6 \pm 0.1.$

Formulas and knowledge bases of this sort are *inconsistent*. In this paper, we assume that information is properly extracted from a set of historic data and hence consistent; (recall that inconsistent information can only be handled in the AM, not the EM). A consistent knowledge base could also be obtained as a result of curation by experts, such that all inconsistencies were removed—see (Khuller et al. 2007; Shakarian et al. 2011) for algorithms for learning rules of this type.

The main kind of query that we require for the probabilistic model is the *maximum entailment* problem: given a knowledge base Π_{EM} and a (non-probabilistic) formula q, identify p, ε such that all valid probability distributions Pr that satisfy Π_{EM} also satisfy $q : p \pm \varepsilon$, and there does not exist p', ε' s.t. $[p - \varepsilon, p + \varepsilon] \supset [p' - \varepsilon', p' + \varepsilon']$, where all probability distributions Pr that satisfy Π_{EM} also satisfy $q : p' \pm \varepsilon'$. That is, given q, can we determine the probability (with maximum tolerance) of statement q given the information in Π_{EM}? The approach adopted in (Nilsson et al. 1986) to solve this problem works as follows. First, we must solve the linear program defined next.

Definition 1 (EM-LP-MIN) Given a knowledge base Π_{EM} and a formula q:

- create a variable x_i for each $w_i \in \mathcal{W}_{EM}(\mathbf{IC}_{EM})$;
- for each $f_j : p_j \pm \varepsilon_j \in \Pi_{EM}$, create constraint:

$$p_j - \varepsilon_j \leq \sum_{w_i \in \mathcal{W}_{EM}(\mathbf{IC}_{EM}) \, s.t. w_i \models f_j} x_i \leq p_j + \varepsilon_j;$$

- finally, we also have a constraint:

$$\sum_{w_i \in \mathcal{W}_{EM}(\mathbf{IC}_{EM})} x_i = 1.$$

The objective is to minimize the function:

$$\sum_{w_i \in \mathcal{W}_{EM}(\mathbf{IC}_{EM}) \, s.t. w_i \models q} x_i.$$

We use the notation $\mathsf{EP\text{-}LP\text{-}MIN}(\Pi_{EM}, q)$ to refer to the value of the objective function in the solution to the **EM-LP-MIN** constraints.

Let ℓ be the result of the process described in Definition 1. The next step is to solve the linear program a second time, but instead maximizing the objective function (we shall refer to this as **EM-LP-MAX**)—let u be the result of this operation. In (Nilsson 1986), it is shown that $\varepsilon = \frac{u-\ell}{2}$ and $p = \ell + \varepsilon$ is the solution to the maximum entailment problem. We note that although the above linear program has an exponential number of variables in the worst case (i.e., no integrity constraints), the presence of constraints has the potential to greatly reduce this space. Further, there are also good heuristics (cf. Khuller et al. 2007; Simari et al. 2012) that have been shown to provide highly accurate approximations with a reduced-size linear program.

Example 4   Consider KB Π'_{EM} from Example 3 and a set of ground atoms restricted to those that appear in that program. Hence, we have:

$$w_1 = \{govCybLab(baja), cybCapAge(baja, 5), mseTT(baja, 2)\}$$
$$w_2 = \{govCybLab(baja), cybCapAge(baja, 5)\}$$
$$w_3 = \{govCybLab(baja), mseTT(baja, 2)\}$$
$$w_4 = \{cybCapAge(baja, 5), mseTT(baja, 2)\}$$
$$w_5 = \{cybCapAge(baja, 5)\}$$
$$w_6 = \{govCybLab(baja)\}$$
$$w_7 = \{mseTT(baja, 2)\}$$
$$w_8 = \emptyset$$

and suppose we wish to compute the probability for formula:

$$q = govCybLab(baja) \vee mseTT(baja, 2).$$

For each formula in Π_{EM} we have a constraint, and for each world above we have a variable. An objective function is created based on the worlds that satisfy the query formula (here, worlds $w_1 - w_4$, w_6, w_7). Hence, EP-LP-MIN(Π'_{EM}, q) can be written as follows:

$$
\begin{aligned}
\max \quad & x_1 + x_2 + x_3 + x_4 + x_6 + x_7 && \text{w.r.t.:} \\
0.7 \leq \quad & x_1 + x_2 + x_3 + x_6 && \leq 0.9 \\
0.1 \leq \quad & x_1 + x_2 + x_4 + x_5 && \leq 0.3 \\
0.8 \leq \quad & x_1 + x_3 + x_4 + x_7 && \leq 1 \\
& x_1 + x_2 + x_3 + x_4 + x_5 + x_6 + x_7 + x_8 = 1
\end{aligned}
$$

We can now solve EP-LP-MAX(Π'_{EM}, q) and EP-LP-MIN(Π'_{EM}, q) to get solution 0.9 ± 0.1. ∎

8.2.2 Analytical Model

For the analytical model (AM), we choose a structured argumentation framework (Rahwan et al. 2009) due to several characteristics that make such frameworks highly applicable to cyber-warfare domains. Unlike the EM, which describes probabilistic information about the state of the real world, the AM must allow for competing ideas—it *must be able to represent contradictory information*. The algorithmic approach allows for the creation of *arguments* based on the AM that may "compete" with each other to describe who conducted a given cyber-operation. In this competition—known as a *dialectical process*—one argument may defeat another based on a *comparison criterion* that determines the prevailing argument. Resulting from this process, the InCA framework will determine arguments that are *warranted* (those that are not *defeated* by other arguments) thereby providing a suitable explanation for a given cyber-operation.

The transparency provided by the system can allow analysts to identify potentially incorrect input information and fine-tune the models or, alternatively, collect more information. In short, argumentation-based reasoning has been studied as a natural way to manage a set of inconsistent information—it is the way humans settle disputes. As we will see, another desirable characteristic of (structured) argumentation frameworks is that, once a conclusion is reached, we are left with an explanation of how we arrived at it and information about why a given argument is warranted; this is very important information for analysts to have. In this section, we recall some preliminaries of the underlying argumentation framework used, and then introduce the analytical model (AM).

Defeasible Logic Programming with Presumptions

DeLP with Presumptions (PreDeLP) (Martinez et al. 2012) is a formalism combining Logic Programming with Defeasible Argumentation. We now briefly recall

$\Theta : \theta_{1a} = evidOf(baja, worm123)$
$\theta_{1b} = evidOf(mojave, worm123)$
$\theta_2 = motiv(baja, krasnovia)$

$\Omega : \omega_{1a} = \neg condOp(baja, worm123) \leftarrow condOp(mojave, worm123)$
$\omega_{1b} = \neg condOp(mojave, worm123) \leftarrow condOp(baja, worm123)$
$\omega_{2a} = condOp(baja, worm123) \leftarrow$
$\phantom{\Omega : \omega_{2a} = }evidOf(baja, worm123), isCap(baja, worm123),$
$\phantom{\Omega : \omega_{2a} = }motiv(baja, krasnovia), tgt(krasnovia, worm123)$
$\omega_{2b} = condOp(mojave, worm123) \leftarrow$
$\phantom{\Omega : \omega_{2b} = }evidOf(mojave, worm123), isCap(mojave, worm123),$
$\phantom{\Omega : \omega_{2b} = }motiv(mojave, krasnovia), tgt(krasnovia, worm123)$

$\Phi : \phi_1 = hasMseInvest(baja) \multimapdotinv$
$\phi_2 = tgt(krasnovia, worm123) \multimapdotinv$
$\phi_3 = \neg expCw(baja) \multimapdotinv$

$\Delta : \delta_{1a} = condOp(baja, worm123) \multimapdotinv evidOf(baja, worm123)$
$\delta_{1b} = condOp(mojave, worm123) \multimapdotinv evidOf(mojave, worm123)$
$\delta_2 = condOp(baja, worm123) \multimapdotinv isCap(baja, worm123)$
$\delta_3 = condOp(baja, worm123) \multimapdotinv motiv(baja, krasnovia), tgt(krasnovia, worm123)$
$\delta_4 = isCap(baja, worm123) \multimapdotinv hasMseInvest(baja)$
$\delta_{5a} = \neg isCap(baja, worm123) \multimapdotinv \neg expCw(baja)$
$\delta_{5b} = \neg isCap(mojave, worm123) \multimapdotinv \neg expCw(mojave)$

Fig. 8.3 A ground argumentation framework

the basics of PreDeLP; we refer the reader to (García and Simari 2004; Martinez et al. 2012) for the complete presentation. The formalism contains several different constructs: facts, presumptions, strict rules, and defeasible rules. Facts are statements about the analysis that can always be considered to be true, while presumptions are statements that may or may not be true. Strict rules specify logical consequences of a set of facts or presumptions (similar to an implication, though not the same) that must always occur, while defeasible rules specify logical consequences that may be assumed to be true when no contradicting information is present. These constructs are used in the construction of *arguments*, and are part of a PreDeLP program, which is a set of facts, strict rules, presumptions, and defeasible rules. Formally, we use the notation $\Pi_{AM} = (\Theta, \Omega, \Phi, \Delta)$ to denote a PreDeLP program, where Ω is the set of strict rules, Θ is the set of facts, Δ is the set of defeasible rules, and Φ is the set of presumptions. In Fig. 8.3, we provide an example Π_{AM}. We now describe each of these constructs in detail.

Facts (Θ) are ground literals representing atomic information or its negation, using strong negation "$\neg$". Note that all of the literals in our framework must be formed with a predicate from the set $\mathbf{P}_{AM}$. Note that information in this form cannot be contradicted.

Strict Rules (Ω) represent non-defeasible cause-and-effect information that resembles a material implication (though the semantics is different since the contrapositive does not hold) and are of the form $L_0 \longleftarrow L_1, \dots, L_n$, where L_0 is a ground literal and $\{L_i\}_{i>0}$ is a set of ground literals.

Presumptions (Φ) are ground literals of the same form as facts, except that they are not taken as being true but rather defeasible, which means that they can be contradicted. Presumptions are denoted in the same manner as facts, except that the symbol $\prec$ is added. While any literal can be used as a presumption in InCA, we specifically require all literals created with the predicate *condOp* to be defeasible.

Defeasible Rules (Δ) represent tentative knowledge that can be used if nothing can be posed against it. Just as presumptions are the defeasible counterpart of facts, defeasible rules are the defeasible counterpart of strict rules. They are of the form $L_0 \prec L_1, \dots, L_n$, where L_0 is a ground literal and $\{L_i\}_{i>0}$ is a set of ground literals. Note that with both strict and defeasible rules, *strong negation* is allowed in the head of rules, and hence may be used to represent contradictory knowledge.

We note that strict rules and facts are necessary constructs as they may not be true in all environmental conditions. We shall discuss this further in the next section with the introduction of an annotation function.

Even though the above constructs are ground, we allow for schematic versions with variables that are used to represent sets of ground rules. We denote variables with strings starting with an uppercase letter; Fig. 8.4 shows a non-ground example.

When a cyber-operation occurs, InCA must derive arguments as to who could have potentially conducted the action. Informally, an argument for a particular actor x conducting cyber-operation y is a consistent subset of the analytical model that entails the atom $condOp(x, y)$. If the argument contains only strict rules and facts, then it is *factual*. If it contains presumptions or defeasible rules, then it *defeasibly derives* that actor x conducted operation y.

Derivation follows the same mechanism of Logic Programming (Lloyd 1987). Since rule heads can contain strong negation, it is possible to defeasibly derive contradictory literals from a program. For the treatment of contradictory knowledge, PreDeLP incorporates a defeasible argumentation formalism that allows the identification of the pieces of knowledge that are in conflict, and through the previously mentioned *dialectical process* decides which information prevails as warranted.

This dialectical process involves the construction and evaluation of arguments that either support or interfere with a given query, building a *dialectical tree* in the process. Formally, we have:

Definition 2 (Argument) An *argument* $\mathcal{A}, L\rangle$ for a literal L is a pair of the literal and a (possibly empty) set of the EM ($\mathcal{A} \subseteq \Pi_{AM}$) that provides a minimal proof for L meeting the requirements: (1) L is defeasibly derived from $\mathcal{A}$, (2) $\Omega \cup \Theta \cup \mathcal{A}$ is not contradictory, and (3) $\mathcal{A}$ is a minimal subset of $\Delta \cup \Phi$ satisfying 1 and 2, denoted $\langle \mathcal{A}, L \rangle$.

Literal L is called the *conclusion* supported by the argument, and $\mathcal{A}$ is the *support* of the argument. An argument $\langle \mathcal{B}, L \rangle$ is a *subargument* of $\langle \mathcal{A}, L' \rangle$ iff $\mathcal{B} \subseteq \mathcal{A}$. An argument $\langle \mathcal{A}, L \rangle$ is *presumptive* iff $\mathcal{A} \cap \Phi$ is not empty. We will also use $\Omega(\mathcal{A}) = \mathcal{A} \cap \Omega$, $\Theta(\mathcal{A}) = \mathcal{A} \cap \Theta$, $\Delta(\mathcal{A}) = \mathcal{A} \cap \Delta$, and $\Phi(\mathcal{A}) = \mathcal{A} \cap \Phi$.

Θ : $\theta_1 = evidOf(baja, worm123)$
$\quad\ \theta_2 = motiv(baja, krasnovia)$

Ω : $\omega_1 = \neg condOp(X,O) \leftarrow condOp(X',O), X \neq X'$
$\quad\ \omega_2 = condOp(X,O) \leftarrow evidOf(X,O), isCap(X,O), motiv(X,X'), tgt(X',O), X \neq X'$

Φ : $\phi_1 = hasMseInvest(baja) \prec$
$\quad\ \phi_2 = tgt(krasnovia, worm123) \prec$
$\quad\ \phi_3 = \neg expCw(baja) \prec$

Δ : $\delta_1 = condOp(X,O) \prec evidOf(X,O)$
$\quad\ \delta_2 = condOp(X,O) \prec isCap(X,O)$
$\quad\ \delta_3 = condOp(X,O) \prec motiv(X,X'), tgt(X',O)$
$\quad\ \delta_4 = isCap(X,O) \prec hasMseInvest(X)$
$\quad\ \delta_5 = \neg isCap(X,O) \prec \neg expCw(X)$

Fig. 8.4 A non-ground argumentation framework

$\langle \mathscr{A}_1, condOp(baja, worm123) \rangle \quad \mathscr{A}_1 = \{\theta_{1a}, \delta_{1a}\}$
$\langle \mathscr{A}_2, condOp(baja, worm123) \rangle \quad \mathscr{A}_2 = \{\phi_1, \phi_2, \delta_4, \omega_{2a}, \theta_{1a}, \theta_2\}$
$\langle \mathscr{A}_3, condOp(baja, worm123) \rangle \quad \mathscr{A}_3 = \{\phi_1, \delta_2, \delta_4\}$
$\langle \mathscr{A}_4, condOp(baja, worm123) \rangle \quad \mathscr{A}_4 = \{\phi_2, \delta_3, \theta_2\}$
$\langle \mathscr{A}_5, isCap(baja, worm123) \rangle \quad \mathscr{A}_5 = \{\phi_1, \delta_4\}$
$\langle \mathscr{A}_6, \neg condOp(baja, worm123) \rangle \quad \mathscr{A}_6 = \{\delta_{1b}, \theta_{1b}, \omega_{1a}\}$
$\langle \mathscr{A}_7, \neg isCap(baja, worm123) \rangle \quad \mathscr{A}_7 = \{\phi_3, \delta_{5a}\}$

Fig. 8.5 Example ground arguments from Fig. 8.3

Note that our definition differs slightly from that of (Simari and Loui 1992) where DeLP is introduced, as we include strict rules and facts as part of the argument. The reason for this will become clear in Sect. 8.3. Arguments for our scenario are shown in the following example.

Example 5 Figure 8.5 shows example arguments based on the knowledge base from Fig. 8.3. Note that the following relationship exists:

$$\langle \mathcal{A}_5, isCap(baja, worm123) \rangle \text{ is a sub-argument of}$$

$$\langle \mathcal{A}_2, condOp(baja, worm123) \rangle \text{ and}$$

$$\langle \mathcal{A}_3, condOp(baja, worm123) \rangle. \qquad \blacksquare$$

Given argument $\langle \mathcal{A}_1, L_1 \rangle$, counter-arguments are arguments that contradict it. Argument $\langle \mathcal{A}_2, L_2 \rangle$ *counterargues* or *attacks* $\langle \mathcal{A}_1, L_1 \rangle$ literal L' iff there exists a subargument $\langle \mathcal{A}, L'' \rangle$ of $\langle \mathcal{A}_1, L_1 \rangle$ s.t. set $\Omega(\mathcal{A}_1) \cup \Omega(\mathcal{A}_2) \cup \Theta(\mathcal{A}_1) \cup \Theta(\mathcal{A}_2) \cup \{L_2, L''\}$ is contradictory.

Example 6 Consider the arguments from Example 5. The following are some of the attack relationships between them: $\mathcal{A}_1$, $\mathcal{A}_2$, $\mathcal{A}_3$, and $\mathcal{A}_4$ all attack $\mathcal{A}_6$; $\mathcal{A}_5$ attacks $\mathcal{A}_7$; and $\mathcal{A}_7$ attacks $\mathcal{A}_2$. $\qquad \blacksquare$

A *proper defeater* of an argument $\langle A, L \rangle$ is a counter-argument that—by some criterion—is considered to be better than $\langle A, L \rangle$; if the two are incomparable according to this criterion, the counterargument is said to be a *blocking* defeater. An important characteristic of PreDeLP is that the argument comparison criterion is modular, and thus the most appropriate criterion for the domain that is being represented can be selected; the default criterion used in classical defeasible logic programming (from which PreDeLP is derived) is *generalized specificity* (Stolzenburg et al. 2003), though an extension of this criterion is required for arguments using presumptions (Martinez et al. 2012). We briefly recall this criterion next—the first definition is for generalized specificity, which is subsequently used in the definition of presumption-enabled specificity.

Definition 3 Let $\Pi_{AM} = (\Theta, \Omega, \Phi, \Delta)$ be a PreDeLP program and let $\mathcal{F}$ be the set of all literals that have a defeasible derivation from Π_{AM}. An argument $\langle \mathcal{A}_1, L_1 \rangle$ is *preferred to* $\langle \mathcal{A}_2, L_2 \rangle$, denoted with $\mathcal{A}_1 \succ_{PS} \mathcal{A}_2$ iff the two following conditions hold:

1. For all $H \subseteq \mathcal{F}$, $\Omega(\mathcal{A}_1) \cup \Omega(\mathcal{A}_2) \cup H$ is non-contradictory: if there is a derivation for L_1 from $\Omega(\mathcal{A}_2) \cup \Omega(\mathcal{A}_1) \cup \Delta(\mathcal{A}_1) \cup H$, and there is no derivation for L_1 from $\Omega(\mathcal{A}_1) \cup \Omega(\mathcal{A}_2) \cup H$, then there is a derivation for L_2 from $\Omega(\mathcal{A}_1) \cup \Omega(\mathcal{A}_2) \cup \Delta(\mathcal{A}_2) \cup H$.
2. There is at least one set $H' \subseteq \mathcal{F}$, $\Omega(\mathcal{A}_1) \cup \Omega(\mathcal{A}_2) \cup H'$ is non-contradictory, such that there is a derivation for L_2 from $\Omega(\mathcal{A}_1) \cup \Omega(\mathcal{A}_2) \cup H' \cup \Delta(\mathcal{A}_2)$, there is no derivation for L_2 from $\Omega(\mathcal{A}_1) \cup \Omega(\mathcal{A}_2) \cup H'$, and there is no derivation for L_1 from $\Omega(\mathcal{A}_1) \cup \Omega(\mathcal{A}_2) \cup H' \cup \Delta(\mathcal{A}_1)$.

Intuitively, the principle of specificity says that, in the presence of two conflicting lines of argument about a proposition, the one that uses more of the available information is more convincing. A classic example involves a bird, Tweety, and arguments stating that it both flies (because it is a bird) and doesn't fly (because it is a penguin). The latter argument uses more information about Tweety—it is more specific—and is thus the stronger of the two.

Definition 4 (Martinez et al. 2012) Let $\Pi_{AM} = (\Theta, \Omega, \Phi, \Delta)$ be a PreDeLP program. An argument $\langle \mathcal{A}_1, L_1 \rangle$ is *preferred to* $\langle \mathcal{A}_2, L_2 \rangle$, denoted with $\mathcal{A}_1 \succ \mathcal{A}_2$ iff any of the following conditions hold:

1. $\langle \mathcal{A}_1, L_1 \rangle$ and $\langle \mathcal{A}_2, L_2 \rangle$ are both factual arguments and $\langle \mathcal{A}_1, L_1 \rangle \succ_{PS} \langle \mathcal{A}_2, L_2 \rangle$.
2. $\langle \mathcal{A}_1, L_1 \rangle$ is a factual argument and $\langle \mathcal{A}_2, L_2 \rangle$ is a presumptive argument.
3. $\langle \mathcal{A}_1, L_1 \rangle$ and $\langle \mathcal{A}_2, L_2 \rangle$ are presumptive arguments, and
   a) $\neg(\Phi(\mathcal{A}_1) \subseteq \Phi(\mathcal{A}_2))$, or
   b) $\Phi(\mathcal{A}_1) = \Phi(\mathcal{A}_2)$ and $\langle \mathcal{A}_1, L_1 \rangle \succ_{PS} \langle \mathcal{A}_2, L_2 \rangle$.

Generally, if $\mathcal{A}, \mathcal{B}$ are arguments with rules X and Y, resp., and $X \subset Y$, then $\mathcal{A}$ is stronger than $\mathcal{B}$. This also holds when $\mathcal{A}$ and $\mathcal{B}$ use presumptions P_1 and P_2, resp., and $P_1 \subset P_2$.

Example 7 The following are relationships between arguments from Example 5, based on Definitions 3 and 4:

$\mathcal{A}_1$ and $\mathcal{A}_6$ are incomparable (blocking defeaters);

$\mathcal{A}_6 \succ \mathcal{A}_2$, and thus $\mathcal{A}_6$ defeats $\mathcal{A}_2$;

$\mathcal{A}_6 \succ \mathcal{A}_3$, and thus $\mathcal{A}_6$ defeats $\mathcal{A}_3$;

$\mathcal{A}_6 \succ \mathcal{A}_4$, and thus $\mathcal{A}_6$ defeats $\mathcal{A}_4$;

$\mathcal{A}_5$ and $\mathcal{A}_7$ are incomparable (blocking defeaters). ∎

A sequence of arguments called an *argumentation line* thus arises from this attack relation, where each argument defeats its predecessor. To avoid undesirable sequences, that may represent circular or fallacious argumentation lines, in DeLP an *argumentation line* is *acceptable* if it satisfies certain constraints (see García and Simari 2004). A literal L is *warranted* if there exists a non-defeated argument $\mathcal{A}$ supporting L.

Clearly, there can be more than one defeater for a particular argument $\langle \mathcal{A}, L \rangle$. Therefore, many acceptable argumentation lines could arise from $\langle \mathcal{A}, L \rangle$, leading to a tree structure. The tree is built from the set of all argumentation lines rooted in the initial argument. In a dialectical tree, every node (except the root) represents a defeater of its parent, and leaves correspond to undefeated arguments. Each path from the root to a leaf corresponds to a different acceptable argumentation line. A dialectical tree provides a structure for considering all the possible acceptable argumentation lines that can be generated for deciding whether an argument is defeated. We call this tree *dialectical* because it represents an exhaustive dialectical analysis (in the sense of providing reasons for and against a position) for the argument in its root. For argument $\langle \mathcal{A}, L \rangle$, we denote its dialectical tree with $\mathcal{T}(\langle \mathcal{A}, L \rangle)$.

Given a literal L and an argument $\langle \mathcal{A}, L \rangle$, in order to decide whether or not a literal L is warranted, every node in the dialectical tree $\mathcal{T}(\langle \mathcal{A}, L \rangle)$ is recursively marked as "D" (*defeated*) or "U" (*undefeated*), obtaining a marked dialectical tree $\mathcal{T}^*(\langle \mathcal{A}, L \rangle)$ where:

- All leaves in $\mathcal{T}^*(\langle \mathcal{A}, L \rangle)$ are marked as "U"s, and
- Let $\langle \mathcal{B}, q \rangle$ be an inner node of $\mathcal{T}^*(\langle \mathcal{A}, L \rangle)$. Then, $\langle \mathcal{B}, q \rangle$ will be marked as "U" iff every child of $\langle \mathcal{B}, q \rangle$ is marked as "D". Node $\langle \mathcal{B}, q \rangle$ will be marked as "D" iff it has at least a child marked as "U".

Given argument $\langle \mathcal{A}, L \rangle$ over Π_{AM}, if the root of $\mathcal{T}^*(\langle \mathcal{A}, L \rangle)$ is marked "U", then $\mathcal{T}^*(\langle \mathcal{A}, h \rangle)$ *warrants* L and that L is *warranted* from Π_{AM}. (Warranted arguments correspond to those in the grounded extension of a Dung argumentation system (Dung 1995)).

We can then extend the idea of a dialectical tree to a *dialectical forest*. For a given literal L, a dialectical forest $\mathcal{F}(L)$ consists of the set of dialectical trees for all arguments for L. We shall denote a marked dialectical forest, the set of all marked dialectical trees for arguments for L, as $\mathcal{F}^*(L)$. Hence, for a literal L, we say it is *warranted* if there is at least one argument for that literal in the dialectical forest

$af(\theta_1) = origIP(worm123, baja) \vee (malwInOp(worm123, o) \wedge (mwHint(worm123, baja) \vee$
$\qquad (compilLang(worm123, c) \wedge nativLang(baja, c))))$
$af(\theta_2) = inLgConf(baja, krasnovia)$
$af(\omega_1) = \text{True}$
$af(\omega_2) = \text{True}$
$af(\phi_1) = mseTT(baja, 2) \vee govCybLab(baja)$
$af(\phi_2) = malwInOp(worm123, o') \wedge infGovSys(krasnovia, worm123)$
$af(\phi_3) = cybCapAge(baja, 5)$
$af(\delta_1) = \text{True}$
$af(\delta_2) = \text{True}$
$af(\delta_3) = \text{True}$
$af(\delta_4) = \text{True}$
$af(\delta_5) = \text{True}$

Fig. 8.6 Example annotation function

$\mathcal{F}^*(L)$ that is labeled "U", *not warranted* if there is at least one argument for literal $\neg L$ in the forest $\mathcal{F}^*(\neg L)$ that is labeled "U", and *undecided* otherwise.

8.3 The InCA Framework

Having defined our environmental and analytical models (Π_{EM}, Π_{AM} respectively), we now define how the two relate, which allows us to complete the definition of our InCA framework.

The key intuition here is that given a Π_{AM}, every element of $\Omega \cup \Theta \Delta \cup \Phi$ might only hold in certain worlds in the set $\mathcal{W}_{EM}$—that is, worlds specified by the environment model. As formulas over the environmental atoms in set $\mathbf{G}_{EM}$ specify subsets of $\mathcal{W}_{EM}$ (i.e., the worlds that satisfy them), we can use these formulas to identify the conditions under which a component of $\Omega \cup \Theta \Delta \cup \Phi$ *can be* true.

Recall that we use the notation $formula_{EM}$ to denote the set of all possible formulas over $\mathbf{G}_{EM}$. Therefore, it makes sense to associate elements of $\Omega \cup \Theta \cup \Phi$ with a formula from $formula_{EM}$. In doing so, we can in turn compute the probabilities of subsets of $\Omega \cup \Theta \Delta \cup \Phi$ using the information contained in Π_{EM}, which we shall describe shortly. We first introduce the notion of *annotation function*, which associates elements of $\Omega \cup \Theta \cup \Phi$ with elements of $formula_{EM}$.

We also note that, by using the annotation function (see Fig. 8.6), we may have certain statements that appear as both facts and presumptions (likewise for strict and defeasible rules). However, these constructs would have different annotations, and thus be applicable in different worlds. Suppose we added the following presumptions to our running example:

$\phi_3 = evidOf(X, O) \prec$, and
$\phi_4 = motiv(X, X') \prec$.

Note that these presumptions are constructed using the same formulas as facts θ_1, θ_2.

Suppose we extend *af* as follows:

$$af(\phi_3) = malwInOp(M, O) \wedge malwareRel(M, M') \wedge mwHint(M', X)$$

$$af(\phi_4) = inLgConf(Y, X') \wedge cooper(X, Y)$$

So, for instance, unlike θ_1, ϕ_3 can potentially be true in any world of the form:

$$\{malwInOp(M, O), malwareRel(M, M'), mwHint(M', X)\}$$

while θ_1 cannot be considered in any those worlds.

With the annotation function, we now have all the components to formally define an InCA framework.

Definition 5 (InCA Framework) Given environmental model Π_{EM}, analytical model Π_{AM}, and annotation function *af*, $\mathcal{I} = (\Pi_{EM}, \Pi_{AM}, af)$ is an **InCA framework**.

Given the setup described above, we consider a *world-based* approach—the defeat relationship among arguments will depend on the current state of the world (based on the EM). Hence, we now define the status of an argument with respect to a given world.

Definition 6 (Validity) Given InCA framework $\mathcal{I} = (\Pi_{EM}, \Pi_{AM}, af)$, argument $\langle \mathcal{A}, L \rangle$ is valid w.r.t. world $w \in \mathcal{W}_{EM}$ iff $\forall c \in \mathcal{A}, w \models af(c)$.

In other words, an argument is valid with respect to w if the rules, facts, and presumptions in that argument are present in w—the argument can then be built from information that is available in that world. In this paper, we extend the notion of validity to argumentation lines, dialectical trees, and dialectical forests in the expected way (an argumentation line is valid w.r.t. w iff all arguments that comprise that line are valid w.r.t. w).

Example 8 Consider worlds $w_1, \ldots, w_8$ from Example 4 along with the argument $\langle \mathcal{A}_5, isCap(baja, worm123) \rangle$ from Example 5. This argument is valid in worlds w_1—w_4, w_6, and w_7.   ∎

We now extend the idea of a dialectical tree w.r.t. worlds—so, for a given world $w \in \mathcal{W}_{EM}$, the dialectical (resp., marked dialectical) tree induced by w is denoted by $\mathcal{T}_w\langle \mathcal{A}, L \rangle$ (resp., $\mathcal{T}_w^*\langle \mathcal{A}, L \rangle$). We require that all arguments and defeaters in these trees to be valid with respect to w. Likewise, we extend the notion of dialectical forests in the same manner (denoted with $\mathcal{F}_w(L)$ and $\mathcal{F}_w^*(L)$, respectively). Based on these concepts we introduce the notion of *warranting scenario*.

Definition 7 (Warranting Scenario) Let $\mathcal{I} = (\Pi_{EM}, \Pi_{AM}, af)$ be an InCA framework and L be a ground literal over $\mathbf{G}_{AM}$; a world $w \in \mathcal{W}_{EM}$ is said to be a *warranting scenario* for L (denoted $w \vdash_{war} L$) iff there is a dialectical forest $\mathcal{F}_w^*(L)$ in which L is warranted and $\mathcal{F}_w^*(L)$ is valid w.r.t w.

Example 9 Following from Example 8, argument $\langle \mathcal{A}_5, isCap(baja, worm123) \rangle$ is warranted in worlds w_3, w_6, and w_7.   ∎

Hence, the set of worlds in the EM where a literal L in the AM *must* be true is exactly the set of warranting scenarios—these are the "necessary" worlds, denoted:

$$nec(L) = \{w \in \mathcal{W}_{EM} \mid (w \vdash_{war} L)\}.$$

Now, the set of worlds in the EM where AM literal L *can* be true is the following— these are the "possible" worlds, denoted:

$$poss(L) = \{w \in \mathcal{W}_{EM} \mid w \nvdash_{war} \neg L\}.$$

The following example illustrates these concepts.

Example 10 Following from Example 8:

$$nec(isCap(baja, worm123)) = \{w_3, w_6, w_7\} \text{ and}$$

$$poss(isCap(baja, worm123)) = \{w_1, w_2, w_3, w_4, w_6, w_7\}. \qquad \blacksquare$$

Hence, for a given InCA framework $\mathcal{I}$, if we are given a probability distribution Pr over the worlds in the EM, then we can compute an upper and lower bound on the probability of literal L (denoted $\mathbf{P}_{L,Pr,\mathcal{I}}$) as follows:

$$\ell_{L,Pr,\mathcal{I}} = \sum_{w \in nec(L)} Pr(w),$$

$$u_{L,Pr,\mathcal{I}} = \sum_{w \in poss(L)} Pr(w),$$

and

$$\ell_{L,Pr,\mathcal{I}} \leq \mathbf{P}_{L,Pr,\mathcal{I}} \leq u_{L,Pr,\mathcal{I}}.$$

Now let us consider the computation of probability bounds on a literal when we are given a knowledge base Π_{EM} in the environmental model, which is specified in $\mathcal{I}$, instead of a probability distribution over all worlds. For a given world $w \in \mathcal{W}_{EM}$, let $for(w) = (\bigwedge_{a \in w} a) \wedge (\bigwedge_{a \notin w} \neg a)$—that is, a formula that is satisfied only by world w. Now we can determine the upper and lower bounds on the probability of a literal w.r.t. Π_{EM} (denoted $\mathbf{P}_{L,\mathcal{I}}$) as follows:

$$\ell_{L,\mathcal{I}} = \text{EP-LP-MIN} \left(\Pi_{EM}, \bigvee_{w \in nec(L)} for(w) \right),$$

$$u_{L,\mathcal{I}} = \text{EP-LP-MAX} \left(\Pi_{EM}, \bigvee_{w \in poss(L)} for(w) \right),$$

and

$$\ell_{L,\mathcal{I}} \leq \mathbf{P}_{L,\mathcal{I}} \leq u_{L,\mathcal{I}}.$$

Hence, we have:

$$\mathbf{P}_{L,\mathcal{I}} = \left(\ell_{L,\mathcal{I}} + \frac{u_{L,\mathcal{I}} - \ell_{L,\mathcal{I}}}{2}\right) \pm \frac{u_{L,\mathcal{I}} - \ell_{L,\mathcal{I}}}{2}.$$

Example 11 Following from Example 8, argument $\langle \mathcal{A}_5, isCap(baja, worm123)\rangle$, we can compute $\mathbf{P}_{isCap(baja,worm123),\mathcal{I}}$ (where $\mathcal{I} = (\Pi'_{EM}, \Pi_{AM}, af)$). Note that for the upper bound, the linear program we need to set up is as in Example 4. For the lower bound, the objective function changes to: $\min x_3 + x_6 + x_7$. From these linear constraints, we obtain: $\mathbf{P}_{isCap(baja,worm123),\mathcal{I}} = 0.75 \pm 0.25$. ∎

8.4 Attribution Queries

We now have the necessary elements required to formally define the kind of queries that correspond to the attribution problems studied in this paper.

Definition 8 Let $\mathcal{I} = (\Pi_{EM}, \Pi_{AM}, af)$ be an InCA framework, $\mathcal{S} \subseteq \mathbf{C}_{act}$ (the set of "suspects"), $\mathcal{O} \in \mathbf{C}_{ops}$ (the "operation"), and $\mathcal{E} \subseteq \mathbf{G}_{EM}$ (the "evidence"). An actor $\mathsf{A} \in \mathcal{S}$ is said to be a *most probable suspect* iff there does not exist $\mathsf{A}' \in \mathcal{S}$ such that $\mathbf{P}_{condOp(\mathsf{A}',\mathcal{O}),\mathcal{I}'} > \mathbf{P}_{condOp(\mathsf{A},\mathcal{O})\mathcal{I}'}$ where $\mathcal{I}' = (\Pi_{EM} \cup \Pi_{\mathcal{E}}, \Pi_{AM}, af)$ with $\Pi_{\mathcal{E}}$ defined as $\bigcup_{c \in \mathcal{E}} \{c : 1 \pm 0\}$.

Given the above definition, we refer to $Q = (\mathcal{I}, \mathcal{S}, \mathcal{O}, \mathcal{E})$ as an *attribution query*, and A as an *answer* to Q. We note that in the above definition, the items of evidence are added to the environmental model with a probability of 1 ± 0. While in general this may be the case, there are often instances in analysis of a cyber-operation where the evidence may be true with some degree of uncertainty. Allowing for probabilistic evidence is a simple extension to Definition 8 that does not cause any changes to the results of this paper.

To understand how uncertain evidence can be present in a cyber-security scenario, consider the following. In Symantec's initial analysis of the Stuxnet worm, they found the routine designed to attack the S7-417 logic controller was incomplete, and hence would not function (Falliere et al. 2011). However, industrial control system expert Ralph Langner claimed that the incomplete code would run provided a missing data block is generated, which he thought was possible (Langner et al. 2011). In this case, though the code was incomplete, there was clearly uncertainty regarding its usability. This situation provides a real-world example of the need to compare arguments—in this case, in the worlds where both arguments are valid, Langner's argument would likely defeat Symantec's by generalized specificity (the outcome, of course, will depend on the exact formalization of the two). Note that Langner was later vindicated by the discovery of an older sample, Stuxnet 0.5, which generated the data block.[1]

InCA also allows for a variety of relevant scenarios to the attribution problem. For instance, we can easily allow for the modeling of non-state actors by extending the available constants—for example, traditional groups such as Hezbollah, which has previously wielded its cyber-warfare capabilities in operations against Israel (Shakarian et al. 2013). Likewise, the InCA can also be used to model cooperation among different actors in performing an attack, including the relationship between non-state actors and nation-states, such as the potential connection between Iran and militants stealing UAV feeds in Iraq, or the much-hypothesized relationship between hacktivist youth groups and the Russian government (Shakarian et al. 2013). Another aspect that can be modeled is deception where, for instance, an actor may leave false clues in a piece of malware to lead an analyst to believe a third party conducted the operation. Such a deception scenario can be easily created by adding additional rules in the AM that allow for the creation of such counter-arguments. Another type of deception that could occur include attacks being launched from a system not in the responsible party's area, but under their control (e.g., see Shadows in the Cloud 2010). Again, modeling who controls a given system can be easily accomplished in our framework, and doing so would simply entail extending an argumentation line. Further, campaigns of cyber-operations can also be modeled, as well as relationships among malware and/or attacks (as detailed in APT1 2013).

As with all of these abilities, InCA provides the analyst the means to model a complex situation in cyber-warfare but saves him from carrying out the reasoning associated with such a situation. Additionally, InCA results are constructive, so an analyst can "trace-back" results to better understand how the system arrived at a given conclusion.

8.5 Open Questions

In this section we review some major areas of research to address to move InCA toward a deployed system.

8.5.1 Rule Learning

The InCA framework depends on logical rules and statements as part of the input, though there are existing bodies of work we can leverage (decision tree rule learning, inductive logic programming, etc.) there are some specific challenges with regard to InCA that we must account for, specifically:

---

[1] http://www.symantec.com/connect/blogs/stuxnet-05-disrupting-uranium-processing-natanz.

- Quickly learning probabilistic rules from data received as an input stream
- Learning of the annotation function
- Identification of the diagnosticity of new additions to the knowledgebase
- Learning rules that combine multiple, disparate sources (i.e. malware analysis and PCAP files, for instance)

8.5.2   Belief Revision

Even though we allow for inconsistencies in the AM portion of the model, inconsistency can arise even with a consistent EM. In a companion paper, (Shakarian et al. 2014) we introduce the following notion of consistency.

Definition 9   InCA program $\mathcal{I} = (\Pi_{EM}, \Pi_{AM}, af)$, with $\Pi_{AM} = \langle \Theta, \Omega, \Phi, \Delta \rangle$, is *Type II consistent* iff: given any probability distribution Pr that satisfies Π_{EM}, if there exists a world $w \in \mathcal{W}_{EM}$ such that $\bigcup_{x \in \Theta \cup \Omega \mid w \models af(x)} \{x\}$ is inconsistent, then we have $Pr(w) = 0$.

Thus, any EM world in which the set of associated facts and strict rules are inconsistent (we refer to this as "classical consistency") must always be assigned a zero probability. The intuition is as follows: any subset of facts and strict rules are thought to be true under certain circumstances—these circumstances are determined through the annotation function and can be expressed as sets of EM worlds. Suppose there is a world where two contradictory facts can both be considered to be true (based on the annotation function). If this occurs, then there must not exist a probability distribution that satisfies the program Π_{EM} that assigns such a world a non-zero probability, as this world leads to an inconsistency.

While we have studied this theoretically (Shakarian et al. 2014), several important challenges remain: How do different belief revision methods affect the results of attribution queries? In particular, can we develop tractable algorithms for belief revision in the InCA framework? Further, finding efficient methods for re-computing attribution queries following a belief revision operation is a related concern for future work.

8.5.3   Temporal Reasoning

Cyber-security data often has an inherent temporal component (in particular, PCAP files, system logs, and traditional intelligence). One way to represent this type of information in InCA is by replacing the EM with a probabilistic temporal logic (i.e. Hansson and Jonsson 1994; Dekhtyar et al. 1999; Shakarian et al. 2011; Shakarian and Simari 2012). However, even though this would be a relatively straightforward adjustment to the framework, it leads to several interesting questions, specifically:

- Can we identify hacking groups responsible for a series of incidents over a period of time (a cyber campaign)?
- Can we identify the group responsible for a campaign if it is not known a priori?
- Can we differentiate between multiple campaigns conducted by multiple culprits in time-series data?

8.5.4 Abductive Inference Queries

We may often have a case where more than one culprit is attributed to the same cyber-attack with nearly the same probabilities. In this case, can we identify certain evidence that, if found, can lead us to better differentiate among the potential culprits? In the intelligence community, this is often referred as identifying *intelligence gaps*. We can also frame this as an abductive inference problem (Reggia and Peng 1990). This type of problems leads to several interesting challenges:

- Can we identify all pieces of diagnostic evidence that would satisfy an important intelligence gap?
- Can we identify diagnostic evidence under constraints (i.e., taking into account limitations on the type of evidence that can be collected)?
- In the case where a culprit is attributed with a high probability, can we identify evidence that can falsify the finding?

8.6 Conclusions

In this paper we introduced InCA, a new framework that allows the modeling of various cyber-warfare/cyber-security scenarios in order to help answer the attribution question by means of a combination of probabilistic modeling and argumentative reasoning. This is the first framework, to our knowledge, that addresses the attribution problem while allowing for multiple pieces of evidence from different sources, including traditional (non-cyber) forms of intelligence such as human intelligence. Further, our framework is the first to extend Defeasible Logic Programming with probabilistic information. Currently, we are implementing InCA along with the associated algorithms and heuristics to answer these queries.

Acknowledgments This work was supported by UK EPSRC grant EP/J008346/1—"PrOQAW", ERC grant 246858—"DIADEM", by NSF grant #1117761, by the National Security Agency under the Science of Security Lablet grant (SoSL), Army Research Office project 2GDATXR042, and DARPA project R.0004972.001.

References

Shadows in the Cloud: Investigating Cyber Espionage 2.0. Tech. rep., Information Warfare Monitor and Shadowserver Foundation (2010)

APT1: Exposing one of China's cyber espionage units. Mandiant (tech. report) (2013)

Altheide, C.: Digital Forensics with Open Source Tools. Syngress (2011)

Dekhtyar, A., Dekhtyar, M.I., Subrahmanian, V.S.: Temporal probabilistic logic programs. In: ICLP 1999, pp. 109–123. The MIT Press, Cambridge, MA, USA (1999)

Dung, P.M.: On the acceptability of arguments and its fundamental role in nonmonotonic reasoning, logic programming and n-person games. Artif. Intell. **77**, pp. 321–357 (1995)

Falliere, N., Murchu, L.O., Chien, E.: W32.Stuxnet Dossier Version 1.4. Symantec Corporation (2011)

García, A.J., Simari, G.R.: Defeasible logic programming: An argumentative approach. TPLP **4**(1–2), 95–138 (2004)

Hansson, H., Jonsson, B.: A logic for reasoning about time and probability. Formal Aspects of Computing **6**, 512–535 (1994)

Heuer, R.J.: Psychology of Intelligence Analysis. Center for the Study of Intelligence (1999)

Khuller, S., Martinez, M.V., Nau, D.S., Sliva, A., Simari, G.I., Subrahmanian, V.S.: Computing most probable worlds of action probabilistic logic programs: scalable estimation for $10^{30,000}$ worlds. AMAI **51**(2–4), 295–331 (2007)

Langner, R.: Matching Langner Stuxnet analysis and Symantic dossier update. Langner Communications GmbH (2011)

Lloyd, J.W.: Foundations of Logic Programming, 2nd Edition. Springer (1987)

Martinez, M.V., García, A.J., Simari, G.R.: On the use of presumptions in structured defeasible reasoning. In: Proc. of COMMA, pp. 185–196 (2012)

Nilsson, N.J.: Probabilistic logic. Artif. Intell. **28**(1), 71–87 (1986)

Rahwan, I., Simari, G.R.: Argumentation in Artificial Intelligence. Springer (2009)

Reggia, J.A., Peng, Y.: Abductive inference models for diagnostic problem-solving. Springer-Verlag New York, Inc., New York, NY, USA (1990)

Shakarian, P., Parker, A., Simari, G.I., Subrahmanian, V.S.: Annotated probabilistic temporal logic. TOCL **12**(2), 14 (2011)

Shakarian, P., Simari, G.I., Subrahmanian, V.S.: Annotated probabilistic temporal logic: Approximate fixpoint implementation. ACM Trans. Comput. Log. **13**(2), 13 (2012)

Shakarian, P., Shakarian, J., Ruef, A.: Introduction to Cyber-Warfare: A Multidisciplinary Approach. Syngress (2013)

Shakarian, P., Simari, G.I., Falappa, M.A.: Belief revision in structured probabilistic argumentation. In: Proceedings of FoIKS, pp. 324–343 (2014)

Simari, G.R., Loui, R.P.: A mathematical treatment of defeasible reasoning and its implementation. Artif. Intell. **53**(2-3), 125–157 (1992)

Simari, G.I., Martinez, M.V., Sliva, A., Subrahmanian, V.S.: Focused most probable world computations in probabilistic logic programs. AMAI **64**(2–3), 113–143 (2012)

Spitzner, L.: Honeypots: Catching the Insider Threat. In: Proc. of ACSAC 2003, pp. 170–179. IEEE Computer Society (2003)

Stolzenburg, F., García, A., Chesñevar, C.I., Simari, G.R.: Computing Generalized Specificity. Journal of Non-Classical Logics **13**(1), 87–113 (2003)

Thonnard, O., Mees, W., Dacier, M.: On a multicriteria clustering approach for attack attribution. SIGKDD Explorations **12**(1), 11–20 (2010)

Chapter 9
The Human Factor in Cybersecurity: Robust & Intelligent Defense

Julie L. Marble, W. F. Lawless, Ranjeev Mittu, Joseph Coyne,
Myriam Abramson and Ciara Sibley

Abstract In this chapter, we review the pervasiveness of cyber threats and the roles of both attackers and cyber users (i.e. the targets of the attackers); the lack of awareness of cyber-threats by users; the complexity of the new cyber environment, including cyber risks; engineering approaches and tools to mitigate cyber threats; and current research to identify proactive steps that users and groups can take to reduce cyber-threats. In addition, we review the research needed on the psychology of users that poses risks to users from cyber-attacks. For the latter, we review the available theory at the individual and group levels that may help individual users, groups and organizations take actions against cyber threats. We end with future research needs and conclusions. In our discussion, we first agreed that cyber threats are making cyber environments more complex and uncomfortable for average users; second, we concluded that various factors are important (e.g., timely actions are often necessary in cyber space to counter the threats of the attacks that commonly occur at internet speeds, but also the 'slow and low' attacks that are difficult to detect, threats that occur only after pre-specified conditions have been satisfied that trigger an unsuspecting

W. F. Lawless (✉)
Paine College, 1235 15th Street, 30901, GA, Augusta, USA
e-mail: wlawless@paine.edu

R. Mittu · J. Coyne · M. Abramson · C. Sibley
Information Technology Division, Naval Research Laboratory,
4555 Overlook Ave SW, 20375 Washington, DC, USA
e-mail: ranjeev.mittu@nrl.navy.mil

J. Coyne
e-mail: joseph.coyne@nrl.navy.mil

M. Abramson
e-mail: myriam.abramson@nrl.navy.mil

C. Sibley
e-mail: ciara.sibley@nrl.navy.mil

J. L. Marble
Advanced Physics Laboratory Senior Human Factors Scientist Asymetric Operations Sector,
Johns Hopkins University, 11100 Johns Hopkins Road, Mailstop MP6 S334,
Laurel, MD 20723, USA
e-mail: julie.marble@navy.mil

© Springer International Publishing Switzerland 2015   173
S. Jajodia et al. (eds.), *Cyber Warfare,* Advances in Information Security 56,
DOI 10.1007/978-3-319-14039-1_9

attack). Third, we concluded that advanced persistent threats (APTs) pose a risk to users but also to national security (viz., the persistent threats posed by other Nations). Fourth, we contend that using "red" teams to search cyber defenses for vulnerabilities encourages users and organizations to better defend themselves. Fifth, the current state of theory leaves many questions unanswered that researchers must pursue to mitigate or neutralize present and future threats. Lastly, we agree with the literature that cyber space has had a dramatic impact on American life and that the cyber domain is a breeding ground for disorder. However, we also believe that actions by users and researchers can be taken to stay safe and ahead of existing and future threats.

9.1   The Cyber Problem

Introduction In our approach to cyber threats, we will review the increasing complexity of, and risks in, the new cyber environment. We will discuss cyber defenses and tools used in defenses, such as the use of engineering to mitigate cyber threats. More fully, we will review and discuss the pervasiveness of cyber-attacks from multiple perspectives: first at the individual level from the perspective of the human attacker and the user, the attacker's target; and second from the perspective of teams and organizations. We end with future research needs and conclusions.

Our Modern Digital Age We live and work in a digital age, where access to information of widely varying values is ubiquitous. However, users fail to comprehend the value of their personal information (e.g., birthdays, on-line browsing behavior, social interactions, etc.) to malicious actors. Information has always been important to survival; the original purpose of the internet was to share the information that would improve global social well-being (Glowniak 1998). The security of information has been defined[1] as "... protecting information and information systems from unauthorized access, use, disclosure, disruption, modification, or destruction ..." Security directly describes how well a system is protected and indirectly the value of the information being protected (Lewis and Baker 2014). However in the modern digital age, sharing information now competes with protecting private information from unintended recipients; the complexity of security has increased to protect information that is deemed private, and the interaction between the complexity of networks and security defenses has led to increasing opacity in the functioning of networks and computers for typical users. Furthermore, as complexity increases with greater security features, systems and protocols, the "increased use of networked systems introduces [even newer] cyber vulnerabilities ..." (Loukas et al. 2013).

Digital space, or cyberspace, for our purposes consists of the three overlapping terrains as determined by Kello (2013, p. 17): (1) the internet (all interconnected computers); (2) the subset of websites comprising the world wide web accessible by only a URL; and (3) a cyber-archipelago of computer systems in theoretical seclusion,

---

[1] From 44 USC § 3542; see http://www.law.cornell.edu/uscode/text/44/3544.

separated from the internet. As Kello notes, these terrains imply that not all threats arrive from the internet, and the cyber-archipelago can only be attacked with access, which emphasizes the role of the human user and the potential for human error with the security of systems. This reduces the target space for malicious actors to access remote and closed targets, each susceptible to different exploits.

Martinez (2014) and others believe that the greatest cyber threats are internal threats from insiders; in particular both malicious dissatisfied actors as well as the unaware insider. Salim (2014), with data from Symantec Corporation's 2013 Internet Security Threat Report,[2] noted that 40 % of data breaches in 2012 were attributed to external hackers and 23 % to accidental data compromise by unaware users. However, for the 40 % of the breaches by hackers, it remains unknown how much of these breaches was due to manipulating users or defenders into an action that produced an exploit.

Cyber threats range over sources and types. For example spear-phishing emails typically target specific individuals or users, while malware is typically directed against websites or processes (e.g., Stuxnet). There are a varying range of malicious actors who work along a continuum of personal and ideological goals and intents, from individual actors, to hacktivists and on through to nation-state actors.

Social media is exploited by malicious actors who use it as a conduit to identify vulnerabilities and targets. Information gleaned from social media can be used to tailor spear-phishing and other exploits. Against the most common attacks (such as phishing email with malicious links or false advertisements that allow the download of malware), the typical defense is training people to "not to click", i.e., to just say "no". However, cyber space is too complex for simple "not to click" defenses; instead, as our arguments will show, multiple defenses that include modeling the cognitive decision-making of attackers and defenders are needed to mitigate the threats in this complex space.

Cyber threats can range from petty cybercrime (such as identity theft) to intense cyber war (for example, Russia's shutdown of media in Ukraine). However, petty crimes like identity theft can be leveraged as part of intense cyber war tactics, such as credit card theft to finance purchase of resources. In the cyber environment, asymmetric[3] capabilities magnify risk, threat and consequence arising even from a single actor; geographically distant adversaries can have significant real-world impacts with little effort and risk, expense or cost. Together, this means that cyber warfare is a new kind of war. After interviewing Pomerantsev, a journalist who wrote about cyberwar in a *Foreign Policy* article, the Washington Post (2014, 5/30) wrote:

> Traditional warfare is very expensive, requiring massive buildups and drains on the state treasury for military campaigns in far-flung locales. The new warfare will be cheap, low-intensity and most likely, waged primarily in cyberspace. Attacks will occur against economic

---

[2] www.symantec.com/about/news/resources/press_kits/detail.jsp?pkid = istr-18.
[3] Asymmetry is a lack of symmetry; e.g., asymmetric warfare is war between belligerents whose relative military power differs significantly, or whose strategy or tactics differs significantly; retrieved from http://en.wikipedia.org/wiki/Asymmetric_warfare.

targets rather than military targets. Taking down a stock market . . . has greater tactical value than taking out a hardened military target. . . . It is the ultimate asymmetric war in which we do not even know who to attack, or how or when.

Cyber warfare can yield "non-linear war" (Pomerantsev 2014), in which a smaller, geographically distant but highly capable opponent is able to have significant impacts on a much larger opponent; furthermore, due to the nature of the cyber environment, traceability of these actions can be limited. In August 2010, (Fox News 2010, 3/8) the U.S. publicly warned about the Chinese military's use of cyber-attacks run by civilian computer experts. These attacks were directed against American companies and government agencies, with the Chinese computer network, "Ghostnet", as one of several identified. The US alleged that these malicious military and civilian teams were developing computer viruses and other cyber capabilities to attack US infrastructure systems where vulnerable (Wall Street Journal 2009, 4/8).

Kello (2013, p. 39) cites Chairman of the Joint Chiefs of Staff Adm Michael Mullen's concern that the cyber tools under development in multiple nations may lead to a 'catastrophic' cyber event. The US is as vulnerable as any other nation or individual, causing the cyber domain to yield newly observable influences on patterns of rivalry (pp. 30–31). Concerning the individual impact of cybercrime, Lewis and Baker (2014) try to keep cyber threats in perspective: "Criminals still have difficulty turning stolen data into financial gain, but the constant stream of news contributes to a growing sense that cybercrime is out of control." While they estimate annual loses at $ 4–600 Billion, a fraction of one percent of global GDP, they go on to add that, today, effects of cybercrime are most notable in the shifts in employment away from highly valuable jobs, in part by damaging company performance and its impact to global growth through damage to national economies and to trade, competition and innovation.

Lewis and Baker (2014) caution that the financial losses may be even larger than they have reported because many cyber events go unreported for many reasons, including a desire to maintain face, protect intellectual property, and corporate privacy. In general, however, not only are most cybercrimes unreported, it is also not unusual for companies to suppress news they think reflects negatively upon them. Recently, for example, based on an internal investigation of General Motors' ignition switch recalls, Valukas (2014) found "a company hobbled by an internal culture that discouraged the flow of bad news". A company may ignore its own security warnings, as apparently occurred in the 2013 Target debit card hack. In this case, the FireEye detection system used by Target could have stopped the malware from acting to send out the stolen data. Apparently, in an instance of what is commonly called "human error", Target's security team turned that function off.[4] But that simplistic finding on the Target security team ignores the complexity of network architecture, and the difficulty of understanding the interactions between tools. Humans do not willingly set themselves up for failure, and generally take the actions that they perceive as

---

[4] See at http://www.businessweek.com/articles/2014-03-13/target-missed-alarms-in-epic-hack-of-credit-card-data.

the most logical in the situation. However, there are few tools to support the performance of cyber defenders that can actively predict the consequences of actions or the emerging features of networks.

9.1.1 Office, Home, and Online Shopping

Cyber threats arise not only in the office, but also in the home, with social media, and with on-line shopping. For an example, Cisco reported[5] that 68 % of users surveyed said they had had computer trouble caused by spyware or adware; 60 % of those were unsure of their problem's origin; 20 % of those who tried to fix the problem said it had not been solved; and for those who had attempted to fix the problem, it cost on average about $ 129 per computer or to restore the system to a previous backup state. In many of these cases, it was simply cheaper to buy a new computer. Cleansing software programs are not always able to find root causes, implying that computer repair requires more technical expertise than the average user is capable. Even bigger problems loom with mobile electronic devices, such as smart phones.

Mobile users fall victim to malware via 'drive-by downloads'[6] from malicious sites, by downloading malware masquerading as desirable software such as an update, or offers for discount coupons and free games. An area of concern for mobile devices is the Quick Response (QR) codes available for users. These codes form a matrix barcode to store alphanumeric characters as a text or URL. A QR code can be scanned with a smartphone's camera as input into a QR reader's app. The QR code directs users to websites, videos, sends text messages and e-mails, or launches other apps. While convenient, the downside is that users are not aware of the content of a QR code until it has been scanned, increasing mobile security risks; further, many users are not aware of the potential commands that can be initiated by QR codes.[7] Malicious-attackers can use these codes to redirect users to malicious websites to download malicious apps that can, for example:

- Make calendars, contacts and credit card information available to cyber-criminals (Washington Post 2014, 6/13).
- Ask for social network passwords; once accessed, social networks can lead to sufficient personal information for identity theft.
- Track locations.
- Send texts to expensive phone numbers; e.g., in Russia (2013) an incident involved a mobile app titled "Jimm" that once installed, sent unwanted expensive texts ($ 6 each).

---

[5] see "Cisco cyber threat reports at http://www.cisco.com/c/en/us/products/security/annual_security _report.html/.

[6] "A drive-by download is when a malicious web site you visit downloads and installs software without your knowledge.", from http://www.it.cornell.edu/security/safety/malware/driveby.cfm.

[7] https://www.bullguard.com/bullguard-security-center/mobile-security/mobile-threats/malicious-qr-codes.aspx.

Recently there has been a rise in the occurrence of "ransom ware" by which a user downloads malware, that, when executed, encrypts the user's hard drive. The malware then notifies the user that in order to re-access the data on the computer, a ransom must be sent. One argument would be to engineer systems that are unbreakable, able to circumvent all attacks, such as credit card scams. But this explosion of engineered responses is untenable. For example, Salim (2014, p. 24) reported that building unbreakable credit card systems is not feasible when faced by resource and time constraints against attackers with ample time, money and protection by other nations. Not only is there a problem with credit cards, air traffic control and stock markets are also affected.

9.1.2 Air Traffic Control

The Inspector General[8] has warned that the U.S. Federal Air Administration's Air Traffic Control (ATC) system is unprepared for cyber threats:

> [In our] report on Federal Aviation Administration (FAA) web applications security and intrusion detection in air traffic control (ATC) systems.... We found that web applications used in supporting ATC systems operations were not properly secured to prevent attacks or unauthorized access. During the audit, our staff gained unauthorized access to information stored on web application computers and an ATC system, and confirmed system vulnerability to malicious code attacks. In addition, FAA had not established adequate intrusion–detection capability to monitor and detect potential cyber security incidents at ATC facilities. The intrusion–detection system has been deployed to only 11 (out of hundreds of) ATC facilities. Also, cyber incidents detected were not remediated in a timely manner.

Addressing ATC's failures, the Inspector General for the Department of Transportation (DOT) criticized DOT for failing to update IT systems as federally required. DOT's information systems are vulnerable to significant security threats and risks.

9.1.3 Stock Markets

Regarding stocks, Lewis and Baker (2014) conclude that "Stock market manipulation is a growth area for cybercrime." Making this threat clear, a hack of an Associated Press Twitter feed sent out a claim of an explosion at the White House, causing the stock market to tumble 100 points within a few seconds before it was identified as false.[9] A deeper concern, seemingly unrelated, is the claim by Lewis (2014) that

---

[8] "Quality control review on the vulnerability assessment of FAA's operations air traffic control system" (2011, 4/15), Project ID: QC-2011-047, from oig.dot.gov; quotes from FederalTimes (2014, 4/25), Government, industry target air traffic cyber-attacks", federaltimes.com.
[9] See at http://nymag.com/daily/intelligencer/2013/04/ap-twitter-hack-sends-stock-market-spinning.html.

millisecond "high-frequency trading" has rigged the stock market. Mary Jo White, Chairman Securities and Exchange Commission, denied that the market was rigged, noting that costs for common stocks had fallen.[10] Despite this incident, the White House requested funds from Congress "to help regulators cope with a technological revolution that has turned stock trading into an endeavor driven and dominated by fast computers".

Time-critical decisions are also an integral aspect to emergency first responders (Loukas et al. 2013) and to the Cyber Response Teams who may also have to fend off a cyber-attack during an emergency response. Based on models of quickening conflict escalation by Mallery (2011), Kello (2013, p. 34) warned:

> Consequently, the interaction domain of cyber conflict unfolds in milliseconds—an infinitesimally narrow response time for which existing crisis management procedures, which move at the speed of bureaucracy, may not be adequate.

9.1.4 Information Concerns

The *Washington Post* (2014) recently reviewed Vodaphone's report about the types of information being gathered by national governments:[11]

> Such systems can collect and analyze almost any information, including the content of most phone calls that flow over the Internet when it's not encrypted. As a result, governments can learn virtually anything people in their nations say or do online and frequently can learn where they are using location tracking, which is built into most cellular networks. The Vodafone report distinguishes between content—words or other information conveyed over its networks—and metadata, which reveals who is contacting whom and what kinds of communication systems they are using.

In its article, the Washington Post (2014) noted that cyber vulnerabilities are being built purposively into modern communication systems, including cell phones:

> Governments have been gaining increasingly intrusive access to communications for at least two decades, when the United States and other nations began passing laws requiring that powerful surveillance capabilities be built directly into emerging technologies, such as cellular networks and Internet-based telephone systems.

9.1.5 The Human Element

The human element is the common thread among all cyber threats. With malicious software, hackers exploit the motivation of users who are simply seeking to achieve

---

[10] *Washington Post* (2014, 6/6), "SEC aims to catch up to trading technology"; http://www.washingtonpost.com/business/economy/sec-aims-to-catch-up-to-trading-technology/2014/06/05/eee8ab06-ece0-11e3-b98c-72cef4a00499_story.html.

[11] http://www.vodafone.com/content/index/media/vodafone-group-releases/2014/law_enforcement_disclosure_report.html.

their goals (e.g., mundane goals like seeking a flight, ordering a book, or responding to an email). Hackers analyze the flow of users' tasks to determine where vulnerabilities can be found, then make decisions on what exploits to run based on their own malicious motivations and intents.

9.2 Overview: Our Approach to the Problem

In our review of cyber threats, we discuss the pervasiveness of cyber problems and the human role as both attacker and target; the lack of awareness by users; cyber defenses and tools; the complexity of the new cyber environment; engineering approaches to mitigate cyber threats; cyber risks; and current research along with theory at the individual and group levels. We end with future research needs and conclusions.

Recognizing the danger from cyber threats, the Federal Communications Commission (FCC) has quietly worked to expand its role among the federal agencies charged with defending the nation's networks from cyber-attack (Washington Post 2014, 6/12). The FCC's initiative follows a set of recommendations for businesses to bolster cyber-defenses issued by the National Institute of Standards and Technology (NIST 2014); NIST has also developed a framework for organizational structure and regulation to increase cyber security.

The classic response to cyber threats has been to focus on deterrence, implying the value of maintaining strong boundaries and increasing the cost of attacks. However, the common focus on deterrence of threats has led to scenarios where we run faster and faster to maintain the same position (i.e., Red Queen scenarios; discussed later) (Section 9.5.1). Consider for a moment password requirements: Kaspersky recommends 23 character passwords, comprising a mix of capital and lower case letters, numbers and special characters.[12] Accepting this recommendation puts an unwieldy cognitive burden on users, creating other vulnerabilities (e.g., recycled passwords, password 'safes'; etc.). Meanwhile, malicious actors informally try to understand the behavior of users even as institutional security policies attempt to limit the behaviors of users. These limits impact the ability of users to achieve their goals, forcing them to seek work-arounds, but yielding even newer vulnerabilities. To get in front of this situation with behavioral modeling, we propose that it is necessary to model the intents and motivations, the cognitions, of both malicious actors and users.

Usually the difference between an offensive and defensive response to a cyber-threat is very clear to both sides. However, notes Kello (2013 p. 32), sometimes a proactive defensive action can be mistaken by a malicious agent as an overt attack, causing the malicious agent to counter the defensive action, creating a cycle that spurs on the cyber arms race.

---

[12] See more at http://usa.kaspersky.com/products-services/home-computer-security/password-manager/?domain=kaspersky.com.

Continued reliance on engineered solutions to cyber incursions neglects a significant aspect of the problem. Okhravi et al. (2011)[13] note that in a contested environment, traditional cyber defenses can prove ineffective against a well-resourced opponent despite hardened systems. They recommend constructing a "moving target" for an active defense. The cyber domain is unique as a human developed environment, and while many tools used to exploit vulnerabilities in the environment are engineered, the selection of targets and implementation of defenses continue to rely on the ability of humans to understand the emerging complexities within this environment.

9.3   Cyber Problems are Pervasive

The breadth of the risks from cyber threats are sketched by Lewis and Baker (2014):

> Simply listing known cybercrime and cyber espionage incidents creates a dramatic narrative. We found hundreds of reports of companies being hacked. In the US, for example, the government notified 3000 companies in 2013 that they had been hacked. Two banks in the Persian Gulf lost $ 45 million in a few hours. A British company reported that it lost $ 1.3 billion from a single attack. Brazilian banks say their customers lose millions annually to cyber fraud.

9.3.1   Risks

Regarding the cyber risks posed to the average person, firm, and our nation, Axelrod and Iliev (2014) conclude that "(t)he risks include financial loss, loss of privacy, loss of intellectual property, breaches of national security through cyber espionage, and potential large-scale damage in a war involving cyber sabotage." Risk has been defined as a measure of the probability and severity of adverse effects (e.g., Lowrance 1976).[14] Applied to cyber threats, risk is the likelihood of a cyber-attack times the consequences of the losses expected from the attack.

Lewis and Baker (2014) note that targets are identified by attackers based on the value of the target and the ease of entry (risk equals consequence times probability; from Kaplan and Garrick 1981). However, given the complexity of cyber networks, the rise of emergent properties in these networks, and the evolution of technologies, it becomes very difficult for defenders and decision makers to provide risk assessments of their networks. What are needed are tools to help defenders understand the strategic value of their systems to attackers, and the risks from a loss of those systems once malicious actors have gained access.

---

[13] The authors are at MIT's Lincoln Laboratories.
[14] This definition comes from the University of Virginia's Center for Risk Management of Engineering Systems; more at http://www.sys.virginia.edu/risk/riskdefined.html.

The difficulty of attribution and prediction of the source (and therefore motivation) of opponents further reduces the ability of defenders to assess risk. Teams of malicious agents can amplify the risks from cyber weapons. Traceability in the cyber environment is difficult, and the anonymity lent by cyber increases the confidence of attackers. To magnify this even further, use of civilian 'militias' is increasingly common (Kello 2013). It is difficult to differentiate these militias from groups acting independently (e.g., Anonymous; see also New York Times (2014, 6/20)).

> Moreover, some countries—notably, Russia and China—increasingly employ cyber "militias" to prepare and execute hostilities. Such use of civilian proxies provides states plausible deniability if they chose to initiate a cyber-attack, but it also risks instigating a catalytic exchange should the lines of authority and communication break down or if agents decide to act alone.

Deception and subterfuge are common in the cyber-environment on the level of individual malicious actors as well as at the nation-state level. Attackers representing nation-states use cyber subterfuge to obtain the innovations they are unable to develop internally on their own (Lewis and Baker 2014), while others combine cyberwar tactics with traditional military strategies to achieve ends ranging from self-promotion to security. Use of deception in cyber exploits further reduces the ability of defenders to estimate risk. This is compounded when the 'average user' cannot foresee the potential impact of what appears to be a simple action (such as following a link in an email from what appears to be a trusted source, when that source has been hacked). Most users are unaware of the risks they face from deception and subterfuge.

9.3.2   Unaware Users

With the recent substantial growth in computing and internet use, the complexity of networks has expanded, increasing the opaqueness of how systems work. Few people know how their computers or the internet protocols work (e.g., who knows what TCP/IP actually does?). Nor are average users always fully aware of the risks arising from even simple actions (such as browsing the net).

It is not uncommon for a single user to have multiple devices; to be safe each device requires protection, implying that each user should have multiple aliases in the cyber environment. However, as Capelle (2014) notes, users take insufficient precautions to protect their data on their devices. He writes,

> ... the Kaspersky-B2B International survey results show that close to 98 % of respondents use a digital device—smartphone, computer or tablet—to carry out financial transactions and 74 % regularly use e-wallets and e-payment systems. However, this increase in the use of mobile payments has not been accompanied by a change in users' security habits. Some 34 % of those surveyed stated for example that they took no security measures when using public WiFi networks, even though 60 % are not certain that the websites they use provide adequate protection for their passwords and personal data. This widespread lack of security reflexes is also evident when it comes to the software versions people use. Fully 27 % of users do not regularly update software on their devices, and so leave themselves open to recurring cyber-attacks.

Reason (2008) states that 'unsafe acts' in cyber can be seen as person-based; that is, arising from aberrant human cognitive processes, such as forgetfulness; or they can be considered from a system perspective. In the system perspective (of a human), humans are assumed to be fallible with errors to be expected. It is necessary for researchers to develop resilient defensive systems to protect against these errors. However, the increasing complexity of our networks increases the risks users face until acceptable defensive actions have been established. The commonness of malware also makes the perception of the impact of the consequence lower—malware slows digital devices, which is annoying; but the perception that users could experience identity theft is underestimated.

These errors can be catastrophic. Kello (2013, p. 23) provides an example of a warning based on a simulation of power-failure in the USA:

> Based on extrapolations of a cyber-attack simulation conducted by the National Academy of Sciences in 2007, penetration of the control system of the U.S. electrical grid could cause "hundreds or even thousands of deaths" as a result of human exposure to extreme temperatures (National Research Council of the National Academies 2012).

This warning was realized within a (Wall Street Journal, 2009, 4/28).

9.3.3 Malware Origination, Repair and Deception

The prevalence of malware makes it difficult to determine where a problem originates; if users cannot figure out the origination of cyber threats, can they be prevented? Attacks against 'average users' often uses deception to gain access. Malicious actors develop malware that leverages deception, requiring exploiters to develop an understanding of user defensive tasks, user decision processes, and a malicious agent's ability to view across the entirety of the network they aim to exploit, for example through impersonation of trusted sources. However, strategic deception is also used in exploits against larger corporate entities. From the media comes an example of the deceptions and misdirection used by criminals acting against banks (USA Today 2014):

> To draw attention away from the massive [money] transfers, the hackers often created a diversion, such as a "denial of service" attack that would bombard the website with traffic in an attempt to shut it down, the law enforcement official said. While the business scrambled to protect its portal, the hackers would push the wire transfer through unnoticed for hours, the official said. By the time the bank realized the money was missing, the hackers had laundered it through so many accounts it became untraceable.

Deception Drones are a new element in US aviation (Los Angeles Times 2014, 6/10). Depending on their mission, they are vulnerable to cyber-attack from novel vulnerabilities. Hartmann and Steup (2013, p. 22): "Events such as the loss of an RQ-170 Sentinel to Iranian military forces . . . [illustrate, possibly, that]:

> . . . a vulnerability of the UAV sensor system with effects on the navigation system was used to attack the GPS system. . . . The GPS-satellite-signal is overlaid by a spoofed GPS-signal

originating from a local transmitter with a stronger signal. The spoofed GPS-signal simulates the GPS-satellite-signal, leading to a falsified estimation of the UAVs current position. Supporters of this theory suppose that Iranian forces jammed the satellite communication of the drone and spoofed the GPS-signal to land the drone safely on an Iranian airfield.

9.3.4 Threat Sources

Threat sources have a wide range, from individual malicious agents and the tools used in attacks against users to nation-state actors running advanced persistent threats over long time frames. Criminal hackers and foreign cyber attackers probe for weaknesses in individuals, firms or institutions in a malicious attempt to understand user goals, motivations, intents and behaviors. Emerging vulnerabilities represent an opportunity to exploit a potential resource. From Axelrod and Iliev (2014), "New vulnerabilities in computer systems are constantly being discovered. When an individual, group, or nation has access to means of exploiting such vulnerabilities in a rival's computer systems, it faces a decision of whether to exploit its capacity immediately or wait for a more propitious time." Vulnerabilities arise from the complexity of networks, and the inability to comprehend the properties from complex interactions, and the human user and defender is lacking the tools to predict from where the next threat will arise.

From a boundary maintenance perspective, cyber criminals seeking vulnerabilities in a target organization's boundaries try to mount attacks without wasting resources by attacking at the points of weakness that they have identified; yet with the low cost of each, multiple attacks may be mounted simultaneously, obscuring the state of the system or the source of an attack to defenders. Vulnerabilities are found by an exploration of a team's or an organization's boundaries, but also, based on interdependence theory, by perturbing a team or an organization to observe how a target behaves inside and outside of its established boundaries (see Section 9.7.5). This is done by malicious agents in order to understand user decisions and responses. Sun Tzu was adapted by Symantec into a quote as "Cyber Sun Tzu" to thwart the legions of cybercriminals we face today (New York Times 2014, 6/21), but it is as true of the tactics utilized by malicious actors against targets: "when the enemy is relaxed, make them toil; when full, make them starve; when settled, make them move."

We ignore the human element of cyber threats at our peril. Cyber threats arise from engineered tools designed to exploit the vulnerabilities of users; the tools are used by intelligent adversaries with a variety of motivations, intents, and goals. Kello (2013, p. 14) points out that vulnerabilities to threats arising from new technologies are often ignored or dismissed because of a failure to grasp the full source or impact of the threat:

> Historically, bad theories of new technology have been behind many a strategic blunder. In 1914, British commanders failed to grasp that the torpedo boat had rendered their magnificent surface fleet obsolescent. In 1940, French strategic doctrine misinterpreted the lessons of mechanized warfare and prescribed no response to the Nazi tank assault. The cyber revolution

is no exception to this problem of lag in strategic adaptation. . . . Circumstances in the lead-up to the U.S. offensive cyber operation known as "Olympic Games," which destroyed enrichment centrifuges in Iran, vividly demonstrate the problem. The custodians of the worm (named Stuxnet by its discoverers) grappled with three sets of doctrinal quandaries: (1) ambiguities regarding the tactical viability of cyber-attack to destroy physical assets; (2) concerns that the advanced code would proliferate to weaker opponents who could reengineer it to hit facilities back home; and (3) anxieties over the dangerous precedent that the operation would set—would it embolden adversaries to unleash their own virtual stock-piles?

While the computer science problems of cyberwar are significant, the human user remains the primary weak link. For example, phishing, spearfishing, spyware, malware, key loggers; attacks made through wi-fi;[15] attacks via mobile phones; email hacking and attacks through linked accounts; use of social media for distributed denial of service attacks; and the use of social media for crowd agitation campaigns to promote hacking of government, military and other agencies. In many respects, these combine to make for a new kind of warfare.

9.4   The Complex Cyber-Environment

Cyber defense in a complex cyber environment is not straightforward. We must realize we are in a war waged across a new terrain and confronted by a new enemy, reducing our likelihood of success. From Sun Tzu (Giles 2007), "If you do not know your enemies nor yourself, you will be imperiled in every single battle." Let's begin by exploring the enemy's battle terrain.

9.4.1   Cyber-Layers

Cyber security and cyber-defense have multiple levels, or strata, of interconnectivity, forming multiplicative relationships between aliases, people, and locations.[16] Malicious agents can target any of the multiple levels. The lowest level is geographic, then the physical infrastructure, the information layer, cyber identity layer, and people layer. The geographic layer on the bottom and the person layer on the top are familiar and are usually combined for military planning operations. The three middle layers are much more fluid and complex. These three layers are continually morphing, advancing and obfuscating. In its layer, information may be shared or unique to identity; people may have multiple cyber identities that can be easily linked or not. The content of a network resides on the information layer. The content consists of email

---

[15] Problems exist with free wi-fi connections. An article in the *New York Times* (2014, 6/4) hoped to protect travelers using free wi-fi: "Make sure that any site you visit has 'HTTPS' in front of the URL; Use a virtual private network, or VPN; Sign up for two-step verification; and Bring only what you need and turn off what you're not using.'

[16] Some of these ideas come from NSA: http://www.nsa.gov/ia/_files/support/defenseindepth.pdf.

messages, files, website, or anything electronically stored or transmitted. The Physical Infrastructure layer represents the physical hardware of cyberspace, the fiber-optic cables, satellites, routers, servers, etc. We discuss the cyber identify layer next.

9.4.2   Malicious Agents

The Cyber Identity layer is probably the most complex. It is how entities are identified on the network. This can be an individual user represented by multiple points of presence, i.e., personal phone, work phone, multiple email addresses, printer, fax, website, blog, etc. Consider that one individual with multiple, complex relationships accessing other levels of the environment can send anything over the internet to any location in the world. However, for most typical users, cyber identities (aliases) are easily linked.

Networks are built for ease of communications, not for security; an inherent design vulnerability. While we are easily able to connect new and different technologies to the net (e.g., homes; cars; weapons), we often do so with minimal concern for securing the network. The convergence of technology and the increasing complexity of these networks pose the challenge of identifying malicious agents and maintaining the situational awareness about their presence on networks.

9.4.3   Social Media

Malicious actors can, and do, leverage social media to gain insight into our behavior. At home (Carley et al. 2013), social media can be leveraged by malicious agents to influence user behaviors in a way that is an indicator of the roles these malicious actors want users to play as part of a staged event, serious enough to warrant an FBI rapid response.[17]

Further emphasizing the need to model human behavior and cognition for vulnerabilities, recent work by Trendmicro[18] indicated that 91 % of hacks begin with some form of phishing. They went on to report that targeting starts by 'pre-infiltration reconnaissance' where individuals are first identified and then profiled via information posted on social networks and the organizations' own websites. Thus, the attacker constructs an email tailored to the target, compelling enough that the target will open the attached file and get infected, most likely with a remote access tool (RAT; also, RATrojan) (Washington Post 2011, 8/3).

---

[17] e.g., from FBI Testimony, a malicious agent was charged with "wire and bank fraud for his role as the primary developer and distributor of the malicious software known as Spyeye"; http://www.fbi.gov/news/testimony/the-fbis-role-in-cyber-security.

[18] See http://www.infosecurity-magazine.com/view/29562/91-of-apt-attacks-start-with-a-spearphishing-email/.

9.5 Engineering Approaches

9.5.1 Red Queen

Engineering approaches to mitigating cyber-threats have led to an arms race. To quote Lewis Carroll, "It takes all the running you can do, to keep in the same place."[19] A never ending arms race means that defenders are always playing catch up, requiring: stronger protocols; stronger encryption; more rigorous password management; automated patching; firewalls; defense-in-depth; intrusion detection systems; and anti-virus software. Yet, the building and maintenance of engineered techniques do not address the most fundamental threats of cyberspace, those arising from human performance.

9.5.2 Blaming Users

The fundamental issue is seeing cyber-security as a problem of computer science and information technology while neglecting the impact of system complexity on users. Cyber-attacks are often called "human" engineering. The common perception from the human engineering perspective is that cyber-security is caused by a lack of discipline, when it is really a cognitive science issue. The typical solution is to blame users, shame them and retrain them; i.e., with case-based solutions. However, the solutions proffered rely on increasingly frustrating and difficult policies implemented at work for each new case, suggesting a lack of teamwork between cyber defenders and users (cf. interdependence theory). Worse, these solutions seldom prevent or uncover new vulnerabilities and new attacks that further exploit cognitive vulnerabilities.

9.5.3 Fulcrum of Power

Users, cyber defenders and malicious actors form a fulcrum of power (Forsythe et al. 2012): Defenders control user behavior through policies and software limitations when they should be limiting the behavior of malicious agents through modeling and prediction (e.g., with Artificial Intelligence, or AI). Users may be unaware of, or indifferent to, the potential sources of risk that they are being protected from by these policies (due to a lack of understanding of the risk consequences); dissatisfied by the agencies that defend them (potentially creating a malicious insider threat); or dissatisfied by the limits a policy places on their ability to perform their job.

---

[19] i.e., Carroll's The Red Queen, in "Through the Looking Glass".

The ability of users to understand the risks they face may be limited due to a lack of communication (e.g., Cisco's[20] report indicated users were often unaware of their organization's security policy), the technical complexity of the network and its sources of risk, or because their work and operations have a higher priority to them in the short term. Security measures may limit or irritate users, causing them to bypass security settings and often inadvertently result in security incidents (e.g., using USB memory sticks). In contrast, those known as "cyber defenders" are more security aware, more able to maintain a smaller cyber footprint, and more likely to follow their organization's policy due to a greater sensitivity to the cyber threats and risks that they face. At work or at home, cyber defenders maintain the sense of vulnerability, leading them to view workable security measures as necessary, a best practice for all users.

From Kello (2013, p. 28), "Therein lies the root dilemma of cyber-security: an impregnable computer system is inaccessible to legitimate users while an accessible machine is inherently manipulable by pernicious code."

9.5.4   User Vulnerability

Within a cyber-network, we argue that the human user is both the greatest source of vulnerability and the greatest resource for a defense. Cyber threats pose a new kind of war where personal information needs to be seen as an asset (not just data) to be protected (NIST 2010). In a newly emerging version of an old threat (recall the PC Cyborg/AIDS Trojan from 1989), accessed by typically entering the system via a downloaded file, then vulnerable personal information or files may be locked away by cybercriminals from users. The New York Times (2014, 6/21) describes how this works:

> Cybercriminals are ... circumventing firewalls and antivirus programs ... [and] resorting to ransomware, which encrypts computer data and holds it hostage until a fee is paid. Some hackers plant virus-loaded ads on legitimate websites, enabling them to remotely wipe a hard drive clean or cause it to overheat. Meanwhile, companies are being routinely targeted by attacks sponsored by the governments of Iran and China. Even small start-ups are suffering from denial-of-service extortion attacks, in which hackers threaten to disable their websites unless money is paid.

Kello (2013, p. 30) tried to highlight the difficulty of defending against cyber-attacks:

> The enormity of the defender's challenge is convincingly illustrated by the successful penetration of computer systems at Google and RSA, two companies that represent the quintessence of technological ability in the current information age. (In 2010, Google announced that sophisticated Chinese agents had breached its systems, and in 2011, unknown parties compromised RSA's authentication products. This was followed by attempts to penetrate computers at Lockheed Martin, an RSA client.)

---

[20] see "Cisco cyber threat reports at http://www.cisco.com/c/en/us/products/security/annual_security _report.html.

Kahneman's (2011) philosophy of mind explains cognitive vulnerabilities by the duality of human thought processes. On the one hand, our associative mind jumps to conclusions by continuously looking for patterns even where none exists; on the other hand, our reasoning self requires concentration and effort to make decisions. The principle of least effort (Zipf 1949) underlies most human judgment and habits, both good habits and bad ones. We quickly develop habits as shortcuts because reasoning takes too much time and effort. Habits make us predictable and vulnerable. As the complexity of our interactions in cyberspace increase, so will our reliance on habits, motivating malicious agents to learn those habits most vulnerable to exploitation.

9.6 Intelligent Adversaries

9.6.1 Changing Tools and Techniques

McMorrow (2010, p. 14) concluded that "[I]n cyber-security there are adversaries, and the adversaries are purposeful and intelligent." The techniques used by malicious actors are constantly changing. As demonstrated by the success of "Cosmo the god", who excelled in creating new disguises for exploits.

> Over the course of 2012, Cosmo and his group UG Nazi took part in many of the highest-profile hacking incidents of the year. UG Nazi, which began as a politicized group that opposed SOPA,[21] took down a bevy of websites this year, including those for NASDAQ, CIA.gov, and UFC.com.[22] It redirected 4Chan's[23] DNS to point to its own Twitter feed. Cosmo pioneered social-engineering techniques that allowed him to gain access to user accounts at Amazon, PayPal, and a slew of other companies. He was arrested in June, as a part of a multi-state FBI sting (Wired 2012).

9.6.2 Using Deception for Defense

There are only so many ways you can deceive and ultimately each new technique is an old technique in new clothes. Yet, there are still users who respond to 'Ethiopian lottery' email.[24] From Sun Tzu (Giles 2007, p. 18), "All warfare is based on deception. Hence, when we are able to attack, we must seem unable; when using our forces, we must appear inactive; when we are near, we must make the enemy believe we are far away; when far away, we must make him believe we are near." As Axelrod and Iliev (2014) claim:

---

[21] Stop Online Piracy Act (SOPA); see http://en.wikipedia.org/wiki/Stop_Online_Piracy_Act.

[22] Ultimate Fighter: see http://www.ufc.com.

[23] An imageboard site; see http://www.networkworld.com/article/2222511/microsoft-subnet/hacktivists-ugnazi-attack-4chan-cloudflare-and-wounded-warrior-project.html.

[24] For a review of lottery and other e-scams, see http://www.fbi.gov/.

> The Stealth of a resource is the probability that if you use it now it will still be usable in the next time period. The Persistence of a resource is the probability that if you refrain from using it now, it will still be useable in the next time period.

To get ahead of the behavioral modeling of the malicious agents who attempt to exploit users, we need a cognitive model of malicious attacker(s).

9.7 Current Research

9.7.1 Theory

In this section, as applied to cyber threats and cyber defenses, we review the cognitive science of individual behavior, cognitive structures for the individual, and unanswered questions for applying cognitive science to individuals in the cyber domain. Second, we review the theory of interdependence to better understand and predict the behavior of teams and organizations and the unanswered questions for interdependent states. Third, we review what is known and not known about communication among teams. We end this section by noting that research is needed on leveraging cognitive models to predict how a malicious agent's motivation and intent influence their selection of a tool to exploit a user.

Behavioral theory is either based on traditional individual methodological perspectives (e.g., cognitive architectures) or, but less often, on groups (i.e., interdependent theory). Methodological individualism assumes that individuals are more stable than labile irrespective of the social interactions in which they engage (Ahdieh 2009). Interdependence theory assumes the opposite, that a state of mutual dependence between the participants of an interaction affects, or skews, the individual beliefs or behaviors of participants; i.e., interdependence changes preferences, no matter how strongly held (Kelley 1992). Further, given the anonymity allowed by the cyber environment, cyber aliases allow for significantly different behaviors as a function of the community surrounding an alias (e.g., when a malicious agent poses "to be from the FBI Director or other top official, it is most likely a scam"[25]).

If the problems with behavioral theory can be solved, then, technological solutions may become feasible. According to Martinez (2014, p. 2) "... the interplay between the human and the machine is paramount to reach timely decisions ... [by] reduc[ing] the information entropy to reach actionable decisions." He believes that one solution "is to identify an architecture that is suitable for machine learning techniques to enable important augmented cognition capabilities in the context of complex decision support systems."

---

[25] http://www.fbi.gov/scams-safety/e-scams.

9.7.2 Attribution

The attribution problem, or identifying the sources of cyber threats, is one of the major defense challenges in cybersecurity due to the pseudonimity of cyberspace. Current cybersecurity efforts are directed toward technical attribution in the development of the black lists of malicious hosts in order to block the propagation of malicious packets and URLs. However, a gap exists between technical and human attribution because malicious software can execute from a remote host. Furthermore, malicious actors exchange, buy, and sell code to be retooled and rewritten, complicating the attribution problem. It is during the reconnaissance phase of an attack, however, that an attacker is most vulnerable to human attribution because of repeated interactions, external or internal, with a target host (Boebert 2010). Detecting malicious intent during an "external" reconnaissance is however a hard problem due to the serendipity of Web browsing. For example, an innocent person might stumble upon a honeypot thereby creating a false positive. Machine learning techniques for authenticating and modeling users in cyberspace from the history of their digital traces address the attribution problem from a behavioral perspective (Abramson 2013, 2014). Current challenges include malicious intent understanding from user interactions in cyberspace.

9.7.3 Cognitive Architectures

Eventually, it may be possible to use cognitive architectures to predict the next moves of malicious actors and agents (e.g., by detecting Advanced Persistent Threats, or APTs,[26] often directed by a government, like espionage by the Chinese and Russians, or the disruptive-Stuxnet by the Americans). Cognitive Science may be useful as a tool to connect media and behavior. Cyberspace is a complex ecosystem requiring a multi-disciplinary scientific approach. By understanding the decision making process, the motivations, and intents of malicious actors, it may be possible to predict the selection of exploits based on the goals of the malicious actor. Conversely, understanding decision processes, motivation and intent may be useful to differentiate the signal of a malicious actor from the false alarms inherent within networks.

Interdisciplinary Once we have identified the human behavior and motivations for a cyber-attack, numerous models exist with different applications, strengths, and utilities. We propose that the first step is to determine what we want to know, and explore the models able to provide that insight. The U.S. Navy explored this problem last year:[27] "Develop and validate a computational model of the cognitive processes from

---

[26] See en.m.wikipedia.org.
[27] Cognitive Modeling for Cyber Defense. Navy SBIR 2013.2. Topic N132–132. ONR; see http://www.navysbir.com/n13_2/N132-132.htm.

cues to actions of the attackers, defenders, and users to create a synthetic experimentation capability to examine, explore, and assess effectiveness of cyber operations."

Behavioral Intent Analysis The characteristics of the network can be thought of as stimulus cues (e.g., Feldman and Lynch 1988). To make sense of, and predict, the environment, humans attempt to find patterns in stimuli. Patterns of the type and number of cues from stimuli yield a belief about the current environment (i.e., a 'guess' or inference about a system's state). Each belief will prime associated motivations that compete against each other (Bernard and Backus 2009). The motivations that will become activated are those with the strongest congruence between the respective motivation and the attitude towards it; those associated with the perceived social norms that favor the motivation; and those where the perception that the action associated with a motivation can be carried out.

An activated motivation primes certain potential intentions (Bernard and Backus 2009). Primed intentions become active when cues supporting the respective intentions are present. Each activated intention primes associated potential behaviors. The potential behavior(s) that ultimately becomes activated is a function of the type and degree of associated affect (positive or negative) and the activated perception. That is, an entity may have an intention to do something, but how the intention is specifically carried out depends, in part, on the emotional state at that point in time.

If we knew the cues affecting a malicious agent, then, based on the types of data being protected, we could infer a set of behavioral intents. If we then applied a model of human cognition to our model of the malicious agent, we could use it to choose from the possible set of exploits. These steps could help us to create a tool that, while not identifying all of the attacks possible, could reduce the uncertainty in the cyber battlespace by identifying for further exploration those cues indicative of specific exploits (e.g., with AI). For example, one way that firms on their own are attempting to identify attackers is with active defenses: From the New York Times (2014, 6/21):

> ... more companies are resorting to countermeasures like planting false information on their own servers to mislead data thieves, patrolling online forums to watch for stolen information and creating "honey pot" servers that gather information about intruders.

We need the development of programs to train users in cognitive defenses against cyber-exploitation and attack. We need multi-layered complex adaptive system models to train users in "cyber-street smarts" to recognize vulnerabilities, attacks, exploitations and suitable defenses. Lastly, we need to develop new "crowd-self-policing" techniques for cyber environments. We should also explore: "Who is vulnerable to what kinds of deception?"; "What makes good deception?" and "How can we detect deception?"

9.7.4 Cyber Security Questions

We argue that the following list represents the key cyber-security questions that need to be answered to address behavioral intent analyses:

Pursued from the Human Dimension:

- How do we measure performance in the cyber domain?
- What factors underlie cyber situation awareness?
- What cognitive and personality attributes characterize better cyber analysts?
- How do we train cyber defenders to be effective?
- What fidelity level is required for effective training?
- What are the characteristics of deception?
- Can we devise a test to discriminate between cyber defenders and ordinary users?

In addition, we provide a list of needed research tools:

- Behavioral modeling of vulnerabilities;
- Cognitively compatible semantic representation of cyber data and system state;
- Autonomous aids to identify situation awareness and the detection of deception; and,
- Communication aides (identifying the information propagating through social media).

9.7.5 Interdependence Theory

Until now, we have addressed cyber threats primarily from an individual perspective. Methodological individualism (e.g., game theory, psychology, learning) focuses on changing the individual in the hope that it may change society (Ahdieh 2009); but methodological individualism has serious shortcomings. For example, game theory remains unproven (Schweitzer et al. 2009). Some of game theory's strongest adherents admit that it is not connected to reality (e.g., Rand and Nowak 2013); yet, despite this disconnect, game theorists conclude that cooperation produces the superior social good (Axelrod 1984), a conclusion supported by a recent review on the theory of human teams (Bell et al. 2012).

That individualism and cooperation do not account for attacks on an organization's boundaries is not surprising. What surprises is how little the traditional focus on individuals has to offer to the science of real organizations. To address cybersecurity from an individual perspective cannot begin to account for the extraordinary time, energy and personnel real groups and organizations devote to defend themselves against all forms of real competition, including cyber-attacks. That is why we continue to develop the theory of interdependence to account for the irrational effects from the interdependence between uncertainty and the incompleteness of meaning that serves to motivate competition (Lawless et al. 2013). In the process, we discover that a large part of the problem with existing social-psychological theory is its overfocus on the individual, especially where it assumes that social reality and cognitive factors are constituted of logically independent and identically distributed (iid) elements. Consequently, through the lens of interdependence, the critical ingredient in group behavior, we can not only study how groups in reality defend themselves, but also, and surprisingly, by unifying theories of cognition and behavior, we can begin to open an unseen window into the individual.

Organizations are systems of interdependence (Smith and Tushman 2005); social behavior is interdependent; and the interaction is characterized by interdependence (Thibaut and Kelley 1959). Interdependence theory was derived from game theory; it was formalized by Thibaut and Kelley, but later abandoned by its surviving author (Kelley 1992); Kelley had been unable to explain why subject preferences, no matter how strong, collected before games were played differed from the actual choices made by subjects during games. Nor has game theory fared well (Schweitzer et al. 2009); even its leading proponents admit that it has no ground truth, that games are not "a good representation of [our] world" (Rand and Nowak 2013, p. 416). Furthermore, no theory of organizations has yet been accepted (Pfeffer and Fong 2005). To counter this weakness in individualism, in this review, we will present the outline of a theory of interdependence.

The topic of deception is integral to cybercrime and offers a natural segue into interdependence theory, built around the idea that all perception leads to a belief that is a construction of reality, an illusion, or, more likely, a combination (Adelson 2000); that physical reality is orthogonal to imagined reality; and that the illusions (or errors) in the beliefs about reality allow challengers to compete against another's construction of reality, thereby generating social dynamics (Lawless et al. 2013). In contrast to the belief in a stable view of reality contingent upon the independent, identically distributed (iid) elements supposedly underpinning situational awareness, the multiple interpretations of reality that commonly arise are derived from socially interdependent situations; instead of stability, interdependence is simulated by a simple bistable image or function. Interdependent states are associated with high levels of uncertainty, indicating that unknowns outweigh ground truth; overriding this uncertainty, as Smallman (2012) has concluded, can produce tragic mistakes.[28] To address this uncertainty for well-defined situations, as in purchasing goods, humans establish social, cultural and legal rules to guide their behaviors. To address the uncertainty arising from ill-defined or poorly defined situations requires teams competing against each other, creating bistable perspectives (e.g., the debates commonly presented before audiences).

Bistability implies the possibility of tradeoffs as teams, groups or organizations make decisions; it is exemplified by scientists arguing over the correct interpretation of data, by politicians arguing over the interpretation of polls, and in the courtroom by attorneys arguing over the facts of a case; e.g., in the latter case, two bistable perspectives are reconstructed before a neutral jury as the two sides help the jury to work through the biases in the opposing perspectives until the better perspective is selected by the jury (Freer and Perdue 1996).

In the bistable view, a state of mutual dependence changes the statistics of interaction, confounding individual effects (Lawless et al. 2013). As with groupthink, teams reduce the degrees of freedom important to independent statistics, resulting

---

[28] E.g., the USS Greenville tragedy in 2001 that broke apart and sunk a Japanese tour boat.

in more power to statistical analyses than should be allowed (Kenny et al. 1998). Team members cooperate to multitask in a state of interdependence (Smith and Tushman 2005). But to multitask, team structures are built with heterogeneous roles of specialists, generating less entropy than a collection of individuals performing the same actions. Why? Interdependence causes a loss in statistical degrees of freedom (dof; see Kenny et al. 1998). Given entropy, S, for $S = k \log W$, as interdependence increases, W decreases, reducing entropy; i.e., S is proportional to $\log W \approx \log (dof)$. Consequently, given $A = U\text{-}TS$, where A is the available energy, U the internal energy, T the temperature, S the entropy, and TS is the energy not available for more work, then the free energy available increases for the structure of a team, a firm or a system to do needed work. Thus, the structure of a well-performing group generates less total entropy than the equal number of individuals performing the same set of tasks (similarly, a heterogeneous cloud is more cost-effective at providing specialized services matched to user needs; in Walters 2014). That is, the structural costs for a team to operate (e.g., coordination paths) are less for the set of individuals who are members of a team than the same individuals working as individuals, the impetus across a weakened market that drives two competitors to merge into a cooperative structure to survive (Lawless et al. 2013). With this information, we can distinguish good and bad team structures. Interestingly, the distinguishability of agents diminishes as the interdependence among them increases.

Assume that a primary goal of living organisms is to survive (Darwin 1973; Kello 2013). Assume also that individuals multitask poorly (Wickens 1992), but that groups perform better than individuals with members performing specialized tasks (Ambrose 2001). Next, assume that well-performing multitasking groups perform better than individuals (Rajivan et al. 2013). Then, if we construe a functional group (e.g., team, firm) as the mechanism that best gathers the resources (energy) needed to survive, in order to minimize entropy losses caused by group formation (Lawless et al. 2013), boundary maintenance becomes an integral factor in survival (Lawless et al. 2014). Unlike low entropy for the formation of best teams, when compared to low-performance teams, we expect that the best performing teams are signified as those that generate maximum entropy, making them more efficient and stable; we do not discuss this further at this time; but see Pressé et al. 2013.

Boundary maintenance entails defending against the threats to a group, including by responding to the risks of cyber threats; viz., the use of "shaming" indicates poor teamwork in the maintenance of their team's boundary. As wealth increases, the maintenance of boundaries becomes stronger. That is, according to Lewis and Baker, "Wealthier countries are more attractive targets for hackers but they also have better defenses. Less-developed countries are more vulnerable." Generalizing, the better a team performs the stronger becomes its boundary.

Predictions and Assessments   Interdependence theory provides a platform for team, organizational, and system predictions and assessments. But, according to interdependence theory, when social agents confront ill-defined problems in states of interdependence, the information derived from them is forever incomplete (Lawless et al. 2013); that is, the information that can be collected from both sides of an interdependent state cannot be used to reconstruct the original state. When outcomes are unpredictable in, say a court, the best result for justice is when legal adversaries in a courtroom are not only competent, but have equal skills and equal amounts of self-interest at stake in the outcome of a trial (Freer and Perdue 1996), exactly the condition for what makes prediction difficult, not only for courtrooms, but with competitive political races, revolutionary science, etc. Thus, in a cyber-exploit, as with any other attack scenario, attackers prefer not to oppose equally capable opponents, at least without some form of advantage (surprise, new weapons or tactics, etc.).

For example,[29] the US Navy, US Marine Corps and the US Coast Guard want to maintain control of the seas. In order to accomplish this goal, they describe "how seapower will be applied around the world to protect our way of life, as we join with other like-minded nations to protect and sustain the global, inter-connected system through which we prosper."

We have studied predictions made under states of interdependence in competitive situations to conclude that they are neither reliable nor valid. However, these predictions become more reliable and valid once an argument has shifted to favor one protagonist over another, thus, ending the state of interdependence, but maybe prematurely when the uncertainty remains high. The message is that the information generated by the interdependence associated with conflict may indicate a problem exists that has yet to be solved.

This phenomenon is more common than recognized. The outcome of the Clinton-Obama competition for the Democratic Nominee for the US Presidency was unclear during January 2008; the matter had been decided by February 2008.[30] Similarly, as of June 2014, predictions for control of the US Senate are no better than 50–50 % for either the status quo or Republican control.[31] If states of interdependence reflect limit cycles (Lawless et al. 2013), then one explanation for the high-levels of uncertainty that may exist comes from the conclusion by Chakrabarti and Ghosh (2013) that the net entropy production (information) for limit cycles is zero.

Interdependence theory poses several new questions:

- How do members of a team during its structural formation align their behaviors to build a group that multitasks better; does structural formation indicate the existence of specialized roles for a team's mission?
- Can we establish, mathematically, the minimum number of members of a team necessary to perform a mission or to defend a firm against a cyber-attack?
- What team characteristics define effective cyber incident response teams?
- Can we develop a tool to measure team performance (Psychophysics and psychometrics; Communication models; entropy heat maps)?
- Can teams be controlled to solve the problems they confront while minimizing mistakes when under competitive threats posed, say, by cyber-attacks?

---

[29] From US Navy, US Marine Corps and US Coast Guard (2007), "A cooperative strategy for 21st Century seapower http://www.navy.mil/maritime/maritimestrategy.pdf.

[30] See the Iowa Electronic Market; www.biz.uiowa.edu/iem/index.cfm.

[31] *Ibid.*

- Do individuals organize best by pooling resources into autonomous groups like teams and firms—Does self-organization lead to better defenses against cyber-attacks?
- What does an organization need to be able to predict its trajectory and assess itself? Viz., which organizations can predict their trajectory? This assumes a leader, but arguably, entities outside of the nation-state do not have a set leader or even set goals (again, Anonymous; see also New York Times 2014, 6/20). Others, like the old Chaos Computer Club did have goals and agendas but individuals still appeared to work consensus style.
- From a theoretical perspective, can a tool be devised to distinguish between good and poor performing teams (e.g., metrics for efficiency; stability; also, considerations of least and maximum entropy)?

9.7.6   Communication Among Teams

Teams organize around multitasking, which requires cooperation among other attributes (Lawless et al. 2013). From the perspective of static self-reports taken after a decision-making event, the larger the group involved in making a decision, the more interdependent it becomes (Lawless et al. 2014); from the perspective of information theory, a team attempts to maximize the flow of information into and out of its team interdependent with the environment by increasing its adaptivity, by minimizing its internal computations on the information flow, and by maximizing the relevance of its response to the environment.

What Makes for Good Teams   Little is known theoretically about what makes for a good team (Bell et al. 2012). Based on small-group studies in the laboratory, good teams communicate together well. Good teams have experienced teammates, underscoring the value of training (Lawless et al. 2013); when joined by a new teammate, a team's performance is disrupted for a period, no matter how proficient is the new member (Bell et al. 2012). The better groups prefer to be cooperative rather than adversarial. However, from the study of the best performing teams away from the laboratory, Hackman (2011) found that the best teams often experienced conflict over issues of disagreement, but that once these issues were worked out, it led them to more creative results.

If the purpose of a team is to multitask (Lawless et al. 2013), thereby giving it more power when the team's [multitasking] actions are united, the mistakes made by a team potentially may be of a larger magnitude than those made by an equal number of independent individuals (e.g., from convergent group biases, like groupthink). Feedback becomes important to help a team act in response to a mistake. To minimize mistakes, the best feedback occurs in settings where challenges are permitted, where mutual self-interests of challengers are at stake (as has been concluded for justice to be served; in Freer and Perdue 1996), and where deliberations based on feedback are witnessed by neutral observers who are in turn able to help revise or modify the original decisions. This happens less with decisions made by the military; but, per Smallman (2012), by possibly reducing mistakes, military decision-making would improve were this information available before decisions are made.

Along the lines proposed by Freer and Perdue that strongly defended arguments best provide justice, Lewis and Baker (2014) reach a somewhat similar conclusion that intellectual property (IP) strongly defended against cybercrime best protects national security:

> We know that balanced IP protection incentivizes growth. This is why nations have, for 150 years, put in place agreements to protect IP. Weak IP protections reduce growth and [encourage] IP theft over the Internet by increasing the scale of theft to unparalleled proportions; this both lowers and distorts global economic growth.

Good Cyber Defender Characteristics   From the perspective of cognitive science, good cyber defenders require tools to support situation awareness. Good defenders are those made aware of the threats against them through better education, training and modeling (e.g., leadership). From the perspective of interdependence theory, in that cyber defense is a critical mission task, good cyber defenders should contribute to the multitasking actions of an organization in a way that optimally contributes to a teams' mission, including teamwork for cyber defense.

9.7.7 Summary

Cyber security is not a single, discrete, static entity. It is a dynamic system of hardware, software and people that experiences continuous change. Modeling cyber security threats becomes extremely hard, unless we take human factors into account and we begin to account for the decision-making processes of attackers and defenders. The kinds of research needed for this system demand a convergence of analyses among the domains of computer science, cognition, information science, mathematics, and networks in natural and social settings. For example, when modeling adversarial intent with respect to planning, proliferating, and potentially using cyber-attacks, researchers must utilize methods ranging across analytical, computational, numerical, and experimental topics to integrate knowledge useful for multi-disciplines, to improve the rapid processing of intelligence, and to rapidly disseminate action information to users.

Other Challenges   To achieve many of the goals we have already discussed, fundamental challenges exist in the cognitive and information cyber-attack sciences:

- Researchers need to explore the attributes of complex, often independent computer and social networks; to explore related motivations for cyber-attacks; and to explore the decision factors used to defend these networks.
- Researchers need a better understanding and prediction of individual and group dynamics associated with the acquisition, proliferation and potential use of cyber-attacks, especially for massive attacks and of the behavior and vulnerabilities of physical and social networks underlying these dynamics.

- Researchers need to develop methods and techniques in response to the challenges of big data to better understand the factors influencing network robustness, dynamics, and concepts of operation, and how the defensive decisions that are made interdependently affect the strategic decisions of adversaries.

Having this cyber knowledge will significantly enhance the situational awareness of cyber-threats. To gain this knowledge, several research directions can be identified and organized into the following categories:

1. Cyber Pre-Attack (e.g., modeling motivation, "mind infections", dark-webs, defensive techniques, and interactions between groups);
2. Cyber Post-Attack (e.g., minimizing impacts of an attack, modeling and preventing cascading failures; providing tools that support understanding of interactions between networks and network elements);
3. Dynamical Interdependent Networks (i.e., networks that function by interacting; e.g., transportation; power); and
4. Computational Capability (e.g., to meet big data challenges; these challenges can be static or dynamic and linear or nonlinear).

In addition, we have identified and listed below known research gaps:

1. Real data is needed to validate models of both networks and cyber motivations, threats, attacks and mitigations;
2. Optimization metrics and the prioritization to select among them are needed;
3. Techniques are needed to incorporate geometric and temporal dynamics for both data collection and responses; and,
4. New models are needed to study human network interactions.

To fill the first gap, collaborations to obtain the sources of data and methods along with cross-testable results are needed for an archive that enables subject matter experts and others from different disciplines to study the archive. For the second gap, interactions are required between network owners and users on the one hand and academics, industry and government on the other to allow a meaningful search for the crucial metrics of cyber-defense performance. The third gap, in temporal dynamics, is currently being addressed from many different angles. The fourth gap, human and network interactions, represents a new area of research that must justify additional resources needed to fund wide-ranging collaborations among researchers across multidisciplinary areas that include computers, cognition, information, mathematics, and networks in natural and social sciences.

9.8   Conclusions

We draw a few conclusions from our review along with a brief discussion.

First, the cyber environment is becoming more and more complex along with the threats affecting cyberspace. For example, "By 2020 Cisco estimates that 99 % of devices (50 billion) will be connected to the Internet. In contrast, currently only around 1 % is connected today." [32] Even defenses are becoming complex, whether a defense is passive or active (e.g., despite our lengthy review of cyber defenses, we omitted numerous defenses, such as the use of encrypting emails, randomly generating passwords,[33] using peer networks to increase security[34], hardening websites, etc.). One of the problems with defending a website against cyber threats is that the relative value of what is being protected increases to cyber-attackers as the defenses they face increase, fueling the arms race between cyber hackers and cyber defenders (Schwartz 2014).

This chapter review is not inclusive of all potential cyber threats. We omitted many threats, such as those for businesses that must handle private personnel information (Washington Post 2014, 6/23).[35]

> But unlike Settles's other [business] experiments ... [with Obamacare] he is still trying to figure some things out—for example, how to safeguard employee information that must now be reported to the Internal Revenue Service, such as the Social Security numbers of children who are covered under their parents' health plans. "We don't want to be liable for that," he said. "What if we get hacked?"

Second, time criticality may be important. Actions can occur at wire speed in cyber, but 'slow and low' attacks like APTs are very difficult to detect and often sit until pre-specified conditions are met. A metric to watch is the cost of the defensive decisions per unit of time per unit of defense resource (from Walters 2014). The implication is that too much cost for cyber defense leads some businesses to settle instead of to defend (i.e., the example we used above where "ransomware" is used by cybercriminals to encrypt a firm's proprietary information and then seeking a fee to decrypt exemplifies the cost of a failed strategy; New York Times 2014, 6/21). Instead of settling, businesses and others must be persuaded that a better strategy is possible with improved defenses (Wall Street Journal 2014, 6/30).

Third, APTs are becoming a larger threat to national defense. For example, Naji (2004), Zarqawi's Islamist strategist "proposed a campaign of constant harassment of Muslim states that exhausted the states' will to resist." (see also The New Yorker 2014, 6/17) Harassment is apparently a characteristic of cyber-attacks against businesses such as when the attackers hold computer assets hostage until their ransom demands are met.

---

[32] e.g., http://communities.intel.com/community/itpeernetwork/blog/2014/02/08/cyber-security-is-not-prepared-for-the-growth-of-internet-connected-devices.

[33] http://csrc.nist.gov/publications/fips/fips181/fips181.txt.

[34] e.g., https://communities.intel.com/community/itpeernetwork/blog/2014/02/13/intel-cyber-security-briefing-trends-challenges-and-leadership-opportunities-cyberstrat14.

[35] See also: "The health care info that was hacked (and bank account info) may have affected contractors as well as both former and current employees. Their names, addresses, birth dates, Social Security numbers and dates of service were also included in the mix." From the *Wall Street Journal* (2014, 6/26), "Montana Breach Affects Up To 1.3 Million As Health Care Data Gets Hacked", http://www.wallstreetotc.com/montana-breach-affects-1-3-million-health-care-data-gets-hacked/24807/.

Fourth, a list of open cognitive science questions was noted that need to be addressed. For example, we need to know, based on cognitive science, the characteristics of good cyber defenders. We need to know the biases of attackers, users and user groups. We also need to explore the steps that can be taken to counter biases to better defend users from cyber-attackers.

Fifth, questions exist also for the interdependence in teams, organizations and systems. From interdependence theory, we need to know how to make teams into better cyber defenders; e.g., based on theory, maintaining the boundaries of good teams should generate less entropy—the evidence, supporting our hypothesis, indicates that the best teams generate less noise, but this evidence is anecdotal (Lawless et al. 2013). We have also found that internally cooperative teams compete better in increasingly competitive environments.[36]

To further develop interdependence theory, we need to better understand the limits of teamwork as cooperation, competition, boundaries, training and technology interact in interdependent environments. We have found that in a competitive world, as teams cooperate to improve their competitiveness, a team's boundaries are strengthened and better maintained (Lawless et al. 2013).

Interdependence theory informs us that boundaries can be maintained by searching for organizational vulnerabilities. Using attacks by "red" teams (Wall Street Journal 2014, 4/28) to search the cyber defenses for vulnerabilities in "blue" teams aids in helping organizations to better defend against cyber-attacks (Schwartz 2014). We agree with Martinez (2014) that system predictions and assessments are currently weak or nonexistent; system defenses need to be practiced and improved and automated where possible (e.g., with AI); and metrics established, measured and reported. Even though we warned that predictions made under interdependent states are clouded by uncertainty, predictions must be made of expected system performance during cyber games, followed by assessments of the metrics for the systems that suffered from red attacks. Comparative analyses of all of the teams playing cyber games need to be assessed and compared against real systems affected by actual cyber-attacks. But, in addition, we want to understand how malicious agents select targets—not just watch them do it. We should be able to create a system that predicts a malicious action before a red team composed of humans enacts a threat. Based on data sets of past cyber threats and defensive actions, predictive cyber threat analytics that predict future threats should become a part of the tool kit used by defenders against malicious actors.

From an individual perspective, cognitive biases form individual vulnerabilities that cyber-attackers attempt to exploit. However, from an interdependent perspective, team training offsets these biases (Lawless et al. 2013). The more competitive is a team, the more able it is to control its biases or limit the extent of their effectiveness

---

[36] Indirectly supporting our conclusion, HHS reported "... that more competition among health plans tends to lower prices ...", *Washington Post* (2014, 6/18), "Federal insurance exchange subsidies cut premiums by average of 76 %, HHS reports"; http://www.washingtonpost.com/national/health-science/federal-insurance-exchange-subsidies-cut-premiums-by-average-of-76percent-hhs-reports/2014/06/17/4f31b502-f650-11e3-a3a5-42be35962a52_story.html.

(e.g., as with varying levels of cyber defenses; as with checks and balances; in Lawless et al. 2013; or as with the use of "red" teams; in Schwartz 2014).

Finally, to optimize defenses against cyber-threats, we must shift our focus from an individual to the interdependent perspective. According to methodological individualism, cooperation produces the superior social good even if punishment is necessary to replace competition with cooperation (Axelrod 1984, p. 8). But, taken to its logical extreme justifies the savagery used by the Islamic State when it forces its people to be more cooperative (e.g., Naji 2004). Moreover, this theoretical perspective cannot wish away the threats and risks posed by cyber-attacks. In contrast, the realism of interdependence theory confirms that competition will remain ever present in the struggle for survival, driving the need for disruptive technology. From Kello (2013, p. 31):

> The revolutionary impact of technological change upsets this basic political framework of international society, whether because the transforming technology empowers unrecognized players with subversive motives and aims or because it deprives states of clear "if-then" assumptions necessary to conduct a restrained rivalry.

Competition and disruptive technology combine to create the very real present and future dangers we face in cyberspace; Again from Kello (2013, p. 32):

> The cyber domain is a perfect breeding ground for political disorder and strategic instability. Six factors contribute to instrumental instability: offense dominance, attribution difficulties, technological volatility, poor strategic depth, and escalatory ambiguity. Another—the "large-N" problem—carries with it fundamental instability as well.

Staying ahead in the race for new technology is important. In the future, Martinez (2014, p. 8) foresees two things for cyber defenders, that tying speech to visual data needs to be improved (e.g., vocal interactions with recommender displays); and that:

> The development of the recommender system . . . is an area of future research applicable to a broad range of applications, including . . . cyber anomaly detection . . . Such an approach will incorporate multiple disciplines in data aggregation, machine learning techniques, augmented cognition models, and probabilistic estimates in reaching the shortest decision time within the courses of action function of a decision support system.

Awareness is increasing of the dangers in cyberspace to Americans and the need to prepare to face those dangers. Recently in the *Wall Street Journal*, Tom Kean and Lee Hamilton (Kean and Hamilton 2014), the former chair and vice chair of the 9/11 Commission, respectively, and now co-chairs of the Bipartisan Policy Center's Homeland Security Project, spoke to these dangers:

> A growing chorus of national-security experts describes the cyber realm as the battlefield of the future. American life is becoming ever more dependent on the Internet. At the same time, government and private computer networks in the U.S. are under relentless cyber-attack. This is more than an academic concern—attacks in the digital world can inflict serious damage in the physical world. Hackers can threaten the control systems of critical facilities like dams, water-treatment plants and the power grid. A hacker able to remotely control a dam, pumping station or oil pipeline could unleash large-scale devastation. As terrorist organizations such as the Islamic State grow and become more sophisticated, the threat of cyber-attack increases as well.

To remain competitive and in business, organizations must be able to defend the proprietary information that they oversee for themselves and their customers in cyberspace (Finch 2014):

> The real game change for many CIOs [Chief Information Officer] is the emerging movement to consider a company's cybersecurity posture when making procurement decisions. To put it bluntly, companies with weaker cybersecurity are increasingly being viewed as less attractive vendors. . . . Already companies that have suffered successful cyber-attacks are finding themselves cut off from revenue streams. Just ask USIS, which performs background investigations for the U.S. government. USIS recently suffered a serious data breach, resulting in the personal information of tens of thousands of government employees being compromised. The response from its federal customers, the Department of Homeland Security and the Office of Personnel and Management, was swift: it was issued "stop-work" orders. And "stop-work" means no money coming in from either DHS or OPM. Worse yet, OPM announced earlier this week that it was not renewing its background check contract with USIS.

References

Abramson, M, (2014), Learning Temporal User Profiles of Web Browsing Behavior, Proceedings of the 6th ASE Conference on Social Computing.

Abramson, M. & Aha D. W. (2013), Authentication from Web Browsing Behavior, FLAIRS Conference.

Adelson, E. H. (2000). Lightness perceptions and lightness illusions. The new cognitive sciences, 2nd Ed. M. Gazzaniga. MIT Press.

Ahdieh, R.G. (2009), Beyond individualism and economics, retrieved 12/5/09 from ssrn.com/abstract=1518836.

Ambrose, S.H. (2001), Paleolithic technology and human evolution, Science, 291, 1748–53.

Axelrod, R. (1984). The evolution of cooperation. New York, Basic.

Axelrod, R. & Iliev, R. (2014), Timing of cyber conflict, PNAS, 111(4): 1–6.

Bell, B. S., Kozlowski, S.W.J. & Blawath, S. (2012). Team Learning: A Theoretical Integration and Review. The Oxford Handbook of Organizational Psychology. Steve W. J. Kozlowski (Ed.). New York, Oxford Library of Psychology. Volume 1.

Bernard, M. & Backus, G. (2009), Modeling the Interaction Between Leaders and Society During Conflict Situations, Sandia National Laboratories; Presented to the System Dynamics Society, Boston; see at: http://www.systemdynamics.org/conferences/2009/proceed/papers/P1382.pdf

Boebert, E. (2010), A survey of challenges in attribution, Proceedings of a workshop on deterring cyberattacks.

Capelle, Q. (2014, 1/24), "Multiple device users insufficiently aware of risks", from http://www.atelier.net/en/trends/articles/multiple-device-users-insufficiently-aware-risks_427025

Carley Kathleen M., et al. (2013), Liu, H., Pfeffer, J., Morstatter, F. & Goolsby, R. "Near real time assessment of social media using geo-temporal network analytics." Advances in Social Networks Analysis and Mining (ASONAM), IEEE/ACM International Conference on. Niagara, ON, Canada, August 25–29, 2013.

Chakrabarti, C.G. & Ghosh, K. (2013), Dynamical entropy via entropy of non-random matrices: Application to stability and complexity in modeling ecosystems, *Mathematical Biosciences*, 245: 278–281.

Darwin, C. (1973) The descent of man. New York, Appleton.

Feldman, J.M. & Lynch, Jr., J.G. (1988), Self-Generated Validity and Other Effects of Measurement on Belief, Attitude, Intention, and Behavior, Journal of Applied Psychology, Journal of Applied Psychology, 73(3): 421–435.

Finch, B.E. (2014, 9/11), CIOs Spur Revenue Generation Through Smart Cybersecurity, the *Wall Street Journal*, http://blogs.wsj.com/cio/2014/09/11/cios-spur-revenue-generation-through-smart-cybersecurity/?KEYWORDS=cyber+threats

Forsythe, C., Silva, A., Stevens-Adams, S.M. & Bradshaw, J. (2012), Human Dimensions in Cyber Operations Research and Development Priorities, SANDIA REPORT, SAND 2012–9188, http://www.jeffreymbradshaw.net/publications/Hum%20Dim%20Cyber%20Workshop%20Final%20Report.pdf

Fox News (2010, 3/8), "FBI Warns Brewing Cyberwar May Have Same Impact as 'Well-Placed Bomb'", from http://www.foxnews.com/tech/2010/03/08/cyberwar-brewing-china-hunts-wests-intel-secrets/

Freer, R. D. & Perdue, W.C. (1996), Civil procedure, Cincinatti: Anderson.

Giles, L. (2007), The art of war by Sun Tzu, Special Edition Books

Hackman, J. R. (2011). "Six common misperceptions about teamwork." Harvard Business Review blogs.hbr.org/cs/

Hartmann, K. & Steup, C. (2013), "The Vulnerability of UAVs to Cyber Attacks—An Approach to the Risk Assessment", in K. Podins, J. Stinessen & M. Maybaum (Eds.), 5th International Conference on Cyber Conflict, NATO CCD COE Publications

Kahneman, D. (2011), "Thinking fast and slow", MacMillan.

Kaplan, S. & Garrick, B.J. (1981), On The Quantitative Definition of Risk, Risk Analysis, 1(1): 11–27.

Kean, T. & Hamilton, L. (2014, 9/10), "A New Threat Grows Amid Shades of 9/11. The nation remains largely unaware of the potential for disaster from cyberattacks", Wall Street Journal, from http://online.wsj.com/articles/tom-kean-and-lee-hamilton-a-new-threat-grows-amid-shades-of-9-11-1410390195

Kelley, H.H. (1992), "Lewin, situations, and interdependence." Journal of Social Issues 47: 211–233.

Kello, L. (2013), "The Meaning of the Cyber Revolution. Perils to Theory and Statecraft", International Security, 38(2): 7–40.

Kenny, D. A., Kashy, D.A., & Bolger, N. (1998). Data analyses in social psychology. Handbook of Social Psychology. D. T. Gilbert, Fiske, S.T. & Lindzey, G. Boston, MA, McGraw-Hill. 4th Ed., Vol. 1: pp. 233–65.

Lawless, W. F., Llinas, James, Mittu, Ranjeev, Sofge, Don, Sibley, Ciara, Coyne, Joseph, & Russell, Stephen (2013). "Robust Intelligence (RI) under uncertainty: Mathematical and conceptual foundations of autonomous hybrid (human-machine-robot) teams, organizations and systems." Structure & Dynamics 6(2).

Lawless, W.F., Mittu, R., Jones, R., Sibley, C. & Coyne, J. (2014, 5/20), "Assessing human teams operating virtual teams: FIST2FAC", paper presented at HFE TAG 68, Aberdeen Proving Ground, May 20–22, 2014.

Lewis, M. (2014), Flash boys: a wall-street revolt. New York: Penguin.

Lewis, J.A. & Baker, S. (2014, June), "Net Losses: Estimating the Global Cost of Cybercrime. Economic impact of cybercrime II," Center for Strategic and International Studies. http://csis.org/files/attachments/rp-economic-impact-cybercrime2.pdf

Los Angeles Times (2014, 6/10), "FAA for the first time OKs commercial drone flights over land". http://www.latimes.com/business/aerospace/la-fi-faa-bp-drone-20140609-story.html

Loukas, G., Gan, D. & Vuong, T. (2013, 3/22), A taxonomy of cyber attack and defence mechanisms for emergency management, 2013, Third International Workshop on Pervasive Networks for Emergency Management, IEEE, San Diego.

Lowrance, W.W. (1976), Of acceptable risk: science and the determination of safety, Kaufmann Publisher.

Mallery, John C. (2011), "Models of Escalation in Cyber Conflict," presentation at the Workshop on Cyber Security and Global Affairs, Budapest, May 31–June 2, 2011, retrieved from http://es.slideshare.net/zsmav/models-of-escalation-and-deescalation-in-cyber-conflict.

Marble, J. (2014, 5/1), "Cognitive science for cybersecurity". Unpublished slides.

Martinez, D., Lincoln Laboratory, Massachusetts Institute of Technology (2014, invited presentation), Architecture for Machine Learning Techniques to Enable Augmented Cognition in the Context of Decision Support Systems. Invited paper for presentation at HCI.

McMorrow, D. (2010), "The Science of Cyber-Security,", Mitre Corp. report JSR-10–102, requested by JASON, retrieved from http://www.fas.org/irp/agency/dod/jason/cyber.pdf

Naji, A.B. (2004), The management of savagery. http://azelin.files.wordpress.com/2010/08/abu-bakr-naji-the-management-of-savagery-the-most-critical-stage-through-which-the-umma-will-pass.pdf

National Research Council of the National Academies (2012), "Terrorism and the Electric Power Delivery System" Washington, D.C.: National Academies Press, p. 16.

New York Times (2014, 6/20), "Hackers Take Down World Cup Site in Brazil"; from http://bits.blogs.nytimes.com/2014/06/20/hackers-take-down-world-cup-site-in-brazil/?_php=true&_type=blogs&_r=0

New York Times (2014, 6/21), "Hacker Tactic: Holding Data Hostage. Hackers Find New Ways to Breach Computer Security".

NIST's Special Publication 800–122 (2010, April), "Guide to Protecting the Confidentiality of Personally Identifiable Information (PII);" from http://csrc.nist.gov/publications/nistpubs/800-122/sp800-122.pdf

NIST (2014, 2/12), "NIST Releases Cybersecurity Framework Version 1.0", http://www.nist.gov/itl/csd/launch-cybersecurity-framework-021214.cfm

Okhravi, H., Haines, J.W. & Ingols, K. (2011), "Achieving cyber survivability in a contested environment using a cyber moving target", *High Frontier Journal*, 7(3): 9–13.

Pfeffer, J., & Fong, C.T. (2005). "Building organization theory from first principles: The self-enhancement motive and understanding power and influence." Org. Science **16**: 372–388.

Pomerantsev, P. (2014, 5/5), "How Putin Is Reinventing Warfare", Foreign Policy, http://www.foreignpolicy.com/articles/2014/05/05/how_putin_is_reinventing_warfare.

Pressé, S., Ghosh, K., Lee, J. & Dill, K.A. (2013), Principles of maximum entropy and maximum caliber in statistical physics, Reviews of Modern Physics, 85: 1115: 1141.

Glowniak J (1998), "History, structure, and function of the Internet; Semin Nucl Med., 28(2):135–44; from http://www.ncbi.nlm.nih.gov/pubmed/9579415

Rajivan, P., Champion, M., Cooke, N.J., Jariwala, S., Dube, G & Buchanan, V. (2013), Effects of teamwork versus group work on signal detection in cyber defense teams. Lecture Notes in Computer Science, 8027: 172–180. P

Rand, D.G. & Nowak, M.A. (2013), Human cooperation, *Cognitive Sciences, 17*(8): 413–425.

Reason, J. (2008), The Human Contribution, Unsafe Acts, Accidents and Heroic Recoveries, University of Manchester, UK: Ashgate.

Salim, H. (2014), "Cyber safety: A systems thinking and systems theory approach to managing cyber security risks". Working Paper CISL#2014–07, Sloan School of Management, MIT.

Schwartz, C. (2014, 6/10), "Program overview/challenges"; presentation to the 2014 Computational methods for decision making gathering, Arlington, VA, 10–12 June 2014.

Schweitzer, F., Fagiolo, G., Sornette, D., Vega-Redondo, F., Vespignani, A., & White, D.R. (2009). "Economic networks: The new challenges." Science **325**: 422–425.

Smallman, H. S. (2012). TAG (Team Assessment Grid): A Coordinating Representation for submarine contact management. SBIR Phase II Contract #: N00014–12-C-0389, ONR Command Decision Making 6.1–6.2 Program Review.

Smith, W. K., & Tushman, M.L. (2005) "Managing strategic contradictions: A top management model for managing innovation streams." Organizational Science **16(5)**: 522–536.

The New Yorker (2014, 6/17), "ISIS's savage strategy in Iraq; www.newyorker.com/online/blogs/comment/2014/06/isis-savage-strategy-in-iraq.html

Thibaut, J.W., & Kelley, H.H., (1959). The social psychology of groups. New York: Wiley.

USA Today (2014, 6/4), "Russian hacker engineered dazzling worldwide crime spree".

Valukas, A.R. (2014, 5/29), "Report to Board of Directors of General Motors Company Regarding Ignition Switch Recalls"; Published by *The Washington Post*. http://www.scribd.com/doc/228338387/Valukas-Report-on-GM-Redacted

Wall Street Journal (2009, 4/8), "Electricity Grid in U.S. Penetrated By Spies", http://www.wsj.com/articles/SB123914805204099085

Wall Street Journal (2014, 4/28), "Europe Begins Its Largest-Ever Cyberwar Stress Test"; http://blogs.wsj.com/digits/2014/04/28/europe-begins-its-largest-ever-cyberwar-stress-test/?KEYWORDS=cyber+threat

Wall Street Journal (2014, 6/30), "Cyber Specter Mandates New CFO-IT Dynamic;" from http://deloitte.wsj.com/riskandcompliance/2014/06/30/cyber-specter-mandates-new-cfo-it-dynamic/?KEYWORDS=cyber+threat

Walters, J.P. (2014, 6/12), "Heterogeneous cloud services"; presentation to the 2014 Computational methods for decision making gathering, Arlington, VA, 10–12 June 2014.

Washington Post (2011, 8/3), "Report on 'Operation Shady RAT' identifies widespread cyber-spying", from http://www.washingtonpost.com/national/national-security/report-identifies-widespread-cyber-spying/2011/07/29/gIQAoTUmqI_story.html

Washington Post (2014, 5/30), "China's cyber-generals are reinventing the art of war", http://www.washingtonpost.com/blogs/innovations/wp/2014/05/30/chinas-cyber-generals-are-reinventing-the-art-of-war/

Washington Post (2014, 6/6), "Vodafone reveals that governments are collecting personal data without limits. Britain's Vodaphone cites several nations [29 nations are cited in its 88 page annex]. Warns that governments have unfettered access", http://www.washingtonpost.com/business/technology/governments-collecting-personal-data-without-limit-says-vodafone/2014/06/06/ff0cfc1a-edb4-11e3-9b2d-114aded544be_story.html.

Washington Post 2014, 6/12), "FCC unveils 'new regulatory paradigm' for defeating hackers", http://www.washingtonpost.com/blogs/the-switch/wp/2014/06/12/fcc-chair-telecom-companies-must-do-more-to-defend-against-hackers/

Washington Post (2014, 6/13), "P.F. Chang's diners have card data stolen", http://www.washingtonpost.com/business/economy/pf-changs-diners-have-card-data-stolen-priceline-to-buy-opentable/2014/06/13/596ab6f4-f2a9-11e3-bf76-447a5df6411f_story.html

Washington Post (2014, 6/23), "As health-care law's employer mandate nears, firms cut worker hours, struggle with logistics", http://www.washingtonpost.com/national/health-science/as-health-care-lawles-employer-mandate-nears-firms-cut-worker-hours-struggle-with-logistics/2014/06/23/720e197c-f249-11e3-914c-1fbd0614e2d4_story.html

Wickens, C. D. (1992). Engineering psychology and human performance (second edition). Columbus, OH, Merrill.

Wired (2012, 11/09), "Teenage Hacker 'Cosmo the God' Sentenced by California Court", retrieved from http://www.wired.com/2012/11/hacker-cosmo-the-god-sentenced-by-california-court/

Zipf, G.K. (1949), *Human behavior and the principle of least effort*, New York: Addison-Wesley.

Chapter 10
CyberWar Game: A Paradigm for Understanding New Challenges of Cyber War

Noam Ben-Asher and Cleotilde Gonzalez

Abstract Cyber-war is a growing form of threat to our society that involves multiple players executing simultaneously offensive and defensive operations. Given that cyber space is hyper dimensional and dynamic, human decision making must also incorporate numerous attributes and must be agile and adaptive. In this chapter, we review how computational models of human cognition can be scaled up from an individual model of a defender operating in a hostile environment, through a pair of models representing a defender and an attacker to multi-agents in a cyber-war. Following, we propose to study the decision making processes that drive the dynamics of cyber-war using a multi-agent model comprising of cognitive agents that learn to make decisions according to Instance-Based Learning Theory (IBLT). In this paradigm, the CyberWar game, assets and power are two key attributes that influence the decisions of agents. Assets represent the key resource that an agent is protecting from attacks while power represents technical prowess of an agent's cyber security. All the agents share the same goal of maximizing their assets and they learn from experience to attack other agents and defend themselves in order to meet this goal. Importantly, they don't learn by using predefined strategies, as many multi-agent models do, but instead they learn from experience according to the situation and actions of others, as suggested by the IBLT's process. This chapter contributes to current research by: proposing a novel paradigm to study behavior in cyber-war, using a well-known cognitive model of decisions from experience to predict what possible human behavior would be in a simulated cyber-war, and demonstrating novel predictions regarding the effects of power and assets, two main contributors to cyber-war.

N. Ben-Asher (✉) · C. Gonzalez
Department of Social and Decision Sciences, Dynamic Decision Making Laboratory,
Carnegie Mellon University, 4609 Winthrop Street, Suite 102,
Pittsburgh, PA 15213, USA
e-mail: noamba@cmu.edu

C. Gonzalez
e-mail: coty@edu.cmu

© Springer International Publishing Switzerland 2015
S. Jajodia et al. (eds.), *Cyber Warfare,* Advances in Information Security 56,
DOI 10.1007/978-3-319-14039-1_10

10.1   Introduction

Cyber-war is not a game; it is a reality. In the past few years, everything we know about war is changing. Military operations used to be planned and executed on the "battlefield" in a three-dimensional world with physical vehicles and weapons, and with enemies we could "see." Cyber-warfare is changing the whole concept of war, what we know about offensive and defensive operations, and just about everything we know about training new soldiers. Cyber-warfare involves multiple units (individual, state-sponsored organizations, or even nations) executing simultaneously offensive and defensive operations through networks of computers. Furthermore, cyber-attacks against people, machines, and infrastructure became a reality and they are taking place here and now. For example, Russia used botnets as part of the military campaign against Georgia in 2008, launching Distributed Denial of Service attacks that silenced Georgian government websites and disabled the government's ability to communicate with its people. The cyber worm 'Stuxnet' that struck the Iranian nuclear facility at Natanz was described by experts as a military-grade cyber missile that targets centrifuges (Farwell and Rohozinski 2011). War is gradually shifting from the physical to the cyber world and they are also taking place in both dimensions in parallel. With the increased dependency on computer systems and networks, however, the assumptions is that the cyber space will be the major battlefield of the future and whomever prevails in the cyber world will prevail in the physical world too. Given the many cyber-physical challenges, it is frightening that we know so little. In many ways, we are unprepared to deal with the new challenges that cyber-war brings to the modern battle field.

In this chapter, we propose one way in which behavioral scientists may contribute to understanding the new challenges of cyber-warfare: the creation of simple formal representation of a representative simulation and experimental paradigms of a cyber-war. As in many everyday situations, decisions in cyber-war are often motivated by human reasons: greed, power, self and common economic interests, friendships and coalitions, etc. Thus, our approach to creating simulated environments in which these motivations may be captured in conjunction with information availability, enabling dynamic decisions to be studied. This is a modest first step towards the development of socio-cognitive theories of decision making in cyber-war.

10.2   Scaling Up: From Individual to Behavioral Game Theory to Behavioral Network Theory

When we make decisions every day, we often rely on our own experiences. Decision from experience (DFE) is an important shift of attention in decision sciences away from the traditional study of decisions from description (Hertwig et al. 2004). DFE represents a natural way of studying how humans adapt and learn to make decisions in the absence of explicitly stated payoffs and probabilities of obtaining those payoffs. And while classical behavioral decision theory focuses on violations of rationality assumptions, DFE helps to understand human behavior in natural environments where one cannot rely on the rationality assumption due to social complexity (Erev and Haruvy 2012). Furthermore, DFE is a way in which a decision maker can utilize own past experience to cope with the inherent uncertainty of a highly complex and dynamic environment. In such situations, it is fairly challenging to provide the decision maker with coherent and comprehensive descriptive information that truly captures the state of the environment.

Different computational models attempt to explain DFE through different mechanisms and with different levels of success. Learning models often emphasize a weighted adjustment process by which the value of a previously observed outcome is combined or updated with a newly observed outcome (e.g., Bush and Mosteller 1955; Erev et al. 2008; Hertwig et al. 2006; March 1996). Reinforcement models of learning are perhaps even more common in the literature. These models often assume that choices are reinforced based on immediate feedback (Erev and Roth 1998; Roth and Erev 1995). More recently, computational models based on the Instance-Based Learning Theory (IBLT) (Gonzalez et al. 2003) have shown robust predictions in a variety of decision making tasks where individuals rely on experience (Lejarraga et al. 2012). IBLT was originally developed to explain and predict learning and decision making in real-time, dynamic decision making environments. The theory has also been used as the basis for developing computational models that capture human decision making behavior in a wider variety of DFE tasks. These include dynamically complex tasks (Gonzalez et al. 2003; Gonzalez and Lebiere 2005; Martin et al. 2004), training paradigms of simple and complex tasks (Gonzalez et al. 2010; Gonzalez and Dutt 2010), simple stimulus-response practice and skill acquisition tasks (Dutt et al. 2009), and repeated binary-choice tasks (Lebiere et al. 2007; Lejarraga et al. 2010). The different applications of the theory illustrate its generality and its ability to capture learning from exploration and DFE in multiple contexts.

Recently, IBL models of learning and decisions from experience have been used in experimentation and to explain human behavior in the detection of cyber-attacks. These models have started to escalate towards behavioral game theoretical science and they are even being used in behavioral network science. Figure 10.1 represents this escalation process. Initially, a single model is constructed to study the cognitive processes that a single decision maker (i.e., the defender) applies when interacting with a controlled environment. At this level, the actions of the attacker are predefined through a set of strategies. In the next level, the attacker is also represented by a cognitive model. Here, both the defender and the attacker have learning mechanisms that allow them to learn from experience and adjust their decisions. When scaling up from an individual decision maker to a pair of decision makers that interact repeatedly, we borrow many concepts from Game Theory and especially from Behavioral Game Theory (BGT). This allows us to observe and examine how behaviors at the pair level evolve and whether stable patterns emerge (i.e., equilibrium) with experience. To capture the complex dynamics of a cyber-war, multiple models interact through a network. In this network, models are not assigned to a specific role, rather they learn from experience regarding their abilities and the abilities of the others. In this setting, models learn through the repeated interaction to play the role of an attacker

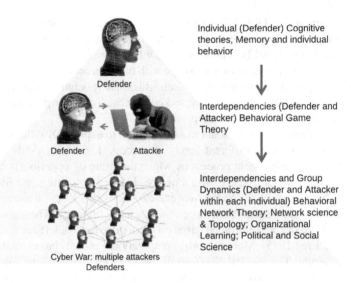

Individual (Defender) Cognitive
theories, Memory and individual
behavior

Interdependencies (Defender and
Attacker) Behavioral Game
Theory

Interdependencies and Group
Dynamics (Defender and Attacker
within each individual) Behavioral
Network Theory; Network science
& Topology; Organizational
Learning; Political and Social
Science

Fig. 10.1 Scaling up from individual decisions to behavioral game theory to network game theory

or a defender depending on their ability and the actions of their opponents. Next, we elaborate and demonstrate each of the levels in the scaling process of cognitive models for cyber-war.

In an initial IBL model, we attempted to represent some of the cognitive processes that cyber analysts confront while detecting cyber-attacks. A security analyst is in charge of defending against intrusions in a network. This analyst is classifying network events captured by an Intrusion Detection System (IDS) as cyber-attacks or not. The work of Dutt and colleagues (Dutt et al. 2011, 2012) used an IBL cognitive model of the recognition and comprehension process needed from a security analyst in a simple cyber-attack scenario. The IBL model first recognizes network events (e.g., execution of an operation on a server, network flows, etc.) as malicious or not based upon the event's situation attributes and the similarity of the events' attributes to past experiences (instances) stored in analyst's memory. Then, the model reasons about a sequence of observed events being a cyber-attack or not, based upon instances retrieved from memory and the risk-tolerance of a simulated analyst. The decisions of the simulated analyst are evaluated based upon two cyber situation awareness metrics: accuracy and the timeliness of analyst's decision actions.

Our recent research attempts to bring together the DFE demonstrations with BGT and social interaction paradigms (Gonzalez et al. 2014b; Oltramari et al. 2013). Cyber security is a non-cooperative "game" that involves strategic interactions between two "players": the defender of the network (e.g., cyber security analyst) and the attacker (e.g., hacker). This is a non-cooperative game because it is assumed that the defender and the attacker act independently, without collaboration or communication with each other. Recent research on adversarial reasoning is now being used and applied to many new and exciting domains, including counter-terrorism, homeland security, health and sustainability, and very recently to cyber security (Shiva et al. 2010). Many technologies based on Game Theory have become available to support the cyber security analyst. For example, a recent survey (Roy et al. 2010) summarizes technical solutions based on Game Theory that are designed to enhance network security. The survey concludes that many of the current game-theoretic approaches to cyber security are based on either static game models or games with perfect or complete information, misrepresenting the reality of the network security context in which situations are highly dynamic and where security analysts must rely on imperfect and incomplete information. Furthermore, although more technologies have become available, they are not implemented to account for the human cognitive factors that influence the behaviors of a defender and an attacker, and these tools are often incomplete and ineffective at supporting the security analyst's job. Thus, the current technology often ignores analysts' cognitive limitations; analysts' understanding of the hacker's strategy and projections of possible actions; and the dynamics of an evolving strategic situation (Gonzalez et al. 2014b).

Another important aspect of social dilemmas and conflict situations is the availability of information to decision makers, which can range from no information about interdependence with others to complete information about the actions of others, their influence on the other's outcomes, and the cultural identities of others. These informational characteristics influence reciprocation, fairness, trust, power, and other social concerns (Ben-Asher et al. 2013b; Martin et al. 2011). Thus, IBL models for DFE were extended to account for social information (Gonzalez et al. 2014a) and descriptive information (Ben-Asher et al. 2013a). Although these are important advancements towards understanding cyber-defense behavior, it is necessary to consider a more dynamic and broader perspective of cyber-warfare. Hence, we extend our research paradigms to multiplayer cyber-war paradigms.

The behaviors at the pair level (e.g., defender-attacker interactions) captured using BGT, which allow us to study the macro-level patterns emerging from micro-level social interactions between the agents may also greatly inform cyber-warfare. Since the predominant focus of developing multi-agent simulations has been for studying social interactions, the assumptions made about individual cognition has been very rudimentary (Sun 2006). Developing slightly more intelligent agents in multi-agent models by leveraging findings from cognitive sciences can provide insights on the interplay between individual cognition and social cognition, and would help develop more ecologically valid models. Our current research leverages existing mathematical representations of human cognition derived from cognitive science literature and from IBLT, and applies them in a multi-agent environment to examine emergent phenomena from cognitive agents engaged in cyber-warfare.

Next, we present an approach to investigate the dynamics in cyber-warfare as a result of investment in cyber security. Using concepts from multi-agent models, BGT, and IBLT, we constructed an n-player cyber security game (CyberWar game) played by cognitive agents. The CyberWar game is a paradigm for simulating a cyber-war in the laboratory, which may be studied with cognitive agents or using human participants. This development is important because cyber-warfare cannot be studied in naturalistic settings. More complex settings to study cyber-warfare are possible but difficult and expensive to conduct (Vigna 2003). Hence, computational modeling and simulations can provide a viable solution to the theoretical study of behavior in cyber-war.

10.3   The CyberWar Game

The CyberWar game aims to capture the characteristics and the dynamics of real-life cyber-warfare, while focusing on the aspects that are important to a decision maker. It is inspired by Hazon, Chakraborty, and Sycara's (2011) n-Player model of social conflict over limited resources. We extended their concept of the game and adapted it to cyber-warfare.

We start by scaling up Alpcan and Baar's (2010) simple security game, as seen in Fig. 10.2 on the left, to accommodate multiple players that can simultaneously decide to attack or not attack each other (Fig. 10.2 on the right). Thus, a player is not assigned to be an attacker of a defender in this game, but it is the player's decision to decide what role to play. In the CyberWar Game, assets and power are two key attributes that influence the decisions of agents. Assets represent the key resource that an agent is protecting from attacks, while power represents the technical prowess of an agent's cyber security. This setting also resembles distributed attacks over the network and incorporates the idea that power can be distributed between multiple goals. Here, the player learns to identify the attacker and who additionally can be a valuable target to attack. For example in Fig. 10.2, Player 1 and Player 3 are likely to attack Player 2. However, if Player 1 invests all the power in the attack without defending from Player 3, Player 3 can take advantage of such situation and attack only Player 1, who has the highest asset's value. Furthermore, unlike many one-shot security games, players here interact repeatedly and can learn from their past interactions with other players.

The CyberWar game takes place in a fully connected network of n players. Each player in the game has two main attributes, *Power* and *Assets*. *Power* represents

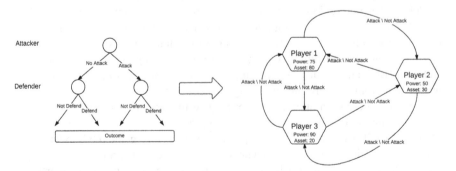

Fig. 10.2 Scaling up from Alpcan and Baar's (2010) simple security game (on the *right*) to a multiplayer CyberWar Game (on the *left*)

the player's cyber security infrastructure, which can be seen as the investment in cyber security. Power influences both the ability to defend against exogenous attacks coming from other players and the ability to initiate attacks against other players. Hence, if player i attacks player j, the outcome of this attack is a function of the players' power (P_i and P_j, respectively). In this game, a player can gain assets only by attacking and winning in a war against another player. The outcome of a war between two players is probabilistic and determined by the ratio between their power: the probability of player i to win a war against player j is:

$$p(i \ win) = 1 - p(j \ win) = \frac{P_i}{P_i + P_j} \tag{10.1}$$

The *Asset* of player j (S_j) can be viewed as the confidential information that a company has and is trying to protect or whatever player i is trying to obtain from player j. Essentially, all players in the CyberWar game share the same goal: to maximize their assets. When a player wins a war, he gains a percentage (g) of the opponent's assets; g represents the severity of the attack. Destructive attacks will have a high g value, whereas less severe attacks will have a low g value. This gives a representation of different types of attacks, as well as the possibility to examine how escalation in the severity of cyber-attacks can influence the dynamics in a network. Considering that player i attacks player j, the possible gains for the attacker is $O_{i,j} = gS_j$, which is equal to the losses incurred by player j from the attack.

Assets not only represent the motivation for a cyber-attack. Assets are also required to initiate an attack and to protect from incoming attacks, whereas losing all assets forces an agent to be suspended from the game for a specific duration. Every war entails costs for the participating agents. There are separate costs for initiating an attack and for defending. When player i attacks player j, the cost of attack (C) is deducted from the assets of the attacking agent. Therefore, the expected gains for player i attacking player j is as follow:

$$U_{i,j} = (P_{i \ win} \times O_{i,j}) - C \tag{10.2}$$

And the expected loss of player j from that attack is:

$$U_{j,i} = -(P_{i \ win} \times O_{i,j}) \tag{10.3}$$

Since a player can attack another player and at the same time be attacked by several other players in any given round of the game, the calculations of gains and losses for each individual player are done sequentially and separately. First, losses from being attacked are calculated, then gains from winning an attack are calculated, and finally gains and losses are summed and the costs of attack and defense are deducted from the remaining assets of the agent.

Therefore, assets change dynamically during the game as a result of each player's actions. A player may also run out of assets and when assets drop below a certain threshold, this player is suspended for a fixed number of trials. This resembles downtime for a network node or service in the cyber-world. During a downtime period, the player cannot engage with other players. After recovering from downtime, a player regains assets which are equal to the initial assets that the player started with in the first trial of the game.

10.3.1 A Cognitive Model of a Cyber-Warrior

For simplicity's sake, many cyber security models tend to adopt an abstract point of view in which multiple attackers and defenders are thought of as a group of attackers and defenders that share the same goal and where the entities in each group operate in a synchronized manner (Alpcan and Baar 2010). In contrast, multiple units in our cyber-war setting can interact without synchronization, each trying to maximize its own gains. Recent efforts to capture this distributed nature involve n-Player models of social conflict that share some similarities with cyber-warfare (Hazon et al. 2011; Kennedy et al. 2010). In parallel, there are attempts to study cyber-attacks and cyber-warfare through agent-based modeling (Kotenko 2005, 2007). However, many of these models use strategic agents that do not aim to replicate human decision making processes. Using a cognitive model of a cyber-warrior aims to bridge this gap; as it provides the ability to examine the human decision making process in a complex environment of n-players. Moreover, the use of a cognitive model allows us to examine the emergence of behaviors and how they evolve overtime through repeated interaction between the agents and to observe how an agent learns about other agents from experience.

To demonstrate the benefits of using cognitive models to capture, analyze, and understand the dynamics of cyber-warfare, we developed an IBL model which represents the decision maker (i.e., an agent) in the CyberWar game. From the agents' perspective, cyber-warfare can be seen as a repeated binary-choice between attacking and not attacking the most profitable opponent in a network. In the CyberWar game, multiple agents with identical cognitive mechanisms and parameters represent multiple decision makers. In each trial, an agent in the game makes a decision of whether or not to attack each of the other agents based on their past experience. Once the agent have identified a likely opponent, it evaluates whether to Attack or Not attack that specific opponent based on the expected payoff for each of the two possible decisions, which is based on the past interactions and outcomes that are stored in memory for that particular type of agent.

10.3.2 Ongoing Research with the CyberWar Game

We combine the CyberWar game with the IBL model of a cyber-warrior to create an ecosystem in which multiple agents with their own cognitive mechanisms and parameters represent multiple decision makers that repeatedly interact. This environment can be used to answer questions regarding the short-term and long-term influence of the investment in cyber security. First, we evaluate how investment in security can influence the assets that an agent gains over time. The focus here is on an agent's ability to acquire and protect assets, and the dynamics of assets over time. Next, we observe how investments in cyber security influence the behavior of an agent. More specifically, we examine how agents learn to become more or less aggressive depending on their investment in cyber security.

The CyberWar game and the cognitive agents were implemented using Netlogo (Wilensky 1999), a multi-agent simulation environment where each agent was an IBL model. Here, we used three levels of power and three levels of assets. The power of an agent was determined by a random draw from a uniform distribution. Low power had the minimum value of 100 and a maximum value of 350. Similarly, medium power ranged between 351 and 700, and high power ranged between 701 and 999. The three levels of initial assets were low, medium, and high assets also corresponded to a random draw from a uniform distribution from the following intervals: 100–350, 351–700, and 701–999. Thus, our environment included 9 different agents, each with a unique combination of power and assets.

Agents could gain and lose assets through attacking other agents. In the current simulation, we examine the interactions when the severity of the cyber-attacks is relatively low, meaning that an agent could gain 20 % of the opponent's assets when winning in a cyber-war. Furthermore, if an agent's assets dropped below 100, that agent was suspended for 10 trials. This represents the downtime in which an agent becomes unavailable due to asset loss. During this period, the agent could neither attack nor be attacked. After recovering from downtime, the agent regained the initial amount of assets it had at the beginning of the simulation. It is important to note that the memory structure of the agent was not reset and as such, the agent could still benefit from the experiences it acquired from previous interactions.

When learning only from experience, instances are created by making a decision and observing its outcome. However, when making the first decision regarding other agents (i.e., a combination of power and assets), an agent had no previous experiences. Thus, to generate expectations from a decision and to elicit exploration of different opponents during the early stages of the interaction, we used prepopulated instances in memory which represents the agent's expectations before having any actual experiences (Ben-Asher et al. 2013; Lejarraga et al. 2012). The prepopulated instances correspond to the possible outcomes from attacking and not attacking other types of agents and contained a fixed value of 500. As the agent accumulated experiences, the activation of these prepopulated instances decayed overtime. Their decay leads to a decrease in the retrieval probability, which in turn lead to a decrease in the contribution of these values to the calculation of the blended value.

To allow the agents to learn from experience and to observe the dynamics of the interactions overtime, we ran 60 simulations each including 2500 trials. For all of the simulations, all the agents shared the same values for the free parameters in the IBL model. The values of σ (noise) and d (decay) were set at 0.25 and 5, respectively (obtained from fitting to a different data set in Lejarraga et al. 2012).

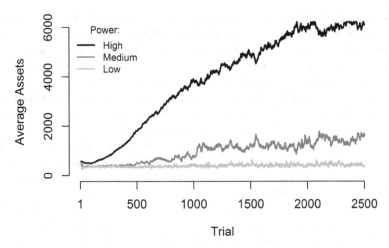

Fig. 10.3 The dynamic of average assets for each level of power as a function trial

To gain a better understanding of the distribution of assets between agents with different levels of power, we examine the dynamics of assets over time. This analysis examines the returns on investment in cyber security. As seen in Fig. 10.3, an agent's power influenced its ability to accumulate assets and the course of its accumulation. High power agents managed to accumulate faster and larger amount of assets compared to all other types of agents. For high power agents, the accumulation started from early stages of the interaction and they maintained a steady increase of assets throughout the interaction. This suggests that initial high investment in cyber security provides agents with the ability to gain an increasing amount of assets. Furthermore, high power agents learned relatively fast regarding their ability to successfully attack other agents and they exploited this ability to accumulate assets.

In contrast to agents with high power, it took about 500 trials before medium power agents were able to accumulate more assets compared to low power agents. Even though agents with medium power managed to accumulate assets, the rate of accumulation was relatively low compared to the rate with which high power agents accumulated assets. This highlights the different outcomes from high and medium investment in cyber security. The benefit from high investment is evident in short-term and long-term interactions, while the benefit from medium investment is only evident in the long-term interaction. Furthermore, not only did high investment in security allow accumulation in earlier stages, the rate of assets growth is faster for high power agents compared to medium power agents. Finally, low power agents did not manage to accumulate assets beyond their initial assets. Considering this finding together with the high probability that low power agents being suspended, it suggests that the low power agents provided the inflow of assets to the ecosystem. After low power agents lost their entire assets to high and medium power agents, they regained assets after recovering from the suspension period. The assets that the low power agents lost were distributed unequally between the high and medium agents, with a noticeable advantage to the high power agents.

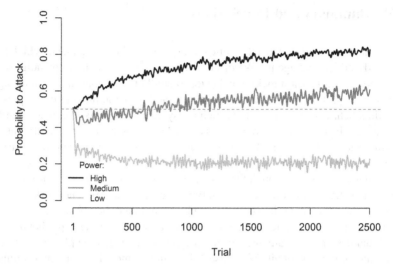

Fig. 10.4 The probability an agent will choose to attack the most beneficial opponent as a function of agents' power and trial

In the current cyber-warfare game, an agent was not defined as an attacker or as a defender. Also, the agent was not provided with any knowledge regarding the way power influenced the likelihood of winning in a cyber-attack. However, agents could learn what action (i.e., attack or not attack) was preferable for them, given their power level. As such, agents could learn from experience to become more aggressive or to avoid attacking other agents in the attempt to maximize their own assets. As illustrated in Fig. 10.4, high power agents gradually learned about their power, and the probability of a powerful agent attacking other agents increased overtime. For medium power agents, we find that initially the probability of attacking other agents drops below chance level. Although for the first 500 trials, it seems that agents with medium power did not tend to be aggressive, their probability of attacking increased gradually above chance level as they accumulated more experiences. Compared to agents with high or medium power, low power agents learned within a few trials to avoid attacking other agents. The learning process of low power agents seems to be faster than that of the other types of agents. When examining the probability of attacking other agents in the last 500 trials, we find that high power agents were more likely ($p = 0.83$) to attack other agents compared to medium ($p = 0.59$) or low ($p = 0.21$) power agents. These results indicate that a high investment in cyber security, which can be utilized to gain assets through cyber-attacks, can promote more aggressive behavior. Furthermore, the weakest agents within a given network quickly learned to avoid conflict with more powerful agents. Thus, two distinct levels of power, high and low, eventually led to the formation of an attackers group and a defenders group. Agent with medium power started the interaction more defensive and increased their aggressiveness overtime. However, compared to the agents with high or low power, the attack behavior of agent with medium power is less predictable.

10.4   Summary and Conclusions

In this chapter, we presented a theoretic multi-player CyberWar game in which play-ers are IBL cognitive agents. We discussed how one may scale up paradigms that study individual decision making behavior to conflict dilemmas and to multi-agent situations, departing from a model of learning and decision making that represents individual behavior. We simulated a rich ecosystem, which takes into account het-erogeneous players with different levels of power and assets that repeatedly interact overtime and can learn from their experiences. The CyberWar game is not restricted to the traditional grouping of attackers and defenders, and the players have motiva-tions and goals rather than predefined roles or strategies. Furthermore, the CyberWar game is not structured around a certain type of cyber-attack or a network topology. Rather it provides a flexible paradigm that helps simulate the evolution of networks over time as players repeatedly interact with one another. In order to predict the com-plex dynamics and the outcomes of the interactions between the players within the constraints of human cognition, we use IBL cognitive models. Through a simulated war, we show that our approach can be applied to efficiently answer a wide range of questions regarding investment in cyber security infrastructure. In particular, we demonstrate how power (i.e., cyber security infrastructure) is the main determinant of the state of a unit during cyber-warfare. We also show how different levels of power lead to different dynamics in the ability to accumulate assets.

The CyberWar Game can also serve as a scalable experimental platform, com-bining human and model players. Incorporating models in an experimental setting provides control over the environment, representing for example aggressive players that attack everybody, greedy players that chase the high assets, or players that are guided by reciprocation. This also allows us to study human response to distributed attacks and examine the evolution of a defensive strategy.

Acknowledgments   This research was partly supported by a Multidisciplinary University Research Initiative Award (MURI; # W911NF-09-1-0525) from Army Research Office and by the Army Research Laboratory under Cooperative Agreement Number W911NF-13-2-0045 (ARL Cyber Se-curity CRA). The views and conclusions contained in this document are those of the authors and should not be interpreted as representing the official policies, either expressed or implied, of the Army Research Laboratory or the U.S. Government. The U.S. Government is authorized to repro-duce and distribute reprints for Government purposes notwithstanding any copyright notation here on. The authors would like to thank Hau-yu Wong, Dynamic Decision Making Laboratory, for help with editorial work in the paper. We also would like to thank Prashanth Rajivan for supporting the implementation of the Netlogo model and helpful inputs.

References

Alpcan T, Baar T (2010) Network security: A decision and game-theoretic approach. Cambridge University Press, Cambridge

Ben-Asher N, Dutt V, Gonzalez C (2013a) Accounting for integration of descriptive and experien-tial information in a repeated prisoner's dilemma using an instance-based learning model. In: Kennedy B, Reitter D, Amant RS (eds) Proceedings of the 22nd Annual Conference on Behavior Representation in Modeling and Simulation, Ottawa, Canada, BRIMS Society

Ben-Asher N, Lebiere C, Oltramari A, Gonzalez C (2013b) Balancing fairness and efficiency in repeated societal interaction. In: Proceedings of the 35th Annual Meeting of the Cognitive Science Society, Humboldt Universität, Berlin, 31 July-3 August 2013

Bush RR, Mosteller F (1955) Stochastic models for learning. John Wiley & Sons: Oxford

Dutt V, Yamaguchi M, Gonzalez C, Proctor RW (2009) An instance-based learning model of stimulus-response compatibility effects in mixed location-relevant and location-irrelevant tasks. In: Howes A, Peebles D, Cooper R (eds) Proceedings of the 9th International Conference on Cognitive Modeling, Manchester, 24–26 July 2009

Dutt V, Ahn Y-S, Gonzalez C (2011). Cyber situation awareness: Modeling the security analyst in a cyber-attack scenario through instance-based learning. In: Li Y (ed) Lecture notes in computer science, vol 6818. Springer, Heidelberg, p 281–293

Dutt V, Ahn Y-S, Ben-Asher N, Gonzalez C (2012) Modeling the effects of base-rate on cyber threat detection performance. In: Rußwinkel N, Drewitz U, van Rijn H (eds) Proceedings of the 11th International Conference on Cognitive Modeling (ICCM 2012). Universitaetsverlag der TU, Berlin, p 88–93

Erev I, Roth AE (1998) Predicting how people play games: Reinforcement learning in experimental games with unique, mixed strategy equilibria. Am Econ Rev 88(4):848–881

Erev I, Glozman I, Hertwig R (2008) What impacts the impact of rare events. J Risk Uncertainty 36(2):153–177. doi:10.1007/s11166–008-9035-z

Erev I, Haruvy E (in press) Learning and the economics of small decisions. In: Kagel JH, Roth AE (eds) The handbook of experimental economics, vol 2. Princeton University Press, Princeton

Farwell JP, Rohozinski R (2011) Stuxnet and the future of cyber war. Survival 53(1):23–40. doi:10.1080/00396338.2011.555586

Gonzalez C, Dutt V (2010) Instance-based learning models of training. Proc Hum Fact Erg Soc An 54(27):2319–2323. doi:10.1177/154193121005402721

Gonzalez C, Lebiere C (2005) Instance-based cognitive models of decision making. In: Zizzo D, Courakis A (eds) Transfer of knowledge in economic decision-making. Macmillan, New York, p 148–165

Gonzalez C, Lerch JF, Lebiere C (2003). Instance-based learning in dynamic decision making. Cognitive Sci 27(4):591–635. doi:10.1016/S0364-0213(03)00031-4

Gonzalez C, Best BJ, Healy AF, Bourne LE Jr, Kole JA (2010) A cognitive modeling account of simultaneous learning and fatigue effects. J Cogn Sys Res 12(1):19–32. doi:10.1016/j.cogsys.2010.06.004

Gonzalez C, Ben-Asher N, Martin JM, Dutt V (2014a) Emergence of cooperation with increased information: Explaining the process with an instance-based learning model. Cognitive Sci (in press)

Gonzalez C, Ben-Asher N, Oltramari A, Lebiere C (2014b) Cognitive Models of Cyber Situation Awareness and Decision Making. In: Wang C, Kott A, Erbacher R (eds) Cyber defense and situational awareness. Springer, (in press

Hazon N, Chakraborty N, Sycara K (2011) Game theoretic modeling and computational analysis of n-player conflicts over resources. In: *Proceedings of the 2011 IEEE International Conference on Privacy, Security, Risk and Trust and IEEE International Conference on Social Computing.* IEEE, Los Alamitos, p 380–387. doi:10.1109/PASSAT/SocialCom.2011.178

Hertwig R, Barron G, Weber EU, Erev I (2004) Decisions from experience and the effect of rare events in risky choice. Psychol Sci 15(8):534–539. doi:10.1111/j.0956–7976.2004.00715.x

Hertwig, R, Barron G, Weber EU, Erev I (2006) The role of information sampling in risky choice. In: Fiedler K, Juslin P (eds) Information sampling and adaptive cognition. Cambridge University Press, New York, p 72–91

Kennedy WG, Hailegiorgis AB, Rouleau M, Bassett JK, Coletti M, Balan GC, Gulden T (2010) An agent-based model of conflict in East Africa and the effect of watering holes. In: Proceedings of the 19th Conference on Behavior Representation in Modeling and Simulation (BRiMS), p 112–119

Kotenko I (2005) Agent-based modeling and simulation of cyber-warfare between malefactors and security agents in internet. In: Merkuryev Y, Zobel R, Kerckhoffs E (eds) Proceedings of 19th European conference on modeling and simulation, Riga Technical University, Riga, 1–4 June 2005

Kotenko I (2007) Multi-agent modelling and simulation of cyber-attacks and cyber-defense for homeland security. In: Proceedings of the 4th IEEE workshop on intelligent data acquisition and advanced computing systems: technology and applications. IEEE, Los Alamitos, p 614–619

Lebiere C, Gonzalez C, Martin M (2007) Instance-based decision making model of repeated binary choice. In: Lewis RL, Polk TA, Laird JE (eds) Proceedings of the 8th International Conference on Cognitive Modeling. Ann Arbor, p 67–72

Lejarraga T, Dutt V, Gonzalez C (2010) Instance-based learning in repeated binary choice. Paper presented at the 31st Annual Conference of the Society for Judgement and Decision Making, St. Louis, 19–22 November 2010

Lejarraga T, Dutt V, Gonzalez C (2012) Instance-based learning: A general model of repeated binary choice. J Behav Decis Making 25(2):143–153

March JG (1996) Learning to be risk averse. Psychol Rev 103(2):309–319. doi:10.1037/0033-295X.103.2.309

Martin MK, Gonzalez C, Lebiere C (2004) Learning to make decisions in dynamic environments: ACT-R plays the beer game. In: Lovett MC, Schunn CD, Lebiere C, Munro P (eds) Proceedings of the Sixth International Conference on Cognitive Modeling, vol 420. Lawrence Erlbaum Associates Publishers, p 178–183

Martin JM, Juvina I, Lebiere C, Gonzalez C (2011) The effects of individual and context on aggression in repeated social interaction. In: Harris D (ed) Engineering psychology and cognitive ergonomics, HCII 2011, LNAI, vol 6781. Springer-Verlag, Berlin, p 442–451

Oltramari A, Lebiere C, Ben-Asher N, Juvina I, Gonzalez C (2013) Modeling strategic dynamics under alternative information conditions. In: West RL, Stewart TC (eds) Proceedings of the 12th international conference on cognitive modeling. ICCM, p 390–395

Roth AE, Erev I (1995) Learning in extensive-form games: Experimental data and simple dynamic models in the intermediate term. Game Econ Behav 8(1):164–212. doi:10.1016/S0899-8256(05)80020-X

Roy S, Ellis C, Shiva S, Dasgupta D, Shandilya V, Wu Q (2010) A survey of game theory as applied to network security. In: Sprague RH Jr. (ed) Proceedings of the 43rd Hawaii international conference on system sciences. IEEE: Los Alamitos

Shiva S, Roy S, Dasgupta D (2010). Game theory for cyber security. In: Sheldon FT, Prowell S, Abercrombie RK, Krings A (eds) Proceedings of the Sixth Annual Workshop on Cyber Security and Information Intelligence Research. ACM, New York, p 34

Sun R (2006) The CLARION cognitive architecture: Extending cognitive modeling to social simulation. In: Sun R (ed) Cognition and multi-agent interaction: From cognitive modeling to social simulation. Cambridge University Press, New York, p 79–99

Vigna G (2003) Teaching hands-on network security: Testbeds and live exercises. J Inf Warfare 3(2):8–25.

Wilensky U (1999) NetLogo. http://ccl.northwestern.edu/netlogo/. Center for Connected Learning and Computer-Based Modeling, Northwestern University, Evanston.

Chapter 11
Active Discovery of Hidden Profiles in Social Networks Using Malware

Rami Puzis and Yuval Elovici

Abstract In this study we investigate the problem of diffusion in social networks, an issue which is relevant in areas such as cyber intelligence. Contrary to related work that focuses on the identification of invisible areas of a social network, our work focuses on finding the most effective nodes for placing seeds in order to effectively reveal hidden nodes in a focused manner. The seeds may consist of malware that propagates in social networks and is capable of revealing hidden invisible nodes. The malware has only limited time to function and operate in stealth mode so as not to alert the hidden node, thus there is a need to identify and utilize the visible nodes that are most effective at spreading the malware across the hidden nodes with minimal effect on the visible nodes. We empirically evaluate the ability of the Weighted Closeness metric (WC) among visible nodes to improve diffusion focus and reach invisible nodes in a social network. Experiments performed with a variety of social network topologies validated the effectiveness of the proposed method.

11.1 Introduction

Extremist organizations all over the world increasingly use online social networks as a form of communication for recruitment and planning. As such, online social networks are also a source of information utilized by intelligence and counter-terrorism organizations investigating the relationships between suspected individuals. Unfortunately, the data extracted from open sources is usually far from being complete due to the efforts of suspects to hide their traces. Intelligence agencies use fake profiles in order to infiltrate the social networks of suspected groups. The first goal of these agencies is to identify all the members of the group. Because the identification process is very complex and slow, there is a need to automate and optimize the process.

R. Puzis (✉) · Y. Elovici
Telekom Innovation Laboratories and Department of Information Systems Engineering,
Ben-Gurion University of the Negev, Beer-Sheva, Israel
e-mail: puzis@bgu.ac.il

Y. Elovici
e-mail: elovici@bgu.ac.il

© Springer International Publishing Switzerland 2015   221
S. Jajodia et al. (eds.), *Cyber Warfare,* Advances in Information Security 56,
DOI 10.1007/978-3-319-14039-1_11

In recent years, online social networks have grown in scale and variability, providing individuals with similar interest opportunities to exchange ideas and network. On the one hand, social networks create new avenues to develop friendships, share ideas, and conduct business. On the other hand, they also serve as an effective tool for plotting crime and organizing extremist groups around the world. Online social networks, such as Facebook, Google+, and Twitter are hard to track due to their massive scale and increased awareness of privacy. Criminals and terrorists strive to hide their traces, particularly in settings in which they can be linked with acts of terrorism, such as social networks

A large portion of recent research in social network analysis has been targeted at recapturing hidden information in social networks. The most popular among these research endeavors is link prediction where the objectives are to detect existing social ties that have not been established within a particular social network or predict future ties (Liben-Nowell and Kleinberg 2007; Hasan et al. 2006). In the security and counter-terrorism domains link prediction can assist in identifying hidden groups of terrorists or criminals (Hasan et al. 2006). For civil applications link prediction can facilitate friend-suggestion mechanisms embedded in online social networks. For example, in bioinformatics, link prediction can be used to find interactions between proteins (Airoldi et al. 2006), and in e-commerce, it can help build recommendation systems.

While link prediction is a widely researched subject, identification of hidden nodes (Eyal et al. 2011), reconstruction of social network profiles, and target oriented crawling (Stern et al. 2013) etc. are equally important intelligence collection tools in the arsenal of private investigators and national security authorities. Most of these tools rely on the collection of publicly available information and are used to infer information to be validated.

In this chapter we focus on the active collection of information by the means of a specially crafted traceable agent (advanced malware) propagating through the social network. The malware identify the infected node's communication with other nodes, and it will try to infect the other nodes as well. Each time the malware reaches a new node, it reports to the operator's command and control server about the existence of the node and the node's connections with other nodes. We assume that this process can reveal all of the hidden nodes. The main challenge is to accomplish this very quickly without being detected. In order to do so there is a need to find a small group of nodes that if infected, will quickly spread the malware and reveal all of the hidden nodes without raising the suspicion of the targets, anti-virus companies, and social network operators.

The remainder of the chapter is structured as follows. In Sect. 2 we present related work on the social networks of terrorists, diffusion and epidemics in social networks, and recapturing missing information in social networks. Section 3 elaborates on the problem of focused diffusion in social networks, while Sect. 4 presents several seed placement strategies. In Sect. 5 the evaluation of seed placement strategies is presented followed by a summary and conclusion in Sect. 6.

11.2   Background and Related Works

11.2.1   Social Networks of Terrorists

During the last two decades social networks have been studied fairly extensively, in the general context of analyzing interactions between people and determining the important structural patterns of such interactions (Aggarwal 2011). In the previous decade, even before September 11, 2001, social network analysis was recognized as a tool for fighting the war against criminal organizations in an age in which there is no well-defined enemy with a formal hierarchical organization (Arquilla and Ronfeldt 2001). Moreover, after the September 11, 2001 events, social network analysis became a well-known mainstream tool to help the fight against terror (Ressler 2006).

Several studies have analyzed terror organization social networks based on graph structural features. In the winter of 2002, Krebs (2001) studied the structural properties of Al-Qaeda's network by collecting publicly available data on the Al-Qaeda hijackers. Rothenberg (2001) conjectured on the structure of the Al-Qaeda network based on public media sources. After the Madrid bombing in March 11, 2004, Rodriguez (2005) used public sources to construct and study the terrorists' network. He showed that the terror organization's network mainly included weak ties that are difficult to detect. In 2004, Sageman used various public sources (largely trial records) to collect and analyze the biographies of 400 terrorists. He discovered that 88 % of the terrorists had family bonds or friendships with the Jihad. In 2005, Basu (2005) studied terrorists' organizations in India. He used social network analysis, such as the betweenness measure, to identify major groups of terrorists and key players. In 2010, Wiil et al. studied a recent Denmark terror plan. By using data mining techniques, they were able to reconstruct the social network of one of the terror plan's conspirators, David Coleman Headley, from public sources.

Attempts to reconstruct the social networks of terrorists requires significant effort mining the Web for publicly available information and free text analysis. In this study, we try to predict links inside social networks in which a substantial number of the network's links data are missing. A similar idea was studied by Dombroski et al. (2003). Their study examined utilizing the inherent structures found in social networks to make predictions about networks based on limited and missing information.

11.2.2   Diffusion and Epidemics in Social Networks

Previous work on diffusion effectiveness in social networks has mainly addressed the centrality of nodes based on the structural qualities of graphs or identifying "invisible" nodes and making diffusion more focused on revealing these nodes.

Kang et al. (2012) presented the notion of "diffusion centrality" (DC) where semantic aspects of the graph, as well as a model of how a diffusive property "p" was used to characterize the centrality of vertices. DC is polynomially computable, and the researchers present a hyper-graph based algorithm to compute DC. A prototype implementation and experiments demonstrate how DC can be computed (using real YouTube data) on semantic social networks of up to 100k vertices in a reasonable amount of time.

Xu et al. (2010) design and evaluate a system that can effectively detect the propagation of Online Social Networking (OSN) worms for which propagation follows the social connections and passively noticeable worm activities are noticeable. By assigning decoy friends to high-degree vertices of OSNs, they construct a surveillance network embedded in the OSN websites. Next, for actual detection they leverage both local and network correlations of worm propagation evidence. Their evaluation on a real-world social graph of Flickr, with two known worms, Koobface and Mikeyy, indicated that the detection system can effectively detect OSN worm propagations in early stages when less than 0.13 % of users are infected. Faghani and Saidi (2009) propose a general model of propagation of Cross Site Scripting (XSS) worms in virtual social network. They examined the effect of the friend-visiting probability in such networks on the propagation of the worms. They analyzed simulation results on Myspace and found support for an analytical propagation model where increasing the probability of visiting friends delays the propagation of XSS worms.

Shakarian et al. (2012) describe a class of problems called Social Network Diffusion Optimization Problems (SNDOPs). SNDOPs have four parts: a diffusion model, an objective function we want to optimize with respect to a given diffusion model, an integer $k > 0$ describing resource that can be placed at nodes, and a logical condition that governs which nodes can have a resource. They performed evaluation on a GREEDY_SNDOP algorithm for two cases of diffusion modes: Tipping models where a given vertex adopts a behavior based on the ratio of how many of its neighbors previously adopted the behavior, and cascade models where a property passes from vertex to vertex solely based on the strength of the relationship between the vertices. Experimental results for solving SNDOP queries showed it could scale to a social network with over 7000 vertices and over 103,000 edges. They also found that SNDOP queries over tipping models can generally be solved more quickly than SNDOP queries over cascading models.

11.2.3   Recapturing Missing Information in Social Networks

Eyal et al. (2011) introduce a new Missing Nodes Identification problem in the context of social networks where missing members in a social network structure must be identified. Towards solving this problem, they present an approach based on clustering algorithms combined with measures from the missing link research. They benchmark five affinity metrics: Almog et al. (2008) employing a Gaussian measure to measure possible node similarity and four affinity measures based on Missing Edge literature. Utilizing two types of problem subsets from a Facebook repository, they empirically compared these five possibilities and found that all five methods provide a good solution relative to a random clustering baseline solution.

Kim and Leskovec (2011) study the broader Network Completion Problem, and present the KronEM algorithms using Konnecker Graphs and an Expectation Maximization (EM) framework to find missing nodes. Their algorithm uses the observed area of the network to fit a model of network structure and then estimates the missing part of the network using the model, re-estimates the parameters and so on. Their experiments on a real network indicated that KronEM and Stochastic blockmodel out-perform the classical link-prediction methods (Adamic-Adar and Degree-Product). Between the two model-based approaches, KronEM is superior to the blockmodel in that it can recostruct the network even when half of the nodes are missing and the network consists of tens of thousands of nodes.

Contrary to the aforementioned literature on the detection of social network worms, locating missing nodes/links in social networks, and computing diffusion centrality, our work focuses on finding the most effective nodes for placing seeds (propagating malware) in terms of revealing the hidden nodes in a focused manner. Opposed to a simple worm that tries to propagate to as many nodes as possible, our malware will try to propagate mainly to nodes that were not known to be connected to the visible node (hidden nodes that were discovered by the malware while running on the computer of the visible node) in order to detect most of invisible nodes before being detected.

11.3   The Problem of Focused Diffusion in Social Networks

Assume a social network where a certain fraction of nodes (profiles) are unknown. Some of these nodes represent individuals marked as target profiles. These target profiles are not available publicly, e.g., due to strict privacy settings. A significant amount of information on the target individuals can be obtained by inspecting the profiles of their social network friends. Unfortunately, this is only possible after we identify the profiles of the targets and learn who their friends are.

Assume a traceable self-propagating agent is injected into the social network in order to perform active monitoring. The goal of active monitoring is to find hidden links in the social network by tracking the propagation of these agents. In order to conceal the network mining activity, such an agent should reach the targets as fast as possible. In this chapter we benchmark several strategies for locating seed profiles on which the diffusive agents should be placed. An agent placed on these seeds should effectively reveal the target profiles while affecting the least possible number of non-targets.

Formally, let $G = (V, E)$ be a social network (Fig. 11.1) where V is the set of nodes that represent profiles and E is the set of undirected links that represent friendship relationships. Let hidden nodes $H \subseteq V$ be a subset of profiles whose privacy settings do not allow for the identification of their friends. We assume that hidden nodes also do not appear in the friend lists of their friends. This means that all links connecting hidden nodes are hidden as well. Let $G' = (V - H, E')$ denotes the visible network where $E' = \{(u, v) \in E \mid u, v \notin H\}$ is a set of visible links.

We model active monitoring as a diffusive process targeted at some hidden nodes (H) as susceptible infective (SI) epidemic diffusion process. Let $I_t \subseteq V$ be a subset of infected profiles in time point t. Each neighbor of these profiles is infected in time

Fig. 11.1 Sample network
with hidden target profiles
(H) and their connections
(*dashed circles* and *lines*).
Solid circles and *lines*
represent the visible network

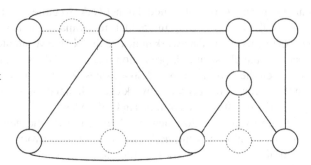

Fig. 11.2 Sample diffusion
process. The black circle
represents a profile infected at
some *t*, gray circles represent
profiles infected at $t + 1$ with a
probability *p*

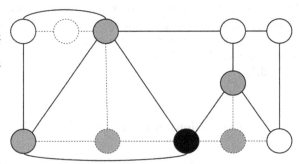

$t + 1$ with a predefined probability p. The prevalence of the infection at time point
t is the size of the set of infected nodes $|I_t|$. We assume that all information on a
profile is revealed, including the friend list, once the node is infected. We denote the
number of hidden nodes that were revealed by the agent as *"revealed"* $R_t = H \cap I_t$.
Intuitively, the quality of the diffusion depends on the growth rate of R_t. We define
a metric named focus ($F_t = |R_t|/|I_t|$) in order to measure the effectiveness of the
diffusion. Normalized focus (*NF*) is the fraction of revealed target nodes (out of all
targets) divided by the fraction of infected nodes (out of all nodes in the network).

For example, assume that in Fig. 11.2, $p = 1$. Then all gray circles are infected
in $t + 1$. In this case, $|I_{t+1}| = 6$, including the node infected at time t and all nodes
infected at time $t + 1$. Two of these nodes are hidden, therefore $|R_{t+1}| = 2$ and
$F_{t+1} = 2/6$. Normalized focus is $NF_{t+1} = \frac{2/3}{6/11} = 1.22$, which indicates that the
diffusion process is moderately focused toward the hidden nodes.

11.4 Seed Placement Strategies

Given the visible network ($G' = \{V - H, E'\}$), the goal is to find a small set of seeds
(initially infected nodes) $I_0 \in V - H$ that result in the most focused diffusion for a
given social network (G). We initially hypothesize that seeds should be as close as
possible to all hidden nodes but at the same time far from most of the known nodes.

Let $dist(s,t)$ denote the distance between s and t in G'. Note that contrary to the work on identifying invisible parts of the network, our work focuses on finding the most effective nodes for placing seeds which in turn will reveal the hidden nodes in a focused manner.

Closeness (C) centrality is a centrality measure based on distances of the given node from everyone else in a social network. We use sum of reciprocal distances as a measure of node closeness.

$$C(v) = \sum_{s \in V-H} \frac{1}{dist(s,v)} \tag{11.1}$$

Assuming high infectivity rate (p), a diffusion starting at vertices with high closeness centrality will spread faster than starting at vertices with low closeness.

A natural extention of closeness to sets of vertices was defined by Everett and Borgatti (1999) as a sum of distances from the group to all nodes outside the group. We deviate slightly from this definition and let Group Closeness (GC) be the sum of reciprocal distances of all nodes from the closest group member. Let $M \subseteq V - H$ be a set of nodes. A distance of a node to a set of nodes is typically defined defined as the distance to the closest set member

$$dist(s,M) = MIN_{v \in M} \{dist(s,v)\} \tag{11.2}$$

Given $dist(s,M)$ GC is simply defined as:

$$GC(M) = \sum_{s \in V-H} \frac{1}{dist(s,M)}. \tag{11.3}$$

Similar to closeness, a set of infectious seeds placed on a set of nodes having the highest GC will cause the infection to spread faster through the network. Unfortunately, a diffusion process optimized for the entire network is not necessarily optimized with regard to the target nodes. Moreover, the prevalence of the infection should be as low as possible while seeds located by maximizing GC maximize the infection prevalence.

Next, we define a variant of group closeness centrality that will result in high values if the group is close to the target vertices and far from all other vertices on average. Let $\delta(v)$ be a weighting function that indicates the importance of the node v. A positive value of $\delta(v)$ means that the diffusion should reach the node v, and the faster the better. A negative value of $\delta(v)$ means that the diffusion should not reach the node v, and if it does, then later is better. A zero value of $\delta(v)$ means that we are indifferent to the infectious state of v. Let T be a set of target nodes. We define the importance of target nodes as unity and manipulate the importance of other nodes using a control variable α.

$$\delta(s) = \begin{cases} 1 & s \in T \\ \alpha & s \notin T \end{cases} \tag{11.4}$$

Fig. 11.3 Number of contacts exposed on Skype and LinkedIn

Fig. 11.4 Sample network from Fig. 11.1 with the number of connections and placeholders to indicate the connections of hidden nodes

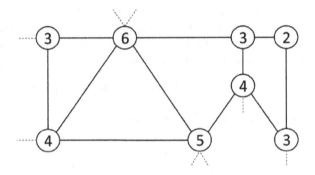

We define the weighted group closeness centrality (WGC) as the sum of reciprocal distances of the group from all nodes in the network, weighted by the importance of the nodes.

$$WGC(M) = \sum_{s \in V-H} \frac{\delta(s)}{dist(s, M)} \tag{11.5}$$

Next, in order to apply WC for the focused diffusion problem, we need to define the target nodes T and the importance weight of non-target nodes α such that $WC(M)$ will be high when nodes in M are close to the hidden nodes and far from other nodes in the network. Naturally, T cannot be the set of hidden nodes (H), but in many cases we know who their neighbors are. Many existing social networks expose the number of contacts a user has even when their identity and other personal information is hidden. LinkedIn and Skype are examples of such networks (see Fig. 11.3).

We define two different seed placement strategies that are based on the notion of weighted group closeness. In the first strategy we set T as the set of all nodes whose reported number of contacts differ from their number of links in the visible network G'. See nodes with connections leading to unknown nodes in Fig. 11.4. In other words we target all nodes who have hidden neighbors.

Fig. 11.5 Sample network with placeholders clustered together according to hidden node reconstruction algorithm

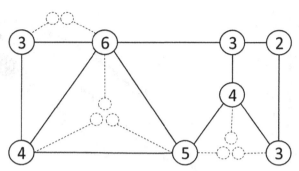

In the second strategy, denoted as RecWGC, we employ node reconstruction techniques to infer hidden nodes (Eyal et al. 2011). Due to the difference in the reported and visible degree of nodes in social networks, it is possible to put placeholders on every connection leading from a visible node to a hidden node. Eyal et al. (2011) employ spectral analysis in order to cluster placeholders. Every cluster of placeholders supposedly represents a single hidden node. Therefore we set T to be the set of clusters when coupling node reconstruction with weighted group closeness.

11.5 Evaluation of Seed Placement Strategies

In addition to finding the set of vertices having maximal C, GC, GWC, and RecWGC as defined in Sect. 4, we also evaluated a few baseline strategies for placing the seeds. Following is a list of the strategies we have used in this study for placing the seeds.

1. Random (Rnd)—Locate the seeds randomly.
2. Group Degree (GD)—Locate the seeds at the set of nodes having the largest Group Degree (Borgatti and Everett 1999). The set is chosen in a greedy manner where each time a vertex that contributes the most to the Group Degree is added.
3. Group Closeness (GC)—Locate the seeds on a set of nodes having the highest Group Closeness (constructed greedily).
4. Weighted Group Closeness (WGC)—Greedily locate the seeds on a set of nodes having the highest WGC where the importance of neighbors of hidden nodes was set to unity and the importance of other nodes was set to $\alpha \in [-2,1]$.
5. Reconstructed Weighted Group Closeness (RecWGC)—Similar to WGC, but the importance of reconstructed nodes (see Fig. 11.5) was set to unity and the importance of all other nodes was set to $\alpha \in [-2,1]$

The strategies were evaluated using a sample of the Facebook social network that was also used for identifying missing nodes by Eyal et al. (2011). The network has 5K nodes and 7.5K undirected edges with up to 35 % of hidden nodes—Hidden Nodes Ratio (HNR) ranging from 0.01 to 0.35. Following the selection of 1–10 seeds we have simulated Susceptible Infected (SI) epidemic diffusion with $p \in [0.05, 0.25]$

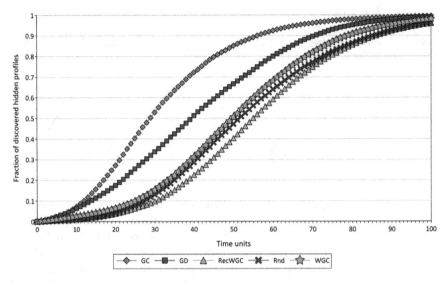

Fig. 11.6 Discovered (infected) hidden profiles as a function of time ($p = 0.1$, HNR $= 0.1$, 4 seeds, $\alpha = -0.3$)

for 100 time units. All the following figures present evaluation results averaged over 30 executions for every experimental setting.

Our evaluation results indicate that while closeness centrality (defined as the sum of reciprocal distances to nodes in the visible network) reveals hidden nodes faster than any other strategy (Fig. 11.6), it also has low normalized focus (NF) throughout the propagation time (Fig. 11.7). We note that for GC, GD, and Rnd the fraction of infected nodes is slightly above the faction of discovered hidden nodes throughout the propagation time. Therefore, their NF values approach unity from the bottom. In contrast, we can see that WGC and RecWGC result in highly focused diffusion, especially during the first stages of the propagation (see Fig. 11.7).

In Figs. 11.6 and 11.7 we present the performance of WGC and RecWGC for $\alpha = -0.3$. Although RecWGC achieves higher NF than WGC, it is more sensitive to the values of α (see Fig. 11.8). WGC results in focused diffusion starting with $\alpha = -0.3$ and lower, while RecWGC performs well for $\alpha \in [-0.6, -0.2]$ and degrades to the performance of GC for other values. Similar degradation can be observed for WGC with $\alpha \geq -0.2$ as can be seen in Fig. 11.9.

Figure 11.10 depicts the maximal and the average NF of RecWGC for different HNR values. As expected it is easier to focus the diffusion process when there are few hidden nodes as can be seen from the sharp degradation in both the maximal and the average NF. The more seeds we use the more hidden nodes can be discovered (see Fig. 11.11 left). One would expect that RecWGC will be able to achieve higher focus by using more seeds. Surprisingly, neither the average NF nor the maximal NF are affected by the number of seeds as depicted in Fig. 11.11 (right).

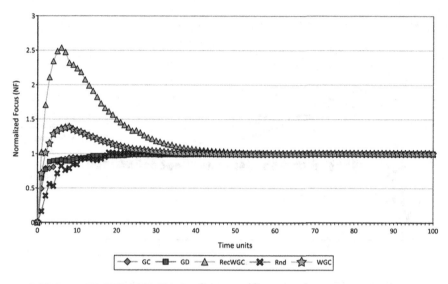

Fig. 11.7 Normalized focus as a function of time ($p = 0.1$, HNR $= 0.1$, 4 seeds, $\alpha = -0.3$)

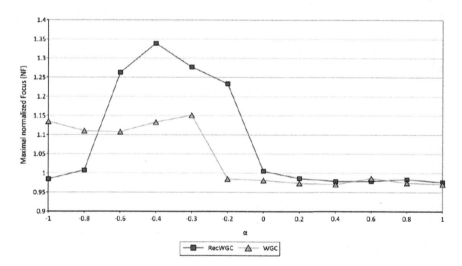

Fig. 11.8 Average normalized focus as a function of α ($p = 0.1$, HNR $= 0.1$, 4 seeds)

Finally we check the sensitivity of RecWGC to the propagation rate (p). Since seeds cannot be all located near the hidden nodes, lower propagation rates result in delayed detection of the hidden nodes. Meanwhile, visible nodes will be infected reducing the NF during the initial stages of the propagation. We can see in Fig. 11.12 that indeed the NF values during the initial propagation stages decrease with the

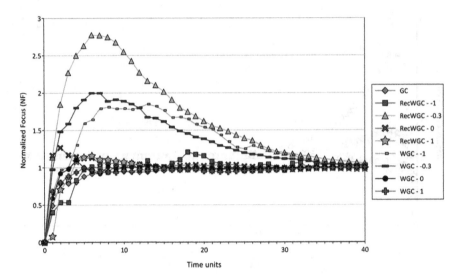

Fig. 11.9 Normalized focus as function of time for WGC and RecWGC compared to GC ($p = 0.1$, HNR $= 0.1$, 4 seeds)

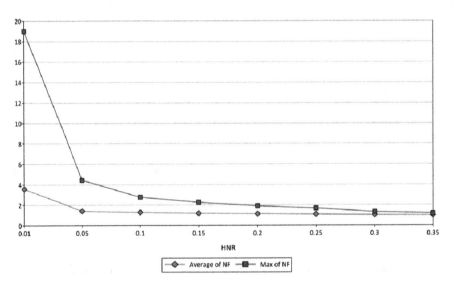

Fig. 11.10 Average and maximal focus as a function of HNR ($p = 0.1$, RecWGC, 4 seeds, $\alpha = -0.3$)

propagation rate (p). For low p values the focus rises slowly reaching the maximal value much later than with high p. Nevertheless, our results indicate that the average normalized focus remains stable for various p values.

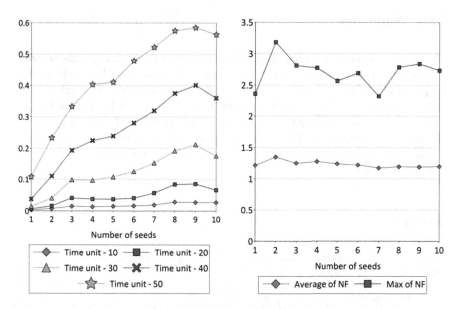

Fig. 11.11 The fraction of discovered hidden nodes (*left*) and the normalized focus (*right*) as the function of the number of seeds ($p = 0.1$, HNR $= 0.1$, RecWGC, $\alpha = -0.3$)

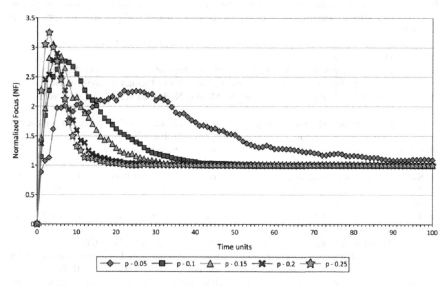

Fig. 11.12 The normalized focus as the function of time for different propagation rates (HNR $= 0.1$, RecWGC, 4 seeds, $\alpha = -0.3$)

11.6   Summary

This chapter focuses on finding the most effective nodes for placing seeds in terms of revealing the hidden nodes in a focused manner. The seeds may be a malware that propagates in social networks and reveals hidden invisible targets. The malware has limited time to function and operate in stealth mode so as not to alert the targets. Thus there is a need to find the visible nodes that are most effective in spreading the malware across the hidden nodes with minimal effect on visible nodes. We empirically evaluated the effectiveness of several seeds placement strategies on a real social network.

References

Aggarwal, C.: Social network data analytics. Springer-Verlag New York Inc (2011)

Airoldi, E., Blei, D., Fienberg, S., Xing, E., Jaakkola, T.: Mixed membership stochastic block models for relational data with application to protein-protein interactions. In: Proceedings of the international biometrics society annual meeting (2006)

A. Almog, Goldberger, J., Y. Shavitt. Unifying unknown nodes in the internet graph using semisupervised spectral clustering. Data Mining Workshops, International Conference on 174–183, 2008

Arquilla, J., Ronfeldt, D.: Networks and netwars: The future of terror, crime, and militancy. 1382. Rand Corp (2001)

Basu, A.: Social network analysis of terrorist organizations in india. In: North American Association for Computational Social and Organizational Science (NAACSOS) Conference, pp. 26–28 (2005)

S. P. Borgatti and M. G. Everett, The centrality of groups and classes, Mathematical Sociology 23(3): 181–201, 1999

Dombroski, M., Fischbeck, P., Carley, K.: Estimating the shape of covert networks. In: Proceedings of the 8th International Command and Control Research and Technology Symposium (2003)

R. Eyal, S. Kraus, and A. Rosenfeld. "Identifying Missing Node Information in Social Networks", AAAI 2011, 2011

M.R. Faghani, H. Saidi. "Malware propagation in online social networks", In proceeding of the 4th IEEE International malicious and unwanted programs (Malware09), Montreal, Canada, 2009

Hasan, M.A., Chaoji, V., Salem, S., Zaki, M.: Link prediction using supervised learning. SDM Workshop of Link Analysis, Counterterrorism and Security (2006)

C. Kang, C. Molinaro, S. Kraus, Y. Shavitt, V. Subrahmanian. "Diffusion Centrality in Social Networks". Proceedings "Advances in Social Network Analysis and Mining (ASONAM)", Istanbul, Turkey, 2012.

M. Kim, J. Leskovec. The Network Completion Problem: Inferring Missing Nodes and Edges in Networks. In SDM '11, 2011.

Krebs, V.: Mapping networks of terrorist cells. Connections 24(3), 43–52 (2001)

Liben-Nowell, D., Kleinberg, J.: The link-prediction problem for social networks. Journal of the American society for information science and technology 58(7), 1019–1031 (2007)

Ressler, S.: Social network analysis as an approach to combat terrorism: Past, present, and future research. Homeland Security Affairs 2(2), 1–10 (2006)

Rodriquez, J.: The march 11th terrorist network: In its weakness lies its strength (2005)

Rothenberg, R.: From whole cloth: Making up the terrorist network. Connections 24(3), 36–42 (2001)

Sageman, M.: Understanding terror networks. Univ of Pennsylvania Pr (2004)

P. Shakarian, M., Broecheler, V.S. Subrahmanian, and C. Molinaro. "Using Generalized Annotated Programs to Solve Social Network Diffusion Optimization Problems," ACM Transactions on Computational Logic, Accepted for publication, 2012.

Stern, R.T., Samama, L., Puzis, R., Beja, T., Bnaya, Z., & Felner, A. (2013, June). TONIC: Target Oriented Network Intelligence Collection for the Social Web. In AAAI.

Wiil, U., Memon, N., Karampelas, P.: Detecting new trends in terrorist networks. In: Advances in Social Networks Analysis and Mining (ASONAM), 2010 International Conference on, pp. 435–440. IEEE (2010)

W. Xu, F. Zhang, and S. Zhu. Toward worm detection in online social networks. In Proceedings of the 25th Annual Computer Security Applications Conference (ACSAC), 2010.

Chapter 12
A Survey of Community Detection Algorithms Based On Analysis-Intent

Napoleon C. Paxton, Stephen Russell, Ira S. Moskowitz and Paul Hyden

Abstract There has been a significant amount of research dedicated to identifying community structures within graphs. Most of these studies have focused on partitioning techniques and the resultant quality of discovered groupings (communities) without regard for the intent of the analysis being conducted (analysis-intent). In many cases, a given network community can be composed of significantly different elements depending upon the context in which a partitioning technique is used or applied. Moreover, the number of communities within a network will vary greatly depending on the analysis-intent and thus the discretion quality and performance of algorithms will similarly vary. In this survey we review several algorithms from the literature developed to discover community structure within networks. We review these approaches from two analysis perspectives: role/process focused (category-based methods) and topological structure or connection focused (event-based methods). We discuss the strengths and weaknesses of each algorithm and provide suggestions on the algorithms' use depending on analysis context.

12.1 Introduction

The nature of communities pervades all aspects of human interaction and this is no different for systems. A functional definition of communities as a "structure of belonging" is provided in (Community 2008). The nature of belonging is critically

N. C. Paxton (✉) · S. Russell · I. S. Moskowitz · P. Hyden
Information Technology Division, Naval Research Laboratory, 4555 Overlook Ave.,
Washington, DC 20375, USA
e-mail: napoleon.paxton@nrl.navy.mil

S. Russell
e-mail: stephen.russell@nrl.navy.mil

I. S. Moskowitz
e-mail: ira.moskowitz@nrl.navy.mil

P. Hyden
e-mail: paul.hyden@nrl.navy.mil

© Springer International Publishing Switzerland 2015   237
S. Jajodia et al. (eds.), *Cyber Warfare,* Advances in Information Security 56,
DOI 10.1007/978-3-319-14039-1_12

essential to any context where the identification of groups, participants or elements is necessary. Not surprisingly, graph and network analytics (system, social, and otherwise) have invested significant resources in methods that enable accurate and timely community identification. Before providing a review of network community detection approaches it is helpful to have a functional definition of network community. Real world networks contain modular structures that contextually define their topology or connectivity. Generally defined as a subset of nodes and edges, these structures often provide invaluable insight into the functionality of the network at large. There are several names for these structures, such as cluster, module, or community (Network analysis 2014; Multiscale ensemble 2012; Community Detection 2014). Although a formal definition has not been widely accepted, the most common description of these structures is a group or cluster of vertices that form a cohesive set apart from the other vertices in a given network (Fortunato 2010). That is, the vertices in the cohesive set (community) occur with a context different from the other vertices in the network. Given this definition of community, it quickly becomes apparent how important the circumstance of the "community" becomes. Thus, the context of the analysis (analysis-intent) will impact the performance of and subsequent comparison across network community detection.

There are many algorithms used to detect community structures within networks. While not comprehensive, in the context of network communities it is not unreasonable to classify these algorithms into four main groups. These groups are null model, hierarchy clustering, statistical inference, and clique based methods (Jin et al. 2013; Social Network Clustering 2011; In search of a network theory 2014; Evans 2010). The literature for these methods tends to focus on what algorithm performs best based on evaluation using a benchmark dataset. However, not much study has been done to examine the results of community detection algorithms given *different* analysis-intents for the same dataset. In this paper we attempt to organize methods in the literature around the four topical areas noted above and compare the strengths and weaknesses of each in the context of two analysis-intents: category-based and event-based.

The rest of the paper is presented as follows: First, we discuss analysis-intent and why it is an important factor in network community detection algorithm performance. Here we discuss two perspectives for analysis: category-based and event-based. Next we discuss the four major categories of community structure algorithms and their strengths and weaknesses as they pertain to category-based community detection and event-based community detection. In this section we also include examples of algorithms that fit each respective category. Each algorithm discussed attempts to address a weakness of its traditional inherited category. After this discussion we conclude the paper.

12.2 Analysis-Intent

When threats or problems occur in a network the typical analyses focus on both the event and attribution. As a result, analyses involving the detection of communities in a network often merge identification/characterization with attribution. Moreover, often the analysis methodology follows this same orientation making it difficult to discern the efficacy of an analytical approach with regard to its applicability to the problem-event *or* the individual/role that was involved. Determining "belonging-ness" based on event features or attributes of attribution may often create overlap. When this distinction is not clearly defined *a priori*. Each time a new community detection algorithm is run on a network, a different set of results may be obtained (Community detection algorithms 2009). The quality of the result is measured based on some ground truth stemming from another analysis of an evaluation dataset that defined which network vertices and nodes should be included within each community (Palla et al. 2005). A deficiency in this approach is that benchmark datasets are typically partitioned into communities in only one way and baselined by an initial, often contextual or manual partitioning scheme. In reality, there frequently exists many vertices-groups (communities) in a network and these communities depend on the desired analysis of the person or organization conducting the community discovery. Because of this, certain algorithms will perform better than others depending on the higher-order purpose of the evaluation.

To highlight the importance of analysis-intent we consider two community detection purposes, category-based and event-based. The goal of a category-based community detection analysis is to identify vertices that are related based on a functional or role-based classification metric. In this case, flow or edge properties (beyond the connection itself) are not important. The only requirement is that two connected vertices are related in some way and that they reside in the same global network definition (they exist in the network of concern). While some sort of logical connection must be defined by the category-based analysis-intent, there is a possibility that these vertices have no *physical* connection at all. The second type of analysis-intent is event-based. The goal of event-based community detection is to identify communities based on observed connection or edge properties. This focus does not require any type of classification that ties any two vertices together. The only requirement is that either the two vertices are connected directly or by a defined chain of events between their neighbors.

Figure 12.1 illustrates the definition of category-based and event-based analysis-intent in the context of a computer network. Figure 12.1 presents the example network of malicious agents that work in tandem on a computer network. This type of network configuration is commonly known as a botnet. Botnets are described in more detail in Dietrich et al. (2013). Although botnets can be significantly more complex, in the figure, we show a simplified botnet containing two botnet controllers that has attacked two victim computers. As with any network activity there are roles and properties related to those roles. Within the figure the master or controlling nodes of the botnet are labeled $\mathbf{M}^1$, the co-opted nodes that carry out the attack are labeled

---

[1] In the botnet scenario depicted in Fig. 12.1 we only consider three layers of nodes (Botmaster, Bots, and Victims). In many cases a fourth layer is present in between the Botmaster and the Bots (Command and Control). We chose not to include this layer for sake of clarity. Also, in many cases the Botmaster layer and the Command and Control layer are the same.

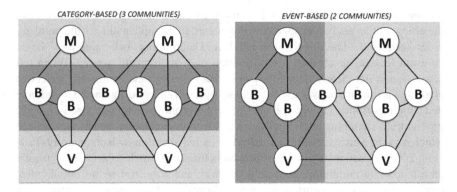

Fig. 12.1 One network, two community partitions based on analysis-intent

B, and the victims nodes labeled **V**. Applying the category-based and event-based definitions partitions the network horizontally and vertically. Examining Fig. 12.1, it is important to note that in the category-based community analysis, there may not be connectivity-defining edges between nodes, e.g. the master nodes, although they belong to the same community.

Network operators are tasked with analyzing the type of network shown in Fig. 12.1 for a variety of reasons. Two common purposes for analysis are to either quickly shut the network down or to discover patterns of its transactions to prevent future attacks. When the goal is to shut the network down, operators would like to quickly identify the nodes that are in control of the network and disable them. As shown in Fig. 12.1, it is possible that the nodes in control of the network never communicate with each other, so community detection algorithms that discover communities based on events alone may not quickly discover the nodes in control of the events. If they do discover these nodes, it is typically through correlation of multiple event-derived communities, which often spans and takes extended amounts of time. When the goal is to discover activity patterns in order to prevent future attacks, the nature or role of the node is much less important. In this case and event-based approach, which is based on connections, is the logical choice over the category based approach which does not focus on the direct communications between nodes.

12.3 Network Community Detection Approaches

As methods to detect communities in networks attempt to solve issues that are common to their detection mechanism, the lines between the different methods tend to blur. This makes it difficult to classify these algorithms as any one type. As Branting pointed out, community detection algorithms are comprised of a utility function and a search strategy (Branting 2011). The utility function determines the quality of the partition between communities. The search strategy specifies a procedure for finding the communities within the network. Here we classify the algorithms based on the latter of the two.

The most widely used methods to detect communities are: Hierarchy Based, Null Model Based, Statistical Inference Based, and Clique Based. Hierarchy based approaches focus mainly on communities that can be put in categories. Null model based approaches focus mainly on communities of equal sizes and a known number of communities. Statistical inference based approaches attempt to identify communities by fitting a generative model to the network data. Clique based approaches find communities based on smaller fully connected sub-graphs discovered in the network. In the following sub-sections we go into more detail on each method.

12.3.1 Hierarchy Based Algorithms

Hierarchy based algorithms consider the community from the perspective of structural or contextual similarity. Common similarity measures used in these approaches include cosine similarity, hamming distance, or the Jaccard index (Chan et al. 2009; Jiashun 2012; Dang and Viennet 2012). In hierarchy based algorithms the similarity between every two vertices within the network are computed based on edge properties and if they are similar enough (typically defined by some threshold value) they are placed within the same community using an $n \times n$ similarity matrix, where n is the number of vertices. The matrix is typically then represented using a dendrogram that can be partitioned using two methods:

1. Divisive: a top down process where groups of vertices are split iteratively by removing edges that connect vertices with low similarity.
2. Agglomerative: a bottom up process where groups of vertices are merged based on high similarity.

12.3.1.1 Divisive Methods

The catalyst algorithm proposed by Girvan and Newman in 2002 uses a hierarchical approach where network communities are given by the graph topology. In the catalyst algorithm the network analysis graph is drawn first by edge centrality. Centrality provides an indicator for the importance of edges, according to an operator selected property or process that can be attributed between vertices. Once edge centrality is computed for each edge, the edge with the largest centrality is removed. Next centrality is recalculated based on the remaining edges and the removal of the edge with the highest centrality is repeated. To the analysis graph built using centrality, the property of betweenness was then applied. Girvan and Newman introduced three options for betweenness: random-walk betweenness, current-flow betweenness, and edge betweenness.

Calculation for random-walk betweenness and current-flow betweenness both have a complexity of $O(n^3)$ for a sparse graph, but edge betweenness has a complexity of $O(n^2)$ for the same graph. It has also been shown that edge betweenness also has better results than the other applications on practical graphs (Newman and Girvan

2004). Edge betweenness is the number of shortest paths between all vertex pairs that run along the edge and is an extension of the concept of site betweenness which was introduced by Freeman in 1977. Inter-community edges have a large value of the edge betweenness because many of the shortest-paths connecting vertices of different communities will pass through them. If there are two or more geodesic paths with the same endpoints that run through an edge, the contribution of each of them to the betweenness of the edge must be divided by the multiplicity of the paths, as one assumes that the signal/information propagates equally along each geodesic path. The betweenness of all edges of the graph can be calculated in a time that scales as $O(m^n)$, or $O(n^2)$ on a sparse $m \times n$ graph, with techniques based on the breadth-first-search (Yoo et al. 2005).

In 2004, Newman and Girvan refined their original algorithm to deal with the extreme scalability problems of the first version. In the original version the authors did not have a utility function to let them know what partitions were best, so the algorithm was only usable for networks with up to 10000 vertices. Even in this case the algorithm was very slow (Hierarchical Block Structures 2014). The new algorithm introduced modularity as a quality measure and this approach has been used extensively since this time (Nascimento 2013).

In 2003 Tyler et al. (Tyler 2013) proposed a modification of the Girvan Newman algorithm to improve the computational speed. Originally, algorithms that compute betweenness have to start from a vertex which is considered the center, and compute the contribution to betweenness from all paths originating at that vertex; the procedure is then repeated for all vertices. In this work Tyler et al. also proposed to calculate the edge betweenness contribution from only a limited number of centers, which are chosen at random. Numerical tests indicate that, for each connected sub-graph it suffices to pick a number of centers growing as the log of the number of vertices of the component. For a given choice of the centers, the algorithm proceeds just like that of Girvan and Newman. The stopping criterion does not require modularity of the partitions, but relies on a particular definition of community. According to such a definition a connected sub-graph with n_0 vertices is a community if the edge betweenness of any of its edges does not exceed n_{0-1}. Indeed, if the sub-graph consists of two parts connected by a single edge, the betweenness value of that edge would be greater than or equal to n_{0-1}, with the equality holding only if one of the two parts consists of a single vertex. Therefore, the condition on the betweenness of the edges would exclude such situations, although other types of cluster structures might still be compatible with it. In this way, in the method of Tyler et al., edges are removed until all connected components of the partition are communities in the sense explained above. The Monte Carlo sampling of the edge betweenness necessarily induces statistical errors. As a consequence, the partitions are in general different for different choices of the set of center vertices. However, the authors showed that, by repeating the calculation many times, the method gives good results on a network of gene co-occurrences, with a substantial gain in computer time. The technique has been also applied to a network of people corresponding via email. In practical examples, only vertices lying at the boundary between communities may not be clearly classified, and be assigned sometimes to a group, sometimes to another. This is actually a nice feature of the method, as it allows identifying overlaps between communities, as well as the degree of membership of overlapping vertices in the clusters they belong to. The algorithm of Girvan and Newman is deterministic and is unable to do this.

In 2007 Sales-Pardo et al. created an algorithm that used this method. Here they created a similarity matrix based on the initial similarity comparison. They called the measure, vertex affinity and it uses modularity as its utility to discover the quality of the communities it discovers. The idea behind this algorithm is the affinity between two vertices is the frequency with which they coexist in the same community in partitions corresponding to local optima of modularity. Each community consists of a group of vertices that cannot increase if it includes one more vertex within the group, including a merging of clusters. The set of optimal clusters is called P_{max}. Next, the algorithm verifies that the network graph as a whole has community structure. In order to do that it calculates a z-score for the average modularity of the partitions in P_{max} with respect to the average modularity of partitions with local modularity optima of the equivalent ensemble of null model graphs. Large z-scores with respect to a threshold indicate meaningful community structure. Once meaningful community structure is found, the affinity matrix is put in a block-diagonal like form by minimizing a cost function expressing the average distance of connected vertices from the diagonal. The blocks correspond to the communities and the recovered partition represents the uppermost organization level. To determine lower levels, one iterates the procedure for each sub-graph identified at the previous level, which is treated as an independent graph. The procedure stops when all blocks found do not have a relevant cluster structure, i.e. their z-scores are lower than the threshold. The partitions delivered by the method are hierarchical by construction, as communities at each level are nested within the communities at higher levels. However, the method my find no relevant partition (no community structure), a single partition (community structure by no hierarchy) or more (hierarchy) and in this respect it is better than most existing methods. The algorithm is not fast, as both the search of local optima for modularity and the rearrangement of the similarity matrix are performed with simulated annealing, but delivers good results for computer generated networks, and meaningful partitions for some real networks.

In 2008 Clauset et al. introduced an algorithm that generates a class of hierarchical random graphs. They define a random hierarchical graph by a dendrogram D, which is the natural representation of the hierarchy, and by a set of probabilities $\{p_r\}$ associated to the $n-1$ internal vertices of the dendrogram. An ancestor of a vertex i is any internal vertex of the dendrogram that is encountered by starting from the "leaf" vertex i and going all the way up to the top of the dendrogram. The probability that vertices i and j are linked to each other is given by the probability pr of the lowest common ancestor of i and j. Clauset et al. searched for the model $(D, \{p_r\})$ that best fits the observed graph topology, by using Bayesian inference as its utility function. The probability that the model fits the graph is proportional to the likelihood:

$$L(D, \{p_r\}) = \prod_{r \in D} P_r^{E_r}(1 - p_r)^{L_r R_r - E_r} \qquad (12.1)$$

Here, E_r is the number of edges connecting vertices whose lowest common ancestor is r, L_r and R_r are the numbers of the graph vertices in the left and right sub-trees descending from the dendrogram vertex r, and the product runs over all internal dendrogram vertices. For the given dendrogram D, the maximum likelihood $L(D)$ corresponds to the set of probabilities $\{p_r\}$, where pr equals the actual density of edges $E_r/(L_r R_r)$ between the two subtrees of r. One can define the statistical ensemble of hierarchical random graphs describing a given graph G, by assigning to each model graph $(D, \{pr\})$ a probability proportional to the maximum likelihood $L(D)$. The ensemble can be sampled by a Markov chain Monte Carlo method. The procedure suggested by Clauset et al. seems to converge to equilibrium roughly in a time $O(n^2)$, although the actual complexity may be much higher. Still, the authors were able to investigate graphs with a few thousand vertices. From sufficiently large sets of model configurations sampled at equilibrium, one can compute average properties of the model, e.g. degree distributions, clustering coefficients. etc., and compare them with the corresponding properties of the original graph. Tests on real graphs reveal that the model is indeed capable to describe closely the graph properties. Furthermore, the model enables one to predict missing connections between vertices of the original graph. This is a very important problem introduced by Liben-Nowell and Kleinberg in 2003. Here edges of real graphs are the result of observations/experiments, that may fail to discover some relationships between the units of the system. From the ensemble of the hierarchical random graphs one can derive the average linking probability between all pairs of graph vertices. By ranking the probabilities corresponding to vertex pairs which are disconnected in the original graph, one may expect that the pairs with highest probabilities are likely to be connected in the system, even if such connections are not observed. Clauset et al. pointed out that their method does not deliver a sharp hierarchical organization for a given graph, but a class of possible organizations, with well-defined probabilities. It is certainly reasonable to assume that many structures are compatible with a given graph topology. In the case of community structure, it is not clear which information can extract from averaging over the ensemble of hierarchical random graphs. Moreover, since the hierarchical structure is represented by a dendrogam, it is impossible to rank partitions according to their relevance. In fact, the work by Clauset et al. questions the concept of "relevant partition", and opens a debate in the scientific community about the meaning itself of graph clustering.

As shown in Girvan and Newman's as well as others' work investigating divisive hierarchical methods, the coupling of centrality and betweenness provides a good hierarchical discriminator for network community detection. However the approach can be computationally intensive for large networks. There may be value in applying hierarchical methods as part of an ensemble approach where the graph resulting from a network community detection methodology creates a reduced size network. Yet the literature focusing on ensemble methods incorporating the technique is sparse.

12.3.1.2   Agglomerative Methods

Hierarchy algorithms that identify communities in an agglomerative fashion used to be the most popular hierarchy based method, but that is debatable today due to the recent popularity of divisive methods. There are algorithms that have an agglomerative property included in their approach, but the main ingredient of the approach is another method. Such is the case with the Girvan and Newman algorithm of 2004 (Clauset et al. 2004), which is based on optimizing modularity and will be discussed method. Although these techniques are currently popular, there are still several current algorithms that use the agglomerative technique for community discovery.

The issue of detecting dynamic communities was addressed by Hopcroft et al. in 2004. Here the authors analyzed snapshots of the citation graph induced by the NEC CiteSeer Database, which covered the period from 1990 to 2001. Here the similarity measure used to compare vertices is based on cosine similarity, which is a well known measure used in information retrieval. Here each snapshot identified the natural communities defined as those communities of the hierarchical tree that are only slightly affected by minor perturbations of the graph, where the perturbation consists in removing a small fraction of the vertices and their edges. The authors found that the best matching natural communities across different snapshots, and in this way they could follow the history of communities. In particular they could see the emergence of new communities, corresponding to new research topics. The main drawback of the method comes from the use of hierarchical clustering, which is unable to sort out meaningful communities out of the hierarchical tree, which includes many different partitions of the graph.

In 2005 Bagrow and Bollt introduced a technique called L-shell. In this procedure communities of any vertex are found. Communities are defined locally, based on a simple criterion involving the number of edges inside and outside a group of vertices. One starts from a vertex-origin and keeps adding vertices lying on successive shells, where a shell is defined as a set of vertices at a fixed geodesic distance from the origin. The first shell includes the nearest neighbors of the origin, the second the next-to-nearest neighbors, and so on. At each iteration, one calculates the number of edges connecting vertices of the new layer to vertices inside and outside the running cluster. If the ration of these two numbers (emerging degree) exceeds some predefined threshold, the vertices of the new shell are added to the cluster, otherwise the process stops. This idea of closing a community by expanding a shell was introduced a year earlier by Costa (MacKay 1995). Here all the shells are centered on hubs. However, in this procedure the number of clusters is preassigned and no cluster can contain more than one hub. Because of the local nature of the process, the L-shell method is very fast and can identify communities very quickly. Unfortunately the method works well only when the source vertex is approximately equidistant from the boundary of its community. To overcome this problem, Bagrow and Bollt suggested to repeat the process starting from every vertex and derive a membership matrix M: the element M_{ij} is one if vertex j belongs to the community of vertex i, otherwise it is zero. The membership matrix can be rewritten by suitably permutating rows and columns based on their mutual distances. The distance between two rows (or columns) is defined as the number of entries whose elements differ. If the graph has a clear community structure, the membership matrix takes a block-diagonal form, where the blocks identify the communities. The method enables one to detect overlaps between communities. Unfortunately this suggestion is much slower because of the rearrangement of the matrix. It requires a computation time of $O(n^3)$. In 2007 Rodrigues et al. improved on the computational time by creating a variant of the Bagrow and Bollt algorithm which examined boundary vertices separately and the first and second nearest neighbors of the running community are investigated simultaneously (Rodrigues et al. 2007).

In 2009, Ahn et al. introduced an agglomerative method called hierarchical link clustering. Here they use a similarity measure for a pair of adjacent edges that expresses the size of the overlap between the neighborhoods of the non-coincident end vertices, divided by the total number of different neighbors of such end vertices. Groups of edges are merged pairwise in descending order of similarity, until all edges are together in the same cluster. The resulting dendrogram provides the most complete information on the community structure of the graph. However, as usual, most of this information is redundant and is an artifact of the procedure itself. So, Ahn et al. introduced a quality function to select the most meaningful partition(s), called partition density, which is essentially the average edge density within the clusters. The method is able to find meaningful clusters in biological networks, like protein-protein and metabolic networks, as well as in a social network of mobile phone communications. It can also be extended to multipartite and weighted graphs.

A more recent algorithm was proposed by Wang et al. in 2011. This algorithm was based on a previous approach from the authors called the HC-PIN algorithm. That algorithm was based on a modified version of edge clustering defined here:

$$CC = \frac{|N_i \cap N_j| + 1}{\min(d_i, d_j)} \tag{12.2}$$

N_i and d_i are the neighbor list and degree of vertex i respectively. As per their algorithm, edge clustering coefficient values are calculated and sorted in descending order for all edges. After that the singletons are merged together by the edges which are sorted in descending order according to edge clustering coefficient values. The problem with this algorithm is if in a PIN, a good cluster has no triangle or has cycle, the edge clustering coefficient formula produces low values for its (cluster's inside) edges. For this reason, the FAG-EC algorithm does not produce accurate communities. This new algorithm introduced a measure called Edge Clustering Value (ECV), which is defined here:

$$ECV = \frac{|N_u \cap N_v|^2}{|N_u| \times |N_v|} \tag{12.3}$$

N_u is the set of neighbors of vertex v. This approach solved the previous problem of inaccurate community clusters, but it still suffers from the issue of not being able to identify overlapping communities.

Overall, hierarchical algorithms are an effective way to analyze networks when the desired result includes communities composed of similar vertices. Many of the newer algorithms, such as the ones we discussed, provide solutions to some of the drawbacks, but in each case there is a drawback in either accuracy or complexity.

An advantage that all hierarchical algorithms have, regardless of the analysis-intent, is that they do not require preliminary knowledge of the number and the size of the communities. This is particularly useful for networks that have communities of varying size, because methods used to estimate the number and size of communities usually group vertices into communities of equal size (Orman et al. 2012). However the trade off is that that agglomerative techniques do not scale well. If distance is used as a similarity measure, the computational complexity is $O(n^2)$ for a single vertex to vertex link and $O(n^2 \log n)$ for the entire graph. This means that when distance is not defined a priori and if the network is of any real-world scale, the computational complexity of these algorithms can become very high and be exacerbated by the computational expense of the similarity measure calculation (Density-based shrinkage 2011).

12.3.1.3 Hierarchy Based Algorithms, Given Analysis-Intent

Category-Based For analysis based on category, hierarchical community discovery is an effective way to segment vertices. Because the communities are defined by similarity, vertices group in to categories naturally around that similarity metric. Of course, the choice of similarity metric (e.g. cosine, jaccard, malhalonobis, etc.) as well as the measure (e.g. betweeness, centrality, other quantitative characteristics, etc.) and how well they are matched in the analysis can significantly impact results and performance. A major weakness of hierarchy based approaches given category oriented analysis-intent is that the there is no contextual discrimination between vertices within the categories beyond the one similarity metric. This means that within a community it is not possible to know which vertex is the most important or how it relates to vertices outside of its community.

Event-Based The research literature is sparse in discussion of the strengths of event-based analysis of network communities using hierarchical methods. This is because a physical or communication defined connection between vertices is not a prerequisite for community construction. Hierarchical methods that consider connections tend to be divisive in nature and remove links that are between vertices and would be along inter-community lines. The connection is only considered after vertices have been clustered based on similarity so the links are not the major factor of what makes a vertex part of a community. Moreover, in agglomerative hierarchical methods, connections are not a factor at all.

12.3.2 Null Model Based Approaches

Null Models are random graphs that match a corresponding graph in some of its structure. In null model algorithms, the fraction of vertex connections that are in the same community as the original/corresponding graph is represented by the following formula:

$$\frac{1}{2m} \sum_{ij \in v} [A_{ij}] \delta(c_i, c_j) \tag{12.4}$$

The formula below is used to derive the expected fraction of vertex connections in a random graph that has the same degree distribution as the original/corresponding graph.

$$\frac{1}{2m} \sum_{ij \in v} \left[\frac{k_i k_j}{2m} \right] \delta(c_i, c_j) \tag{12.5}$$

The algorithm by Newman and Girvan in 2004 was the original algorithm to use the null model method. In this approach, the connections of the null model are edges of the null model network are redrawn (rewired) at random under the constraint that the degree and vertex count remained the same as the corresponding graph; essentially exercising the null model with constraints from the original/corresponding graph.

Exercising a null model is the basic concept underlying the modularity optimization network-community detection technique, where null models represent different network connection configurations. Configuration models describe a network with n vertices, where each vertex m has a degree value of D_m. In the configuration model each communication, represented by an edge, is split into two halves. Each half is called a stub and is rewired randomly with any other stub in the global network, including itself. When modularity is used to discover communities, the number of edges inside the group of vertices in the original graph has to exceed the expected number of internal edges found in the same group of vertices represented in its corresponding null model and this number is an average over all possible rewired realizations of the null model.

In 2009, Shen et al. introduced an approach which attempted to detect overlaps using null models. Here they suggested the definition:

$$Q = \frac{1}{2m} \sum_{ij} \frac{1}{O_i O_j} \left(A_{ij} - \frac{k_i k_j}{2m} \right) \delta(C_i, C_j) \tag{12.6}$$

O_i is the number of communities including vertex i. The contribution of each edge to modularity is then the smaller, the larger the number of communities including its end vertices (Shen et al. 2009).

Another null model based algorithm that addressed the problem of overlapping communities was proposed by Nicosia et al. in 2009. Here they considered directed un-weighted networks, starting from the general expression:

$$Q_{ov} = \frac{1}{m} \sum_{c=1}^{n_c} \sum_{i,j} \left[r_{ijc} A_{ij} - s_{ijc} \frac{k_i^{out} k_j^{in}}{m} \right] \tag{12.7}$$

k_i^{in} and k_j^{out} are the in-degree and out-degree of vertices i and j respectfully, the index c labels the communities and $r_{ijc} = s_{ijc} = \delta_{c_i c_j c}$, where c_i and c_j correspond to the communities of i and j. In this case, the edge ij contributes to the sum only if $c_i = c_j$, as in the original definition of modularity. For overlapping communities, the coefficients are $a_{i,c}$, $a_{j,c}$ for vertices i and j. We can also assume $r_{ijc} = F(a_{i,c} a_{j,c})$, where F is some function. The term s_{ijc} is related to the null model of modularity, and it must be handled with care. In modularity's original null model, edges are formed by joining two random stubs, so one needs to define the membership of a random stub in the various communities. If we assume that there is no correlation a priori between the membership coefficients of any two vertices, we can assign a stub originating from a vertex i in community c the average membership corresponding to all edges which can be formed with i. On a directed graph we have to distinguish between outgoing and incoming stubs, so one has

$$\beta^{out}_{i\to,c} = \frac{\sum_j F\left(\alpha_{i,c}, \alpha_{j,c}\right)}{n} \tag{12.8}$$

$$\beta^{in}_{i\leftarrow,c} = \frac{\sum_j F\left(\alpha_{j,c}, \alpha_{i,c}\right)}{n} \tag{12.9}$$

where α is the membership of i in c and one can write the following general expression for modularity

$$Q_{ov} = \frac{1}{m} \sum_{c=1}^{n_c} \sum_{i,j} \left[r_{ijc} A_{ij} - \frac{(\beta^{out}_{i\to,c} k^{out}_i)(\beta^{in}_{j\leftarrow,c} k^{in}_j)}{m} \right] \tag{12.10}$$

The question now becomes the choice of the function $F(\alpha_{i,c}, \alpha_{j,c})$. If the formula above is to be an extension of modularity to the case of overlapping communities, it satisfy the general properties of classical modularity. For instance, the modularity value consisting of the whole network as a single cluster should be zero. It turns out that large classes of functions yield an expression for modularity that fulfills this requirement. Otherwise, the choice of F is rather arbitrary and good choices can be only tested a posteriori, based on the results of optimization. A similar approach was introduced in 2009 by Papadopoulos et al. called Bridge Bounding (Papadopoulos et al. 2009). The main difference in the approaches is here the cluster around a vertex grows until one hits the boundary edges.

An example of a null model based algorithm other than modularity optimization was presented by Reichardt and Bornholdt in 2006. Here the authors showed that it was possible to reformulate the problem of community detection as the problem of finding the ground state of a spin glass model. Here each vertex is labeled by a Potts spin variable σ_i, which indicates the cluster including the vertex. The basic principle of the model is that edges should connect vertices of the same class (i.e. same spin state, whereas vertices of different classes (i.e. different spin states) should be disconnected (ideally). So, one has to energetically favor edges between vertices in the same class, as well as non-edges between vertices in different classes, and penalize edges between vertices of different classes, along with non-edges between vertices in the same class. The resulting Hamiltonian of the spin model is:

$$H(\{\sigma\}) = -\sum_{i<j} J_{ij}\, \delta(\sigma_i, \sigma_j) = -\sum_{i<j} J(A_{ij} - \gamma\, p_{ij})\delta((\sigma_i, \sigma_j)) \tag{12.11}$$

where J is a constant expressing the coupling strength, A_{ij} are the elements of the adjacency matrix of the graph, $\gamma > 0$ a parameter expressing the relative contribution to the energy from existing and missing edges, and p_{ij} is the expected number of links connecting i and p_{ij} is the expected number of links connecting i and j for a null model graph with the same total number of edges m of the graph considered. The system is considered a spin glass because as the couplings J_{ij} between spins are both ferromagnetic (on the edges of the graph, provided γpij < 1) and antiferromagnetic (between disconnected vertices, as $A_{ij} = 0$ and $J_{ij} = -J\gamma pij < 0$). The multiplicative constant J is irrelevant for practical purposes, so in the following we set $J = 1$. The range of the spin-spin interaction is infinite, as there is a non-zero coupling between any pair of spins. It is important to note that while this method is similar to modularity, this method is much more general than modularity, since both the null mode and the parameter γ can arbitrarily be chosen.

An algorithm to identify communities in bipartite graphs was presented by Barber et al. in 2008 (Danon et al. 2005). Here, suppose that the two vertex classes (red and blue) are made out of p and q vertices, respectively. The degree of a red vertex i is indicated with k_i, that of a blue vertex j with d_j. The adjacency matrix A of the graph is in block off-diagram form, as there are edges only between red and blue vertices. Because of that, Barber assumes that the null model matrix P, whose element P_{ij} indicates as usual the expected number of edges between vertices i and j in the null model, also has the block off-diagonal form:

$$P = \begin{bmatrix} O_{p\times p} & \bar{P}_{p\times q} \\ \bar{P}^T_{q\times p} & O_{q\times q} \end{bmatrix} \tag{12.12}$$

where the O are square matrices with all zero elements and $\bar{P}_{ij} = \frac{k_i d_j}{m}$, as in the null model of standard modularity (though other choices are possible). According to Barber, spectral optimization of modularity gives excellent results for bi-partitions, but its performance worsens when the number of clusters is unknown, and this is usually the case.

The resolution limit problem, which null based algorithms suffer from, are well documented. In general, many graphs with community structure usually contain communities that are diverse in size (Palla et al. 2005; Clauset et al. 2004; Guimera et al. 2003). If two small sub-graphs happen to be connected by a few false edges, modularity will put them in the same cluster even if they have nothing to do with each other. As mentioned before, the issue lies with the null model itself and the implicit assumption that each vertex can interact with every other vertex, which implies that each part of the graph knows about every other part of the graph. This is not always the case. A better assumption is that each vertex has a limited view of the graph as a whole, and interacts with that small local portion. Several algorithms have addressed this issue, such as Li et al. (2008); Fortunato and Barthelemy (2007); Ruan and Zhang (2008); and Berry et al. (2009). In Berry et al. weighted graphs are considered in which intra-cluster edges have a weight of 1, and inter-cluster edges have a weight of ϵ. They concluded that clusters with internal strength w_s may remain undetected if

$w_s < \sqrt{W_\epsilon/2} - \epsilon$, where W is the total strength of the graph. So, the resolution limit decreases when ϵ decreases. The authors used this result to show that by properly weighting the edges of a given un-weighted graph, it becomes possible to detect clusters with very high resolution by still using modularity optimization.

Although algorithms such as the one proposed by Berry et al. show promise in reducing the resolution limit problem, the weakness still persists. Research in this area is ongoing. Because of this problem, approaches based on modularity optimization is moderate at best when attempting to identify communities based on observed events. Communities constructed from observed events tend to vary in size and it is inevitable that some of these communities will be lost under the current options available from modularity optimization. When the intent of the analysis is category-based, this method can yield positive results. This is because many modulation optimization techniques are paired with hierarchical clustering methods that naturally group vertices in classes of similar categories. The only issue to consider is the tradeoff between accuracy of detection and computational speed since many of the more accurate techniques utilize global optimization techniques such as simulated annealing which tend to be very slow.

Null model algorithms provide reliable results due to the high degree of permutations, suggesting why many network community detection algorithms apply modularity in some way. Despite their popularity, null model algorithms have some drawbacks. A well-known issue involves a resolution limit, which makes it difficult for modularity to discover small communities. Null model approaches have an intrinsic problem because the number of connections between the original graph and the null model graph are compared as part of methodology. The null model graph assumes that each vertex can get attached to any other vertex in the network, but if the network is large this is an unreasonable assumption that does not reflect reality. From a practical perspective, as the network size grows, the expected number of connections between two groups of vertices decrease in size. If the network is large enough, the expected number of edges between the two groups of vertices could be smaller than one that would make the modularity value high. This would result in an inclusive community being defined where one does not exist, as the algorithm would merge the two groups even though they should not be merged. Since smaller groups of vertices would always merge together, small communities may never be discovered. Within the literature there have been several approaches proposed to resolve this issue and these approaches will be discussed later in the paper.

12.3.2.1   Null Model Based Algorithms, Given Analysis-Intent

Category-Based   Null model approaches can be effective in discerning network community for category-based analysis intent. However the presumption is that an appropriate metric is selected that will discriminate the categories. Because null model approaches exploit all possible vertices' connections if the metric can discriminate between communities, then even non-existing edges can be detected as part of the community.

Event-Based   Null based algorithms generally are effective at identifying communities of equal size in an event-based analysis context. However in this context, they do not generally detect small communities well. Identifying both large and small communities are of importance when conducting an analysis based on observed events, so null model algorithms may not be the ideal sole choice for this type of analysis. Like the hierarchical algorithms, the null model approach may be complementary with other algorithms in this context. Due to its potentially high computational costs, in an ensemble network community detection configuration, if possible null model approaches should be applied after network scale reduction techniques.

12.3.3   Statistical Inference Based Algorithms

Network community detection algorithms based on statistical inference aim to deduce properties of network communities beginning with a set of observations to validate hypotheses of how vertices are (or are expected to be) connected to each other. Algorithms using this technique identify communities by attempting to find the best fit of a model to graph generated from observations. Like other statistical techniques, the model assumes that vertices have some sort of classification based on characteristics that are available in the observations. In the context of network community detection, this method was detailed by Mackay (1995). Mackay's work was the pioneering work bridging information theory and machine learning to describe communication processes in network community detection. As a result, many of the subsequent methods in the literature find their grounding in Mackay's methods.

As there are many types of statistical inference there are several algorithms that use this statistical methods such as Bayesian inference (Morup and Schmidt 2012), block-modeling (Karrer and Newman 2011), model selection (Hierarchical Block Structures 2014), and generalized information theory (MacKay 1995). Bayesian inference uses observations to estimate the probability that a hypothesis is true. Block modeling decomposes a graph in classes of vertices with common properties. Vertices are usually grouped in classes of structural or regular equivalence. Vertices are said to have structural equivalence when two or more vertices have the same neighbors. Regular equivalence is when vertices of one class share similar connection patterns to vertices of another class. Model selection is, as the name suggests, the applying of several models (hypotheses) and evaluating the observables for the best fit. In Information theory algorithms, the communities that are discovered are considered a compressed description of the graph as a whole.

An advantage all algorithms that use this method has is they have the ability to address issues of statistical significance directly. This is because the clustering of communities is based on statistical properties exhibited by the vertices and the links that bind them together.

Efforts to use inference based community detection methods have not been around as long as the other methods, but recently there has been a lot of attention directed at using these techniques. In this section we will focus on several methods that have become popular recently. These include Bayesian, block modeling, model selection, and information theory based methods.

In 2008, Hofman and Wiggins proposed a Bayesian based approach to community detection. Here they modeled a graph with community structure as in the planted partition problem, in that there are two probabilities θ_c and θ_d that there is an edge between vertices of the same or different clusters, respectively (Hofman and Wiggins 2008). The unobserved community structure is indicated by the set of labels $\rightarrow_\sigma$ for the vertices; π_r is again the fraction of vertices in group r. The conjugate prior distributions $p(\vec{\theta})$ and $p(\vec{\pi})$ are chosen to be Beta and Dirichlet distributions. The most probable number of clusters K^* maximizes the conditional probability $p(\{K|A\})$ that there are K clusters, given the matrix A. Here Hofman and Wiggins assume that the prior probability $p(K)$ on the number of clusters is a smooth function, therefore maximizing $p(\{K|A\})$ amounts to maximizing the Bayesian evidence $p\{A|K\} \propto p(K|A)/p(K)$, obtained by integrating the joint distribution $p(A, \vec{\sigma}|\vec{\pi}, \vec{\theta}, K)$, which is factorizable, over the model parameters $\vec{\theta}$ and $\vec{\pi}$. The integration can be performed exactly only for small graphs. The complexity of the algorithm was estimated at $O(n^\alpha)$, with $\alpha = 1.44$ on synthetic graphs. Here the main cause for the high complexity comes from the high memory requirements. This method is powerful, since it does not to know the number of clusters before beginning the analysis and the edge probabilities do not need to be guessed but instead are inferred by the procedure.

Another, more recent, Baysian based approach was introduced by Psorakis et al. in 2011 (Psorakis 2011). Here the authors proposed an algorithm called Bayesian NMF. Where NMF stands for Non-negative Matrix Factorization. It is a feature extraction and dimensionality reduction technique in machine learning that has been adapted to community detection. NMF approximately factorizes the feature matrix V into two matrices with the non-negativity constraint as $V \approx WH$, where V is $n \times m$, W is $n \times k$, H is $k \times m$, and k is the number of communities provided by users. W represents the data in the reduced feature space. Each element $w_{i,j}$ in the normalized W quantifies the dependence of vertex i with respect to community j. In the algorithm presented by Psorakis et al., the matrix V, where each element V_{ij} denotes a count of the interactions that took place between two vertices i and j, is decomposed via NMF as part of the parameter inference for a generative model. An issue with this approach is, traditionally NMF is inefficient with respect to both time and memory constraints due to the matrix multiplication. In the version used by Psorakis et al., the worst-case time complexity is $O(kn^2)$, where k denotes the number of communities.

A method based on block modeling was presented by Airoldi et al. in 2008. Here the authors introduced the concept of mixed membership. This technique factorized the adjacency matrix into a low dimensional space expressing patterns of directed social relationships between blocks of vertices. According to the generative process, for each pair of vertices group membership is sampled for both for the source and the destination: the link is generated by sampling from the binomial distribution which encodes the probability of observing a directed connection between the considered groups. Since membership assignments are drawn independently for each possible link, users can belong to multiple groups.

In a recent method, introduced by Barbieri in 2013, the authors present a community detection algorithm that fits a stochastic generative block model to an observed social graph and a metric called a cascade (2013). A cascade of an item i is a sequence of pairs (user, timestamp) recording which vertices adopt i and at which time. In the CCN model, each observation is assumed to be the result of a stochastic process where a given user u acts in the network according to a set of topics/communities which also represent user interests. Given a community c, the degree of involvement of user u to that community is governed by two parameters, $\pi_u^{c,\,s}$ and $\pi_u^{c,\,d}$, where $\pi_u^{c,\,s}$ measures the degree of active involvement of u in c, while $\pi_u^{c,\,d}$ measures the degree of passive involvement of u in c. Using twitter as an example, a hypothetical user u which uses the micro blogging platform for three specific interest: (i) network science and data mining, (ii) the city of Barcelona, and (iii) the rock legend Bruce Springsteen. While on the first topic u is actively posting, using the platform for communicating with other researchers, in the other two topics u is just passively listening: for sake of information needs, u follows users which are good information sources for events happening in Barcelona and users which are authorities for whatever concerns Bruce Springsteen. The users that are good sources of information usually have a large number of followers and are, in some sense, influential. In the second and third community, u might re-tweet some pieces of information, but it is quite unlikely that u would produce some original information. Going back to our parameters we can expect u to have both high $\pi_u^{c,\,s}$ and $\pi_u^{c,ds}$. Not surprising u has many followers in the first community and almost no followers in the other two communities. This is a key observation behind this model: the likelihood of u posting something on a topic, the likelihood of this information being further propagated, and the likelihood of u having followers interested in that topic, are all strongly correlated. In this model they are jointly represented by the parameter $\pi_u^{c,\,s}$. Similarly, they model the likelihood of having an incoming arc in a community and the likelihood of being influenced by other users in that community with the parameter $\pi_u^{c,\,d}$. This is how they achieve the jointly modeling of the social graph and the set of cascades. Another important aspect of this algorithm is one user can belong to more than one community, but a link is usually explainable because of a unique topic. This overlap allows information to be shared across multiple communities. This algorithm was tested on real-world datasets with accurate results, but very slow. The learning time is slow due to (i) the extreme computational burden of the update equations δ_u^k and γ_v^k, and (ii) the fact that the M step is an improvement, rather than an optimization step. The GEM procedure typically exhibits a slower convergence rate than the standard EM procedure: the result is that the learning phase requires additional iterations, and each iteration is extremely computationally heavy.

Another block model based approach that was introduced in 2013 was introduced by Chen et al. to address dynamic networks (2013). The inspiration behind this algorithm comes from the fact that many algorithms change over time, such as IP networks and even social groups. In this approach the authors introduce a concept called overlapping temporal communities (OTC). Here vertices can belong to multiple communities at any given time and those communities can persist over time as well. The algorithm works by first adopting an optimization-based approach to OTC Detection using the following:

$$max$$

$$\{Y^t\} \quad \sum_{t=1}^{T} f_{A^t(Y^t)} \tag{12.13}$$

$$s.t. \quad \sum_{t=1}^{T-1} d_{A^{t+1}, A^t}\left(Y^{t=1}, Y^t\right) \leq \delta$$

$$Y^t \text{ represents a cover, } t = 1, \ldots, T.$$

Here $f_{A^t(Y^t)}$ is the snapshot quality, which serves two purposes: (1) it measures how well the cover Y^t reflects the network A^t, i.e., the closeness between the assigned similarity level encoded in Y^t and the observed similarity level in A^t, and (2) it prevents the algorithm from over-fitting, e.g., generating duplicate communities or many small communities overlap with each other. The function $d_{A^{t+1}, A^t(Y^{t+1}, Y^t)}$ is a distance function that measures the difference between the covers at time $t+1$ and t. Consequently, the first constraint in the above formulation ensures that the covers evolve smoothly over time. Tests with this approach show that even small networks are detectable using the temporal overlap capability of this algorithm. The total memory space complexity is $O(E + nrT)$. The total complexity based on time is: $O(nr^2T + Mr^2E + MnrT)$. When the number of clusters r is bounded, both the space and time complexity scale linearly in E and nT which is considered very efficient. The limitation of this approach is based on the utility function it uses to identify valid partitions, which is essentially the same as modularity. As we discussed earlier, modularity has a well-defined issue with resolution limit.

In 2007, Rosvall and Berstrom introduced a method based on information theory which a partition of a graph in communities represents a synthesis Y of the full structure that a signaler sends to a receiver, who tries to infer the original graph topology X from it. The best partition corresponds to the signal Y that contains the most information about X. This can be quantitatively assessed by the minimization of the conditional information $H(H|Y)$ of X given Y:

$$H(X|Y) = \log\left[\prod_{i=1}^{q}\left(\frac{n_i(n_i-1)}{l_{ii}^2}\right)\prod_{i>j}\binom{n_in_j}{l_{ij}}\right] \tag{12.14}$$

where q is the number of clusters, n_i the number of vertices in cluster i, l_{ij} the number of edges between clusters i and j. We remark that, if one imposes no constraints on q, H(X|Y) is minimal in the trivial case in which $X = Y$ (H(X|X) = 0). This solution is not acceptable because it does not correspond to a compression of information with respect to the original data set. One has to look for the ideal tradeoff between a good compression and a small enough information H(X|Y). The Minimum Description Length (MDL) principle provides a solution to the problem, which amounts to the minimization of a function given by H(X|Y) plus a function of the number n of vertices, m of edges and q of clusters. Here the quality of the discovered community is a function of the complexity of the community structure together with the mutual information between the community structure and the graph as a whole. The best community structure is the one that minimizes the sum of the number of bits needed to represent the community structure and the number of bits needed to represent the entire graph given the community structure. Here community detection consists of finding the community structure that leads to the minimum description length representation of the graph, where description length is measured in number of bits. Simulated annealing performs the optimization. As a result, Rosvall and Berstrom's method is slow and should be limited to graphs with up to about 10^4 vertices. However, faster techniques may be used even if they imply a loss in accuracy. According to the results discovered, this approach is superior to modularity optimization when communities are made up of different sizes.

Rosvall and Bergstrom also proposed an information theory based algorithm in 2008 which had the goal of finding an optimal compression of information needed to describe the process of information diffusion across a graph with respect to the full adjacency matrix (Rosvall and Bergstrom 2008). Here a random walk method is chose as a proxy of information diffusion. A two level description, in which one gives unique names to important structures of the graph and to vertices within the same structure, but the vertex names are recycled among different structures, leads to a more compact description than by simply coding all vertices with different names. This is similar to the procedure usually adopted in geographic maps, where the structures are cities and one usually chooses the same names for streets of different cities, as long as there is only one street with a given name in the same city. Huffman coding (Rosvall and Bergstrom 2008) is used to name vertices. For the random walk, the above-mentioned structures are communities, as it is intuitive that walkers will spend a lot of time within them, so they play a crucial role in the process of information diffusion. Graph clustering turns them into the following coding problem: finding the partition that yields the minimum description length of an infinite random walk. Such description length consists of two terms, expressing the Shannon entropy of the random walk within and between clusters. Every time the walker steps to a different cluster, one needs to use the codeword of that cluster in the description, to inform the decoder of the transition. Clearly, if clusters are well separated from each other, transitions of the random walker between clusters will be infrequent, so it is advantageous to use the map, with the clusters as regions, because in the description of the random walk the codewords of the clusters will not be repeated many times, while there is a considerable saving in the description due to the limited length of the codewords used to denote the vertices. Instead, if there are no well-defined clusters and/or if the partition is not representative of the actual community structure of the graph, transitions between the clusters of the partition will be very frequent and there will be little or no gain by using the two-level description of the map. Combining a greedy search with simulated annealing achieves the minimization of the description. This makes the process slow; similar to other methods that use simulated annealing.

An information theory based algorithm that was applied to directed weighted-graphs by Rosvall et al. in 2009. In the case of weighted graphs, a teleportation probability is introduced as a utility method instead of random walk to guarantee ergodicity. The partitions of directed graphs obtained by the method differ from those derived by optimizing the directed version of the Newman-Girvan modularity alogrithm because the approach identifies pairwise relationships between vertices and does not capture flows.

12.3.3.1   Statistical Inference Based Algorithms, Given Analysis-Intent

Category-Based   Statistical inference based algorithms are arguably the best way to identify communities based on category because the information used to discover the communities are encoded into the graph based on categories.

Event-Based   Communities that are focused on observed events are also discovered well using several forms of statistical inference based algorithms for the same reason as the category intent, meta data about the vertex or link is encoded and therefore available to use in the analysis. Because of this problem, we can discover a wealth of information about the semantics of connections in and out of the communities. An important obstacle of this approach is the complexity of the calculation for both time and memory requirements. This type of analysis can be quite slow depending on the level of detail desired in the analysis.

12.3.4   Clique Based Algorithms

Methods that use cliques to discover communities are based completely on observed connections. Here communities are created by fully connected sub-graphs called cliques, where a clique or combination of maximal cliques makes up a community. Cliques became popular due to their ability to identify overlaps within communities, which is a natural occurrence in real-world communities (Palla et al. 2005) and tends to intrinsically support both category-based and event-based analysis-intent. Many clique based approaches suffer from a dependence on discovering all cliques within a network. This has been proven to be a NP-complete problem.

  A widely used community detection approach is called the clique percolation method, which was introduced by Palla et al. in 2005. This algorithm builds communities in a natural way by first identifying all the maximal cliques in a network for some value of k and then the cliques percolate into each other if they are adjacent. In order to be adjacent, the percolating cliques must share $k - 1$ vertices. For example, a clique composed of three vertices is a triangle and in order for another clique to percolate into the triangle it has to have at least two vertices. The sub-community based construction allows sharing of vertices, so they may have overlap. Also, some vertices may be connected even if they do not belong to adjacent k-cliques. To identify k-cliques, an algorithm must keep entries of a clique by clique overlap matrix O, which is an $n_c \times n_c$ matrix, n_c being the number of cliques. Here O_{ij} is the number of vertices shared by cliques i and j. Limitations of the approach include the complexity involved in discovering maximal cliques, which grows exponentially with the size of the graph and is considered an NP-Complete problem. According to the authors this limitation has not hindered community discovery in some relatively large networks. The algorithm is also considered relatively fast due to the limited number of cliques in sparse graphs with up to 10^5 vertices.

The clique percolation algorithm was extended to bipartite graphs by Lehmann et al. in 2008. Here the term bi-clique is introduced as a sub-graph $K_{a,b}$ if each of a vertices of one class are connected with each of b vertices of the other class. Two cliques $K_{a,b}$ are adjacent if they share a clique $K_{a-1,b-1}$, and a $K_{a,b}$ clique community is the union of all $K_{a,b}$ cliques that can be reached from each other through a path of adjacent $K_{a,b}$ cliques. Once again finding all N_c bi-cliques is a NP-complete problem. This is primarily due to the fact that the number of bi-cliques grows exponentially with the size of the graph in the same way as k-cliques.

A fast version of the clique percolation method was introduced by Kumpula et al. in 2008. In this algorithm, the graph is initially empty and edges are added sequentially one by one. Whenever a new edge is added, one checks whether new k-cliques are formed, by searching for $(k-2)$ cliques in the subset of neighboring vertices of the endpoints of the inserted edge. A graph Γ^* is required to be built, where the vertices are $(k-1)$ cliques and edges are set between vertices corresponding to $(k-1)$ cliques which are sub-graphs of the same k-clique. At the end of the process, the connected components of Γ^* correspond to the searched k-clique communities. The technique has a time complexity which is linear in the number of k-cliques of the graph, so it can vary a lot in practical applications. Despite this variability, SCP has proven to be much faster than CPM. The biggest advantage of SCP over CPM is due to the implementation for weighted graphs. SCP inserts edges in decreasing order of weight, which allows the algorithm to only be applied once, instead of many times for the CPM.

12.3.4.1 Clique Based Algorithms, Given Analysis-Intent

Category-Based Cliques build communities by observing direct connections and building fully connected sub-graphs called cliques. This method can identify categories, but will need to first discover every clique first. As mentioned earlier, discovering cliques is computationally expensive and is much more efficient in other methods.

Event-Based Events are the result of a series of multiple direct connections. Since clique based methods are built from direct connections, they are ideal for discovering events.

12.4 Conclusion

Each algorithm/approach/method surveyed had strengths and weaknesses that depended on the intent of the analysis. Overall, hierarchical and modularity based methods perform best when the analysis-intent is category-based. This is because these two methods naturally group vertices into classes based on a chosen form or metric of similarity. The clique based method is ideal for event-based analysis. This is because communities are built from observed connections and not similarity. Algorithms based on statistical inference were effective on both intents depending on the chosen method for community finding. Overall, there is no one algorithm that is perfect for every situation so in order to get the best results you must first carefully identify the type of result you expect.

As mentioned before, the literature for community detection methods tends to focus on the evaluation of algorithms using a benchmark dataset in one context. In this chapter we emphasize the importance of considering analysis intent or multiple contexts as a determining factor when choosing the best algorithm for detecting communities. For example, if a null model-based algorithm is compared to a clique based approach, the null model algorithm would likely perform better than the clique based approach when the analysis-intent is to discover categories. On the other hand, the clique based approach would likely perform better when searching for communities composed of a chain of events. For these reasons we believe considering analysis-intent in the decision making process of choosing a community detection method should be a required practice. The appendix in Sect. 6, displays a grid of community detection algorithms/approaches surveyed. Each algorithm has been evaluated on its ability to address certain intent criteria. In the future we will use this list to create new algorithms that are tailored for the analysis intent at hand.

12.5 Appendix

Method	Authors	Approach/Algorithm Name	Shallow Hierarchy	Varying community sizes	Few Roles (categories)	High Similarity (clustering)	High Node Degree	Directional	Weighted
Information Theory-Based	Pascal Pons 2005	Walktrap	high	low	high	high	high	high	low
	Sun et al., 2007	Parameter-free Mining of Large Time-evolving Graphs (MDL Based)	moderate	high	high	low	low	high	low
	Coizmadia, 2003	N++	high	moderate	high	high	high	low	low
	Roxvall and Bergstrom, 2007	Information Theoretic Framework	high	high	high	moderate	moderate	low	low
	Ziv et al., 2005	Network Information Bottleneck	high	low	high	moderate	moderate	low	low
	J. Rissanen	Modeling by shortest data description	high	moderate	low	high	low	low	low
	Mackay, 2003	Statistical Inference-Generative models	high	moderate	high	moderate	low	low	low
	Branting, 2008	Minimizing description length	high	low	low	high	moderate	low	low
	Zhang et al. 2007	Spectral mapping and fuzzy clustering	high	low	low	high	moderate	low	high
	Mitrovic and Tadic 2009	Spectral modeling	high	low	low	high	low	low	high
	Donetti and munoz 2004	Elegent eigenvector based spectral algorithm	high	low	low	high	moderate	low	high
	Hue et. ol., 2008	Graph Clustering technique	high	low	low	high	low	low	high
	Hughes, 1995.	Random walk algorithm	high	low	low	high	low	low	high
	Li et. al, 2008.	Synchronized clusters	high	low	low	high	low	low	high
	Nowicki and Snijder 2001	Generative community method	high	low	low	high	low	low	high
Null Model Based	Costellano et. al, 2004	Centrality based method	high	low	low	high	low	low	high
	Meo et. Al, 2012	The Louvain method	low	low	low	moderate	moderate	low	low
	Newman, 2006	Leading eigenvector method	low	low	low	high	moderate	low	low
	Kawadia anc Sreenivasan, 2012	Sequential greedy method	low	low	low	high	moderate	low	low
	Reichardt and White, 2007	Blockmodeling approach	low	low	moderate	high	moderate	high	moderate
	Duch and Arenas, 2005	extremal optimization	low	low	low	high	moderate	low	low
	Blondel, 2008	Modularity optimization	low	low	low	moderate	moderate	low	low
	Schuetz and Caflisch 2008	Modularity optimization	low	low	low	moderate	moderate	low	low
	Xiang et. al, 2009	Modularity optimization	low	low	low	moderate	moderate	low	low
	Massen and Doye 2005	Modularity optimization	low	low	low	moderate	moderate	low	low
	Guimera et. al, 2004	Modularity optimization	low	low	low	moderate	moderate	low	low
	Medus et. al, 2005	Modularity optimization	low	low	low	moderate	High	low	low
	Lehmann and Hansen 2007	Modularity optimization	low	low	moderate	moderate	moderate	high	moderate
	Arenas et al 2007	Modularity on directed graphs	low	low	moderate	low	high	moderate	moderate
	Leicht and Newman 2008	Modularity on directed graphs	low	low	moderate	moderate	moderate	moderate	low
Hierarchical Based	Nicosia et al. 2009	Community overlap based method on directed graphs	moderate	moderate	moderate	moderate	moderate	moderate	low
	Lancichinetti et. al, 2009	Overlap and Hierarchy based Algorithm	moderate	high	moderate	high	moderate	moderate	low
	Bu et al, 2014	Greedy modularity optimization	moderate	low	high	moderate	high	low	Low
	Baumes et. al 2005	IS and Iiake found in	moderate	high	high	moderate	high	low	low
	Xie and Szymanski, 2013	Label propagation	moderate	moderate	Moderate	moderate	moderate	low	low
	Nepusz et al. 2008	Vertex Similarity	moderate	moderate	Moderate	high	low	low	low
	Girvan and Newman, 2002	Girvan and Newman algorithm	high	moderate	high	high	low	low	low
Clique Based	Pollner, Palla, and Vicsek, 2012	CFinder	moderate	moderate	high	high	high	low	moderate
	Eppstein and Strash, 2011	Bron-Kerbosch algorithm	high	high	moderate	moderate	high	low	low
	Koch, 2006	Bron-Kerbosch algorithm	moderate	high	moderate	moderate	high	low	low
	Qian, Zhang, and Yang, 2007	Hybergraph	moderate	high	moderate	high	high	moderate	low

References

Block, P., Community: The Structure of Belonging, Berrett-Koehler, 2008.

Laut, I., Rath, C., Worner, L., Nosenko, V., Zhdanov, S., Schablinski, J., Block, D., Thomas, H., and Morfill, G., Network analysis of three-dimensional complex plasma clusters in a rotating electric field. Physical Review E, 2014. **89**(2).

Kim, E, Hwang, D, and Ko, T., Multiscale ensemble clustering for finding modules in complex networks. Physical Review E, 2012. **85**(2): p. 026119.

Scibetta, M., Boano, f., Revelli, R., and Ridolfi, L., Community Detection as a Tool for District Metered Areas Identification. Procedia Engineering, 2014. **70**: p. 1518.

Fortunato, S., *Community detection in graphs*. Physics Reports, 2010. **486**: p. 99.

Jin, D., et al., *Extending a configuration model to find communities in complex networks*. Journal of Statistical Mechanics: Theory and Experiment, 2013. **2013**(09): p. P09013.

Jia, Y., Garland, M., and Hart, J., Social Network Clustering and Visualization using Hierarchical Edge Bundles. Computer Graphics Forum, 2011: p. no.

Leydesdorff, L. and Ahrweiler, P., In search of a network theory of innovations: Relations, positions, and perspectives. Journal of the Association for Information Science and Technology, 2014: p. n/a.

Evans, T.S., *Clique graphs and overlapping communities*. Journal of Statistical Mechanics: Theory and Experiment, 2010. **2010**(12): p. P12037.

Community detection algorithms: A comparative analysis. Physical Review E, 2009. **80**(5): p. 056117.

Branting, K.L., Context-Sensitive Detection of Local Community Structure, Social Network Analysis and Mining, 1869–5450:1–11, Springer (2011)

Palla, G., et al., Overlapping community detection in networks: The state-of-the-art and comparative study. ACM Computing Surveys (CSUR), 2005. **435**(7043): p. 5.

Dietrich, C.J., C. Rossow, and N. Pohlmann, CoCoSpot: Clustering and recognizing botnet command and control channels using traffic analysis. Computer Networks, 2013. **57**(2): p. 475–486.

Chan, S.-Y., P. Hui, and K. Xu. Community *Detection of Time-Varying Mobile Social Networks*. in *1st International Conference on Complex Sciences: Theory and Applications* (*Complex 2009*). 2009. Shanghai, China: Springer.

Jiashun, J. *FAST COMMUNITY DETECTION BY SCORE*. 2012; Available from: arXiv:1211.5803.

Dang, T.A. and E. Viennet. *Community Detection based on Structural and Attribute Similarities*. in *The Sixth International Conference on Digital Society*. 2012. Valencia, Spain: IARIA.

Girvan, M. and M.E.J. Newman, *Community structure in social and biological networks*. Proceedings of the National Academy of Sciences, 2002. **99**(12): p. 7821–7826.

Newman, M.E.J. and M. Girvan, *Finding and evaluating community structure in networks*. Physics Review E, 2004. **69**(026113).

Freeman, L.C., A Set of Measures of Centrality Based on Betweenness. Sociometry, 1977. **40**(1): p. 7.

Yoo, A., et al. *A Scalable Distributed Parallel Breadth-First Search Algorithm on BlueGene/L*. in *ACM/IEEE Conference on Supercomputing*. 2005. Washington, D.C.

Ward, J.H., *Hierarchical grouping to optimize an objective function*. Journal of the American Stastical Association, 1963. **58**.

Orman, G.K., V. Labatut, and H. Cherifi, *Comparative evaluation of community detection algorithms: a topological approach*. Journal of Statistical Mechanics: Theory and Experiment, -2012. **2012**(08): p. P08001.

Huang, J., Sun, H., Han, J., Feng, B., *Density-based shrinkage for revealing hierarchical and overlapping community structure in networks*. Physica A Statistical Mechanics and its Applications, 2011. **390**(11): p. 2160.

MacKay, D.J.C., *Information Theory, Inference, and Learning Algorithms*, ed. C.U. Press. Vol. 1. 1995, Cambridge: Cambridge Univeristy Press. 640.

Morup, M. and M.N. Schmidt, *Bayesian community detection.* Neural Computation, 2012.

Karrer, B. and M.E.J. Newman, *Stochastic blockmodels and community structure in networks.* Physics Review E, 2011. **83**(016107): p. 11.

Hierarchical Block Structures and High-Resolution Model Selection in Large Networks. Physical Review X, 2014. **4**(1).

Nascimento, M. and Pitsoulis, L., *Community detection by modularity maximization using GRASP with path relinking.* Computers & Operations Research, 2013.

Tyler, J.R., D.M. Wilkinson, and B.A. Huberman. *Email as spectorscopy: automated discovery of community structure within organizations.* in *International Conference on Communities and Technologies.* 2003. Kluwer Academic, Dordrecht.

Sales-Pardo, M., et al., *Extracting the hierarchical organization of complex systems.* National Academy of Sciences, 2007. **104**(39).

Clauset, A., C. Moore, and M.E.J. Newman, *Hierarchical structure and the prediction of missing links in networks.* 453, 2008. **7191**(98).

Liben-Nowell, D. and J. Kleinberg. *The Link-Prediction Problem for Social Networks.* in *Twelfth International Conference on Information and Knowledge Management.* 2003. New York, NY: ACM.

Clauset, A., M.E.J. Newman, and C. Moore, *Finding community structure in very large networks.* Physical Review E, 2004. **70**(066111).

Hopcroft, J., et al., *Natural Communities in Large Linked Networks.* Proceedings of the National Academy of Sciences, 2004. **101**(5249).

Bagrow, J.P. and E.M. Bollt, *A local method for detecting communties.* Physical Review E, 2005. **72**(046108).

Rodrigues, F.A., G. Travieso, and L.d.F. Costa, *Characterization of complex networks: A survey of measurements.* International Journal of Modern Physics C, 2007. **18**(937).

Ahn, Y., J.P. Bagrow, and S. Lehmann. *Communities and Hierarchical Organization of Links in Complex Networks.* 2009; Available from: arxiv:0903.3178.

Wang, J., et al., *A Fast Hierarchical Clustering Algorithm for Functional Modules Discovery in Protein Interaction Networks.* IEEE/ACM Transactions on Computational Biology and Bioinformatics, 2011. **8**(3).

Shen, H.-W., X.-Q. Cheng, and J.-F. Guo, *Quantifying and identifying the overlapping community structure in networks.* Journal of Statistical Mechanics: Theory and Experiment, 2009. **2009**(07): p. P07042.

Nicosia, V., et al., *Extending the definition of modularity to directed graphs with overlapping communities.* J. Stat. Mech., 2009(P03024).

Papadopoulos, S., et al. *Bridge Bounding: A Local Approach for Efficient Community Discovery in Complex Networks.* 2009; Available from: arXiv:0902.0871.

Reichardt, J. and S. Bornholdt. *Stastical Mechanics of Community Detection.* 2006; Available from: arXiv:cond-mat/0603718.

Barber, M.J., et al., *Searching for communities in bipartie networks.* In Proceedings of 5th Jagna International Workshop on Stochastic and Quantum Dynamics of Biomolecular Systems, 2008.

Danon, L., et al., *Comparing community structure identification.* Journal of Statistical Mechanics: Theory and Experiment, 2005. **2005**(September 2005).

Guimera, R., et al., *Community analysis in social networks.* Physics Review E, 2003. **68**(065103).

Li, J.Z., et al., Worldwide Human Relationships Inferred from Genome-Wide Patterns of Variation. Science, 2008. **319**(5866).

Fortunato, S. and M. Barthelemy, *Resolution limit in community detection.* Proceedings of the National Academy of Sciences, 2006. **104**(1).

Ruan, J. and W. Zhang, *Identifying network communities with a high resolution.* Physics Review E, 2008. **77**(016104).

Berry, J.W., et al. *Tolerating the Community Detection Resolution Limit with Edge Weighting.* Physics and Society 2009; Available from: arxiv.org/abs/0903.1072.

Hofman, J. and C. Wiggins, *Bayesian approach to network modularity*. Physical review letters, 2008. **100**(258701).

Psorakis, I., Roberts,S., Ebden, M., and Sheldon, B., Overlapping Community Detection Using Bayesian Non-Negative Matrix Factorization, Phys., Rev. E83, June 2011

Pisorakis, I., Roberts, S., Ebden, M., and Sheldon, B., *Overlapping community detection using Bayesian non-negative matrix factorization*. Physical Review E, 2011. **83**(6): p. 066114.

Airoldi, E., et al., *Mixed membership stochastic blockmodels*. Journal of Machine Learning Research, 2008. **9**.

Barbieri, N., F. Bonchi, and G. Manco. *Cascade-based Community Detection*. in *Proceedings of the sixth ACM International Conference on Web Search and Data Mining*. 2013. New York, NY: ACM.

Chen, Y., V. Kawadia, and R. Urgaonkar. *Detecting Overlapping Temporal Community Structure in Time-Evolving Networks*. 2013; Available from: arXiv:1303.7226.

Rosvall, M. and C.T. Bergstrom, *An information-theoretic framework for resolving community structure in complex networks*. Proceedings of the National Academy of Sciences, 2007. **104**(18): p. 7327–7331.

Rosvall, M. and C. Bergstrom, *Maps of random walks on complex networks reveal community structure*. National Academy of Sciences, 2008. **105**(4).

Rosvall, M., D. Axelsson, and C.T. Bergstrom, *The map equation*. The European Physical Journal Special Topics, 2009. **178**.

Lehmann, S., M. Schwartz, and L.K. Hansen, *Biclique communities*. Physical Review E, 2008. **78**(016108).

Kumpula, J.M., et al., *Sequential algorithm for fast clique percolation*. Physical Review E, 2008. **78**(026109).

Chapter 13
Understanding the Vulnerability Lifecycle for Risk Assessment and Defense Against Sophisticated Cyber Attacks

Tudor Dumitraş

Abstract The security of deployed and actively used systems is a moving target, influenced by factors that are not captured in the existing security models and metrics. For example, estimating the number of vulnerabilities in source code does not account for the fact that cyber attackers never exploit some of the discovered vulnerabilities, in the presence of reduced attack surfaces and of technologies that render exploits less likely to succeed. Conversely, some vulnerabilities are exploited stealthily before their public disclosure, in zero-day attacks, and old vulnerabilities continue to impact security in the wild until all vulnerable hosts are patched. As such, *we currently do not know how to assess the security of systems in active use*. In this chapter, we report on empirical studies of security in the real world, using field data collected on 10+ million real hosts that are targeted by cyber attacks (rather than on honeypots or in small-scale lab settings). Our empirical findings and the novel metrics we evaluate on this field data will enable a more accurate assessment of the risk of cyber attacks, by taking into account the vulnerabilities and attacks that matter most in practice.

13.1 Introduction

In systems that are *deployed and actively used*, security is a moving target as attackers exploit new vulnerabilities (to subvert the system's functionality), vendors distribute software updates (to patch vulnerabilities and to improve security) and users reconfigure the system (to add functionality). Measuring the security of such systems is challenging. Many security metrics have been proposed, including the total count of vulnerabilities in source code, the severity of these vulnerabilities, the size of the attack surface and the time window between the vulnerability disclosure and the release of a patch. System administrators often rely on these metrics to assess the risk associated with vulnerabilities, while developers use them as guidelines for improving software security. However, practical experience suggests that the existing security metrics and models exhibit a low level of correlation with vulnerabilities

T. Dumitraş (✉)
Electrical and Computer Engineering Department, University of Maryland,
College Park, MD, USA
e-mail: tdumitra@umiacs.umd.edu

© Springer International Publishing Switzerland 2015
S. Jajodia et al. (eds.), *Cyber Warfare,* Advances in Information Security 56,
DOI 10.1007/978-3-319-14039-1_13

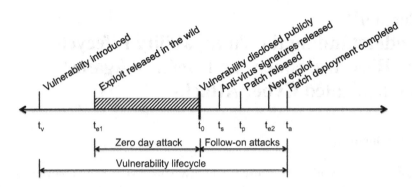

Fig. 13.1 Events in the vulnerability lifecycle

and attacks and do not provide an adequate assessment of security (Shin et al. 2011; Zimmermann et al. 2010). This highlights the fact that our ability to assess the security of systems that are deployed and actively used is currently limited by the metrics we employ.

For example, the Common Vulnerabilities and Exposures (CVE) consortium maintains a database with extensive information about vulnerabilities—including technical details and the disclosure dates—that is a widely accepted standard for academia, governmental organizations and the cyber security industry (CVE 2012). The Common Vulnerability Scoring System (CVSS) defines a static score for each vulnerability, which includes exploitability metrics (Access Vector, Access Complexity and Authentication) and impact metrics (Confidentiality Impact, Integrity Impact, and Availability Impact). The National Institute of Standards and Technology (NIST) recommends CVSS scores as the reference assessment method for software security (Quinn et al. 2010).

However, the CVSS "exploitability" subscore is not a good predictor for which vulnerabilities are exploited in the real world (though, most exploited vulnerabilities do have high exploitability (Allodi and Massacci 2012), and the CVSS-based risk evaluation does not fit the real attack data, as observed in the wild Allodi (2013). For instance, estimating the number and severity of vulnerabilities in source code does not account for the fact that cyber attackers never exploit some of the discovered vulnerabilities, in the presence of reduced attack surfaces and technologies that render exploits less likely to succeed. Conversely, some vulnerabilities are exploited stealthily before their public disclosure, in zero-day attacks, and old vulnerabilities continue to impact security in the wild until all vulnerable hosts are patched.

Figure 13.1 illustrates the vulnerability lifecycle. A vulnerability is created when the earliest application version that includes the (yet-unknown) vulnerability is released (t_v). A vulnerability is disclosed when its existence is publicly advertised. By convention, the disclosure date is considered the "day zero" in the vulnerability lifecycle, as this is the date when the security community becomes aware of the vulnerability ($t_0 \geq t_v$). Several exploits may be created for a vulnerability during its lifecycle. The exploits may be released before or after disclosure (t_{e1}, t_{e2}); those released before disclosure are known as *zero-day attacks* ($t_{e1} < t_0$). Once the vulnerability is disclosed, anti-virus vendors release new signatures for detecting the exploit (t_s), and the vendor releases a new version that patches the vulnerability (t_p). The vulnerable host population starts decaying when the patch is released, but the vulnerability ceases to have an impact only after all vulnerable hosts worldwide have been patched (t_a).

In this chapter, we focus on characterizing the vulnerability lifecycle empirically, using data resources (described in Sect. 14.4) that are generally available to the research community. Specifically, we show that zero-day attacks are more prevalent than previously thought and they go on undetected for 312 days on average (Sect. 13.4.1), that the volume of attacks exploiting them increases by up to 5 orders of magnitude after disclosure (Sect. 13.4.2) and that fewer than 35 % of the vulnerabilities discovered are exploited in the wild (Sect. 13.4.3). We discuss the implications of these findings for public policy and the future security technologies, and we reflect on a number of open research questions that will require further empirical studies conducted at scale (Sect. 14.6).

13.2   Related Work

The total number of vulnerabilities present in source code and their severity, as represented by the Common Vulnerability Scoring System (CVSS), are commonly used security metrics. For example, Rescorla (2005) analyzed the number of vulnerabilities disclosed for 4 operating systems in order to determine whether the practice of vulnerability disclosures leads to reliability growth over time. Ozment et al. (2006) study the rate of vulnerability finding in the foundational code of OpenBSD and fit the data to a vulnerability growth model in order to estimate the number of vulnerabilities left undiscovered. Clark et al. (2010) examine the challenge of finding vulnerabilities in new code and show that the time to discover the first vulnerability is usually longer than the time to discover the second one (a phenomenon they call the "honeymoon effect"). Several studies employ vulnerability counts as an implicit measure of security. Shin et al. (2011) evaluate code complexity, code churn and the developer activity to determine the vulnerable code locations in Linux. Bozorgi et al. (2010) propose a machine learning approach for predicting which vulnerabilities will be exploited based on their CVSS scores. In consequence, the National Institute of Standards and Technology (NIST) recommends CVSS scores as the reference assessment method for software security (Quinn et al. 2010). Based on an empirical analysis, Ransbotham et al. suggest that vulnerabilities in open source software have an increased risk of exploitation, diffuse sooner and have a larger volume of exploitation attempts than closed source software (Ransbotham 2010). In contrast to these contributions, we focus on security metrics that reflect the security of systems in their deployment environments.

Frei studied zero-day attacks by combining publicly available information on vulnerabilities disclosed between 2000–2007 by analyzing three exploit archives, popular in the hacker community (Frei 2009). This study showed that, on the disclosure date, an exploit was available for 15 % of vulnerabilities and a patch was available for 43 % of vulnerabilities (these percentages are not directly comparable because they are computed over different bases—all vulnerabilities that have known exploits and all vulnerabilities that have been patched, respectively). The study also found that 94 % of exploits are created within 30 days after disclosure. However, the exploits included in public archives are proofs-of-concept that are not always used in real-world attacks. Shahzad et al. conduct a similar study, but on a larger data set Shahzad et al. (2012). In this work, the authors analyze how the type and number of vulnerabilities change during the period of their analysis window. McQueen et al. (2009) analyze the lifespan of known zero-day vulnerabilities in order to be able to estimate the real number of zero-day vulnerabilities existed in the past. In contrast to this previous work, we analyze field data, collected on real hosts targeted by cyber attacks, to understand the prevalence and duration of zero-day attacks before vulnerabilities are disclosed, and we conduct a real-world analysis rather than make statistical estimations.

Symantec analysts identified 8–15 zero-day vulnerabilities each year between 2006–2011 (Symantec Corporation 2012). For example, 9 vulnerabilities were used in zero-day attacks in 2008, 12 in 2009, 14 in 2010 and 8 in 2011. The 14 zero-day vulnerabilities discovered in 2010 affected the Windows operating system, as well as widely used applications such as Internet Explorer, Adobe Reader, and Adobe Flash Player. These vulnerabilities were employed in high-profile attacks, such as Stuxnet and Hydraq. In 2009, Qualys analysts reported knowledge of 56 zero-day vulnerabilities (Qualys, Inc. 2009). In contrast, to these reports, we propose a technique for identifying zero-day attacks automatically from field data available to the research community, and we conduct a systematic study of zero-day attacks in the real world. In particular, we identify 11 vulnerabilities, disclosed between 2008–2011, that were not known to have been used in a zero-day attack.

Most prior work has focused on the entire window of exposure to a vulnerability, first defined by Schneier (2000). Arbaugh et al. evaluated the number of intrusions observed during each phase of the vulnerability lifecycle and showed that a significant number of vulnerabilities continue to be exploited even after patches become available (Anderson et al. 2000). Frei compared how fast Microsoft and Apple react to newly disclosed vulnerabilities and, while significant differences exist between the two vendors, both have some vulnerabilities with no patch available 180 days after disclosure (Frei 2009). A Secunia study showed that 50 % of Windows users were exposed to 297 vulnerabilities in a year and that patches for only 65 % of these vulnerabilities were available at the time of their public disclosure (Frei 2011). Moreover, even after patches become available, users often delay their deployment, partly because of the overhead of patch management and partly because of the general observation that the process of fixing bugs tends to introduce additional software defects. For example, a typical Windows user must manage 14 update mechanisms to keep the host fully patched (Frei 2011), while an empirical study suggested that over 10 % of security patches have bugs of their own (Beattie 2002).

While the market for zero-day vulnerabilities has not been studied as thoroughly as other aspects of the underground economy, the development of exploits for such vulnerabilities is certainly a profitable activity. For example, several security firms run programs, such as HP's Zero Day Initiative and Verisign's iDefense Vulnerability Contributor Program, that pay developers up to $ 10,000 for their exploits (Greenberg 2012; Miller 2007), with the purpose of developing intrusion-protection filters against these exploits. Between 2000–2007, 10 % of vulnerabilities have been disclosed through these programs (Frei 2009). Similarly, software vendors often reward the discovery of new vulnerabilities in their products, offering prizes up to $ 60,000 for exploits against targets that are difficult to attack, such as Google's Chrome browser (Google Inc. 2012). Moreover, certain firms and developers specialize in selling exploits to confidential clients on the secretive, but legal, market for zero-day vulnerabilities. Industry sources suggest that the market value of such vulnerabilities can reach $ 250,000 (Miller 2007; Greenberg 2012). In particular, the price of exploits against popular platforms, such as Windows, iOS or the major web browsers, may exceed $ 100,000, depending on the complexity of the exploit and on how long the vulnerability remains undisclosed (Greenberg 2012).

13.3   Data Resources

Understanding the vulnerability lifecycle requires rigorous empirical research, using real-world data about cyber attacks. Unfortunately, unlike in other research communities where data sets have sometimes outlived the system for which they were collected, the data sets used for validating cybersecurity research are often forgotten after the initial publication referencing them. This is the result of scientific, ethical, and legal challenges for publicly disseminating security-related data sets, necessarily include sensitive and potentially dangerous information.

In this chapter, we take advantage of the Worldwide Intelligence Network Environment (WINE), a platform for data intensive experiments in cyber security (Dumitras and Shou 2011). WINE was developed at Symantec Research Labs for sharing comprehensive field data with the research community. WINE samples and aggregates multiple terabyte-size data sets, which Symantec uses in its day-to-day operations, with the aim of supporting open-ended experiments at scale. The data included in WINE is collected on a representative subset (Papalexakis et al. 2103) of the hosts running Symantec products, such as the Norton Antivirus. These hosts do not represent honeypots or machines in an artificial lab environment; they are real computers, in active use around the world, that are targeted by cyber attacks. WINE also enables the reproduction of prior experimental results, by archiving the reference data sets that researchers use and by recording information on the data collection process and on the experimental procedures employed.

We correlate the WINE data sets with information from additional sources: the National Vulnerability Database (NVD), (http://nvd.nist.gov/) the Open Sourced Vulnerability Database (OSVDB) (2012), Symantec's descriptions of anti-virus

signatures (http://www.symantec.com/security_response/landing/azlisting.jsp) and
intrusion-protection signatures (http://www.symantec.com/security_response/attack
signatures/), and a Symantec data set with dynamic analysis results for malware
samples.

NVD is a database of software vulnerabilities which is widely accepted for vulnerability research. Similarly, OSVDB is a public database that aggregates all the
available sources of information about vulnerabilities that have been disclosed since
1998. Because the Microsoft Windows platform has been the main target for cyber
attacks over the past decade, we focus on vulnerabilities in Windows or in software
developed for Windows. The information we collected from OSVDB includes the
discovery, disclosure and exploit release date of the vulnerabilities. To complete the
picture of the vulnerability lifecycle, we collect the patch release dates from Microsoft and Adobe Security Bulletins (Microsoft: Microsoft security bulletins 2012;
Adobe Systems Incorporated 2012).

Threat Explorer is a public web site with up-to-date information about the latest
threats, risks and vulnerabilities. In addition, it provides detailed historical information about most threats for which Symantec has generated anti-virus signatures.
From these details, we are only interested in the malware class of the threat (e.g.,
Trojan, Virus, Worm), the signature generation date and associated CVE identifier(s),
if the threat exploits known vulnerabilities. For example, we build the ground truth
for our zero-day attack investigation by combining information from OSVDB and
Symantec Threat Explorer to prepare a list of threats along with the vulnerabilities
they exploit.

In this chapter, we analyze three WINE data sets: *anti-virus telemetry*, *intrusion-
protection telemetry* and *binary reputation*. The anti-virus telemetry data records
detections of known threats for which Symantec generated a signature that was
subsequently deployed in an anti-virus product. The anti-virus telemetry data in
WINE was collected between December 2009 and August 2011, and it includes 225
million detections that occurred on 9 million hosts. From each record, we use the
detection time, the associated threat label, the hash (MD5 and SHA2) of the malicious
file, and the country where the machine resides. We use this data in three ways: to
link the threat labels with malicious files (Sect. 13.4.1), to assess the continued
impact of zero-day vulnerabilities after they are publicly disclosed (Sect. 13.4.2)
and to estimate the fraction of hosts that are attacked using vulnerability exploits
(Sec. 13.4.3).

The intrusion-prevention (IPS) telemetry dataset within WINE provides information about attacks detected in network streams, i.e. a series of network packets
that: (1) carry malicious code, and (2) have not been prevented by other existing
defenses (e.g. network or OS firewall). The IPS telemetry in WINE was collected
between August 2009 and December 2013, and it includes 300 million detections
that occurred on 6 million hosts. Each IPS entry contains the signature ID for the
threat detected, a machine ID, a platform string and a timestamp for the event. We
use this data for estimating the fraction of hosts that are attacked using vulnerability
exploits (Sect. 13.4.3).

The binary reputation data, on the other hand, does not record threat detections.
Instead, it reports all the binary executables—whether benign or malicious—that

have been downloaded on end-hosts around the world. The binary reputation data in WINE was collected since February 2008, and it includes 32 billion reports about approximately 300 million distinct files, which were downloaded on 11 million hosts. Each report includes the download time, the hash (MD5 and SHA2) of the binary, and the URL from which it was downloaded. These files may include malicious binaries that were not detected at the time of their download because the threat was unknown. We note that this data is collected only from the Symantec customers who gave their consent to share it. The binary reputation data allows us to look back in time to get more insights about what happened before signatures for malicious binaries were created. Therefore, analyzing this data set enables us to discover zero-day attacks conducted in the past (Sect. 13.4.1).

In recent years, most exploits are embedded in non-executable files such as *.pdf, *.doc, *.xlsx 2011). Because the binary reputation data only reports executable files, it is not straightforward to find out whether a non-executable exploit was involved in a zero-day attack or not. To analyze non-executable exploits, we try to identify a customized malicious binary that was downloaded after a successful exploitation, and we then search the binary in the binary reputation data. To this end, we search the dynamic analysis data set to create a list of binaries that are downloaded after the exploitation phase.

13.4 Characterizing the Vulnerability Lifecycle

In this section, we analyze the data sets described in Sec. 14.4 in order to answer several open questions about the vulnerability lifecycle:

- *How prevalent are zero-day attacks, and for how long can they go on undetected?* (Sect. 13.4.1)
- *What happens with these exploits after disclosure?* (Sect. 13.4.2)
- *How many vulnerabilities are exploited in the wild?* (Sect. 13.4.3)

13.4.1   The Prevalence and Duration of Zero-Day Attacks

A *zero-day attack* is a cyber attack exploiting a vulnerability that has not been disclosed publicly. There is almost no defense against a zero-day attack: while the vulnerability remains unknown, the software affected cannot be patched and anti-virus products cannot detect the attack through signature-based scanning. For cyber criminals, unpatched vulnerabilities in popular software, such as Microsoft Office or Adobe Flash, represent a free pass to any target they might wish to attack, from Fortune 500 companies to millions of consumer PCs around the world. For this reason, the market value of a new vulnerability ranges between $ 5000–250,000 (Greenberg 2012; Miller 2007). Examples of notable zero-day attacks include the 2010 Hydraq trojan, also known as the "Aurora" attack that aimed to steal information

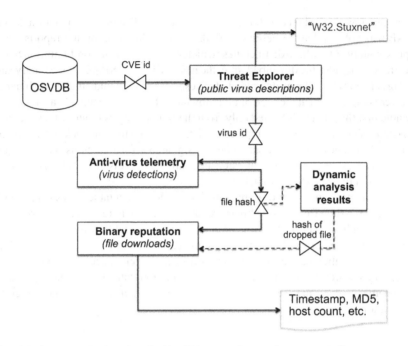

Fig. 13.2 Overview of our method for identifying zero-day attacks systematically

from several companies (Lelli 2010), the 2010 Stuxnet worm, which combined four zero-day vulnerabilities to target industrial control systems (Falliere 2011), and the 2011 attack against RSA (Rivner 2011). Unfortunately, very little is known about zero-day attacks because, in general, data is not available until *after* the attacks are discovered. Prior studies relied on indirect measurements (e.g., analyzing patches and exploits) or the post-mortem analysis of isolated incidents, and they do not shed light on the the duration, prevalence and characteristics of zero-day attacks.

Figure 13.2 illustrates our analysis method (Bilge and Dumitraş 2012), which has five steps: building the ground truth, identifying exploits in executables, identifying executables dropped after exploitation (optional phase), analyzing the presence of exploits on the Internet, and identifying zero-day attacks.

Building the Ground Truth We first gather information about vulnerabilities in Windows and in software running on the Windows platform by querying OSVDB and other references about disclosed vulnerabilities (e.g., Microsoft Bulletins). For all the vulnerabilities that are identified by a CVE number we collect the discovery, disclosure, exploit release date and patch release dates. We then search Symantec's Threat Explorer for these CVE numbers to identify the threats that exploit these vulnerabilities. Each threat has a name (e.g., W32.Stuxnet) and a numerical identifier, called *virus_id*. We manually filter out the *virus_id*s that correspond to generic virus detections (e.g., "Trojan Horse"), as identified by their Threat Explorer descriptions (Symantec Corporation 2012). This step results in a mapping of threats to their corresponding CVE identifiers, $Z_i = \{virus\_id_i, cve\_id_i\}$, which are our candidates for the zero-day attack study. Note that some $virus\_id$s use more than one vulnerability, therefore in Z_i it is possible to observe the same $virus\_id$ more than once.

Identifying Exploits in Executables In the second stage our aim is to identify the exploits that are detected by each $virus\_id$ in Z so that we can search for them in the binary reputation data. The anti-virus telemetry data set records the hashes of all the malicious files identified by Symantec's anti-virus products. We represent each file recorded in the system with an identifier ($file\_hash\_id$). Certain $virus\_id$s detect a large number of $file\_hash\_id$s because of the polymorphism employed by malware authors to evade detection. This step results in a mapping of threats to their variants, $E_i = \{virus\_id_i, file\_hash\_id_i\}$.

Identifying Executables Dropped After Exploitation When exploits are embedded in non-executable files, we can find their $file\_hash\_id$s in the anti-virus telemetry data but not in the binary reputation data. To detect zero-day attacks that employ such exploits, we query the dynamic analysis data set for files that are downloaded after successful exploitations performed by the $file\_hash\_id$s identified in the previous step. This step also produces a mapping of threats to malicious files, but instead of listing the exploit files in E we add the dropped binary files. This may result in false positives because, even if we detect a dropped executable in the binary reputation data before the disclosure date of the corresponding vulnerability, we cannot be confident that this executable was linked to a zero-day attack. In other words, the executable may have been downloaded using other infection techniques. Therefore, this step is optional in our method.

Analyzing the Presence of Exploits on the Internet Having identified which executables exploit known cve_ids, we search for each executable in the binary reputation data to estimate when they first appeared on the Internet. Because the binary reputation data indicates the *presence* of these files, and not whether they were executed (or even if they could have executed on the platform where they were discovered), these reports indicate attacks rather than successful infections. As some $virus\_id$s match more than one variant, the first executable detected marks the start of the attack. After this step, for each $virus\_id$ in Z we can approximate the time when the attack started in the real world.

Identifying Zero-Day Attacks Finally, to find the $virus\_id$s involved in zero-day attacks we compare the start dates of each attack with the disclosure dates of the corresponding vulnerabilities. If at least one of the $file\_hash\_id$s of a threat $Z_i = \{virus\_id_i, cve\_id_i\}$ was downloaded before the disclosure date of cve_id_i, we conclude that cve_id_i is a zero-day vulnerability and that $virus\_id_i$ performed a zero-day attack.

Prevalence of Zero-Day Attacks We apply this method to analyze the zero-day attacks that occurred between 2008 and 2011 (Bilge and Dumitraş 2012). We identify 18 zero-day vulnerabilities: 3 disclosed in 2008, 7 in 2009, 6 in 2010 and 2 in 2011.

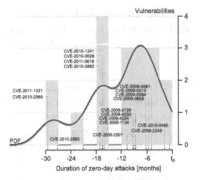

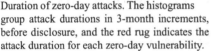

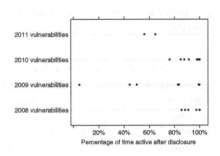

Duration of zero-day attacks. The histograms group attack durations in 3-month increments, before disclosure, and the red rug indicates the attack duration for each zero-day vulnerability.

Percentage of the period after the disclosure date that zero-day vulnerabilities are still exploited. Each dot corresponds to an antivirus signature. 100% means that a vulnerability exploit was still in use at the time of our experiment.

a

b

Fig. 13.3 Impact of zero-day vulnerabilities, before and after disclosure

While the exploit files associated with most vulnerabilities were detected by only one anti-virus signature—typically a heuristic detection for the exploit—there are some vulnerabilities associated with several signatures. For example, CVE-2008-4250 was exploited 8 months before the disclosure date by Conficker (also known as W32.Downadup) (Porras et al. 2009) and four other worms.

To determine whether these vulnerabilities were already known to have been involved in zero-day attacks, we manually search all 18 vulnerabilities on Google. From the annual vulnerability trends reports produced by Symantec (Symantec Corporation 2008, 2009, 2010, 2011, 2012) and the SANS Institute (2009), as well as blog posts on the topic of zero-day vulnerabilities, we found out that 7 of our vulnerabilities are generally accepted to be zero-day vulnerabilities. For example, CVE-2010-2568 is one of the four zero-day vulnerabilities exploited by Stuxnet and it is known to have also been employed by another threat for more than 2 years before the disclosure date (17 July 2010). Most of these vulnerabilities affected Microsoft and Adobe products. Overall, 60% of the zero-day vulnerabilities we identify in our study were not known before, which suggests that there are many more zero-day attacks than previously thought—perhaps more than *twice as many*.

Duration of Zero-Day Attacks The zero-day attacks we identify lasted between 19 days (CVE-2010-0480) and 30 months (CVE-2010-2568), and the average duration of a zero-day attack is 312 days. Figure 13.3a illustrates this distribution. 16 of the zero-day vulnerabilities targeted fewer than 150 hosts, out of the 11 million hosts in our data set. On the other hand, 2 vulnerabilities were employed in attacks that infected thousands or even millions of Internet users. For example, Conficker exploiting the vulnerability CVE-2008-4250 managed to infect approximately 370 thousand machines without being detected over more than two months. This example illustrates the effectiveness of zero-day vulnerabilities for conducting stealth cyber attacks.

We also ask the question whether the zero-day vulnerabilities continued to be exploited up until the end of our experimentation period. Figure 13.3b shows the distribution of the time that we continue to detect anti-virus signatures linked to these vulnerabilities, expressed as a percentage of the time between disclosure and the time of writing. The figure suggests that zero-day vulnerabilities do not loose their popularity after the disclosure date. While two vulnerabilities, CVE-2009-1134 and CVE-2009-2501, ceased to have an impact after being exploited over a year, 58 % of the anti-virus signatures were still active at the time of our experiment. This suggests that the vulnerability lifecycle is often longer than 4 years.

While linking exploits to dropped executables through the dynamic analysis of malware samples may produce false positives, we repeat our experiments taking this data set into account, to see if we can identify more zero-day vulnerabilities. We do not detect additional zero-day attacks in this manner, but this optional step allows us to confirm 2 of the zero-day vulnerabilities that we have already discovered.

Interpretation of the Results The method described in this section primarily detects zero-day attacks delivered through executable files, because we use the binary reputation data (which tracks only binary executables) to approximate the start dates of attacks. Moreover, as WINE includes data from a sample of the set of hosts submitting telemetry to Symantec—which is itself a sample all the hosts on the Internet—we may be underestimating the duration of the attacks. We therefore caution the reader that our results for the duration of zero-day attacks are best interpreted as *lower bounds*.

13.4.2 Zero-day Vulnerabilities After Disclosure

To learn what happens after the disclosure of zero-day vulnerabilities, we investigate the volume of attacks exploiting these vulnerabilities over time. Specifically, we analyze the variation of the number of malware variants, as they emerge in the wild, and of the number of times they are detected. Figure 13.4a shows how many downloads (before the disclosure date) and detections (after the disclosure date) of the exploits for the zero-day vulnerabilities were observed until the last exploitation attempt. The number of attacks increases 2–100,000 times after the disclosure dates of these vulnerabilities.

Figure 13.4b shows that the number of variants (files exploiting the vulnerability) exhibits the same abrupt increase after disclosure: 183–85,000 more variants are detected each day. One reason for observing a large number of new different files that exploit the zero-day vulnerabilities might be that they are repacked versions of the same exploits. However, it is doubtful that repacking alone can account for an increase by up to 5 orders of magnitude. More likely, this increase is the result of the extensive re-use of field-proven exploits in other malware.

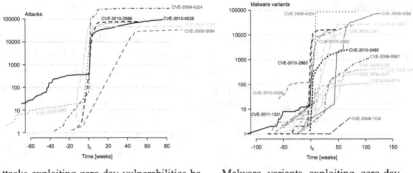

Attacks exploiting zero-day vulnerabilities before and after the disclosure (time = t_0).

Malware variants exploiting zero-day vulnerabilities before and after disclosure (time = t_0).

a   **b**

Fig. 13.4 Impact of vulnerability disclosures on the volume of attacks. We utilize logarithmic scales to illustrate an increase of several orders of magnitude after disclosure

Figure 13.5 shows the time elapsed until all the vulnerabilities disclosed between 2008 and 2011 started being exploited in the wild. Exploits for 42 % of these vulnerabilities appear in the field data within 30 days after the disclosure date. This illustrates the fact that the cyber criminals watch closely the disclosure of new vulnerabilities, in order to start exploiting them, which causes a significant risk for end-users.

13.4.3 The Exploitation Ratio of Product Vulnerabilities

While some vulnerabilities are exploited before their public disclosures, and some continue to be exploited for years afterward, other vulnerabilities are never exploited in the field. Figure 13.6 illustrates this problem. The number of vulnerability exploits is not proportional to the total number of vulnerabilities discovered in Windows OSes, and the two metrics follow different trends (as suggested by the trend lines in Figure 13.6). Additionally, there is no apparent correlation between the number of vulnerabilities discovered, and the size of the OS code. [1] This suggests the existence of deployment-specific factors, yet to be characterized systematically, that influence the security of systems in active use.

We propose several metrics (Nayak et al. 2014), derived from field-gathered data, that capture the notion of whether disclosed vulnerabilities get exploited.

---

[1] Approximate lines of code, in millions: Windows 2000 $\simeq$ 30, Windows XP $\simeq$ 45, Windows Server 2003 $\simeq$ 50, Windows Vista, Windows 7 > 50 (http://bit.ly/RKDHIm; http://bit.ly/5LkKx, http://tek.io/g3rBrB).

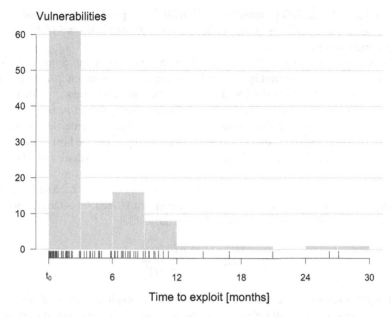

Fig. 13.5 Time before vulnerabilities disclosed between 2008–2011 started being exploited in the field. The histograms group the exploitation lag in 3-month increments, after disclosure, and the red rug indicates the lag for each exploited vulnerability. The zero-day attacks are excluded from this figure

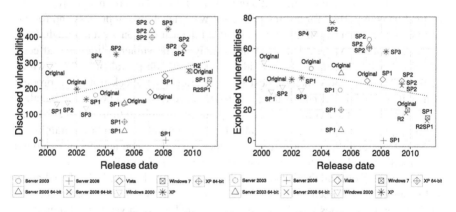

a All vulnerabilities disclosed publicly. **b** Vulnerabilities exploited in the wild.

Fig. 13.6 Number of vulnerabilities disclosed and exploited for Microsoft Windows over 11 years of releases, estimated using NVD (http://nvd.nist.gov/) and WINE. No clear trend exists for total number of vulnerabilities disclosed but number of vulnerabilities actually exploited in the field decreases with newer operating systems

1. *Count of vulnerabilities exploited in the wild.* For a product p, we consider the number of vulnerabilities known to have been exploited in the wild, $\left| V_p^{ex} \right|$, to be an important metric.

   We combine information from NVD (http://nvd.nist.gov/) and Symantec's signature databases (http://bit.ly/1hCw1TL; Symantec Corporation 2012) to obtain the subset of a product's disclosed vulnerabilities that have been exploited.

   V_p is the set of vulnerabilities listed in NVD that affect product p, and V_p^{ex} is the subset of these vulnerabilities referenced in at least one Symantec signature.

   Prior research has suggested that these signatures represent the best indicator for which vulnerabilities are exploited in real-world attacks (Allodi and Massacci 2012).

2. *Exploitation ratio.* The exploitation ratio is the proportion of disclosed vulnerabilities for product p that have been exploited up until time t. This metric captures the likelihood that a vulnerability will be exploited.

$$ ER^p(t) = \frac{\left| V_p^{ex}(t) \right|}{\left| V_p(t) \right|} $$

Exploitation Ratio Table 13.1 shows the number of exploited vulnerabilities and the exploitation ratio for all OSes and products in our study. The exploitation ratios shown include vulnerabilities disclosed and exploited as of the end of the product's support period, or as of 2014 if the product is presently supported. We account for *progressive* and *regressive* vulnerabilities (Clark et al. 2010) separately. A progressive vulnerability is a vulnerability discovered in version N that does not affect version $N - 1$ or previous versions, while a regressive vulnerability is one found in version N that affects at least one of the previous versions. The progressive-regressive distinction is important for evaluating the software development process and for understanding the security of the new code added in each version—even though, from the users' point of view, it is important to study all the vulnerabilities that affect a product version. The table also includes the exploitation prevalence, EP^p, which helps to illuminate how likely a host is to experience an attack if a given product is installed. EP^p is defined as the proportion of the hosts with product p installed that experienced at least one attack targeting one of p's vulnerabilities. Note that this metric captures information not revealed by the exploitation ratio or the number of exploited vulnerabilities. For instance, Reader 9 has the same number of exploited vulnerabilities as IE 8, but its exploitation prevalence is far higher.

In aggregate, over all the software products we analyzed, about 15 % of the known vulnerabilities have been exploited in real-world attacks. Note, however, that the exploitation ratio varies greatly across products and between versions of a product. This highlights the pitfall of employing the number and severity of vulnerabilities as a measure of security: a product with many high-impact vulnerabilities in NVD would be considered insecure, even if its exploitation ratio is lower than for other products. To further investigate whether the total count of vulnerabilities models the security of a software product, we compare the distributions of the disclosed and exploited vulnerabilities for each product using the Kolmogorov-Smirnov test

Table 13.1 Exploitation ratio and exploitation prevalence of products. $ER(yr)$: exploitation ratio of the product for all vulnerabilities up to the year yr. EP_P: the ratio of machines experiencing an attack over the number of machines having the product installed. NA indicates that no machines in WINE had the product installed

Year	Product	$ER^p(yr)$	$ER^p_{Prog}(yr)$	$\left|V_p^{ex}\right|$	$\left|V_p^{prog,ex}\right|$	EP^p
2006	IE 5	0.12	0.14	27	25	NA
2010	IE 6	0.17	0.16	73	33	0.035
2013	IE 7	0.13	0.07	36	4	0.002
2013	IE 8	0.13	0.15	29	10	0.0004
2009	Office 2000	0.32	0.32	27	27	NA
2013	Office 2003	0.35	0.36	43	21	0.0002
2013	Office 2007	0.27	0.18	18	2	0
2013	Office 2010	0.25	0	5	0	0
2009	Windows XP	0.21	0.15	39	8	NA
2006	Windows XP SP1	0.28	0.31	41	11	0.026
2010	Windows XP SP2	0.23	0.27	73	16	0.011
2014	Windows XP SP3	0.13	0.07	58	12	0.047
2012	Windows Vista	0.21	0.09	39	5	0.005
2011	Windows Vista SP1	0.16	0.06	40	6	0.004
2014	Windows Vista SP2	0.11	0.06	39	2	0.011
2014	Windows 7	0.07	0.25	20	2	0
2014	Windows 7 SP1	0.07	0	15	0	0.004
2008	Adobe Reader 5	0.18	0.2	4	1	NA
2008	Adobe Reader 6	0.22	0.17	5	1	NA
2009	Adobe Reader 7	0.17	0.09	11	4	0.177
2011	Adobe Reader 8	0.16	0.15	29	18	0.180
2013	Adobe Reader 9	0.11	0.10	29	10	0.242
2014	Adobe Reader 10	0.08	0.04	13	1	0.0002
2014	Adobe Reader 11	0.06	0	5	0	0

(http: //www.itl.nist.gov/div898/handbook/index.htm). The results suggest that we cannot reject the null hypothesis that the number of vulnerabilities and the number of exploits are drawn from the same distribution, at the $p = 0.05$ significance level, for any of the products studied. However, some differences stand out. For example, IE 5 has nearly three times as many reported vulnerabilities as Office 2000. Nevertheless, both have a similar number of exploited vulnerabilities. This is reflected in the much higher exploitation ratio for Office. This is one example of how field-gathered data which reflects the deployment environment can complement more traditional security metrics.

Another trend visible in Table 13.1 is that the latest versions of each product have a lower absolute number of exploited vulnerabilities than earlier versions (except in the case of IE). For instance, Windows 7 has fewer exploited vulnerabilities than Windows Vista, and Reader versions 10 and 11 have fewer than versions 8 and 9. One factor that has likely contributed to this decrease is the introduction of security technologies by Microsoft and Adobe that make exploits less likely to succeed, even in the presence of vulnerabilities (e.g., address space layout randomization and sandboxing). Another likely contributing factor is the commoditization of the underground malware industry, which has led to the marketing of exploit kits that bundle a small number of effective attacks for wide-spread reuse.

13.5 Discussion

Knowing which vulnerabilities are exploited in the wild will allow system administrators to prioritize patching based on empirical data, rather than relying exclusively on the CVSS scores for this task. Moreover, the exploitation ratios of different products can be incorporated in quantitative assessments of the risk of cyber attacks against enterprise infrastructure. These metrics enable an assessment of the security of software products in their deployment environments. For example, we observe that the exploitation ratio tends to decrease with newer versions. Large drops in the exploitation ratio for progressive vulnerabilities seem to be associated with the introduction of security technologies, such as ASLR and DEP in Windows Vista or the protected mode in Adobe Reader 10. Interestingly, anecdotal evidence suggests that cyber criminals are starting to feel the effects of this scarcity of exploits. While zero-day exploits have traditionally been employed in targeted attacks (Bilge and Dumitraş 2012), in 2013 the author of the Blackhole exploit kit advertised a $100,000 budget for purchasing zero-day exploits (Krebs 2013). The zero-day exploit for CVE-2013-3906 was nicknamed the "dual-use exploit" after being employed both for targeted attacks and for delivering botnet-based malware (FireEye 2013).

Our findings also provide new data for the debate on the benefits of the full disclosure policy. This policy is based on the premise that disclosing vulnerabilities to the public, rather than to the vendor, is the best way to fix them because this provides an incentive for vendors to patch faster, rather than to rely on security-through-obscurity (Schneier 2000). This debate is ongoing (Anderson and Moore 2006; Bollinger 2004; Schneier 2003, 2004), but most participants agree that disclosing vulnerabilities causes an increase in the volume of attacks. Indeed, this is what the supporters of full disclosure are counting on, to provide a meaningful incentive for patching. However, the participants to the debate disagree about whether trading off a high volume of attacks for faster patching provides an overall benefit to the society. For example, Schneier initiated the debate by suggesting that, to mitigate the risk of disclosure, we should either patch all the vulnerable hosts as soon as the fix becomes available, or we should limit the information available about the vulnerability (Schneier 2000). Ozmet et al. concluded that disclosing information about vulnerabilities improves system security (Ozment and Schechter 2006), while Rescorla et al. could not find the same strong evidence on a more limited data set (Rescorla 2005). Arora et al. (2004) and Cavusoglu et al. (2004) analyzed the impact of full disclosure using techniques inspired from game theory, and they reached opposite conclusions about whether patches would immediately follow the disclosure of vulnerabilities.

The root cause of these disagreements lies in the difficulty of quantifying the real-world impact of vulnerability disclosures and of patch releases without analyzing comprehensive field data. We take a first step toward this goal by showing that the disclosure of zero-day vulnerabilities causes a significant risk for end-users, as the volume of attacks increases by up to 5 orders of magnitude. However, vendors prioritize which vulnerabilities they patch, giving more urgency to vulnerabilities that are disclosed or about to be disclosed. In consequence, between 2000–2007 the percentage of vulnerabilities that have a patch available on their disclosure date has grown by more than 5 times, and few vulnerabilities still lack a patch 3 months after their disclosure (Frei 2009). Meanwhile, attackers stockpile zero-day exploits and use them only as needed (O'Gorman and McDonald 2012), and early disclosures reduce the value of these exploits; indeed, some fees for new exploits are paid in installments, with each subsequent payment depending on the lack of a patch (Greenberg 2012). Additional research is needed for quantifying all the aspects of the full disclosure trade-off, e.g., by measuring how quickly vulnerable hosts are patched in the field, following vulnerability disclosures.

13.5.1 Open Questions

Our empirical studies presented in this chapter represent a first step toward understanding the security of systems that are deployed and actively used. To improve security against sophisticated cyber attacks, we must further answer several research questions:

- *What deployment-specific factors affect security?* Such factors could include interactions among different software components, multiple product lines running side-by-side, the effects of prior cyber attacks and the user behavior, as just a few examples.
- *How to assess the risk of cyber attacks against critical infrastructures?* A more accurate assessment will require new metrics, such as the rate of vulnerability exploitation in the wild, the size of the exercised attack surface of systems in operation, and the patch-deployment rate and lifecycle.
- *How to detect sophisticated attacks?* To achieve this, we need new threat models, based on field data about attacker behavior, as well as an understanding of how current security systems fail in the field.
- *How does malware propagate, in enterprise networks and across the Internet?* The propagation patterns of malicious software have been studied primarily in

the context of flash worms (Kumar et al. 2005; Staniford et al. 2002), which achieved high propagation rates by scanning randomly-generated permutations of the IPv4 address space. However, these techniques are infeasible in the larger address space of the IPv6 protocol, and recent worms involved in targeted attacks, such as Stuxnet (Falliere et al. 2011), Duqu (Symantec Corporation 2011) and Flame (CrySyS Lab: sKyWIper 2012), were designed to propagate more slowly, in order to evade detection.

- *How do cyber stockpiles decay, over time?* Recent industry reports (for example O'Gorman and McDonald (2012)) suggest that advanced attack groups stockpile zero-day exploits and use them as needed. However, the value of these exploits decays over time because the vulnerabilities may be discovered independently. The literature includes conflicting numbers for this rate of decay; for example, a study of the Chrome and Firefox vulnerability reward programs suggest rediscovery rates between 2.25 and 4.7 % (Finifter et al. 2013), while in our study of zero-day attacks 60 % of the vulnerabilities identified were not previously known to have been used in zero-day attacks (Bilge and Dumitraş 2012), suggesting that they were discovered and disclosed independently of these attacks.

As in our studies of exploitation ratios and zero-day attacks, answering these additional research questions will require empirical studies conducted at scale, using comprehensive field data.

13.6   Conclusions

We conduct empirical studies of security in the deployment environment, focusing on several phases of the vulnerability lifecycle. Our findings include the fact that fewer than 35 % of the vulnerabilities discovered are exploited in the wild, that the average duration of zero-day attacks is approximately 10 months and that the attacks exploiting these vulnerabilities increase by up to 5 orders of magnitude and, in some cases, continue for more than 4 years. This suggests that evaluating the security of systems in lab conditions, at development-time, fails to capture deployment-specific factors that affect security in important ways. We propose several metrics not provided in any existing databases, such as the exploitation ratio and the milestones of the vulnerability lifecycle (e.g. the start of the zero-day attack), and we show how to measure them using field data available to the research community. These metrics can provide the information needed for a more accurate assessment of the risk of cyber attacks against critical infrastructures. This information will empower users and administrators to assess and mitigate risks by taking into account the vulnerabilities and attacks that matter most in practice.

Acknowledgements   This research would not have been possible without the WINE platform, built and made available to the research community by Symantec. Our results can be reproduced by utilizing the reference data sets WINE 2012-003 and WINE-2014-001, archived in the WINE infrastructure.

References

Adobe Systems Incorporated: Security bulletins and advisories. http://www.adobe.support/ security/ (2012)

Allodi, L.: Attacker economics for internet-scale vulnerability risk assessment. In: Proceedings of Usenix LEET Workshop (2013)

Allodi, L., Massacci, F.: A preliminary analysis of vulnerability scores for attacks in wild. In: CCS BADGERS Workshop. Raleigh, NC (2012)

Anderson, R., Moore, T.: The economics of information security. In: Science, vol. 314, no. 5799 (2006)

Arbaugh, W.A., Fithen, W.L., McHugh, J.: Windows of vulnerability: A case study analysis. IEEE Computer 33(12) (2000)

Arora, A., Krishnan, R., Nandkumar, A., Telang, R., Yang, Y.: Impact of vulnerability disclosure and patch availability - an empirical analysis. In: Workshop on the Economics of Information Security (WEIS 2004) (2004)

Beattie, S., Arnold, S., Cowan, C., Wagle, P., Wright, C.: Timing the application of security patches for optimal uptime. In: Large Installation System Administration Conference, pp. 233–242. Philadelphia, PA (2002). URL http://www.usenix.org/events/lisa02/tech/beattie.html

Bilge, L., Dumitraş, T.: Before we knew it: an empirical study of zero-day attacks in the real world. In: ACM Conference on Computer and Communications Security, pp. 833–844 (2012)

Bollinger, J.: Economies of disclosure. In: SIGCAS Comput. Soc. (2004)

Bozorgi, M., Saul, L.K., Savage, S., Voelker, G.M.: Beyond heuristics: learning to classify vulnerabilities and predict exploits. In: KDD. Washington, DC (2010)

Cavusoglu, H.C.H., Raghunathan, S.: Emerging issues in responsible vulnerability disclosure. In: Workshop on Information Technology and Systems (2004)

Clark, S., Frei, S., Blaze, M., Smith, J.: Familiarity breeds contempt: The honeymoon effect and the role of legacy code in zero-day vulnerabilities. In: Proceedings of the 26th Annual Computer Security Applications Conference, ACSAC '10, pp. 251–260. ACM, New York, NY, USA (2010). . URL http://doi.acm.org/10.1145/1920261.1920299

CrySyS Lab: sKyWIper (a.k.a. Flame a.k.a. Flamer): A complex malware for targeted attacks. Tech. rep., Budapest University of Technology and Economics (2012). URL http://www.crysys.hu/skywiper/skywiper.pdf

CVE: A dictionary of publicly known information security vulnerabilities and exposures. http://cve.mitre.org/ (2012)

Dumitraş, T., Shou, D.: Toward a standard benchmark for computer security research: The Worldwide Intelligence Network Environment (WINE). In: EuroSys BADGERS Workshop. Salzburg, Austria (2011)

Falliere, N., O'Murchu, L., Chien, E.: W32.Stuxnet dossier. Symantec Whitepaper (2011). URL http://www.symantec.com/content/en/us/enterprise/media/security_response/whitepapers/ w32_stuxnet_dossier.pdf

Finifter, M., Akhawe, D., Wagner, D.: An empirical study of vulnerability rewards programs. In: Proceedings of the ACM Conference on Computer and Communications Security. Washington, DC (2013)

FireEye: The Dual Use Exploit: CVE-2013-3906 Used in Both Targeted Attacks and Crimeware Campaigns. http://bit.ly/R3XQQ4 (2013)

Frei, S.: Security econometrics: The dynamics of (in)security. Ph.D. thesis, ETH Zürich (2009)

Frei, S.: End-Point Security Failures, Insight gained from Secunia PSI scans. Predict Workshop (2011)

Google Inc: Pwnium: rewards for exploits (2012). http://blog.chromium.org/2012/02/pwnium-rewards-for-exploits.html

Greenberg, A.: Shopping for zero-days: A price list for hackers' secret software exploits. Forbes (2012). http://www.forbes.com/sites/andygreenberg/2012/03/23/shopping-for-zero-days-an-price-list-for-hackers-secret-software-exploits/

Krebs, B.: Crimeware author funds exploit buying spree. http://bit.ly/1mYwlUY (2013)

Kumar, A., Paxson, V., Weaver, N.: Exploiting underlying structure for detailed reconstruction of an internet-scale event. In: Internet Measurment Conference, pp. 351–364 (2005)

Lelli, A.: The Trojan.Hydraq incident: Analysis of the Aurora 0-day exploit. http://www.symantec.com/connect/blogs/trojanhydraq-incident-analysis-aurora-0-day-exploit (2010)

McQueen, M.A., McQueen, T.A., Boyer, W.F., Chaffin, M.R.: Empirical estimates and observations of 0day vulnerabilities. In: Hawaii International Conference on System Sciences (2009)

Microsoft: Microsoft security bulletins. http://technet.microsoft.com/en-us/security/bulletin (2012)

Microsoft Corp.: A history of Windows. http://bit.ly/RKDHIm

Miller, C.: The legitimate vulnerability market: Inside the secretive world of 0-day exploit sales. In: Workshop on the Economics of Information Security. Pittsburgh, PA (2007)

National Institute of Standards and Technology: Engineering statistics handbook. http://www.itl.nist.gov/div898/handbook/index.htm

Nayak, K., Marino, D., Efstathopoulos, P., Dumitraş, T.: Some vulnerabilities are different than others: Studying vulnerabilities and attack surfaces in the wild. In: Proceedings of the 17th International Symposium on Research in Attacks, Intrusions and Defenses. Gothenburg, Sweeden (2014)

National Vulnerability Database. http://nvd.nist.gov/

O'Gorman, G., McDonald, G.: The Elderwood project. Symantec Whitepaper (2012)

OSVDB: The open source vulnerability database. http://www.osvdb.org/ (2012)

Ozment, A., Schechter, S.E.: Milk or wine: does software security improve with age? In: 15th conference on USENIX Security Symposium (2006)

Papalexakis, E.E., Dumitras, T., Chau, D.H.P., Prakash, B.A., Faloutsos, C.: Spatio-temporal mining of software adoption & penetration. In: IEEE/ACM International Conference on Advances in Social Networks Analysis and Mining (ASONAM). Niagara Falls, CA (2103)

Porras, P., Saidi, H., Yegneswaran, V.: An anlysis of conficker's logic and rendezvous points. http://mtc.sri.com/Conficker/ (2009)

Qualys, Inc.: The laws of vulnerabilities 2.0. http://www.qualys.com/docs/Laws_2.0.pdf (2009)

Quinn, S., Scarfone, K., Barrett, M., Johnson, C.: Guide to adopting and using the security content automation protocol (SCAP) version 1.0. NIST Special Publication 800-117 (2010)

Ransbotham, S.: An empirical analysis of exploitation attempts based on vulnerabilities in open source software (2010)

Rescorla, E.: Is finding security holes a good idea? In: IEEE Security and Privacy (2005)

Rivner, U.: Anatomy of an attack (2011). http://blogs.rsa.com/rivner/anatomy-of-an-attack/ Retrieved on 19 April 2012

SANS Institute: Top cyber security risks - zero-day vulnerability trends. http://www.sans.org/top-cyber-security-risks/zero-day.php (2009)

Schneier, B.: Cryptogram september 2000 - full disclosure and the window of exposure. http://www.schneier.com/crypto-gram-0009.html (2000)

Schneier, B.: Locks and full disclosure. In: IEEE Security and Privacy (2003)

Schneier, B.: The nonsecurity of secrecy. In: Commun. ACM (2004)

Shahzad, M., Shafiq, M.Z., Liu, A.X.: A large scale exploratory analysis of software vulnerability life cycles. In: Proceedings of the 2012 International Conference on Software Engineering (2012)

Shin, Y., Meneely, A., Williams, L., Osborne, J.A.: Evaluating complexity, code churn, and developer activity metrics as indicators of software vulnerabilities. IEEE Trans. Software Eng. 37(6), 772–787 (2011)

Staniford, S., Paxson, V., Weaver, N.: How to 0wn the Internet in your spare time. In: USENIX Security Symposium, pp. 149–167 (2002)

Symantec Attack Signatures. http://www.symantec.com/security_response/attacksignatures/

Symantec Corporation: Symantec global Internet security threat report, volume 13. http://eval.symantec.com/mktginfo/enterprise/white_papers/b-whitepaper_internet_security_threat_report_xiii_04-2008.en-us.pdf (2008)

Symantec Corporation: Symantec global Internet security threat report, volume 14. http://eval. symantec.com/mktginfo/enterprise/white_papers/b-whitepaper_internet_security_threat_report_ xv_04-2010.en-us.pdf (2009)

Symantec Corporation: Symantec global Internet security threat report, volume 15. http://msisac. cisecurity.org/resources/reports/documents/SymantecInternetSecurityThreatReport2010.pdf (2010)

Symantec Corporation: Symantec Internet security threat report, volume 16 (2011)

Symantec Corporation: W32.Duqu: The precursor to the next Stuxnet. Symantec Whitepaper (2011). URL http://www.symantec.com/content/en/us/enterprise/media/security_response/ whitepapers/w32_duqu_the_precursor_to_the_next_stuxnet_research.pdf

Symantec Corporation: Symantec Internet security threat report, volume 17. http://www. symantec.com/threatreport/ (2012)

Symantec Corporation: Symantec threat explorer. http://www.symantec.com/security_response/ threatexplorer/azlisting.jsp (2012)

Symantec.cloud: February 2011 intelligence report. http://www.messagelabs.com/mlireport/ MLI_2011_02_February_FINAL-en.PDF (2011)

TechRepublic: Five super-secret features in Windows 7. http://tek.io/g3rBrB

Wikipedia: Source lines of code. http://bit.ly/5LkKx

Zimmermann, T., Nagappan, N., Williams, L.A.: Searching for a needle in a haystack: Predicting security vulnerabilities for windows vista. In: ICST, pp. 421–428 (2010)

Chapter 14
Graph Mining for Cyber Security

B. Aditya Prakash

Abstract How does malware propagate? How do software patches propagate? Given a set of malware samples, how to identify all malware variants that exist in a database? Which human behaviors may lead to increased malware attacks? These are challenging problems in their own respect, especially as they depend on having access to extensive, field-gathered data that highlight the current trends. These datasets are increasingly easier to collect, are large in size, and also high in complexity. Hence data mining can play an important role in cyber-security by answering these questions in an empirical data-driven manner. In this chapter, we discuss how related problems in cyber-security can be tackled via techniques from graph mining (specifically mining network propagation) on large field datasets collected on millions of hosts.

14.1 Introduction

Graphs—also known as networks—are powerful tools for modeling processes and situations of interest in real-life like social-systems, cyber-security, epidemiology, biology etc. How do contagions spread in population networks? How stable is a predator-prey ecosystem, given intricate food webs? How do rumors spread on Twitter/Facebook? Answering all these big-data questions involves the study of aggregated dynamics over complex connectivity patterns. Understanding such processes will eventually enable us to manipulate them for our benefit e.g., understanding dynamics of epidemic spreading over graphs helps design more robust policies for immunization.

Questions such as how blackouts can spread on a nationwide scale, how social systems evolve on the basis of individual interactions, or how efficiently we can search data on large networks like those of blogs or web-sites are all also related to dynamical phenomena on networks. Hence, progress here holds great scientific as well as commercial value.

B. Aditya Prakash (✉)
Department of Computer Science, Virginia Tech., Blacksburg, VA 24061, USA
e-mail: badityap@cs.vt.edu

© Springer International Publishing Switzerland 2015
S. Jajodia et al. (eds.), *Cyber Warfare,* Advances in Information Security 56,
DOI 10.1007/978-3-319-14039-1_14

In the security sphere, such problems include understanding the propagation of malware (e.g. estimating the number of machines infected) and the temporal characteristics of benign files. To answer such problems security researchers and analysts need comprehensive, field- gathered data that highlights the current trends in the cyber threat landscape. Today, cyber security research requires experiments conducted at scale, using field data that is updated continuously. However, owing to ethical and legal concerns for sharing data on cyber attacks, security research has traditionally been validated through experiments on synthetically-generated traces or on small data sets (McHugh 2000; Camp et al. 2009). Because the cyber security landscape changes frequently, synthetic data sets become obsolete faster than in other fields, and the performance of new security technologies tested on such data sets is difficult to relate to the results expected in the real world. Moreover, certain types of specialized attacks are rare evens that cannot be observed easily; for example, a recent study has suggested that zero-day exploits, which target undisclosed software vulnerabilities, are typically found on fewer than 0.002 % of the hosts connected to the Internet (Bilge and Dumitraş 2012). Such attacks cannot be studied systematically using data collected from only a few hundreds or even a few thousands hosts.

However getting access to large-scale data is not enough. Researchers who use such datasets must understand the properties of the data, to assess the selection bias for their experiment and to draw meaningful conclusions. Every corpus of field data is likely to cover only a subset of the hosts connected to the Internet, and we must understand how to extrapolate the results, given the characteristics of the data sets analyzed.

In this chapter, we discuss how sophisticated graph mining techniques paired with the right kind and scale of telemetry data, can help in answering challenging problems in security. We first survey related work in Sect. 14.2. We then describe some of our recent advancements in mining so-called cascades and more general network-based propagation processes, with theoretical, algorithmic and empirical results (Sect. 14.3). Next, we discuss how to use these new results and large-scale security data resources (Sect. 14.4) to model malware propagation and understand the effects of sampling on models learnt from the datasets (Sect. 14.5). We specifically show that propagation of high-volume malicious files have a characteristic rise-fall pattern. which can be succinctly described using a parsimonious model. We further demonstrate that this is preserved under sampling as well. We then discuss the implications of our results (in Sect. 14.6), some future security research questions where graph and data mining can help, and finally conclude in Sect. 14.7.

14.2   Related Work

Graph mining is a very active research area in recent years. Representative works include patterns and "laws" discovery e.g., power law distributions (Faloutsos et al. 1999; Leskovec et al. 2005), small world phenomena (Milgram 1967); (Albert et al. 1999), and numerous other regularities. We review more related work in context of four parts: virus propagation, diffusion processes and data mining for security.

14.2.1 Virus Propagation

Epidemic Thresholds See Hethcote (2000) for a recent survey of standard epidemiological models like SIR, SIS etc. The class of epidemiological models that are most widely used are the so-called *homogeneous models* (Bailey 1975; McKendrick 1925; Anderson and May 2002). A homogeneous model assumes that every individual has equal contact to others in the population, and that the rate of infection is largely determined by the density of the infected population. Kephart and White (1991, 1993) were among the first to propose epidemiology-based models (KW model) to analyze the propagation of computer viruses. The KW model provides a good approximation of virus propagation in networks where the contact among individuals is sufficiently homogeneous. Various structured (hierarchical) topologies have also been analyzed (Hethcote 1984). However, there is overwhelming evidence that real networks (including social networks Domingos and Richardson 2001, router and AS networks (Faloutsos et al. 1999, and Gnutella overlay graphs Ripeanu et al. 2002) deviate from such homogeneity-they follow a power law structure instead. Pastor-Satorras and Vespignani studied viral propagation for such power-law networks (Pastor-Satorras and Vespignani 2001, 2002). They developed an analytic model for the Barabási-Albert (BA) power-law topology (Barabási and Albert 1999). However, their derivation depends on some assumptions which does not hold for many real networks (Kumar et al. 1999; Faloutsos et al. 1999). Pastor-Satorras et al. (2002) also proposed an epidemic threshold condition, but this uses the "mean-field" approach, where all graphs with a given degree distribution are considered equal. Newman (2005) studied the epidemic thresholds for multiple competing viruses on special, *random* graphs. Finally, except for Chakrabarti et al. (2008) and Ganesh et al. (2005) who gave the threshold for the SIS model on arbitrary undirected networks, none of the earlier work focuses on epidemic thresholds for *arbitrary, real* graphs. Time-evolving graphs have been rarely analyzed in literature, with most studies being simulation studies (Barrett et al. 2008).

Immunization Briesemeister et al. (2003) focus on immunization of power law graphs. They focus on the random-wiring version (that is, standard preferential attachment), versus the "highly clustered" power law graphs. Their simulation experiments on such synthetic graphs show that such graphs can be more easily defended against viruses, while random-wiring ones are typically overwhelmed, despite identical immunization policies. Cohen et al. (2003) studied the *acquaintance* immunization policy and showed that it is much better than random, for both the SIS as well as the SIR model. For random power law graphs, they also derived formulae for the critical immunization fraction, above which the epidemic is arrested. Madar et al. (2004) continued along these lines, mainly focusing on the SIR model for scale-free graphs. They linked the problem to bond percolation, and derived formulae for the effect of several immunization policies, showing that the "acquaintance" immunization policy is the best. Both works were analytical, without studying any real graphs. Hayashi et al. (2003) study the case of a growing network, and they derive analytical formulas for such power law networks (no rewiring). They introduce the SHIR model (Susceptible, Hidden, Infectious, Recovered), to model computers under e-mail virus attack and derive the conditions for extinction under random and under targeted immunization, always for power law graphs with no rewiring. Apart from analysis only on structured topologies, all the existing immunization strategies mentioned before assume: (1) *full* immunity-once a node is immunized, it is completely removed from the graph; (2) binary allocation (i.e., each node would need at most 1 antidote); and (3) *symmetric* immunization-once applied, an antidote affects both incoming and outgoing edges.

14.2.2   Diffusion Processes on Graphs

There are a lot of dynamic process on graphs, all of which are related to virus propagation. Here, we survey the related work, including (a) Blogs and propagations, (b) information cascade and (c) marketing and product penetration.

Blogs and Propagations There is a lot of work on blogs, trying to model link behavior in large-scale on-line data (Adar and Adamic 2005; Kumar et al. 2003). The authors note that, while information propagates between blogs, examples of genuine cascading behavior appeared relatively rare. This may, however, be due in part to the Web-crawling and text analysis techniques used to infer relationships among posts (Adar and Adamic 2005; Gruhl et al. 2004).

There are several potential models to capture the structure and behavior of the *blogosphere*. This is defined as the set of blogs, their postings, and their pointers to other blogs/postings/web-pages.

Gruhl et al. (2004) showed that for some topics, their popularity remains constant in time ("chatter") while for other topics the popularity is more volatile ("spikes").

Kumar et al. (2003) analyze community-level behavior as inferred from blogrolls—permanent links between "friend" blogs. In follow-up work, Kumar et al. (2006) studied several topological properties of link graphs in communities, discovering that "star" topologies are frequent. Kempe et al. (2003) focused on finding the most influential nodes in a network, under the threshold-model of influence. Richardson and Domingos (2002) introduced the concept of *network value* of a customer, which is valuable for viral marketing.

Information Cascade Information cascades are phenomena in which an action or idea becomes widely adopted due to the influence of others, typically, neighbors in some network (Bikhchandani et al. 1992; Goldenberg et al. 2001; Granovetter 1978). Also, cascades on random graphs using a threshold model have been theoretically analyzed (Watts 2002) before.

Marketing and Product Penetration Rogers (2003) studied how people adopt a new product: New adopters follow a Bell curve over time, therefore saturation follows an S-curve. The Bass Model for diffusion (Bass 1969) fits this data to a model. The Bass model includes parameters for pricing and advertising effects, and matches product sales data for a wide variety of products. Like most analytic work, the Bass model ignores the topology, and assumes that all adopters have equal probability of influencing each of the non-adopters.

Virus propagation is closely related to these important dynamic processes on graphs.

14.2.3 Data Mining for Security

Much research has tried to model malware propagation. In July 2001, the Code Red worm infected 359,000 hosts on the Internet in less than 14 h (Moore et al. 2002). Code Red achieved this by probing random IP addresses (using different seeds for its pseudo-random number generator) and infecting all hosts vulnerable to an IIS exploit. Staniford et. al. (2002, 2004) analyzed the Code Red worm traces and proposed an analytical model for its propagation. They also argue that optimizations like hit-list scanning, permutation scanning can allow a worm to saturate 95 % of vulnerable hosts on the Internet in less than 2 s. Such techniques were subsequently employed by worms released in the wild, such as the the Slammer worm (Moore et al. 2003) (infected 90 % of all vulnerable hosts within 10 min) and the Witty worm (Weaver and Ellis 2004).

Gkantsidis et al. study the dissemination of software patches through the Windows Update service and find that approximately 80 % of hosts request a patch within a day after it is released; the number of hosts drops by an order of magnitude during the second day, and is further reduced by factor of 2 in day three (Gkantsidis et al. 2006). Additionally, (Wang et al. 2002; Lad et al. 2005; Li et al. 2006) conducted measurement studies into routing instability in Broder Gateway Protocol (BGP) routers caused by catastrophic events, such as worm outbreaks or power outages. Other recent research also includes using machine learning methods like belief propagation on the file-machine graph (Chau et al. 2011) to infer files' reputations (say malicious or benign).

14.3 Cascade Mining

In this section, we state some of our recent results in mining propagation processes. Later in the next section we will describe the security datasets we analyzed, and then our results. Our work is arguably the first to present a systematic study of propagation and immunization of single as well as multiple viruses on arbitrary, real and time-varying networks as the vast majority of the literature focuses on structured topologies, cliques, and related un-realistic models.

14.3.1   Theory: Tipping Points and Competition

We tackled important questions like understanding *the tipping point* behavior of epidemics and predicting *who-wins* among competing viruses/products, which have immediate and broad applications.

14.3.1.1   Epidemic Thresholds for Static and Dynamic Graphs

The main question we answer is: will there be an epidemic, given the graph and the virus propagation model? We showed (Prakash et al. 2011) (see Fig. 14.1) that the threshold condition is (λ_1 is the first eigenvalue of the connectivity matrix, C is a virus-model dependent constant): $\lambda_1 \cdot C < 1$, for (a) *any* graph; and (b) *all* propagation models in standard literature (more than 25 from canonical texts, including the AIDS virus *H.I.V.*, and the award-winning Independent Cascade model). We also showed (Prakash et al. 2010; Valler et al. 2011) that the epidemic threshold of the "flu-like" SIS model on *any set* of time-varying graphs depends only on the largest eigenvalue of a so-called 'system' matrix'.

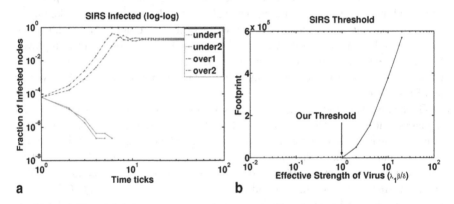

Fig. 14.1 The tipping-point exactly matches our prediction: simulation results on a massive social-contact graph PORTLAND (31 mil. edges, 1.5 mil. nodes) and the SIRS model (temporary immunity like pertussis). **a** Plot of Infected Fraction of Population vs Time (log-log). Note the qualitative difference in behavior- *under* (*green*) the threshold and *above* (*red*) the threshold. **b** *Footprint* (expected final epidemic size) vs Effective Strength (lin-log). Notice our prediction is exactly at the take-off point

14.3.1.2   Mutually Exclusive Competing Viruses

Given two competing products (or memes or diseases) such as iPhone/Android (or common flu/avian flu), and 'word of mouth' adoption of them, which product will 'win', in terms of highest market share? We prove the surprising result (Prakash et al. 2012) that, under realistic conditions, for *any* graph, the stronger virus completely wipes-out the weaker virus ('winner-takes-all'). We demonstrate it through case-studies using real data too.

14.3.1.3   Co-existence with Competing Viruses

What happens when the competing viruses are not mutually exclusive (e.g., IE and Chrome)? We show (Beutel et al. 2012) that there is a phase-transition: if the competition is harsher than a critical threshold, then 'winner-takes-all', otherwise, the weaker virus survives.

14.3.2   Algorithms: Immunization, Edge-Placement, Finding Culprits

We have also developed *fast and effective algorithms* for a variety of tasks w.r.t. propagation, many of which naturally arise in epidemiology ('vaccination programs'), social media ('detecting rumor sources') and cyber security ('designing worms').

14.3.2.1   Fractional Immunization

Given a fixed amount of medicines with partial impact, how should they be distributed? Collaborating with domain experts, we studied controlling the spread of bacteria between hospitals through patient transfers, by distributing scarce infection-control resources (which only have partial impact on any hospital) (Prakash et al. 2013). We formulated the problem, and developed SMARTALLOC, a near-optimal and fast algorithm. Figure 14.2 demonstrates our algorithm on the network of MEDICARE patient transfers.

14.3.2.2   Complete Immunization and Edge-placement

Given a large network, like a computer communication network, which k nodes should we remove (or monitor, or immunize), to make it as robust as possible against a computer virus attack? Our previous work on thresholds in various settings (Prakash et al. 2010, 2011) gave a clear optimization goal: minimize the leading eigenvalue of the adjacency matrix for static graphs. Making careful approximations, we exploited the *submodular* structure of the set of possible solutions, getting provably near-optimal algorithms for static graphs (Tong et al. 2010) and fast heuristics for dynamic graphs (Prakash et al. 2010). Which edges should we add or delete in order to speed-up (marketing) or contain (diseases, malware) a dissemination? We proposed (Tong et al. 2012) NETMELT and NETGEL, near-optimal, near linear-time algorithms to solve these problems as well, in spite of the intrinsic

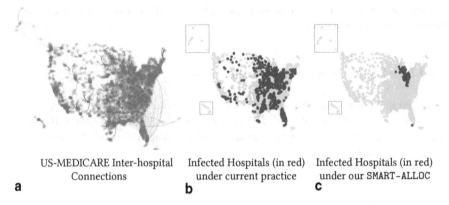

US-MEDICARE Inter-hospital Connections	Infected Hospitals (in red) under current practice	Infected Hospitals (in red) under our SMART-ALLOC
a	**b**	**c**

Fig. 14.2 Our proposed SMARTALLOC method has *6x fewer* infections (*red circles*): (**a**) The US-MEDICARE network of hospitals overlayed on a map. (**b**) Infected hospitals after a year (365 days) under current practice. (**c**) Similarly, under SMARTALLOC. The current practice allocates equal amounts of resource to each hospital

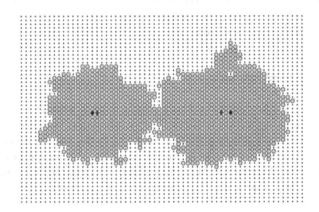

Fig. 14.3 Culprits Example: A snapshot of a 2D grid in which an infection has been spreading (according to the SI model). Infected nodes are represented via *grey circles*, while *Grey dots* are uninfected. The 2 *Blue stars* denote the true seeds. The 2 *Red diamonds* denote the seeds automatically discovered by NETSLEUTH. Clearly NETSLEUTH recovers the correct seeds both in *number* (two) and *location* (being spatially very close to the true seeds)

quadratic complexity of adding possible edges. We also studied the two problems and our methods theoretically and the equivalence between different strategies (edge vs. node-deletion).

14.3.2.3 Finding Culprits of Epidemics

Can we identify sources of rumors on Twitter? We developed (Prakash et al. 2012) a highly efficient algorithm NETSLEUTH to reliably identify nodes in networks from which an infection started to spread. As an example, consider Fig. 14.3. It depicts an example grid-structured graph, in which a subgraph has been infected by a stochastic process starting from two seed nodes. The plot shows the true seed nodes, as well as the seed nodes automatically identified by NETSLEUTH; it finds the correct number of seed nodes, and places these where a human would; in fact, the discovered seeds have a higher likelihood for generating this infected subgraph than the true seed nodes.

14.3.3   Empirical Studies: Building Better Models

We studied numerous real-datasets to build better models in domains such as propagation of memes in online media and competing tasks in everyday life. We also show how to use such models for varied challenging applications like forecasting trends activity. While models in epidemiology have been widely studied and accepted, the models describing exactly how information diffuses in online media is uncertain. Here we ask a very simple question: How quickly does a piece of news spread over these media? How does its popularity diminish over time? Does the rising and falling pattern follow a simple universal law? We propose SPIKEM (Matsubara et al. 2012), a concise yet flexible model, which *generalizes* and *unifies* previous models and observations, and excels at challenging tasks like *forecasting, spotting anomalies* etc. We show the power of SPIKEM through the analysis of more than 7.2 GB of real data.

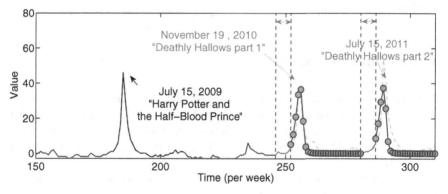

Fig. 14.4 SPIKEM at work: Results of "what-if" forecasting for the Harry Potter series. We trained parameters by using **a** the first spike around July 15, 2009 (*black solid line*), and **b** access volume two months before the release (*blue lines* with *double arrows* around time $t = 250, 280$) and then, forecasted the following two spikes (*red lines*)

14.4   Datasets

Next, we describe some cyber-security specific datasets we used to measure how files propagate in cyber-space.

Symantec's WINE data is collected from real-world hosts running their consumer anti-virus software. Users of Symantec's consumer product line have a choice of opting-in to report telemetry about the security events (e.g. executable file down-loads, virus detections) that occur on their hosts. The events included in WINE are representative of events that Symantec observes around the world (Papalexakis and Dumitraş 2013). WINE enables reproducible experimental results by archiving the reference data sets that researchers use and by recording information on the data collection process and on the experimental procedures employed.

We analyze the complete set of events recorded in the *binary reputation* and *anti-virus telemetry* data sets from WINE during the entire month of June 2011. WINE does not include user identifiable information.

14.4.1   Anti-virus Telemetry

Anti-virus (AV) telemetry records detections of known malware for which Symantec generated a signature that was deployed in an anti-virus product. As commercial security products generally aim for low false-positive rates, we have a high degree of confidence that the files detected in this manner are indeed malicious. From each record, we use the detection time, the associated threat label, the hash (MD5 and SHA2) of the malicious file detected and the manner of the detection (signature scanning or behavioral features extracted from an execution of the file on the end host). Each record indicates that the anti-virus has blocked an attack that may have resulted in an infection.

14.4.2   Binary Reputation

The binary reputation data records all binary executables—benign or malicious—that were downloaded/copied on end-hosts worldwide. From each record we extract the time stamp of the file creation event, the country in which the host is located, the hash (MD5 and SHA2) of the binary, and the URL from which it was downloaded (if available).

Starting from the raw data available in WINE, we define a reference data set with the following pieces of information:

- File occurrence counts spanning a whole month (June 2011), both for legitimate files and malware.
  (File SHA2 ID, Occurrences, Timestamp)
- Counts of personal computers where telemetry is collected, for each country, spanning June 2011. This piece of data is both in aggregate form and in a daily basis. The attributes of this dataset are:
  (Country ID, count, Timestamp)
- The lifetime of malicious URLs as crawled by humans using these personal computers during June 2011. This dataset consists of records of the form:
  (URL, First-seen Timestamp, Last-seen Timestamp)

For each one of the aforementioned datasets, we possess both *before* and *after* sampling versions. As noted before, however, even the *before* sampling parts of the dataset may be viewed as a sample of the real world, since the hosts that use Symantec software are a subset (or a sample) of all the machines that exist in the Internet.

The WINE database is updated continuously with data feeds used in production by Symantec, and the data is sampled on-the-fly as the files are loaded on the database. Each record includes an anonymous identifier for the host where the data was collected. The WINE sampling scheme selects all the records that include a pre-determined sequence of bits at a pre-determined position in the host identifier, and discards all the other records. In consequence, WINE includes either all the events recorded on a host or no data from that host at all. Because the host identifier is computed using a cryptographic hash, the distribution of its bits is uniform, regardless of the distribution of the input data. This sampling strategy was chosen because it accommodates an intuitive interpretation of the sampled subset: the WINE data represents a slice of the Internet, just like the original data set is a (bigger) slice of the Internet. To study the effects of sampling, we compare the sampled data in WINE with the original data set for the month of June 2011.

Comment   The data included in WINE is collected on a representative subset of the hosts running Symantec products, such as the Norton Antivirus. These hosts do not represent honeypots or machines in an artificial lab environment; they are real computers, in active use around the world, that are targeted by cyber attacks.

14.5   Characterizing File Propagation

Here we ask the following two main questions:

- *How do executable files propagate temporally?*
- *What is the effect of sampling?*

14.5.1   Temporal Propagation Patterns

A worm that propagates through buffer-overflow exploits (e.g., the Blaster worm from 2003) will exhibit a propagation rate different from another malware that spread through drive-by-downloads. Computing this propagation rate, which is analogous to the *basic reproduction number* R_0 from epidemiology, allows analysts to assess the threat introduced by the malware. Additional patterns of the time series that describes the evolution of the number of infections provide further clues regarding the behavior of the malware; for example, a surge of infections hours after Microsoft's

Patch Tuesday[1] may point to the use of automated techniques for reverse-engineering security patches into working exploits.

Our proposed analysis and modelling (Papalexakis and Dumitraş 2013), with respect to the temporal propagation pattern, works for high volume files, i.e. files that have enough samples of occurrences such that any form of (meaningful) modelling is feasible. As "high volume" files we consider all files with more than 1000 occurrences in distinct machines. In Fig. 14.5 we show that the file popularity (and hence its volume) follows a power law.

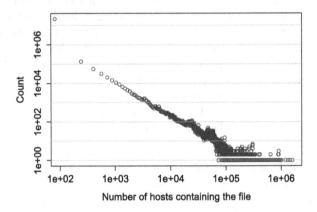

Fig. 14.5 Distribution of file popularity among machines. We observe that the popularity of a file, which also reflects its volume on the database, follows a power law

In Fig. 14.6, we illustrate the propagation pattern of six high volume files coming from several, major software vendors. For instance, these files can be either patches of already existing software, or new software binaries; such files (e.g. security patches) tend to become highly popular very early in their lifetime. In fact, in Fig. 14.6 we observe, for all those popular files, a steep *exponential rise* which follows shortly after they initially appear on the Internet.

This exponential rise is followed by, what appears to be a *power-law drop*. Intuitively, this observation makes sense: A few days after a new security patch by a major software vendor appears, nearly all users download it right away and only a few people tend to download it a couple of days after its release date; moreover, nearly nobody downloads the file one or two weeks after it has been released. We henceforth refer to this pattern as the SHARKFIN pattern, due to the resemblance of the spike to an actual shark fin. Later (see Sect. 14.5.1.1) we describe our SHARKFIN model which can fit and describe these spikes succinctly.

Moreover, Fig. 14.6 also captures a *daily periodicity* in the files' propagation pattern. An intuitive explanation for this periodic behavior may be that a large number of these files are security patches, which are very often downloaded automatically;

---

[1] Each month's second Tuesday, on which Microsoft releases security patches.

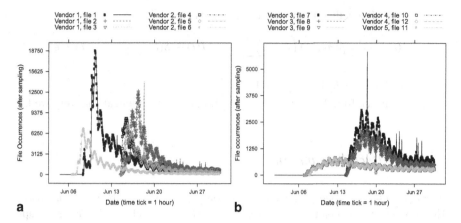

Fig. 14.6 Propagation of high volume files, before and after sampling (the symbol markers correspond to the sampled data, while the lines correspond to the original data scaled down by the sampling rate). These files all follow the SHARKFIN pattern that we describe on the main body of the text: A spike that grows exponentially and drops as a power law

this would explain the relative increase of occurrences in a periodic manner, since the auto-update software usually runs the update at a standard time.

14.5.1.1   The SHARKFIN Model

Our observations above suggest similar patterns to what we had found in case of rise and fall patterns in social media (Fig. 14.4). Hence we propose to re-purpose the SPIKEM model we discussed in the previous section to model the temporal propagation of the executable files. We call our model SHARKFIN.

The SHARKFIN model assumes a total number of N un-informed population ('bloggers' or 'machines') that can be informed ('infected') by the file/hashtag. Let $U(n)$ be the number of such machines that are *not* infected at time n; $I(n)$ be the count of machines that got infected up to time $n - 1$; and $\Delta I(n)$ be count of machines infected exactly at time n. Then $U(n+1) = U(n) - \Delta I(n+1)$ with initial conditions $\Delta I(0) = 0$ and $U(0) = N$.

Additionally, we let β as the 'infectivity' (essentially popularity) of a particular file. We assume that the popularity of a file at any particular person drops as a specific power-law based on the elapsed time since the file infected *that person* (say τ) i.e. $f(\tau) = \beta\tau^{-1.5}$. Finally, we also have to consider one more parameter for the model: the "external shock", or in other words, the first appearance of a file: let n_b the time that this initial burst appeared, and let $S(n_b)$ be the size of the shock (count of infected machine).

Finally, to account for periodicity, we define a periodic function $p(n)$ with three parameters: P_a, as the strength of the periodicity, P_p as the period and P_s as the phase shift.

Putting it all together, the SHARKFIN model is

$$\Delta I(n+1) = p(n+1) \left(U(n) \sum_{t=n_b}^{n} (\Delta I(t) + S(t)) \, f(n+1-t) + \epsilon \right)$$

where $p(n) = 1 - \frac{1}{2} P_a \left(\sin \left(\frac{2\pi}{P_p} (n + P_s) \right) \right)$.

As we can see from Fig. 14.7, our model SHARKFIN fits the real data very well.

14.5.2 Effects of Sampling

As mentioned before, we are typically given only a sample from the WINE database. How do the observed patterns and properties of the dataset change? Can we extrapolate from the sample to the entire dataset? Suppose we are given a sampled subset of the occurrences of a file, each accompanied with a time-stamp, as in the previous subsection. The sampling procedure is the same as before (see Sect. 14.4). It is important for someone who works on a sample to be able to reconstruct the original propagation pattern of a file, given that sample. How can we reconstruct the original, before sampling, propagation pattern of that particular file? Does the reconstruction resemble the original pattern?

As we investigated in the previous section, we can successfully model the propagation pattern of legitimate files before sampling, as in Fig. 14.6(a). In Fig. 14.6 we observe that sampling does not severely alter the SHARKFIN shape of the time-series, at least for such popular, high volume files; the sampled time series seems to have consistently lower values than the before sampling ones, which is to be expected due to sampling (even though our sampling is per machine and not per file occurrence).

The main idea of our extrapolation technique lies exactly in the observation above. Since sampling has displaced the sampled time-series by a, roughly, constant amount, we follow these two simple steps:

1. Multiply every point of the sampled time series by the sampling factor, in order to displace it to, roughly, the same height as the original time-series.
2. Fit the model that we introduce previously (SHARKFIN) on the multiplied time-series.

More formally, following the same notation as before, and denoting the sampling rate by s, we need to minimize the following function: $\min_\theta \sum_{n=1}^{T} (s X(n) - \Delta I(n))^2$

In Fig. 14.7(a & b), we show the result of the proposed approach, for two popular, high volume files, by major software vendors. We can see that our extrapolation is perfectly aligned with the model of the data *before* sampling, which renders our simple scheme successful. On top of that, both models (before and after sampling), as we also demonstrated on Fig. 14.6 fit the original data very well.

As in modelling, here we employ RSE in order to further assess the quality of our extrapolation (by measuring the RSE between the original sampled vector of observations, and the extrapolated one). The median RSE was 0.0741; the mean RSE was 0.2377 ± 0.3648. We see that for the majority of files, the extrapolation quality is very high, demonstrating that our extrapolation scheme, using SHARKFIN, is successful for high density files.

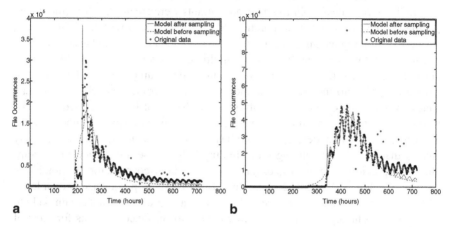

Fig. 14.7 **(a)** & **(b)**: In these Figures we show (i) our extrapolation after sampling, (ii) our modelling before sampling, and (iii) the original data before sampling, for two different, popular, legitimate files. We see that the extrapolation and the model before sampling are almost perfectly aligned, justifying our approach. Additionally, we see that they both fit very well the original data. The median RSE in this case was 0.0741

14.6   Discussion

The increasing ability to collect large datasets has enabled us to develop and test increasingly sophisticated models and algorithms. Will a specific YouTube video go viral? Given a who-contacts-whom network and a virus propagation model, can we predict whether there will be an epidemic? Which are the best nodes (people, computers etc.) to immunize, to slow down and prevent an epidemic as soon as possible? These are all propagation-based questions that deal with large complex phenomena on graphs or networks. Propagation processes on networks can give rise to a very rich macroscopic behavior, leading to a challenging and exciting research questions. Such problems are central in surprisingly diverse areas: from cyber security, epidemiology and public health, product marketing to information dissemination. Understanding such problems will eventually help us manipulating and controlling them. For example, our findings allow us to characterize how malware or benign files propagate via security telemetry. This can lead to new line of work into preventing attacks. We can empirically quickly identify benign files from malicious files by using their unique propagation patterns, or understand how to prevent attacks by estimating the number of hosts reached by worms and by security updates. Similar to controlling disease spreading via vaccination, we can ask how to administer software patches 'optimally'.

Our findings have also shown the importance of sampling. Big data is difficult to transfer and analyze: hence sampling can be bring down the computational running time of many tasks. The velocity of data collection (say in security telemetry) is very high: more than *403 million* malware variants were created in 2011 (more than a million a day) (Symantec Corporation 2012). Hence faced with these high rates, on-the-fly sampling techniques can enable open-ended analyses and experiments.

More broadly, increasingly there are multiple opportunities for machine learning and data mining techniques in cyber security. For example, WINE has provided unique insights into the prevalence and duration of zero-day attacks. A zero-day attack exploits one or more vulnerabilities that have not been disclosed publicly. Knowledge of such vulnerabilities gives cyber criminals a free pass to attack any target, while remaining undetected. WINE has enabled a systematic study of zero-day attacks that has shown, among other findings, that these attacks are more common than previously thought and that they go on undiscovered for 10 months on average (Bilge and Dumitraş 2012). Quantifying these properties had been a long-standing open question, because zero-day attacks are rare events that are unlikely to be observed in honeypots or in lab experiments; for instance, exploits for most of the zero-day vulnerabilities identified in the study were detected on fewer that 150 hosts out of the 11 million analyzed.

14.6.1 Open Questions

There are several interesting research questions that lie ahead, which can leverage the recent explosion in the amount of available data.

- *How to cluster malware variants?* As mentioned before, there are millions of malware variants appearing every day—how to identify all the variants of a given malware that exist in our database using a graph of similar malware? Clustering is a classic data mining problem, but without access to malware source code (which is very hard to get) static analysis methods can not be used.
- *How can we deploy software patches?* A big advantage of modeling how malware spread is to use our models to manipulate the propagation, say by deploying patches, and/or other monitoring software.
- *How to identify malicious files faster?* A faster (and more accurate) identification will enable more proactive protection against zero-day threats. We need to explore more empirical approaches here again, which do not just rely on threat identification and/or source code for detection of novel malware.
- *What human factors lead to increased attacks?* While human users are often considered to be the weakest link in security systems, the risks associated with typical day-to-day computing habits are not well understood. Given security telemetry,

an interesting problem would be to find statistical proxies of human behaviors which are related to increased malware reports on a machine.

- *Networks with attributes:* Not all connections are important e.g. some are much more likely to lead to transmission of infection than others. In this chapter, we gave an abstracted model for malware and file spreading. However, especially for malware spreading via more sophisticated methods (like Stuxnet Falliere et al. 2011), having auxiliary features like historical attributes, textual information, geographical information, can greatly enhance these models.

14.7   Conclusions

We discussed how graph mining together with large scale datasets can help answer challenging research questions in cyber security. We first showed several of our recent results in the field of large-graph cascade mining like finding epidemic thresholds in arbitrary graphs, designing fast and effective immunization algorithms and developing simple but powerful models using detailed datasets. We then proposed how these advancements can be applied to model executable file propagation accurately using the WINE datasets via the SHARKFIN model. We also explored how to learn the model taking into account the fact that the datasets are typically sampled. These models can be used for detecting malicious files faster as well as improving security products more generally. We finally concluded with several open questions in security where big-graph mining can potentially an important role by leveraging the recent explosion in tera-byte scale datasets.

Acknowledgements   The WINE platform data analyzed here is available for follow-on research as the reference data set WINE-2012-006. Based on work partly supported by the Army Research Laboratory under grant number W911NF-09-2-0053, the National Science Foundation under grant numbers IIS-1017415 and IIS-1353346 and by the Maryland Procurement Office under contract H98230-14-C-0127.

References

Adar, E., Adamic, L.A.: Tracking information epidemics in blogspace. (2005)

Albert, R., Jeong, H., Barabási, A.L.: Diameter of the World-Wide Web. Nature **401**, 130–131 (1999)

Anderson, R.M., May, R.M.: Infectious diseases of humans: Dynamics and control. Oxford Press (2002)

Bailey, N.: The Mathematical Theory of Infectious Diseases and its Applications. Griffin, London (1975)

Barabási, A.L., Albert, R.: Emergence of scaling in random networks. Science **286**, 509–512 (1999)

Barrett, C.L., Bisset, K.R., Eubank, S.G., Feng, X., Marathe, M.V.: Episimdemics: an efficient algorithm for simulating the spread of infectious disease over large realistic social networks pp. 1–12 (2008)

Bass, F.M.: A new product growth for model consumer durables. Management Science **15**(5), 215–227 (1969)

Beutel, A., Prakash, B.A., Rosenfeld, R., Faloutsos, C.: Interacting viruses in networks: can both survive? In: Proceedings of the 18th ACM SIGKDD international conference on Knowledge discovery and data mining, KDD '12, pp. 426–434 (2012)

Bikhchandani, S., Hirshleifer, D., Welch, I.: A theory of fads, fashion, custom, and cultural change in informational cascades. Journal of Political Economy **100**(5), 992–1026 (1992)

Bilge, L., Dumitras, T.: Before we knew it: An empirical study of zero-day attacks in the real world. In: ACM Conference on Computer and Communications Security. Raleigh, NC (2012)

Briesemeister, L., Lincoln, P., Porras, P.: Epidemic profiles and defense of scale-free networks. WORM 2003 (2003)

Camp, J., Cranor, L., Feamster, N., Feigenbaum, J., Forrest, S., Kotz, D., Lee, W., Lincoln, P., Paxson, V., Reiter, M., Rivest, R., Sanders, W., Savage, S., Smith, S., Spafford, E., Stolfo, S.: Data for cybersecurity research: Process and "wish list". http://www.gtisc.gatech.edu/files_nsf10/data-wishlist.pdf (2009)

Chakrabarti, D., Wang, Y., Wang, C., Leskovec, J., Faloutsos, C.: Epidemic thresholds in real networks. ACM TISSEC **10**(4) (2008)

Chau, D.H.P., Nachenberg, C., Wilhelm, J., Wright, A., Faloutsos, C.: Polonium : Tera-scale graph mining for malware detection. In: SIAM International Conference on Data Mining (SDM). Mesa, AZ (2011)

Cohen, R., Havlin, S., ben Avraham, D.: Efficient immunization strategies for computer networks and populations. Physical Review Letters **91**(24) (2003)

Domingos, P., Richardson, M.: Mining the network value of customers. In: KDD, pp. 57–66 (2001)

Falliere, N., O'Murchu, L., Chien, E.: W32.Stuxnet dossier. Symantec Whitepaper (2011). http://www.symantec.com/content/en/us/enterprise/media/security_response/whitepapers/w32_stuxnet_dossier.pdf

Faloutsos, M., Faloutsos, P., Faloutsos, C.: On power-law relationships of the internet topology. SIGCOMM pp. 251–262 (1999)

Ganesh, A., Massoulié, L., Towsley, D.: The effect of network topology on the spread of epidemics. In: IEEE INFOCOM. IEEE Computer Society Press, Los Alamitos, CA (2005)

Gkantsidis, C., Karagiannis, T., Vojnovic, M.: Planet scale software updates. In: SIGCOMM, pp. 423–434 (2006)

Goldenberg, J., Libai, B., Muller, E.: Talk of the network: A complex systems look at the underlying process of word-of-mouth. Marketing Letters (2001)

Granovetter, M.: Threshold models of collective behavior. Am. Journal of Sociology **83**(6), 1420–1443 (1978)

Gruhl, D., Guha, R., Liben-Nowell, D., Tomkins, A.: Information diffusion through blogspace. In: WWW '04 (2004). www.www2004.org/proceedings/docs/1p491.pdf

Hayashi, Y., Minoura, M., Matsukubo, J.: Recoverable prevalence in growing scale-free networks and the effective immunization. arXiv:cond-mat/0305549 v2 (2003)

Hethcote, H.W.: The mathematics of infectious diseases. SIAM Review **42** (2000)

Hethcote, H.W., Yorke, J.A.: Gonorrhea transmission dynamics and control. Springer Lecture Notes in Biomathematics **46** (1984)

Kempe, D., Kleinberg, J., Tardos, E.: Maximizing the spread of influence through a social network. In: KDD '03 (2003)

Kephart, J.O., White, S.R.: Directed-graph epidemiological models of computer viruses. In: Proceedings of the 1991 IEEE Computer Society Symposium on Research in Security and Privacy, pp. 343–359 (1991)

Kephart, J.O., White, S.R.: Measuring and modeling computer virus prevalence. In: Proceedings of the 1993 IEEE Computer Society Symposium on Research in Security and Privacy, pp. 2–15 (1993)

Kumar, R., Novak, J., Raghavan, P., Tomkins, A.: On the bursty evolution of blogspace. In: WWW '03: Proceedings of the 12th international conference on World Wide Web, pp. 568–576. ACM Press, New York, NY, USA (2003).

Kumar, R., Novak, J., Tomkins, A.: Structure and evolution of online social networks. In: KDD '06: Proceedings of the 12th ACM SIGKDD International Conference on Knowedge Discover and Data Mining, pp. 611–617. New York (2006)

Kumar, S.R., Raghavan, P., Rajagopalan, S., Tomkins, A.: Trawling the web for emerging cyber-communities. Computer Networks **31**(11-16), 1481–1493 (1999)

Lad, M., Zhao, X., Zhang, B., Massey, D., Zhang, L.: Analysis of BGP Update Burst During Slammer Attack. In: The 5th International Workshop on Distributed Computing (2005)

Leskovec, J., Kleinberg, J., Faloutsos, C.: Graphs over time: Densification laws, shrinking diameters and possible explanations. In: Conference of the ACM Special Interest Group on Knowledge Discovery and Data Mining. ACM Press, New York, NY (2005)

Li, J., Wu, Z., Purpus, E.: CAM04-5: Toward Understanding the Behavior of BGP During Large-Scale Power Outages. Global Telecommunications Conference, 2006. GLOBECOM '06. IEEE pp. 1–5 (Nov. 2006)

Madar, N., Kalisky, T., Cohen, R., ben Avraham, D., Havlin, S.: Immunization and epidemic dynamics in complex networks. Eur. Phys. J. B **38**(2), 269–276 (2004)

Matsubara, Y., Sakurai, Y., Prakash, B.A., Li, L., Faloutsos, C.: Rise and fall patterns of information diffusion: model and implications. In: Proceedings of the 18th ACM SIGKDD international conference on Knowledge discovery and data mining, KDD '12, pp. 6–14 (2012)

McHugh, J.: Testing intrusion detection systems: A critique of the 1998 and 1999 DARPA intrusion detection system evaluations as performed by Lincoln Laboratory. ACM Transactions on Information and System Security **3**(4), 262–294 (2000)

McKendrick, A.G.: Applications of mathematics to medical problems. In: Proceedings of Edin. Math. Society, vol. 44, pp. 98–130 (1925)

Milgram, S.: The small-world problem. Psychology Today **2**, 60–67 (1967)

Moore, D., Shannon, C., Claffy, K.C.: Code-red: a case study on the spread and victims of an internet worm. In: Internet Measurement Workshop, pp. 273–284 (2002)

Moore, D., Paxson, V., Savage, S., Shannon, C., Staniford, S., Weaver, N.: Inside the Slammer worm. Security & Privacy, IEEE **1**(4), 33–39 (2003)

Newman, M.E.J.: Threshold effects for two pathogens spreading on a network. Phys. Rev. Lett (2005)

Papalexakis, E.E., Dumitras, T., Chau, D.H., Prakash, B.A., Faloutsos, C.: Spatio-temporal mining of software adoption & penetration. In: 2013 IEEE/ACM International Conference on Advances in Social Networks Analysis and Mining (2013)

Pastor-Satorras, R., Vespignani, A.: Epidemic dynamics and endemic states in complex networks. Physical Review E **63**, 066,117 (2001)

Pastor-Satorras, R., Vespignani, A.: Epidemic dynamics in finite size scale-free networks. Physical Review E **65**, 035,108 (2002)

Prakash, B.A., Tong, H., Valler, N., Faloutsos, M., Faloutsos, C.: Virus propagation on time-varying networks: Theory and immunization algorithms. ECML-PKDD (2010)

Prakash, B.A., Chakrabarti, D., Faloutsos, M., Valler, N., Faloutsos, C.: Threshold conditions for arbitrary cascade models on arbitrary networks. In: ICDM (2011)

Prakash, B.A., Beutel, A., Rosenfeld, R., Faloutsos, C.: Winner takes all: Competing viruses or ideas on fair-play networks. WWW (2012)

Prakash, B.A., Vreeken, J., Faloutsos, C.: Spotting culprits in epidemics: How many and which ones? In: ICDM (2012)

Prakash, B.A., Adamic, L.A., Iwashyna, T.J., Tong, H., Faloutsos, C.: Fractional immunization in networks. In: SDM, pp. 659–667 (2013)

Richardson, M., Domingos, P.: Mining knowledge-sharing sites for viral marketing (2002). citeseer.ist.psu.edu/richardson02mining.html

Ripeanu, M., Foster, I., Iamnitchi, A.: Mapping the gnutella network: Properties of large-scale peer-to-peer systems and implications for system design. IEEE Internet Computing Journal **6**(1) (2002)

Rogers, E.M.: Diffusion of Innovations, 5th Edition. Free Press (2003). http://www.amazon.ca/exec/obidos/redirect?tag=citeulike09-20&path=ASIN/0743222091

Staniford, S., Moore, D., Paxson, V., Weaver, N.: The top speed of flash worms. In: WORM, pp. 33–42 (2004)

Staniford, S., Paxson, V., Weaver, N.: How to 0wn the internet in your spare time. In: Proceedings of the 11th USENIX Security Symposium, pp. 149–167. USENIX Association, Berkeley, CA, USA (2002). http://dl.acm.org/citation.cfm?id=647253.720288

Symantec Corporation: Symantec Internet security threat report, volume 17. http://www.symantec.com/threatreport/ (2012)

Tong, H., Prakash, B.A., Eliassi-Rad, T., Faloutsos, M., Faloutsos, C.: Gelling, and melting, large graphs by edge manipulation. In: CIKM (2012)

Tong, H., Prakash, B.A., Tsourakakis, C.E., Eliassi-Rad, T., Faloutsos, C., Chau, D.H.: On the vulnerability of large graphs. In: ICDM (2010)

Valler, N., Prakash, B.A., Tong, H., Faloutsos, M., Faloutsos, C.: Epidemic spread in mobile ad hoc networks: Determining the tipping point. IFIP NETWORKING (2011)

Wang, L., Zhao, X., Pei, D., Bush, R., Massey, D., Mankin, A., Wu, S., Zhang, L.: Observation and Analysis of BGP Behavior under Stress. In: IMW (2002)

Watts, D.J.: A simple model of global cascades on random networks. In: Proceedings of the National Academy of Sciences of the United States of America, vol. 99, pp. 5766–5771 (2002)

Weaver, N., Ellis, D.: Reflections on Witty: Analyzing the attacker. ;login: The USENIX Magazine **29**(3), 34–37 (2004)

Chapter 15
Programming Language Theoretic Security in the Real World: A Mirage or the Future?

Andrew Ruef and Chris Rohlf

Abstract The last decade has seen computer security rise from a niche field to a household term. Previously, executive level responses to computer security were disbelief and dismissal, while today the responses are questions of budget and risk. Computer security is a complicated issue with many moving parts and it is difficult to present a coherent view of its issues and problems. We believe that computer security issues have their root in programming languages and language runtime decisions. We argue that computer intrusion, malware, and network security issues all fundamentally arise from tradeoffs made in programming language design and the structure of the benign programs that are exploited. We present a case for addressing fundamental computer security problems at this root, by using advancements in programming language technology. We also present a case against relying on advancements in programming language technology, arguing that even when using the most sophisticated programming language technology available today, attacks are still possible, and that the current state of research is insufficient to guarantee security. We also discuss practical issues relating to the implementation of large-scale reforms in software development based on advancements in programming language technology.

15.1 Introduction

Hacking is characterized as secretly gaining unauthorized access to a computer system for purposes of causing damage or stealing information. This act is at the root of the theft and sale of personally identifiable and financial information, and has inspired research efforts, product development, and public policy all aiming to prevent it. The ease of hacking has led to a global grey market that trades in all aspects of the commodities acquired through hacking.

A. Ruef (✉)
Trail of Bits, New York, USA
e-mail: awruef@cs.umd.edu

C. Rohlf
Yahoo Inc. New York, USA
e-mail: Chris.Rohlf@leafsr.com

© Springer International Publishing Switzerland 2015
S. Jajodia et al. (eds.), *Cyber Warfare,* Advances in Information Security 56,
DOI 10.1007/978-3-319-14039-1_15

What enables the act of hacking? All interactions with information in a computer system are brokered by computer programs. Those programs are written by major technology companies or open source software developers with the best of intentions. However, the developers of these programs accidentally introduce errors into the programs, and then those errors are discovered and used by hackers to gain unauthorized access to information. The process of identifying these errors, or vulnerabilities, in software is a common thread throughout all instances of data theft of individuals or companies.

A *vulnerability* is a property of software, such as the GNU/Linux kernel or the Firefox web browser, that can result in undefined behavior. The software itself is decidedly not malicious and was created with the best of intentions. However, due to oversight or programmer error, it contains a bug whose properties are advantageous to an attacker. Usually, these bugs are referred to as *memory safety* or *memory corruption* errors. In contrast, an *exploit* is a system or piece of software that uses a vulnerability to attack a victim's computer, usually for the purpose of injecting a new program into the victim's computer.

Knowledge of vulnerabilities is important in information security. This knowledge proceeds through a series of phases. Vulnerabilities exist when a programmer creates them, but generally the programmer does not know that they have introduced a vulnerability. At some point in the future, the vulnerability is discovered. If an attacker discovers this vulnerability, then the attacker has the option of creating an exploit for the vulnerability and using the exploit to attack computers. It is also possible that a defender discovers the same vulnerability, and then patches it. A vulnerability that an attacker has discovered but a defender has not is typically known as a *zero day vulnerability*.

One important distinction in discussing fixes to bugs is in attacker goals. Broadly, an attacker can have two goals: intrusion or denial. An intrusive attacker tries to gain unauthorized access to information, or information sources, that they would not otherwise have privilege to access. Intrusive attackers could try to make a change, for example website defacement, or to steal information, for example theft of personal financial information. A denying attacker tries to deny the use of a service or system to other users, for example taking e-mail servers offline. We are largely concerned with intrusive attackers and the mechanisms that attackers can use to exceed their assigned privilege and access or modify information.

Another distinction is in the means of an attack. Dangerous attacks that scale thanks to automation and involve the exploitation of software. Other types of attacks that result in the theft of data stem from *social engineering*. These attacks involve the compromise of software systems that manage data through the human operators of the system, for example persuading a help desk technician to reset a password for a victim's account. As we will see, many existing problems can have an element of social engineering to them, however, attackers' powers greatly increase with the exploitation of vulnerabilities. Additionally, the exploitation of vulnerabilities represents a more effective and scalable attack vector than persuading individual people to carry out an attacker's plans.

Therefore, the landscape of threats that we consider is one where the battleground for control of data is inside of legitimate applications that companies and governments run to control the data; attackers operate in this field through those legitimate applications as well as software that they write to exploit and manage compromised computers. Attackers that deal with vulnerabilities in software for the purpose of stealing information are currently very potent, as vulnerabilities are plentiful in software. However, their potency is contingent upon the availability of vulnerabilities and exploits.

Previous analyses (Guido 2011, Hutchins et al. 2011) 1 attacker kill chain and discovered that attackers use a small number of exploits in their attacks, proportional to the other building blocks of attacks. Attackers in one presented model (Guido 2011) compose a variety of resources together to carry out attacks: they acquire domain names and generate fake web sites, identify e-mail addresses and send malicious e-mails, re-purpose or discover vulnerabilities in software and associated exploits for those vulnerabilities, create malicious software to install on compromised computers, and manage servers for this malicious software to connect to that allow the attackers to administer compromised computers.

Of these different attacker resources, the vulnerabilities and exploits are the fewest in number (Guido 2011), and they are also more difficult for an attacker to manage and plan around. The discovery of a vulnerability requires both the presence of a vulnerability and a sufficiently intelligent act of analysis to identify the vulnerability. Malicious software can be created in a vacuum, but software exploits are inexorably linked to open source or commercial software that is actively supported by developers. Any vulnerability discovered by an attacker can also be discovered and patched by a defender, without knowledge of the attacker's discovery of same vulnerability. While malicious software can be modified to avoid detection by antivirus software, software exploits are not generally similarly modifiable.

From this perspective, the approach of an attacker when they carry out an attack is to present to your computer systems with specifically chosen pieces of information for processing. The attacker chooses these pieces of information with the foreknowledge of a vulnerability in your computer systems, such that the information is tailored to take advantage of that vulnerability. However, the attackers' ability to attack is entirely dependent on the presence and knowledge of those vulnerabilities. So, in a sense, the defender has two problems. The first problem is the existence of their attacker, which transcends problems in computer science. However, the first problem is meaningless without the second problem, which is the existence of vulnerabilities in the defender's software. Frequently, we try to explain the computer security dynamic via analogies to the physical world. The requirement of vulnerabilities is a fundamental property of the cyber attacker-defender exchange where real-world analogies break down. In the physical world, a defender may mitigate their insecurity by building a taller wall; an attacker can respond with a taller ladder. In contrast, in computer software, an attacker cannot respond to the mitigation of a vulnerability and must abandon the attack. Without knowledge of a specific vulnerability, and an exploit for that vulnerability, there is nothing an attacker can do to gain access to protected information.

In short, the presence of software vulnerabilities is within our influence, however, the presence of attackers is not. One interpretation of this dynamic is that it makes sense to address fundamental problems of computer security when programs are created and to explore what specifically about the construction of programs leads to the presence of vulnerabilities.

It is with this in mind that we turn our attention to the study of prior intrusions, and the role that vulnerable software played in that course of those intrusions. Later, we examine what results are possible from changing the way that we build software with security resilience in mind, and what current limitations exist in building software with this resilience.

15.2   Case Studies

After examination of past attacks, and consideration of today's security ecosystem, we believe that software vulnerabilities are at the core of today's security problems and that efforts taken to address the presence of vulnerabilities in software will address the root of the problem and not its symptoms.

The following case studies highlight a trend that we have observed while examining attacker activities post-mortem. Attackers use an exploit in a piece of software written in an unsafe language to gain access to otherwise private information and then their attack spreads in scope using other techniques that rely on this information. The attacker carries out at least one action that relies on flaws specifically in memory-unsafe software that processes arbitrary input.

15.2.1   HBGary

In early 2011, security consulting company HBGary was very publicly hacked by the hacking collective Anonymous. The compromise severely disrupted HBGary's business and resulted in the disclosure of all external and internal HBGary email correspondence. We will examine how the attack occurred in detail and what role software played in this attack (Peter Bright N.D.).

HBGary's electronic infrastructure was small and straightforward. The company hosted their email with Google via the Google Apps service, which is extremely secure, and they had only a few websites, all of which were internally administered by HBGary employees and contractors. How would an adversary proceed from scratch to all email from HBGary's Google Apps accounts? This attack began with a compromise of one of the websites that HBGary maintained. This compromise occurred due to a SQL injection vulnerability in the content management system (CMS) that powered one of HBGary's websites. This vulnerability that was exploited by Anonymous gave them access to the server that the CMS was running on and all the information it contained. This vulnerability represents a type of vulnerability that arises due to insecure programming languages and has plagued web applications for decades. A SQL injection is a type of error where an external program—a database—expects to receive a query from a web application. However, an attacker is able to write additional code in the query that is then executed by the database application. This is possible because, in the dynamically and loosely typed web languages that CMSs are frequently written in, there is no distinction between a program, data, and input. For example, PHP is a programming language that has frequently resulted in the introduction of SQL injection vulnerabilities, and PHP encouraged this by providing an interface to programmers for executing database queries that allowed programmers to dangerously combine the data that consisted of a query and the data (code) that was provided by an attacker. In contrast, a strongly statically typed language like Haskell has frameworks that will refuse to compile a program if the Haskell type checker indicates that input data may be used inappropriately in a query to a database.

In the timeline of the HBGary compromise, the exploitation of this CMS was the only known exploitation of a vulnerability in software. However, this exploitation was crucial to the further successes of Anonymous in obtaining data from HBGary. The server did not contain any information that was of interest to Anonymous, except for usernames and passwords for the HBGary employees who added content to the CMS. One of those usernames was for a senior level employee at HBGary, and that employee used the same username-password combination within the CMS that he used for his HBGary Google Apps email account. This allowed Anonymous to log in to this individual's email account, where they then discovered that he was an administrator of the Google Apps email infrastructure. Each of these events following the exploitation represents an embarrassing breach of basic computer security protocol (re-using passwords between services, not having role level separation of accounts, using insecurely stored passwords in a database). However, none of these lapses would have been relevant had there not also been a vulnerability present in the CMS that allowed its compromise.

The exploitation of HBGary's CMS also highlights another advantage of using exploits as opposed to other forms of coercion or compromise, which is that it can occur with no knowledge or cooperation of the victim. In attack case studies like this, the use of vulnerabilities in software diminishes the ability for the victim to understand in a timely manner what has happened to them, and thus to prepare an effective response.

15.2.2 RSA

Next we consider the compromise of the security product company RSA that led to widespread revocation of keying material and authentication tokens. This compromise also began with a memory corruption vulnerability that was in Flash. A specific employee at RSA was sent an email with a spreadsheet attachment; the spoofed sender of the email, the subject of the email, and the name of the spreadsheet were all plausible to the recipient of the email. The recipient opened the email, thus allowing the Flash exploit embedded in the spreadsheet to compromise that employee's computer. From this employee's computer, and with that employee's privileges on RSA's network, the attackers were then able to copy private keys used in the RSA SecureID system (RSA n. d.).

Flash is written in C^{++}, which is a low-level language with manual memory management, and has a long history of vulnerabilities. In low level languages, like C^{++}, the programmer is responsible for allocating and describing regions of memory within the computer, and managing those regions of memory over time. It is the programmer's responsibility to ensure that, when manipulating memory, they do not read or write outside the bounds of an object and that they only use objects that they have initialized themselves. The specific vulnerability that allowed for the compromise of RSA was a temporal memory safety violation within the Flash virtual machine in which the C^{++} code for the virtual machine used memory that had it had not initialized, but had instead been initialized by the attacker. In contrast, memory managed languages, like Java or Haskell, do not allow the programmer to use objects that they have not themselves initialized. If the virtual machine had been written in one of these languages, this vulnerability could not have existed and therefore this attack would not have been possible.

As in the HBGary incident, in this incident there were other security failures. Email communications in RSA were not authenticated via a public key infrastructure, and it is generally taught as security hygiene to employees to not open attachments received via email. However, despite those failures, had it not been for the presence of a vulnerability in Flash, the attacker would not have had the option to compromise RSA.

15.2.3   Heartbleed

The world was shocked in 2014 by the discovery of the vulnerability in the OpenSSL library that was named by its discoverers 'Heartbleed'. This vulnerability allowed for an attacker to read arbitrary memory present on a server running OpenSSL. This is especially damaging in OpenSSL's primary use case because the ability to read arbitrary memory would allow an attacker to read the private key of an OpenSSL server, thus allowing the attacker to decrypt all messages sent and received by that server. Additionally, this vulnerability would allow an attacker to read information that had been processed by the server in the recent past. The severity of this situation is amplified because in the instance where a system would use OpenSSL, there is a clear need for the privacy and security of data manipulated by that server.

This was especially shocking because OpenSSL was previously considered to have been subjected to intense scrutiny, and was regarded as high quality code. However, it did have a reputation for being obtuse and difficult to understand, and it's possible that the scrutiny of auditors was not as thorough as it was generally believed. This is a known problem with software security reputation, where people will assign a degree of trustworthiness to a particular piece of software based on how frequently vulnerabilities are discovered in that software. However, if no vulnerabilities are discovered for a long period of time, it is not immediately clear if that is because the software has no vulnerabilities or because no one is looking hard enough.

This particular vulnerability allowed the attacker to read beyond the bounds of an existing allocated object, though it did not allow writing. The act of reading beyond the bounds of an object has no effect on the operation of a traditional low-level computer program, thus the use of this vulnerability prior to its disclosure would most likely have gone totally unnoticed. This vulnerability is entirely due to OpenSSL being written in C. Had OpenSSL been implemented in a language with memory management, this vulnerability would not have been possible.

The Heartbleed bug could have resulted in the compromise of bank accounts, health medical records, or essentially any secret information accessible via the internet. In the wake of the vulnerability's disclosure, online services that used OpenSSL (such as Google, Yahoo, Amazon, Facebook, LinkedIn, NetFlix, USAA, Healthcare.Gov, Dropbox, and so on) (Mashable 2014) generally required that their customers change their passwords and authenticating information.

The Heartbleed vulnerability was effectively impossible to detect and, now that its details are known, is still extremely difficult to detect—so it is effectively impossible for organizations that might have been victims to even know that they were victims. This is in contrast to attack methodologies that rely on interactions with administrators of information systems. These interactions can leave a trail that can be followed by investigative personnel.

15.2.4   Software Is the Problem

Given the evidence that the problem is in software, we ask, is it possible to address the security problem entirely in software by applying programming language technology that ensures program security? There has been some academic work in programming language theory and security that shows promise, but it has either transitioned very slowly or not at all into the real world. The authors now present a case for, and a case against, the application of programming language theory to software security.

15.3   The Case for Security Enforcement via Programming Languages

We can use techniques from formal methods and strong type checking to create systems that have extremely strong security guarantees. These techniques can identify existing and prevent the creation future memory error vulnerabilities, and can make securing applications against higher-level errors easier. This effort has already produced some success stories that show us a way forward to creating formally secure systems.

One success story is the CompCert certified compiler. CompCert's goal is to create a formally verified compiler that has a strong guarantee of generating assembly code whose semantics are faithful to the semantics of the source code. CompCert is partially written in the theorem-prover Coq, which allows for the formal verification of components of CompCert. This formal verification allows for strong mathematical statements that the code written only does what the author of the code identified the code should do.

John Regehr at the University of Utah conducted an experiment to identify bugs in modern, popular compilers. They created a program, called CSmith (Yang 2011), that itself automatically wrote billions of different valid C source codes automatically. This type of program is referred to as a *fuzzer*, it creates inputs that stress test different corner cases of a programs operation. In the case of CSmith, the inputs it produces are C programs. Each of these C programs was then compiled by a suite of different compilers, and the resulting programs executed. If the same C source code, compiled by two different compilers, produced a different output, then one of the compilers is faulty.

The CSmith experiment tested six compilers, including industry standard compilers like Microsoft Visual C, gcc, and clang, however only 11 errors were found in CompCert (Yang 2011). Of course, this does not mean that CompCert is wholly free of errors, but this stands in contrast to the other tested compilers, in which hundreds of errors were discovered with fuzz testing. Additionally, the errors identified in CompCert were all in the unproven components, no defects were identified in the proven components of CompCert.

Fuzzing is also used to identify bugs in web browsers. For example, Google uses fuzzing to identify bugs in the Chrome web browser. What if we applied techniques of formal verification and proof of correctness to web browsers? It is suspected that the "Elderwood gang" identified vulnerabilities in Internet Explorer using a fuzzer (Guido 2013). What if a web browser was as resilient to fuzzing as CompCert is? The formal proof of software does not mean the software is entirely bug free, however it does render redundant a bug-finding technique that attackers use to identify vulnerabilities.

Another success story is the Java programming language. Security practitioners have disdain for security properties of the Java runtime, however this disdain is unfounded when talking about programs written in the Java programming language. The security of Java can be complicated; to unpack it we have to consider the security of the Java runtime and the Java programming language separately.

The Java Virtual Machine (JVM) is written in C, which does not guarantee spatial or temporal memory safety the way that the Java language itself does. Additionally, the JVM attempts to enforce strong security guarantees about the containment of untrusted Java programs that a user downloads and executes within their browser (McGraw et al. 1997). Attacks have been found in implementation details both in the low-level implementation of the JVM and the sandboxing mechanism. However, this attack scenario is only valid when an attacker can cause their victim to execute a provided Java program (Oh 2012).

This limitation has not prevented attackers from using vulnerabilities in the JVM to compromise computers. However, vulnerabilities in the JVM that are specific to running attacker-chosen programs generally do not create vulnerabilities when running Java programs that were created in good faith. There have been extremely few vulnerabilities present in the Java ecosystem that introduce vulnerabilities into good-faith Java programs. The Java programming language also guarantees spatial and temporal memory safety, so programmers do not have to worry about introducing memory corruption bugs when they write Java programs.

We can see this directly if we compare two mature web servers: Tomcat, and IIS. Tomcat is written in Java, while IIS is written in C and C^{++}. Both Tomcat and IIS also have about a decade of history to consider for security relevant. If we consider the vulnerabilities publically disclosed in both, there have been 23 code execution and 48 denial of service vulnerabilities in IIS, while there have been 1 code execution and 19 denial of service vulnerabilities in Tomcat. Tomcat has had many other types of errors leading to information disclosure or authentication bypasses, however Tomcat has simply not had the same difficulty that IIS has had with memory safety.

Java programs are not immune to bugs, but they are immune to the types of memory corruption bugs that we identified earlier as being the first step to compromise in many intrusions. Consider the following thought experiment: in an alternate universe without Java, all of the business-specific back-end and middleware programs that would be written in Java are instead written in C^{++}. Programs in both our universe and the alternate universe have bugs, however in the alternate non-Java universe there are more memory corruption bugs that lead to attacks. This suggests that perhaps language-theoretic security has already had some victories.

Other work has argued that code injection vulnerabilities in software are violations of *full abstraction* (Abadi 1999). This implies that if compilation of a source language to a target language, for example C to X86, can be proven to be fully abstract, then the resulting program is by definition free of code injection vulnerabilities. Some work has been done in this area (Fournet et al. 2013); extensions of this work could lead to the development of compilers that produce programs which are provably absent of memory errors.

One discovered means of providing full abstraction and removing code injection vulnerabilities is *control flow integrity*, or CFI (Abadi et al. 2005). This serves as a transformation of the original program into a new program that checks the program as it runs to ensure that the program running is the same as the program that was compiled, with respect to control flow. Some practical CFI schemes exist, however they have not been adopted at scale due to the performance penalty of the current implementations.

Some flaws will always be present, and software will never be bug free. For example, we can develop languages that by design do not permit memory corruption errors, however entirely different design principles are necessary to deny information leakage. In many cases, a program betraying a sensitive variable or value is as bad as a program permitting code injection via memory corruption, for example a password checking program or secure e-mail program.

However, research into these topics has been active for the past forty years and some exciting systems have been both theorized about and practically instantiated. It is possible that, once we have dispatched memory errors as a cause of concern in our programs that we can focus on higher-level errors that previously we would have ignored.

For example, there have been research projects that use *dependent typing* to enforce security invariants on programs with complicated state machines. The TLS protocol is one such state machine, and a research effort has formally verified an implementation of TLS using a type system, in the miTLS project (Bhargavan et al. 2014). What is especially heartening is that during the development of this implementation, the miTLS team discovered a new class of vulnerabilities against the TLS protocol. The miTLS codebase is written in F#, a functional language running on a managed runtime, so it does not have the spatial and temporal memory safety issues that C or C^{++} does. It also has the invariants of the TLS protocol encoded into the type system, providing a strong guarantee that the implementation matches the specification.

This style of development can be extended to other types of correctness invariants. Other work has focused on the creation of programming languages and systems that are resilient against leaking information. In these systems, information about the secrecy of variables is encoded into the type system. Programs that could leak sensitive information to low security channels are not allowed to type-check or compile.

A practical instantiation of one of these systems is the Jeeves programming language (Yang et al. 2012). This programming language provides tools for the programmer to describe privacy and security polices for variables and enforces those polices as the program runs. This language has been used to implement a conference management system, which enforces privacy policies between authors and reviewers.

Other systems are trying to make it easier for developers to formally prove their C applications. The Frama-C system is an open source software analysis system that allows for annotation and formal proofs of correctness of C programs.

Another success story for formal verification and large scale software development was the seL4 micro-kernel (Gerwin et al. 2009). This micro-kernel has been proven to be correct with respect to its specification. This system has not been stress tested the way that CompCert has, and it's development did take a significant amount of time, however it is an unambiguous win to have developed a verified operating system kernel.

Additionally, Intel is currently adding memory bounds checking operations into processor hardware (Zamyatin 2013; Nagarakatte et al. 2014). The MPX extension to the Intel CPU would allow for the CPU to efficiently check whether or not a memory reference operation was within the bounds of the object being referenced. These extensions were designed with performance in mind so that their addition to new applications would have low overhead, and this has been born out in initial experiments. With integration into compilers the addition of memory protection to newly compiled programs would be transparent to the software developer and require no annotation or cooperation. These extensions would ensure spatial memory safety.

There are also new research projects that investigate the creation of entirely new CPU architectures to support information security and safety (Pierce 2013). These systems can provide low level information flow control and assure memory safety as well as information flow safety.

We can measure the success of some attempts to enforce spatial memory safety by examining data, such as in the Microsoft Software Vulnerability Exploit Trends (Yang et al. 2012) report, which studies types of vulnerabilities discovered in Microsoft products. In the 2013 report we can see that in 2006, 40 % of the discovered vulnerabilities involved spatial corruption, whereas in 2012 that share had fallen to 8 %, possibly due to a combination of advances in program analysis technology and runtime mitigation strategies. In contrast, the percentage of temporal memory safety vulnerabilities increased from 10 % in 2006–30 % in 2012. These changes indicate that our defenses have successfully mediated prior exploits and attackers have moved on to new exploit varieties, indicating that our software-theoretic defensive strategy is influencing attacker behavior at a very fundamental level (Swamy Shivaganga et al. 2013).

We will always struggle with errors in software. However, programming language technology has been working to both remove more classes of errors from software, via type checking and verification, and lessen the impact of errors when they occur, via language design that guarantees spatial and temporal memory safety.

15.4 The Case Against Security Enforcement via Programming Languages

Theoretical programming language security is a mirage as long as it is designed to run on insecure systems, interact with untrusted parties, and process untrusted data. For many years type-safe languages have promised solutions to the problems that plague ubiquitous languages such as C/C^{++}. These solutions include the promise to eliminate memory safety issues such as buffer overflows and type confusions. Here we show that all too often these solutions are either built on top of fundamentally insecure designs such as just-in-time code generation or are entirely impractical for real world use.

This raises the question: 'Why then, is C/C^{++} still so widely used?'. The answer is simply user demand. The rate at which code is committed on popular applications such as Chrome and Firefox is growing every year. Nowhere is this more evident than the so called 'browser wars' where the first browser vendor to implement a new feature or portion of a web specification gains market share. Changing the programming language these applications are written in is simply not feasible in a short amount of time. There exists an enormous amount of libraries for these languages that implement everything from PNG parsing to compression of data. So in the interim we are left with dealing with these languages and the unique security problems they present (http://lists.x.org/archives/xorg-announce/2014-January/002389.html).

The current state-of-the-art in defending against memory safety exploits is to patch vulnerabilities, detect exploits, and raise attacker costs. The latter is by far the most effective approach thus far and is normally implemented through reducing deterministic program behavior. Its effectiveness becomes self evident when one examines the number of in-the-wild exploits discovered for widely used hardened software such as Chrome. The two most effective protections are Address Space Layout Randomization (ASLR) and Data Execution Prevention (DEP). These protections can of course be defeated with enough resources but this helps to reduce the number of potential threat actors. The beauty of these protections is that they work on machine code compiled from both legacy and new source code on operating systems that we all use today. However in recent years the security research community has proved that with enough vulnerabilities in a program memory protections can be defeated. This is primarily accomplished through writing exploits that chain together primitives such as memory disclosure and code execution.

Two recent advancements in programming language-based security have been defeated through research: randomization with diversity, and control flow integrity.

Binary diversity was a promising area of research into radically increasing the difficulty of exploiting low-level memory vulnerabilities. A specially created compiler would produce a uniquely randomized program for every customer that wanted to install the program. This was made to scale by hosting the compiler in the cloud (Jackson et al. 2011). Then, any attacker that discovered a vulnerability in this program would have to create an exploit that would work despite the specific executable code of the program. However, a group at Stanford published work that did just this—in their "Blind Return Oriented Programming" (Bittau et al. 2014) paper they used the timing and termination behavior of a program of unknown low-level structure to leak out facts about the program and then exploit it.

Since its introduction, control flow integrity suffered from an unacceptable loss of performance. Recent research (Zhang et al. 2013) sought to improve the performance of CFI and it succeeded. However, it was then discovered that the compromises made to improve the performance of CFI as a technique resulted in compromises to the security of CFI as a whole, allowing for program injection exploits despite the use of CFI (Göktas et al. 2014).

It can be argued that type safety has provided memory corruption free programs for years. Ruby, Python, C#, and Java are four great examples of high level type-safe languages that aren't plagued by these issues and are still accessible to the developer community. But when one looks deeper we see flawed language interpreter implementations written in C/C^{++} that suffer from the same core issues (http://bugs.python.org/issue20246). However these languages and their type safety models only solve a portion of security issues. Programs written in these languages still suffer from broken logic, fail-open conditions, integer conversion (C#), authentication and authorization weaknesses, and little researched areas of memory safety vulnerabilities such as JIT mis-compilation (http://leafsr.com/Attacking_Clientside _JIT_Compilers_Paper.pdf). We see evidence of this all over, particularly in the incidents mentioned in our introduction.

JIT mis-compilation is perhaps the strongest argument against type safety as a way of eliminating all memory safety security vulnerabilities. Much like all programming languages, type safe languages require compilation to machine code in order to work. This process can either be done AOT (Ahead Of Time) or JIT (Just In Time). The latter is a process that happens at runtime during execution of the program where a higher level representation of the program (typically a bytecode) is translated into native code, written into memory, and executed directly. This has the potential to be a fragile process that must include security considerations from the beginning. Often the code that is emitted is tied to a specific object in memory, or at the least a specific subset or class of objects. Even assuming the type system is perfect, if the code emitted is incorrect due to a logic vulnerability then a memory safety vulnerability becomes possible (http://blogs.technet.com/b/srd/archive/2011/06/14/ms11–044 -jit-compiler-issue-in-net-framework.aspx; https://bugzilla.mozilla.org/show_bug. cgi?id=635295; http://bugs.java.com/bugdatabase/view_bug.do?bug_id=7056380).

15.5 Practical Considerations

When considering language-based defenses that require the creation of new programming languages and then the implementation of new systems in those programming languages, we must contend with a long track record of failure to adopt. Past efforts by Microsoft to rewrite large amounts of existing code in new languages have largely met with failure. The challenge to successfully execute such a rewrite is very real: if it took effectively decades to produce the software that you currently run, it would take at least a proportional amount of time to reproduce that software using a new language. Additionally, the rewrite effort is not finished until all unsafe portions of code have been fully encapsulated by or replaced by the new programming language: any use of old, unsafe code introduces the theoretical possibility of a vulnerability, so incremental work has limited utility. The largest-scale systems that have been formally verified to date have been in the scope of operating system kernels and compilers, so the ramifications of rewriting billions of lines of code inside of new languages have not been fully explored. Unforeseen issues could arise that would result in failure of completion of the rewrite, or require modifications to the theory or underlying implementation of the new languages and technology.

Because of the expense and effort required to perform such drastic overhauls to our existing systems, and our past failures at such overhauls, it is unlikely that future efforts will be attempted voluntarily. The current regulatory and liability frameworks in the United States do not create clear incentives for software vendors to create reliable software. These same structures also do not incentivize companies that use information technology to select vendors with security in mind. For example, though both HBGary's and RSA's primary commodity was information security expertise, their compromise did not result in loss of business.

However, at least one company is attempting a voluntary overhaul. Mozilla has created a new programming language, Rust, which is designed to be both fast and memory-safe. They are using this language to write a new web browser called Servo. If written entirely in Rust, Servo would, by design, contain none of the vulnerabilities that plague existing web browsers.

15.6   Conclusion

Our security problems are a consequence of errors in applications. Errors in applications lead to exploits used by intrusive attackers to compromise computers. Exploits have been shown in the past to be a weak point in attacker methodology, so focusing defensive efforts on increased application security seems like an efficient strategy to increase computer security.

Type and memory safe languages offer one path to remove many types of vulnerabilities from our software. Using these technologies we can be sure that our applications are free of spatial and temporal memory safety errors.

Type safe languages go a long way to help prevent and eliminate memory safety issues however these are not the only security vulnerabilities affecting programs today. Furthermore type safety doesn't begin to solve the problem posed by JIT mis-compilation which can be the result of a variety of causes.

References

Abadi, Martin, Protection in Programming-Language Translations, Lecture Notes in Computer Science Volume 1603, 1999, pp 19–34

Abadi, Martín, et al. "Control-flow integrity." Proceedings of the 12th ACM conference on Computer and communications security. ACM, 2005.

Benjamin C. Pierce. The SAFE Machine: An Architecture for Pervasive Information Flow, June 2013. Invited talk at Computer Security Foundations Symposium (CSF).

Bhargavan, Karthikeyan, et al. "Proving the TLS Handshake Secure (as it is)." IACR Cryptology ePrint Archive 2014 (2014): 182.

Bittau, Andrea, et al. "Hacking blind." Proceedings of the 35th IEEE Symposium on Security and Privacy. 2014.

Fournet, Cedric; Swamy, Nikhil; Chen, Juan; Dagand, Pierre-Evariste; Strub, Pierre-Yves; Livshits, Benjamin, Fully Abstract Compilation to JavaScript, POPL 2013

Göktas, Enes, et al. "Out of control: Overcoming control-flow integrity." IEEE S&P. 2014.

Guido, Dan "A Case Study of Intelligence-Driven Defense" IEEE Security & Privacy November/December 2011, p 67–70

Guido, Dan Elderwood and the Department of Labor Hack, May 13, 2013 http://blog.trailofbits.com/2013/05/13/elderwood-and-the-department-of-labor-hack/

Hutchins, Eric M, Cloppert, Michael J, Amin, Rohan M "Intelligence-Driven Computer Network Defense Informed by Analysis of Adversary Campaigns and Intrusion Kill Chains", Lockheed Martin Technical Report. 2011 http://www.lockheedmartin.com/content/dam/lockheed/data/corporate/documents/LM-White-Paper-Intel-Driven-Defense.pdf

Jackson, Todd, et al. "Compiler-generated software diversity." Moving Target Defense. Springer New York, 2011. 77–98.

Klein, Gerwin, et al. "seL4: Formal verification of an OS kernel." Proceedings of the ACM SIGOPS 22nd symposium on Operating systems principles. ACM, 2009.

Mashable, April 9, 2014 http://mashable.com/2014/04/09/heartbleed-bug-websites-affected/

McGraw, Gary; Felten, Edward Understanding the keys to Java security—the sandbox and authentication, JavaWorld May 1, 1997 http://www.javaworld.com/article/2076945/java-security/understanding-the-keys-to-java-security—the-sandbox-and-authentication.html

Nagarakatte, Santosh, Milo MK Martin, and Steve Zdancewic. "WatchdogLite: Hardware-Accelerated Compiler-Based Pointer Checking." Proceedings of Annual IEEE/ACM International Symposium on Code Generation and Optimization. ACM, 2014

Nagaraju, Swamy Shivaganga and Craioveanu, Cristian and Florio, Elia and Miller, Matt, Software Vulnerability Exploitation Trends, Microsoft, 2013

Oh Jeong Wook Recent Java exploitation trends and malware, Black Hat USA 2012 https://media.blackhat.com/bh-us-12/Briefings/Oh/BH_US_12_Oh_Recent_Java_Exploitation_Trends_and_Malware_WP.pdf

Peter Bright, N.D. ArsTechnica http://arstechnica.com/tech-policy/2011/02/anonymous-speaks-the-inside-story-of-the-hbgary-hack/. Accessed 15 Feb 2011

RSA FraudAction Research Labs. n. d. https://blogs.rsa.com/anatomy-of-an-attack. Accessed 01 April 2011

Yang, Xuejun; Chen, Yang; Edie, Eric; Regehr, John, Finding and Understanding Bugs in C Compilers, PLDI 2011 http://www.cs.utah.edu/~regehr/papers/pldi11-preprint.pdf

Yang, Jean, Kuat Yessenov, and Armando Solar-Lezama. "A language for automatically enforcing privacy policies." ACM SIGPLAN Notices. Vol. 47. No. 1. ACM, 2012.

Zamyatin, Igor, Intel® Memory Protection Extensions (Intel® MPX) support in the GNU toolchain, Intel July 22, 2013 https://software.intel.com/en-us/blogs/2013/07/22/intel-memory-protection-extensions-intel-mpx-support-in-the-gnu-toolchain

Zhang, Chao, et al. "Practical control flow integrity and randomization for binary executables." Security and Privacy (SP), 2013 IEEE Symposium on. IEEE, 2013.

Printed in the United States
By Bookmasters